John Wesley

A Theological Journey

Kenneth J. Collins

Abingdon Press
Nashville

JOHN WESLEY
A THEOLOGICAL JOURNEY

Copyright © 2003 by Abingdon Press

This book is printed on acid-free paper.

Library of Congress Cataloging-in-Publication Data

Collins, Kenneth. J.
   John Wesley : a theological journey / Kenneth J. Collins
      p. cm.
Includes bibliographical references.
   ISBN 0-687-02788-8 (pbk. : alk. paper)
   1. Wesley, John, 1703–1791.   2. Methodist Church—Doctrines
3. Theology, Doctrinal.   I. Title.

BX8495.W5   C7535   2003
230'.7'092—dc21

                                                                2002015284
ISBN 13: 978-0-687-02788-0

08 09 10 11 12—10 9 8 7
MANUFACTURED IN THE UNITED STATES OF AMERICA

*To the Worldwide Church that is
Methodism in Commemoration
of the Three Hundredth Anniversary
of the Birth of John Wesley*

Contents

Acknowledgments

I would like to thank Dr. Kenneth Cain Kinghorn of Asbury Theological Seminary who helped in the selection of suitable pictures for this work. I would also like to thank Drs. Allan Coppedge and Laurence Wood, both of Asbury Theological Seminary, who read the manuscript and offered many helpful comments.

CHAPTER ONE

The Puritan and Anglican Heritage

The Epworth Church

During the reign of Elizabeth I (1533–1603), an energetic and deeply principled movement emerged in the English church that took exception to both the Act of Uniformity and the use of the *Book of Common Prayer*, the very staples of the Elizabethan settlement. In time, Thomas Cartwright and others became popularly known as Puritans (though Cartwright himself had rejected the designation) because they sought to purify the Church of England from its Roman Catholic vestiges in terms of both doctrine and polity. In particular, many of the Puritans sought not only to eliminate episcopacy, but also to cleanse the English church from numerous ceremonies, vestments, and customs that harkened back to the Middle Ages and that, in their judgment, helped render the gospel opaque.

Although a considerable number of Puritans had hopes of working within the Anglican Church to effectuate suitable reforms, as the reign of Elizabeth progressed many were becoming increasingly doubtful of these efforts, especially when the queen crushed the Presbyterian movement in 1593. Serious tensions within both church and society continued well into the seventeenth century and were exacerbated by William Laud, an Anglican prelate, who attempted to undo many of the Puritans' earlier labors. Among other things, Laud tried to reintroduce pre-Reformation liturgical practices such as stained glass windows, crucifixes, and altar rails; he moved the Communion table from the nave to the east end of the choir; and he even admitted, to the great dismay of the Puritans, who had been deeply influenced by Reformed theology, that the Church of Rome itself was a true church because it received the Scriptures as a rule of faith and both sacraments.

The fortunes of the Puritans improved in time with the calling of the Long Parliament in 1640, the imprisonment of Archbishop Laud the following year (Charles I had elevated him to Archbishop of Canterbury in 1633), and the surprising military successes of Oliver Cromwell, leader of the New Model Army and Puritan champion. However, the Puritan interregnum from 1640 to 1660, during which Cromwell emerged as Lord Protector with considerable power and the Puritans enjoyed greater freedom to exercise their will, this period, which should have been one of marked improvement, was actually deeply resented by many of the common folk simply because they chafed under the Puritan ethos and ethic. Add to this the horror of the Rump Parliament's execution of Charles I in 1649 and many of the English were more than ready for the restoration of the monarchy in 1660, though Charles II was not formally crowned until 1661.

At first, with the coronation of Charles Stuart, the possibility of something other than a mere restoration of the Anglican Church appeared to be in the offing; and the Savoy Conference in 1661 had even considered uniting the Presbyterians with the Church of England. The Conference, however, broke up with little effect, and Parliament proceeded to impose a number of debilitating restrictions on those dissenters who would not conform to the Anglican Church. To illustrate, the Corporation Act, passed in 1661, restricted membership of corporations to members of the Church of England; the Act of Uniformity of 1662 imposed a revised *Book of Common Prayer* and required "unfeigned assent and consent"[1] by its ministers to its contents; the Conventicle Act of 1664 forbade meetings for worship (other than in the Anglican form) in private houses or in the open; the Five Mile Act, passed the following year, ordered dissenting ministers not to come within five miles of a corporate town or "to preach to any assembly without having sworn an oath against rebellion";[2] and the Test Act of 1673 excluded all Roman Catholics from public office.

During the subsequent reign of James II, the fear of Roman Catholicism was so great that William of Orange and his wife, Mary Stuart, the daughter of James II, were invited to the English throne in 1688 in what has been called the Glorious Revolution. Moderate and sensible in many respects, King William promulgated the Toleration Act the following year, which afforded dissenters freedom of worship provided that they continued to affirm the doctrine of the Trinity. With this measure of religious liberty and freedom of conscience in place, dissent as a distinct movement would continue in English religious life well into the next century, such that by the time of 1715, when John Wesley was but a boy, its numbers were in the range of a quarter of a million out of a total population of more than five million.[3]

The Maternal Legacy

The theological setting in which John Wesley thrived as a child was marked, of course, by Anglicanism; but it was also shaped, to some extent, by a heritage of dissent mediated to him through the lineage of both his mother and father. Some of Susanna Wesley's relatives, for example, were gifted and energetic leaders who had departed from the Church of England in the name of piety and reform. Indeed, Susanna's grandfather on her mother's side had been an earnest and serious Puritan from his youth. Growing up in Pembrokeshire, the young John White entered Jesus College, Oxford, in 1607 or so and after completing his studies was admitted to the bar. By 1640, he became a member of Parliament, a Puritan stronghold by this time, and set his course in opposition to the established church. In recognition of his strong Puritan sentiments and his gifts for leadership, John White was appointed the chairman of the Committee for Religion and eventually became a member of the historic Westminster Assembly of Divines.[4]

But Susanna's Puritan relations were even closer. Dr. Samuel Annesley, her father, had graduated from Queens College, Oxford, where he received his B.A. and M.A. degrees in 1639 and 1644, respectively; and he was subsequently honored with the Doctor of Laws degree in 1648. Devout and serious in many respects and pursuing a long and deeply held call to ministry, Samuel Annesley was ordained by presbyters in 1644 and began his ministerial career on board a man-of-war as its chaplain.[5] Sensing a call to a more orderly and stable life, the young cleric soon settled down in the parish of Cliffe in Kent. By 1652, Samuel Annesley was ministering in London and was well known for the nonconformist convictions of his gifted preaching as well as for the meetinghouse that he had established in Little St. Helen's.[6] Six years later, in 1658, the prominent rector became the Vicar of St. Giles, Cripplegate, a position from which he was ejected in 1662 for his failure to conform to the Anglican Church. Dr. Annesley remained in London, steadfast in his convictions, where he served as the "patriarch of Dissent" until his death on December 31, 1696. Interestingly enough, John Wesley thought so well of many of his grandfather's theological convictions that he reproduced a sermon from this seventeenth-century leader in his own *A Christian Library,* a collection of some of the best pieces on practical divinity. The words of Dr. Annesley that follow, in their emphasis on holiness, faith working by love, as well as the role of the Holy Spirit in the Christian life, could have just as easily flowed from the pen of John Wesley. Dr. Annesley writes:

> Remember these two words, though you forget all the rest of the Sermon, viz., "CHRIST and Holiness, Holiness and CHRIST": interweave these all manner of ways, in your whole conversation. . . .
>
> It is serious Christianity that I press, as the only way to better every condition: it is Christianity, downright Christianity, that alone can do it: it is not morality without faith; that is but refined Heathenism: it is not faith without morality; that is but downright hypocrisy: it must be a divine faith, wrought by the HOLY GHOST, where GOD and man concur in the operation; such a faith as works by love, both to GOD and man; a holy faith, full of good works.[7]

The twenty-fifth and last child of Dr. Annesley, and the one to whom he left his papers before he died, was Susanna, who was born in London on January 20, 1669. Growing up in a godly setting where religious matters were often discussed, Susanna developed some spiritual disciplines that would serve her well throughout life. The mother of Methodism became, among other things, a good steward of time and set apart regular periods for meditation and self-examination, so typical of her Puritan heritage. In addition, as a young child, Susanna most likely kept a spiritual journal in which she would chronicle the state of her soul before a holy and forgiving God, the pages of the journal becoming her confessional. In fact, so important were the elements of personal piety to the youngest Annesley, that she later confessed to her son Samuel Wesley Jr. that "when I was in my father's house . . . I used to allow myself as much time for recreation as I spent in private devotion."[8]

Beyond these elements of practical divinity, it is clear that Susanna, both as a child and later as an adult, kept a strict Puritan Sabbath, in which all unnecessary labors were put aside and the day was observed in all manner of seriousness and in due devotion to the Most High, a practice that she later passed along to her children and especially to her son John. Indeed, when Wesley articulated the characteristics of "notorious sinners" in his treatise *The Principles of a Methodist Farther Explained* in 1746, it was, in a real sense, the voice of his own mother that resounded in the cautionary words: "The remainder were gross, open sinners, common swearers, drunkards, *sabbath-breakers*, whoremongers, plunderers, robbers, implacable, unmerciful, wolves and bears in the shape of men. Do you desire instances of more 'notorious sinners' than these?"[9]

Though Susanna would retain many elements of her Puritan heritage, she nevertheless decided at a tender age—not quite thirteen—to become a part of the religious establishment, a member of the Church of England. Considering the dispute between the dissenters and the Anglicans as best as she was able, the young child evidently concluded with good and sufficient reasons the nature of her future course.[10] Later as an adult, Susanna took the trouble to draw up a detailed account of this earlier transition, but her narrative was unfortunately consumed in the flames of the great Wesley house fire that erupted in February 1709.

A person of deep character and strong willed in many respects, Susanna had offended the sensibilities of her husband, Samuel, when she had not offered the proper "Amen" to his prayer for

King William, the chief protagonist of the Glorious Revolution.[11] As noted earlier, William of Orange and his wife, Mary Stuart, had displaced the "Catholic" James II from the English throne in 1688. Such a turn of events was distasteful, to say the least, for those English people, like Susanna, who had been schooled on the notion of the divine right of kings. Indeed, with politics and religion so intimately connected since the time of Henry VIII and the English Reformation, it is little wonder that, on the one hand, Susanna had such reservations about King William and, on the other hand, her husband could find them troubling—so much so that he took a rash vow to this effect: "Sukey, if that be the case, we must part, for if we have two Kings, we must have two beds."[12] With the kind of stubbornness that emerges only from a deeply principled person, Samuel abandoned his wife and children and headed for London. Just how long Samuel actually forsook his family is a point well disputed,[13] but what is clear is that the neglectful husband and father eventually returned to the Epworth parsonage without having received the kind of assurances from Susanna that he had demanded in his vow.[14] Within a year after Samuel's return, John Wesley was born on June 17, 1703.[15]

The English Puritans, as Newton aptly notes, were characterized by "their intense pastoral care, their concern for family religion, and their efforts to bring every member of a household or congregation to a personal appropriation of God's grace"—elements that just as accurately describe Susanna's own care for her burgeoning brood.[16] Like her Puritan ancestors, Susanna not only recommended the works of Richard Baxter as conducive to spiritual growth and maturation, but also stressed, along with her husband, Samuel, daily reading and meditation on the Bible as a suitable means of grace. Every morning at the Epworth rectory, for example, the Wesley family read psalms as well as chapters from the Old and New Testaments, the household being filled with the Word, the very sounds of salvation.

Something of a disciplinarian, Susanna cared for her children according to rule and method. For instance, all of the Wesley children, except Kezzy, were taught to read when they were five years old; and a single day was allotted to the task of learning the alphabet, a task that John and others accomplished quiet easily though Mary and Anne took a day and a half. Moreover, on each day of the week, Susanna had a private talk with one of her children according to a fixed pattern: on Monday with Mollie, on Tuesday with Hettie, on Wednesday with Nancy, on Thursday with John, on Friday with Patty, on Saturday with Charles, and on Sunday with Emilia and Sukey.[17] Six hours a day were spent at school, at which instruction was serious and thorough and loud talking and boisterous play were strictly forbidden—rules that would in a similar fashion find their way into John Wesley's own educational practices at Kingswood.

Upon reflection in his later years, John Wesley was so impressed with his mother's educational practices and discipline that he asked her to collect the principal rules that she had observed in their family. In a letter to her son on July 24, 1732, Susanna details her method: When the children turned a year old, and some even before this, they were taught to "fear the rod, and to cry softly; by which means they escaped abundance of correction they might otherwise have had."[18] Even before her children could speak, Susanna adds, she stressed the importance of the Lord's Day, that it must be distinguished from all other days—a precept that was, no doubt, a reminder of her own earlier origins. Beyond this, as soon as the children had "grown pretty strong," they were limited to three meals a day so that drinking and eating between meals was never allowed. Indeed, the Wesley children were always put into a "regular method of living," which included such matters as dressing, undressing, changing linen, and so on.[19] Elsewhere in this same letter, and in a summary fashion, Susanna underscores the element that is absolutely necessary for the inculcation of piety and for the proper foundation of a religious education:

> In order to form the minds of children, the first thing to be done is to conquer their will. . . . I insist upon conquering the wills of children betimes, because this is the only foundation for a religious education. When this is thoroughly done, then a child is capable of being governed by the reason of its parent, till its own understanding comes to maturity.[20]

In addition, Susanna listed the various "bylaws" that were part of the Epworth household, which include the following:

(1) Whoever was charged with a fault, of which they were guilty,

if they would ingenuously confess it, and promise to amend, should not be beaten. This rule prevented a great deal of lying. . . .
(2) That no sinful action, as lying, pilfering, playing at church, or on the Lord's day, disobedience, quarreling, etc., should ever pass unpunished.
(3) That no child should ever be chid or beat twice for the same fault. . . .
(4) That every single act of obedience . . . should be always commended, and frequently rewarded, according to the merits of the cause.
(5) That if ever any child performed an act of obedience, or did anything with an intention to please, though the performance was not well, yet the obedience and intention should be kindly accepted, and the child with sweetness directed how to do better for the future.
(6) That [property] be inviolably preserved, and none suffered to invade the property of another in the smallest matter, though it were but of the value of a farthing, or a pin. . . .
(7) That promises be strictly observed; and a gift once bestowed, and so the right passed away from the donor, be not resumed. . . .
(8) That no girl be taught to work till she can read very well; and then that she be kept to her work with the same application, and for the same time, that she was held to in reading. This rule also is much to be observed; for the putting children to learn sewing before they can read perfectly is the very reason why so few women can read fit to be heard, and never to be well understood.[21]

In light of such counsel, modern writers have criticized Susanna's educational practices as unduly harsh and rigorous. But John Wesley evidently did not think so. In fact, in his later years, Wesley repeatedly cautioned against the unholy triumvirate of "pride, self-will, and love of the world," especially in his sermons, as well as against the pernicious nature of self-will in particular, which is the desire to live according to human autonomy, in which one's own will and desires, rather than the gracious and loving will of God, become the chief guides of life. Indeed, so appreciative was Wesley of his mother's earlier counsel and discipline that in later life he wrote to her the following:

If you can spare me only that little part of Thursday evening which you formerly bestowed upon me in another manner, I doubt not but it would be as useful now for correcting my heart as it was then for . . . forming my judgment.[22]

On February 9, 1709, an inferno consumed the Epworth rectory, and John Wesley just barely escaped with his life, falling into his rescuer's arms as the roof collapsed, which sent flames, smoke, and debris into the night sky. Though Wesley was to remember this horrific event quite well, sometimes even referring to himself as "a brand plucked from the burning" (Zech. 3:2), it was Susanna who first clearly discerned the providential care of God in this deliverance:

> I do intend to be more particularly careful of the soul of this child, that Thou hast so mercifully provided for, than ever I have been, that I may do my endeavor to instill into his mind the principles of Thy *true* religion and virtue.[23]

With the destruction of the rectory, and with no suitable dwelling to house the entire family, the Wesley children were scattered among neighbors and friends. After the rectory was rebuilt and the children were together once more, Susanna was initially dismayed because she became aware that in the interim, they had taken on several bad habits by learning some common, perhaps even vulgar, songs and by growing careless about the Sabbath. Immediately, Susanna began a reform in order to cleanse her sons and daughters of these practices and to inculcate noble and holy virtues—those, in other words, most in accord with Christian grace and with life in an English rectory.

Susanna, by all accounts, was a godly, even serious, woman who not only employed the means of grace on a regular basis, but also often enjoyed devotional or spiritual literature. Her interests in this last area were quite broad, reflecting the maturity of her judgment; and Susanna could just as easily recommend the works of Castaniza as those of Richard Baxter and Henry Scougal. Accordingly, a few years after the great house fire, in 1711 or so, Susanna read the work of the Halle Pietist Ziegenbalg, whose account of two Danish Moravian missionaries and their labors in Tranquebar (in Tamil Nâdu) deeply moved her. At this time, and perhaps as a consequence of this reading in its display of undaunted courage and witness, Susanna herself underwent "a deep emotional and spiritual experience" and was thereby both prepared and emboldened to employ her numerous gifts and graces for ministry despite the opposition from her own eighteenth-century setting.[24] To illustrate, in 1712, when Samuel Wesley headed to Convocation and left his curate, Mr. Inman, to preach at the Epworth church in his absence—as was his practice under such circumstances—Susanna was so displeased with the lack of sound spiritual teaching in the pulpit and with the curate's repeated laborious harangues on the duty of Christians to pay their debts (whether the text was Romans 1:19 or Matthew 5:19 made little difference), that she began to hold evening services in her kitchen in order to minister to the needs of the people. In these services—at one point almost two hundred people attended (perhaps standing in the doorways and outside in the yard)—psalms were sung, prayers were read, and a sermon drawn from Samuel's library shelves was recited by Susanna to the edification of all. Mr. Inman chafed under Susanna's able and steady leadership, especially since her evening services were better attended than his morning ones. He, therefore, wrote a letter to Samuel and complained bitterly about Susanna's inappropriate actions.

Conventional in many respects and concerned with good order, Samuel asked his wife to end immediately the kitchen services, these informal gatherings that had so inflamed his curate. Susanna, not easily dissuaded in anything, considered the matter very carefully and responded to her husband's request by engaging in some serious theological reflection—reflection that Samuel, himself, ultimately found convincing. Susanna wrote:

> If you do, after all, think fit to dissolve this assembly, do not tell me that you desire me to do it, for that will not satisfy my conscience; but send me your positive command, in such full and express terms as may absolve me from all guilt and punishment, for neglecting this opportunity of doing good, when you and I shall appear before the great and awful tribunal of our LORD JESUS CHRIST.[25]

John Wesley, no doubt, participated in these house meetings—inaccurately described by some as "conventicles"—and thereby saw a living example of a functional definition of ministry, one that deemed it far better to minister to the needs of the common people—even if it gave offense to the prejudices of the day—than to watch the harvest rot on the ground for want of laborers. This was a lesson that Wesley had learned at the hands of his gifted and courageous mother, and it would help to shape his own understanding of gospel ministry in the days ahead.

The Paternal Legacy

The Puritan heritage of John Wesley was considerable not only on his mother's side of the family, but on his father's side as well. To illustrate, Bartholomew Westley, his great-grandfather, who had studied physics and divinity at university, was ejected from his parish at Allington, just north of Bridport, on St. Bartholomew's day, August 24, 1662, for his failure to conform to the Anglican Church. Driven from the Bridport area by the Five Mile Act, Bartholomew most likely returned to Charmouth, where he bought some property the following year.[26]

Bartholomew's son John Westley was of similar Puritan sentiments. While studying at New Inn Hall, Oxford, for example, where he received his B.A. in 1654 and his M.A. in 1657, Westley had the good fortune to make the acquaintance of the great Puritan divine John Owen, who was then Vice Chancellor of the university. Edmund Calamy, the famous historian of English Nonconformity, maintained that Westley's proficiency in Oriental languages as well as his devout and serious life at the university brought him to the attention of the Vice Chancellor. After graduation, Westley was associated with a "gathered church" at Melcombe Regis; and he later accepted a call to the parish of Winterbourne Whitchurch, Dorset, near Blanford, having been approved by the Triers, Oliver Cromwell's Board of Commissioners, which examined every candidate for ministry.

After the restoration of the Stuart line in 1661, with the ascension of Charles II to the English throne, John Westley began to suffer increasing difficulties. He was charged, for instance, with "diabolically railing" in the pulpit against the Stuart monarchy and with praising Cromwell. Beyond this, he was accused of teaching false and pernicious doctrines—a serious charge for any minister to face. And so when Westley refused to use the *Book of Common Prayer* during the summer of 1661, he was promptly thrown into prison. The following year, he was back in the pulpit, and, like his father, Bartholomew, he was ejected from his parish (as were over two thousand others) for his failure to conform. He preached his farewell sermon at Whitchurch on the text "And now, brethren, I commend you to God, and to the word of his grace" (Acts 20:32) to a weeping, brokenhearted congregation. Westley recovered somewhat from this censure and settled in Preston, a base from which he pastored a congregation in Poole. By 1666, the dissenting minister was so firm in his convictions that he was now defying the Five Mile Act in Preston itself. And when he died some years later as a relatively young man, it was perhaps the poverty, the struggles, and the exclusion that had taken their toll.

In the following century, 1765 to be exact, John Wesley inserted a lengthy conversation in his journal between his grandfather, John Westley, and Gilbert Ironside, Bishop of Bristol, in which the young dissenting pastor offers an apologetic for his views and demonstrates, quite clearly, that his ministry had "both a divine call and a divine blessing."[27] In fact, so impressed was Wesley with the faithful witness of his paternal heritage that he reflected on this wonder to his brother Charles in a letter on January 15, 1768, in which he opined: "It is highly probable one of the three will stand before the Lord. But, so far as I can learn, such a thing has scarce been for these thousand years before, as a son, father, grandfather, *atavus, tritavus*, preaching the gospel, nay, and the genuine gospel, in a line."[28] Sadly, some of John Westley's contemporaries were not so kind. Indeed, the Vicar of Preston refused to bury him in the churchyard, and so the exact date and place of his entombment are not known.[29]

John Westley's most famous child, and the one who later changed the family named to Wesley, was a boy named Samuel. Born at Winterbourne Whitchurch in 1662 not long after the expulsion, Samuel was educated, first, privately and then, later, at a dissenting academy, the Free School in Dorchester. Afterward, he attended Newington Green, where the foundations for an excellent classical education were laid. These dissenting academies, which provided an alternative to the establishment, arose directly out of the disabilities suffered under the Clarendon Code. Thomas Secker, who later became the Archbishop of Canterbury, described them as "an extraordinary place of education."[30] In fact, so valued were these schools that even some Anglicans sent their children to them in order to avoid, as Samuel Wesley had put it, "the debauchery of the universities."[31]

While at Newington Green, under the careful direction of Charles Morton, Samuel was given the task of refuting an Anglican argument against dissenters. Surprisingly enough, in the process of preparing his response, Samuel came to the conclusion that the Anglicans had actually been right in their major criticisms. For one thing, Samuel was deeply offended at the defense offered by dissenters concerning the execution of King Charles I. Add to this his disgust at their "calf's head club,"[32] as well as his dislike of the intolerance of many dissenters, and we can begin to understand what strong passions had been aroused in Samuel at the time and why he subsequently left dissent in order to enter the very church that had persecuted not only his grandfather, but his own father as well.

Determined and resolute in his newly found convictions, Samuel Wesley set out for Exeter College, Oxford, in 1683, where he enrolled as a servitor, that is, as a poor scholar who would meet his costs, in part, by serving older students. A good student with a scholarly bent, Samuel received his Bachelor of Arts degree in June 1688, and his master's degree, supposedly from Corpus Christi College, Cambridge University in 1694. His acceptance into the Anglican Church was reaffirmed, and his gifts and graces for ministry were acknowledged by his ordination to deacon in 1688 by Dr. Sprat, Bishop of Rochester, and to the priesthood in 1689 by Dr. Compton, the Bishop of London.

The paths of Samuel Wesley and Susanna Annesley, so similar in many respects, finally crossed in 1682, perhaps for the first time, at the wedding of Susanna's sister to John Dunton, the noted bookseller. Enjoying a lengthy period of courtship, the couple were married in the parish church of St. Marylebone on November 12, 1688. After the wedding, Samuel served as a curate at St. Botolph's for a brief period; and then to improve his meager income, he signed on for a six-month naval chaplaincy, leaving his pregnant wife behind. After he returned, Samuel filled another curacy, this time at Newington Butts, Surrey. Finally, Samuel and Susanna settled into the rectory at South Ormsby in Lincolnshire in 1691, a position secured for them through the good graces of the Marquis of Normanby. During this period, Samuel added to his paltry income by publishing in the *Athenian Gazette* and elsewhere. Around 1696 or so, the Wesleys moved from South Ormsby to Epworth in Lincolnshire, where Samuel served as rector. There is evidence to suggest that Samuel believed he had received this appointment at the request of no one less than Queen Mary in appreciation for a work that he had published in defense of the Glorious Revolution. However, since Queen Mary died in 1694, about two years or so before the appointment at Epworth, the queen must have expressed her intention on this matter shortly before her demise—if Samuel's reckoning was indeed correct.

Earnest and devout in many respects, Samuel participated in the religious society movement in England. The first of these societies, which sought to "fortify and supplement . . . parochial organizations,"[33] arose in London in 1678 through the efforts of Anthony Horneck, an immigrant Lutheran minister. A couple of years later, *The Country Parson's Advice to His Parishioners* championed the ongoing merits of these beneficent groups; and thus the moral and spiritual climate was laid for the creation of the Society for the Reformation of Manners in 1691. This last society served both to encourage and to empower the Justices of the Peace in England as they performed their many duties in the enforcement of the law and in the maintenance of good public order, especially with respect to the elimination of "profaneness and debauchery."[34] By 1699, the Society for the Reformation of Manners had already spawned the Society for Promoting Christian Knowledge (SPCK), an intentional group that not only circulated sound Christian literature, but also promoted various educational institutions. A couple of years later, the Society for the Propagation of the Gospel (SPG) was created, and it soon became a vital missionary arm of the Anglican Church, particularly in the colonies. All of these societies, which constituted a kind of benevolent empire, received the warm support of several prominent Anglican clergy, Archbishop Tenison and Bishop Beveridge among them.

On a more personal level, these religious societies issued a call to a more godly and holy life. In particular, they fostered "a high-Church piety"[35] that depended on a rigorous study of Scripture; they recommended the reading of suitable devotional literature; and they required a higher standard of morality from its members illustrated by its amelioration of the plight of the poor. In fact, so impressed was Samuel Wesley with the design and purpose of these societies that in 1700 he set up a small religious association in Epworth. In a letter to the parent society in London, Samuel expressed the various duties of his circle of friends in the following way:

> First to pray to God; secondly, to read the Holy Scriptures and discourse upon religious matters for their mutual edification; and thirdly, to deliberate about the edification of our neighbor and the promoting of it.[36]

Earlier, in 1698, Samuel had preached before the Society for the Reformation of Manners in London on the same text that his son John Wesley would employ some sixty-five years later before the same society. And although, as Richard P. Heitzenrater aptly points out, there is no evidence that John Wesley participated as a child in the society at Epworth,[37] the later direction of his life clearly suggests that Wesley was not only familiar with the substance of these pietistic circles, especially in terms of their design to foster holiness of heart and life, but also well acquainted with their methods, particularly in terms of the use of small, intentional, face-to-face meetings that fostered both accountability and honesty, the very staples of spiritual maturity.

John Wesley's Early Life

Though the influence of the Epworth rectory on the Wesley children in the form of lessons, prayers, and parental discipline obviously cannot be denied, we must also remember that in the case of John Wesley, as with his brother Charles, such influence was relatively short lived. Nominated for the Charterhouse School in London by the Duke of Buckingham, John matriculated at this institution—which was once a Carthusian monastery—as a gown-boy in January 1714 when he was but ten years old. A favorite of Thomas Walker, the schoolmaster, John Wesley was well liked at the school though he had to suffer, from time to time, the same indignities that all the younger students experienced at the hands of the older ones, namely, the practice of the boys of the higher classes of Charterhouse taking the portion of meat from the younger ones.

When Wesley was in his mid-thirties he would recall the days of a relatively carefree youth at Charterhouse, of a boy who was presumptuously satisfied with his own religious life. For example, in his autobiographical narrative that precedes his Aldersgate account of May 24, 1738, Wesley observes:

> The next six or seven years were spent at school; where, outward restraints being removed, I was much more negligent than before even of outward duties, and almost continually guilty of outward sins, which I knew to be such, though they were not scandalous in the eye of the world. However, I still read the Scriptures, and said my prayers, morning and evening. And what I now hoped to be saved by, was, (1) *not being so bad as other people;* (2) *having still a kindness for religion;* and (3) *reading the Bible, going to church, and saying my prayers.*[38]

This is a very revealing narrative, for although it obviously represents the perspective of a man looking back on his youth—and is no doubt colored by that later vantage point—it nevertheless displays the same kind of sensitivity and religious judgment of Luther in the sixteenth century or of Kierkegaard in the nineteenth. Like Luther who preceded him, Wesley's conscience was not easily put aside, and he was hardly satisfied with the conventional religion of his Charterhouse days. Indeed, the round of religious duties, which included the means of grace, left him simply with a "kindness for religion." And though the young Wesley was clearly not plagued by the overbearing scruples of the monastic Luther, he began to evidence pangs of conscience that others hardly or rarely felt. Moreover, like Kierkegaard who followed him, Wesley was as a perplexing, even a mysterious, figure because he doubted and called into question precisely what others so readily assumed, namely, what it means to be a Christian. For one thing, why was Wesley in retrospect not satisfied with the religious staples of his life at Charterhouse such as praying, reading the Bible, and going to church as his peers evidently were? That is, what did Wesley see that others did not; and perhaps more important, why did he long for it so?[39]

Because of his taste for scholarship, Samuel Wesley Sr. eagerly sought whatever educational opportunities he could afford for his children, and so he was naturally well pleased with the direction

of his son Charles's education, which eventually included attendance at the Westminster School in London, an academy at which
his brother Samuel Jr. was already an usher. Soon John would be
ready for the university, and his somewhat ambitious father hoped
to ensure that he would gain entrance to no place less than Oxford
University. With such a design in mind, Samuel arranged a meeting between his son and Dr. Sacheverell who supposedly could
provide a handsome recommendation. But from all reports the
meeting between the well-connected scholar and the hopeful student did not go well. The doctor looked at the small stature of John
Wesley and declared: "You are too young to go to the University;
you cannot know Greek and Latin yet. Go back to school."[40]
Wesley's response to such flippancy was immediate and frank: "I
looked at him as David looked at Goliath, and despised him in my
heart. I thought, 'If I do not know Greek and Latin better than you,
I ought to go back to school indeed.' "[41]

Despite Dr. Sacheverell's gloomy assessment, John Wesley was
admitted to Christ Church, Oxford, in July 1720. As a gown-boy
and graduate of Charterhouse, Wesley was entitled to forty
pounds a year for three years and one hundred pounds for the
fourth year.[42] But this sum was hardly sufficient for an Oxford student, and so both Susanna and Samuel sent funds from time to
time. Despite such support, John—perhaps taking after his
father—was frequently in debt. Knowing that her son was occasionally troubled and dispirited at Christ Church due to his financial situation, Susanna offered words of both comfort and
assurance: "Be not discouraged; do your duty, keep close to your
studies, and hope for better days; perhaps, notwithstanding all, we
shall pick up a few crumbs for you before the end of the year."[43]

Lively and engaging, with a keen mind and a sharp wit, Wesley
had several friends at Christ Church with whom he often took
meals. His youthful manner was easy and light, marked by a taste
for both conversation and the diversions of the day. Like many other
students, Wesley frequented the coffeehouse, rowed on the river,
and played backgammon, billiards, chess, cards, and tennis. And on
those rare occasions when both time and resources permitted, he
would attend the theater. Here was a young man, in other words,
who was obviously enjoying his youth, who was exploring an array
of activities with a sense of wonder and ease. The seriousness and

the meticulous use of time, so characteristic of the mature Wesley, would only come later. Indeed, it would take reading Jeremy Taylor's *Rules and Exercises of Holy Living and Holy Dying* shortly after his residence at Christ Church, among other things, to precipitate such a change. And yet elements of that later seriousness, especially in the area of religion, were present even during this earlier period.

Reflecting the godly influence of both Susanna and Samuel, the Epworth rectory had prepared Wesley well for his days at Oxford. For one thing, the Puritan heritage, the concern for discipline, principle, and good order so evident in his earlier familial setting, evoked in Wesley an ardent desire for exacting moral rectitude in his own life.[44] Indeed, the time would come when that early environment, that curious mix of Puritan discipline and Anglican sensibilities, would bear remarkable fruit. In the meantime, however, Wesley was left not only with pious desires, but also with a rigor in matters of religion that those closest to him, such as his brother Samuel Jr., could only find troubling. Thus, toward the end of 1721, while Wesley was at Christ Church, Samuel cautioned John about his intensity of discipline in study as well as in religion, saying, "Your soul is too great for your body."[45] This would prove to be wise counsel, indeed, but it would take years, and much pain along the way, before Wesley understood its meaning.

CHAPTER TWO

The End of Religion

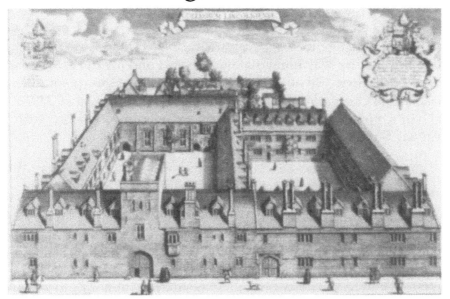

Lincoln College, Oxford, 1675

Toward the end of his residence at Christ Church, as he was maturing in several respects, John Wesley began to think seriously about taking Anglican orders. And though he in retrospect maintained that it was his father, Samuel, who pressed him to enter into ministry, it was actually Susanna who had raised the issue for the first time.[1] "I heartily wish you were in Orders," she wrote in September 1724, "and could come and serve one of [Samuel Sr.'s] churches. Then I should see you often, and could be more helpful to you than 'tis possible to be at a distance."[2]

Later, in February 1725, Susanna counseled her son to make a thorough examination of himself "that you may know whether you have a reasonable hope of salvation by Jesus Christ, that is, whether you are in a state of faith and repentance or not."[3] This matter deserves great attention, she cautioned, "but especially those designed for the clergy ought above all things to make their calling and election sure."[4] Indeed, so eager was Susanna for her son to become an Anglican priest, to make religion "the business of [his] life,"[5] that she exclaimed,

> I think the sooner you are a deacon the better, because it may be
> an inducement to greater application in the study of practical
> divinity, which of all others I humbly conceive is the best study
> for candidates for Orders.[6]

When Samuel, however, first learned of what John and Susanna
had in mind, he was immediately opposed and sent his son this
word of caution: "By all this you see I'm not for your going over
hastily into Orders. When I'm for your taking 'em, you shall know
it."[7] In a poignant letter that reveals something of her life with
Samuel, Susanna confided to John in February 1725,

> 'tis an unhappiness almost peculiar to our family, that your
> father and I seldom think alike. I approve the disposition of your
> mind, I think this season of Lent the most proper for your prepa-
> ration for Orders.[8]

Nevertheless, this unhappiness of which Susanna wrote was not to
last long for by the next month Samuel had already changed his
mind—for whatever reason—and hoped that John would enter
orders that summer. Earlier, Samuel had urged his son to consider
very carefully the proper motivation for ministry which should
include, among other things, three principal springs: "The glory of
God, and the service of his *church*, in the edification and salvation
of our *neighbor*."[9] And in a subsequent letter, composed in March
1725, Samuel promised that he would gather up some money for
his son's orders and "something more."[10]

During the time John Wesley was considering his call to the ministry of the Church of England, he encountered a "religious
friend," that is, one who helped him "to alter the whole form of
[his] conversation, and to set in earnest upon a new life."[11] Just
who was this religious friend who played such an important role
in Wesley's life? One clue to this puzzle can perhaps be found in
Wesley's habit of visiting the rectory at Stanton where he was
friendly with Sally Kirkham, the rector's daughter. However, as
one author notes, an equally strong case can be made for Robin
Griffiths, the son of the Reverend John Griffiths of Broadway,
Worcestershire, in the Cotswold Hills.[12] At any rate, this religious
friend, whoever it was, helped Wesley see the importance of
inward holiness, the goal of religion, for which he now prayed.

Sometime before 1725, Wesley had fallen among "some Lutheran and Calvinist authors," whose confused accounts magnified faith to such an extent that they invariably undermined the importance of obedience and the rest of the commandments of God.[13] Wesley later attributed this confusion among some continental Protestants to their "overgrown fear of popery, being so terrified with the cry of 'merit and good works' that they plunged at once into the other extreme."[14] This error of "solafidianism," the magnifying of faith out of all proportion, threw Wesley into a quandary for a time, "not being able to find out what the error was, nor yet to reconcile this uncouth hypothesis either with Scripture or common sense."[15] The encounter with his religious friend in 1725, no doubt, helped matters somewhat, but it was perhaps Wesley's reading habits during this period that provided a greater measure of both insight and relief.

à Kempis and Taylor

In the spring of 1725, Wesley began to focus his studies on the Pietists of the holy living tradition. In May of that year, for example, he wrote to his mother, indicating that he had been advised lately to read over Thomas à Kempis.[16] This medieval monk's work, *The Imitation of Christ*, had already become a spiritual classic by the eighteenth century even though Bellarmine and others had raised questions about its authorship a full century earlier. At any rate, Thomas Hemerken, the reputed author, was born in the German city of Kempten. He was subsequently educated in the school at Deventer run by the Brethren of Common Life, a group that, under the leadership of Gerhard Groote, placed a premium on the inner life of the soul and on the necessity of imitating the life of Christ by loving one's neighbor as oneself. As a director of spiritual life, Thomas à Kempis was greatly in demand, and his counsel followed that of Groote, the founder of the movement, and Florentius Radewijns, his successor.

Though Wesley was deeply appreciative of the spirituality expressed in *The Imitation of Christ*, especially in its emphasis on inward religion, his letters to his mother in May and June of 1725 show that he was concerned about the harshness of some of the teachings of this spiritual classic, in particular that we should supposedly be "perpetually miserable" in the world.[17] Susanna offered a detailed and sophisticated reply to her son's queries and revealed that she took à Kempis "to have been an honest, weak man, that had more zeal than knowledge, by his condemning all mirth or pleasure as sinful and useless, in opposition to many direct and plain texts of Scripture."[18] But in these same letters, Susanna also helped her son sift the wheat from the chaff, so to speak, in order that he might realize the importance of discipline as well as the necessity of prudential rules in the Christian life, those rules, in other words, that are suggested by reason as one reflects on the high goal and calling of being in Christ. In her letter on June 8, 1725, Susanna elaborates:

> Take this rule. Whatever weakens your reason, impairs the tenderness of your conscience, obscures your sense of God, or takes off your relish of spiritual things; in short, whatever increases the strength and authority of your body over your mind, that thing is sin to you, however innocent it may be in itself.[19]

A couple of months later, Wesley explored this same topic with his father, Samuel, who offered counsel remarkably similar to Susanna's:

> And 'tis no wonder if contemplative men, especially when wrapped in a cowl, and the darkness of seraphical divinity . . . when they observed how mad the bulk of the world was (as they still will be) for sensual pleasures, should run the matter too far o' the contrary extreme, and attempt to persuade us to have no senses at all or that God made 'em to very little purpose: an opinion not very improper for these who fancy they can and do believe transubstantiation.[20]

Nevertheless, for all his concern about à Kempis's imbalance, Samuel added in this same letter: "Mortification is still an indispensable Christian duty. The world's a siren, and we must have a care of her."[21]

John Wesley's own high valuation of *Imitation of Christ*, despite his erstwhile criticisms, is revealed in his later work *A Plain Account of Christian Perfection*, produced in 1766, in which the elderly Wesley reflects upon his earlier spiritual development:

I met with Kempis's "Christian's Pattern." The nature and extent
of inward religion, the religion of the heart, now appeared to me
in a stronger light then ever it had done before. I saw that giving
even all my life to God (supposing it possible to do this, and go
no further) would profit me nothing, unless I gave my heart, yea,
all my heart, to Him. I saw that simplicity of intention, and purity
of affection, one design in all we speak and do, and one desire
ruling all our tempers, are indeed the wings of the soul, without
which she can never ascend to the mount of God.[22]

Here, then, Wesley evidently saw quite clearly the nature and extent
of inward religion for the first time, that is, the importance of giving
all his heart to God as well as the beauty of simplicity of intention.
In other words, he was becoming much more sensitive, spiritually
speaking, and was now able to discern, in a way he had not done
before, not only the subtle rhythms of the heart, but also the importance of the unseen, the eternal. What à Kempis, the medieval monk,
had taught Wesley, then, was that vital religion ever begins with the
transformation of the heart, with the alteration of the tempers of the
deepest recesses of our being. This is a hidden work and often misprized by the world; but through the empowering grace of God,
these veiled affections, so mysterious and obscure, can become quite
manifest, even resplendent, in the love of God and neighbor.

At about the same time that Wesley was reading à Kempis, he
became acquainted with the writings of Jeremy Taylor, especially
with his *Rules and Exercises of Holy Living and Holy Dying* (1650–1651).
Born and raised in Cambridge, Jeremy Taylor, a conscientious
Caroline divine, was a protégé of Archbishop William Laud and a
chaplain to King Charles I. After the collapse of the monarchy,
Taylor found sanctuary as a chaplain on the estate of Lord and
Lady Carbery at Golden Grove. In time, Taylor was made an
Anglican bishop (of Down, Connor, and Dromore), as well as vice-
chancellor of Trinity College, Dublin. Gifted in many ways, Taylor
was one of the last in a line of what can be called a golden age of
preachers that began with Donne and Andrews. Taylor's *Rules and
Exercises of Holy Living and Holy Dying*, penned at Golden Grove,
like many of his other writings, breathed an air of simplicity, seriousness, and practicality that was indicative of much of seventeenth-
century English spirituality. Ever concerned with the laity of the
Church of England, Taylor, for the most part, targeted his

efforts toward those who were not being served well by the local clergy.

In Taylor's writings, Wesley found once again, but in a slightly different way, what he had discovered in à Kempis, namely, the significance of purity of intention as well as the importance of thorough dedication to God. Accordingly, in reading several parts of *Holy Living and Holy Dying*, Wesley later reflected:

> I was exceedingly affected; that part in particular which relates to purity of intention. Instantly, I resolved to dedicate all my life to God, all my thoughts, and words, and actions; being thoroughly convinced, there was no medium; but that every part of my life (not some only) must either be a sacrifice to God, or myself, that is, in effect, to the devil.[23]

In this context, then, the Christian life is understood as devotion, as an entire dedication and consecration to the will of God. Here the Most High is the One toward whom the highest affections and tempers of the heart are directed. The Almighty is the goal, the *telos*, the very perfection of our being.

Though Wesley had learned much from this Caroline divine, all was not well. In fact, one of Wesley's female companions at the time remarked that Taylor's *Holy Living and Holy Dying*

> almost put her out of her senses when she was fifteen or sixteen years old because he seemed to exclude all from being in a way of salvation who did not come up to his rules, some of which are altogether impracticable.[24]

To illustrate, in this work there were twenty-three rules for the employment of time; ten for directing the intention; and eight for signs of purity of intention among several others. In light of this counsel, one of the first rules of holy living that John Wesley adopted was the meticulous use of time, "the most visible consequence of Taylor's advice was Wesley's beginning to keep a diary as a record and measure of his progress in holy living."[25]

Beyond these difficulties, Wesley struggled with Taylor's notion of assurance—or rather the lack thereof—as well as with the Anglican bishop's estimation of humility. Concerning the former, Wesley related to his mother, Susanna, that he could not accept the idea that "a true penitent must all the days of his life pray for pardon, and never think the work completed till he dies."[26] Wesley reasoned that "if we can never have any certainty of our being in a state of salvation," as Taylor had suggested, "good reason it is that every moment should be spent, not in joy, but fear and trembling."[27] Given such judgments, Wesley could only conclude, "God deliver us from such a fearful expectation as this."[28] Concerning the latter difficulty, the estimation of humility, Wesley neither believed that Bishop Taylor was sufficiently clear on this topic, nor considered it a virtue "to think ourselves the worst in every company." This kind of humility, Wesley maintained, cannot be pleasing to God, "since it does not flow from faith, without which it is impossible to please him."[29]

So then, through encountering a religious friend and through reading à Kempis and Taylor (as well as Robert Nelson's *The Practice of True Devotion* and William Beveridge's *Private Thoughts Upon Religion*[30]), Wesley not only began to clear up the confusion as a result of his earlier reading of the well-meaning, wrong-headed Germans, but also, more important, underwent what can best be described as a spiritual awakening. In other words, during 1725, Wesley understood for the first time that holiness is the end or goal of religion. He realized that true religion entailed not simply outward exercise or duty, but also the tempers and affections of the heart; that it embraced not simply works of mercy, but works of piety as well; and that scriptural Christianity encompassed not merely external exercises, a round of labors, and duties, but also inward transformation especially in terms of devotion and dedication to God. All this and more Wesley learned as he prepared for ordination. It was truly a remarkable year.

When the elderly John Wesley reflected back on his awakening in the pivotal year of 1725, he couched it in the language of real Christianity. That is, he explored his earlier religious experience along the lines of the distinction between being a nominal Christian and being a real one. For example, in his sermon "In What Sense We Are to Leave the World," Wesley states:

When it pleased God to give *me* a settled resolution to be not a *nominal* but a *real* Christian (being then about two and twenty years of age) my acquaintance were as ignorant of God as myself. But there was this difference: I knew my own ignorance; they did not know theirs. I faintly endeavoured to help them; but in vain. Meantime I found by sad experience that even their *harmless* conversation (so called) damped all my good resolutions. But how to get rid of them was the question, which I resolved in my mind again and again. I saw no possible way, unless it should please God to remove me to another college.[31]

This passage, written in 1784, expresses the same judgments and sentiments of those of the young Wesley during the year 1725. The continuity here not only is striking, but also reinforces the notion that on one level, the early Wesley was quite dissatisfied not only with his own early Christian experience, but with that of others as well. Some of Wesley's peers, at Oxford and elsewhere, may have been content, even self-satisfied, in their Christian walk; but clearly Wesley was not. Therefore, biographers who gloss over this early period, who discern an untroubled continuity from the Epworth rectory to Wesley's public ministry later on, must ignore significant evidence to the contrary—and much of it from Wesley's own pen. Clearly, the discontent of Wesley, along with his yearning for the deeper things of God, mark him as one who desired spiritual growth as a *movement* from one realization of grace to the next, who welcomed, in other words, what our own age has called a spiritual journey.

Wesley's Early Understanding of Faith

Though Wesley, by the time he was twenty-two, understood the end or goal of religion in the midst of its beliefs, doctrines, sacraments, works of piety and mercy, and the like, he did not yet comprehend the proper means to realize the goal of holiness, how to actualize, in other words, in the warp and woof of life, the high ideals that had so captivated both his imagination and his religious sensibilities. To illustrate, in a letter to his mother on July 29, 1725, Wesley has a limited and largely undeveloped view of the nature of faith as is evident in the following: "Faith is a species of belief," and belief is defined "as an assent to a proposition upon rational grounds. Without rational grounds there is therefore no belief, and consequently no faith."[32] Elsewhere, in this same letter, Wesley writes very much as a child of the Enlightenment, as one who greatly values the operations and substantiating power of discursive reason: "As I understand faith to be an assent to any truth upon rational grounds, I don't think it possible without perjury to swear I believe anything, unless I have rational grounds for my persuasion."[33] Moreover, through his readings of John Norris, Samuel Clarke, and others, Wesley felt justified in his own affirmations that the divine testimony is the most reasonable of all evidence whatsoever, and that "faith must necessarily at length be resolved into reason."[34] Susanna offered a subtle, but no less significant, corrective in her subsequent letters and shifted the locus of authority from reason to the trustworthiness of God:

> You are somewhat mistaken in your notion of faith. . . . The true measure of faith is the authority of the revealer, the weight of which always holds proportion with our conviction of his ability and integrity. Divine faith is an assent to whatever God has revealed to us, because he has revealed it.[35]

John's response to these observations demonstrates, quite clearly, that he was convinced by Susanna on this larger issue: "I am, therefore, at length come over entirely to your opinion," he exclaims, "that saving faith (including practice) is an assent to what God has revealed because He had revealed it and not because the truth may be evinced by reason."[36]

But even with this modification of his understanding of faith in 1725, the year of his spiritual awakening, Wesley continued to focus on one aspect of faith, namely, assent. Granted, assent is ever an aspect of vital, redeeming faith, but it can in no way be deemed the whole. That is, mere intellectual assent to the truths of the Christian faith, whether such truths be sustained by reason or by an appeal to the authority of God, can never by itself be satisfactory for it may leave the dispositions and affections of the heart virtually untouched. Assent, then, must ever be joined with trust, a trust that holds to God as the locus of all value, the orienting center of human life. *Fides*, in other words, must ever be accompanied by *fiducia*. Beyond this, faith must be embraced as a spiritual sense, as a means to discern the things of God as depicted, for example, by the author of the book of Hebrews. Put another way, faith must be seen as an organ of spiritual knowledge, that it is, in a real sense, the "seeing eye," the "hearing ear," of spiritual discernment. However, it would take several years before Wesley would comprehend all three elements of the nature of faith aright: as assent, as trust, and as a spiritual sense. In the meantime, he sought various ways and approaches, some of which he later rejected, to realize the holiness that had so captivated him.

Developments at Oxford

With the blessings of Susanna and Samuel, John Wesley was finally ordained deacon of the Church of England on September 19, 1725. Bishop Potter, the son of a Yorkshire merchant, officiated. The night before his ordination, in a way typical of many English Puritan divines, Wesley recorded in his diary "the first results of what soon became regular Saturday evening self-examinations."[37] Among other things, he listed "boasting, [being] greedy of praise, intemperate sleep . . . [and] heat in arguing."[38] Various resolutions to amend his life appeared in the diary from time to time as well as a listing of the occasions when such resolutions were simply neglected or outright broken. Indeed, so intent was Wesley on bringing greater order and regularity to his religious life that in October 1726 he made a "summary" resolution that he would henceforth "once a day read over the last week's resolutions."[39]

The newly ordained Wesley continued his studies at Oxford and was elected a Fellow of Lincoln College on March 17, 1726, to the great pleasure of his father: "What will be my fate before the summer is over, God knows; but wherever I am, my Jacky is Fellow of Lincoln."[40] Most of the colleges at Oxford during this period were dominated by Tories, although a few, such as Exeter and Jesus, entertained Whig sentiments.[41] It was the Jacobite reputation of much of the university, among other things, that kept Whig numbers small, the lowest point being reached during the 1750s.[42] In terms of religion, Oxford was remarkably traditional, even conservative, since it was rooted in "the ideals of seventeenth-century High Church divines"; and some of its colleges had a cherished history of combating heresy.[43] Lincoln College, for instance, arose in the Middle Ages specifically to oppose the Lollards; and its founding was portrayed by Wesley in terms of the task to "overturn all heresies, and defend the Catholic faith."[44]

In November 1726, Wesley was elected yet again, but this time as Greek lecturer and moderator of the classes at Lincoln. As a

Greek lecturer, Wesley expounded upon selected passages of the New Testament to his undergraduate students. As a moderator, he presided over the daily "disputations" at the college, which were forums for the critical examination of various topics. Studious and disciplined in many respects, Wesley received his Master of Arts degree on February 14, 1727, and he delivered three lectures: one on the souls of animals, a second on Julius Caesar, and a third on the love of God. The lectures were well received and naturally enhanced Wesley's reputation at the college. Unfortunately, these early discourses have all been lost.

Shortly before Wesley received his master's degree at Lincoln, he wrote to his mother in January 1727 and looked to her, once again, for guidance in the area of practical divinity. Having drawn up a scheme of studies from which he did not intend to depart, Wesley related to Susanna that he had "perfectly come over to [her] opinion, that there are many truths it is not worth while to know."[45] Speculative studies, then, theological or otherwise, were quietly put aside. Susanna replied to her son in a subsequent letter and expressed her hearty approval:

> Your drawing up for yourself a scheme of studies highly pleases me, for there is nothing like a clear *method* to save both time and labour in anything. . . . 'Tis certain there are very few that will persevere in a regular course.[46]

Earlier, in a letter to his older brother Samuel Jr., Wesley had noted that "leisure and I have taken leave of one another: I propose to be busy as long as I live."[47] Accordingly, Wesley's energy and drive, always considerable, now had an even more focused direction.

But this January 1727 correspondence with his mother is valuable for another reason; for in it Wesley gives evidence, once again, of the seriousness with which he took the Christian faith, that he was in earnest to know, in an experiential and practical way, its deepest riches. Recounting an earlier conversation that he had with Robin Griffiths, who had earlier matriculated at New College, Oxford, while Wesley was at Christ Church, Wesley observes:

> About a year and a half ago I stole out of company at eight in the evening with a young gentleman with whom I was intimate. As we took a turn in an aisle of St. Mary's Church, in expectation of

a young lady's funeral with whom we were both acquainted, I asked him if he really thought himself my friend, and if he did, why he would not do me all the good he could. He began to protest, in which I cut him short by desiring him to oblige me in an instance which he could not deny to be in his own power—to let me have the pleasure of making him a whole Christian, to which I knew he was at least half persuaded already; that he could not do me a greater kindness, as both of us would be fully convinced when we came to follow that young woman.[48]

To be a "whole Christian," rather than a half one, was Wesley's desire for his closest friends, Robin Griffiths among them, and for himself as well. Such an emphasis made Wesley appear earnest to his friends and eccentric to his enemies. How could a rector's son at Lincoln *not* be a whole Christian? The logic was inescapable for some though it was doubted by Wesley himself.

William Law

In August 1727, Wesley left the comfortable environment of Oxford and headed for Lincolnshire to serve as his father's curate at Epworth and at Wroote. In this pastoral setting, Wesley saw little fruit to his ministry, but he continued to read spiritual and devotional literature. In 1729 or so, Wesley encountered William Law's *Christian Perfection* and *A Serious Call to a Devout and Holy Life*. Educated at Emmanuel College, Cambridge, William Law had been elected a fellow in 1711, the year of his ordination. When the Elector of Hanover and great-grandson of James I of England was invited to the throne in 1714 as George I, Law refused to acknowledge the legitimacy of this monarch and thereby lost his fellowship and retired to King's Cliffe. Law recovered somewhat, began to associate with the Gibbon family at Putney in 1727, and eventually became the tutor of Edward Gibbon, the father of the famous historian.

In reading this well-known Anglican, Wesley explored and then appropriated three keen insights. First of all, he now came to realize the extensiveness of the moral law, its "exceeding height and breadth and depth," and as a consequence he "cried to God for help and resolved not to prolong the time of obeying him as [he] had never done before."[49] As was his practice at the time, Wesley matched this spiritual insight with further resolutions and exclaimed:

> And by my continued endeavour to keep his whole law, inward
> and outward, to the utmost of my power, I was persuaded that I
> should be accepted of him, and that I was even then in a state of
> salvation.[50]

Such a resolve was actually a prescription for a deep and long-lasting malaise in Wesley's life, for it, in effect, made obedience to the moral law the basis of acceptance, a frustrating impossibility for any aspirant. Put another way, this approach made sanctification the ground of justification.

Second, Wesley expressed what he had learned through reflecting upon the writings of William Law in a now familiar idiom. Thus, several years later, in his *Plain Account of Christian Perfection*, he points out:

> A year or two after, Mr. Law's "Christian Perfection" and
> "Serious Call" were put into my hands. These convinced me,
> more than ever, of the absolute impossibility of being half a
> Christian; and I determined, through his grace (the absolute
> necessity of which I was deeply sensible of) to be all-devoted to
> God, to give him all my soul, my body and my substance.[51]

Few can mistake the seriousness and the ardor that are present in these words. Wesley wanted nothing less than to give all to God: body, soul, and all his possessions in an act of thoroughgoing consecration. Again, he desired to place all that he was, all that he would ever become, on the altar of the Most High.

Third, both William Law's *Christian Perfection* and *Serious Call* had a strong ascetic bent to them; and although Wesley objected to some of this counsel, it is likely—given his larger theological journey—that he was to some extent influenced by just such an emphasis. In his *Christian Perfection*, for example, Law set aside the most innocent amusements as a waste of time; he allowed little place for the appreciation of beauty and delight; and he cast doubts upon learning as a suitable goal of a dedicated life.[52] Similarly, in his *Serious Call*, Law stressed the need for acts of renunciation and mortification, some of which were quite dour and severe, an emphasis that may have been mediated to him by John Tauler and John Ruysbroeck, but which was eventually passed to Wesley.

So then, through reading the triumvirate of à Kempis, Taylor, and Law, Wesley came to understand quite clearly the end or goal of religion, which is sanctification or holiness, that is, loving God and neighbor in all sincerity and devotion and with suitable affection. He saw, for example, that purity of intention, often neglected in conventional and external religion, is ever vital in serving a God of holy love and in embracing one's neighbor. He also realized, in a way many of his contemporaries had not, that in this service, he must be devoted to the Most High in a thoroughgoing fashion, ever mindful of the divine will as expressed in the moral law, a law that extends to all his thoughts, words, and actions.

Equally important as the content of Wesley's breakthrough was its source. Indeed, as a young man, Wesley learned what constitutes the substance of holiness or sanctification not at the feet of Eastern Fathers—though he would later *explicate* this teaching by means of their writings—but at the feet of western divines: one a Roman Catholic mystic and the other two earnest Anglican leaders.[53] In fact, Wesley's readings during this pivotal period are dominated by western and Anglican voices that include, among others, John Norris, Bishop Atterbury, Francis Hutcheson, Bishop George Bull, Samuel Clarke, William Lowth, Fénelon, Bishop Browne, Anthony Horneck, and, of course, Thomas à Kempis, Jeremy Taylor, and William Law.[54] Consequently, the considerable and lasting appropriation here with respect to holiness is a *western* one and is deeply rooted in and sustained by rich Anglican sensibilities that were broad enough to take into account the fruits of both Catholics and Anglicans, and wise enough to be grounded, in important ways, in the Caroline divinity of the seventeenth century. And though there has been much contemporary discussion of the virtual equivalence of eastern notions of *theosis* and Wesley's understanding of *sanctification*, as this present work progresses, it will become increasingly apparent that there are important differences to be noted as well, differences that reflect Wesley's own distinct eighteenth-century ecclesiastical location.[55]

The First Rise of Methodism: Oxford

Wesley went up to Oxford in July 1728, where he remained for a few months, and was ordained priest in the Church of England on September 22 by Dr. Potter, the same bishop who had ordained him deacon. Shortly after his ordination, Wesley returned to Epworth and Wroote to assist his father in pastoral duties. In the meantime, Charles Wesley was pursuing his studies at Christ Church, Oxford, where he began to attend the weekly sacrament and to encourage some of his friends to do the same. A letter from Charles to his brother John in January 1729 revealed just what an inhospitable place Christ Church could be for those who took their religion seriously:

> Christ Church is certainly the worst place in the world to begin a reformation in; a man stands a very fair chance of being laughed out of his religion at his first setting out, in a place where 'tis scandalous to have any at all.[56]

Nevertheless, Charles and a few others continued their pious activities at the university, and a report from him in May 1729 motivated Wesley to visit Christ Church and this small group, which included Charles, of course, as well as William Morgan and occasionally Robert Kirkham. The members of this fledgling society not only attended the sacrament regularly, but also prayed, studied together, and engaged in religious conversation. The seeds of what would later become Oxford Methodism were now being planted. Toward the end of the summer, however, the group broke up as John and Charles went to Epworth and the others to their homes.

In October 1729, Dr. Morley, the rector of Lincoln, pointed out to Wesley that it was necessary for fellows to fulfill their duties at the college, not in absentia, but in person. The "interest of [the] college and obligation to statute,"[57] Dr. Morley cautioned, required Wesley's return as well as the resumption of his duties—despite Samuel's need of a curate. So then, after attending to his affairs, Wesley headed for Oxford in November of that year; and he, along with his brother Charles and William Morgan, continued where they had left off during the summer by meeting on a regular basis and by striving to keep the precepts of the university. Soon Robert Kirkham joined their number once again. The little band was eventually referred to as "The Holy Club," "Godly Club," "Bible Moths," and "Supererogation Men." The term "Methodist" came later when John Bingham, of Christ Church, observed there was "a new set of Methodists" springing up among them.[58]

Curiously enough, there is some dispute among historians as to what the name "Methodist" originally meant, for the evidence is ambiguous. For example, when John reminisces about the movement in his sermon "On Laying the Foundation of the New Chapel," he associates the name with an ancient group of physicians who began to flourish at Rome during the time of Nero and who thought that "all diseases might be cured by a specific method of diet and exercise."[59] The name was also used, however, in the seventeenth century in a sermon at Lambeth in reference to " 'plain packstaff Methodists,' who despised all rhetoric."[60] However, as Heitzenrater aptly points out, "Wesley never associated the title 'Methodist' with the nomenclature of the previous generation's theological disputes, apparently being unfamiliar with the obscure usage."[61] And to complicate matters further, Charles Wesley not only suggests a different dating for the initial use of the name Methodist than John ("This gained *me* the harmless name of Methodist. In half a year *after this* my brother left his curacy at Epworth and came to our assistance."), but he also offers a different clue as to its meaning and contends that it was "bestowed upon himself and his friends because of their strict conformity to the method of study prescribed by the statutes of the University."[62]

Whatever the source of the term "Methodist," those called by this name eventually came to include—besides the Wesleys— William Morgan, Robert Kirkham, John Clayton, George Whitefield, Benjamin Ingham, James Hervey, J. Broughton, John Whitelamb, John Gambold, Westley Hall, and Charles Kinchin, among others.[63] From the very beginning this little religious society had focused on works of piety such as prayer, reading the Scriptures, and receiving the Lord's Supper as important means of grace; but with the addition of John Clayton to the group, there was also an increasing emphasis on keeping the fasts (on Wednesdays and Fridays) of the ancient church. An older man with a taste for learning, Clayton was the son of a Manchester bookseller and eventually became a good patristic scholar. Stressing the significance of primitive Christianity, Clayton introduced the Wesleys to the teachings of such Manchester Nonjurors as Thomas Deacon and John Byrom. Wesley was, of course, already familiar with the High Church ideals of seventeenth-century divinity and with the views of the Anglican Robert Nelson;[64] but Clayton helped Wesley and others see the value of the so-called *Apostolic Constitutions,* which stressed not only the importance of fasting, but also baptism by immersion and various eucharistic practices,[65] especially the practice of frequent Communion. In fact, in 1732, the year in which Clayton joined the Methodists, Wesley made an extract of Robert Nelson's *The Great Duty of Frequenting the Christian Sacrifice.*[66]

In terms of works of mercy, a constant concern as well, William Morgan augmented the Methodist practice by enjoining the Wesleys and others to visit the Oxford prisons, the Castle and the Bocardo in particular. Here they not only prayed with the prisoners and administered communion, but also distributed pious books such as *The Whole Duty of Man, The Christian Monitor,* and *The Companion to the Altar.*[67] As a part of their ongoing discipline and stewardship, the Oxford Methodists cut off all needless expense so that they could be of greater service to the poor. In fact, Wesley noted that it was the practice of the early Methodists to give away all that they had after they had provided for their own necessities. A clue to John Wesley's own behavior at the time perhaps can be found in his sermon "The More Excellent Way," in which he notes:

> One of them [the Oxford Methodists] had thirty pounds a year. He lived on twenty-eight, and gave away forty shillings. The next year receiving sixty pounds, he still lived on twenty-eight, and gave away two-and-thirty. The third year he received ninety pounds, and gave away sixty-two. The fourth year he received a hundred and twenty pounds. Still he lived on twenty-eight, and gave to the poor ninety-two. Was not this a more excellent way?[68]

Wesley's later reflections on the rise of Oxford Methodism are also significant because in them he underscores the importance he attached to being a scriptural Christian where the Bible constitutes the basic standard or norm of his life. In his *Plain Account of Christian Perfection,* for example, he states: "In the year 1729, I began not only to read, but to study, the Bible, as the one, the only standard of truth, and the only model of pure religion."[69] Elsewhere, in his sermon "On God's Vineyard," Wesley points out:

> From the very beginning, from the time that four young men united together, each of them was *homo unius libri*—A man of one book. . . . They had one, and only one, rule of judgment. . . . They were one and all determined to be *Bible-Christians.*[70]

Naturally, there were other ways of being a Christian in the eighteenth century, especially within the context of a large state church like the Church of England; but Wesley and the Oxford Methodists had chosen "the more narrow way." For their trouble, they were mocked by their classmates, ridiculed on occasion, and called "Bible moths" and "Bible bigots."

While Oxford Methodism was taking shape, Wesley continued his responsibilities as a fellow, tutor, and moderator of the classes. Evidence from his diary indicates that during this period, Wesley was reading selections from German pietistic works, especially the works of Bartholomew Ziegenbalg and August Hermann Francke. Like his mother, Susanna, Wesley found Ziegenbalg's account of the labors of two Danish missionaries both edifying and instructive. Like many continental Protestants, Wesley cherished Francke's *Nicodemus* (or *A Treatise on the Fear of Man*), a work that had been translated into English by Anton Wilhelm Böhme in 1706.[71] In fact, not only did Wesley recommend this work to several of his students at Oxford, John Robson in particular, but he also later published it, in an abridged version, in his *Christian Library*.

The central theme of *Nicodemus* was clearly congenial to Wesley's purpose, for it described, in various ways, the necessity of overcoming the fear of humanity through the power of gracious faith. In this treatise, for instance, Francke warned his fellow ministers: "A fearful Minister reproves common people boldly; but when he is to speak to great and honorable persons, his mouth is gagged."[72] And the grand excuse for not speaking honestly and forthrightly was to be found in the fear—to use Francke's own words—"of getting an ill name."[73] In addition, clustering around the main topic of the fear of humanity were the ancillary themes of the fear of suffering, "flinching from the cross,"[74] and the lack of self-denial[75]—all of which often led to failure in the pulpit. The antidote, then, for such vapid preaching, whereby one could be delivered from the fear of humanity, was the exercise of a vital faith in God, which entailed an honest consideration of one's true spiritual state. Francke cautioned his followers:

> The first and most necessary of all means is a constant and earnest endeavor to free ourselves from the most dangerous deceitfulness of our own hearts. Nothing is a more fatal hin-

drance of a man's salvation, than the false conceit that he is already a Christian.[76]

Moreover, Francke underscored the salutary effect of preaching on inward religion[77] and holiness: "There is no true faith," he wrote, "without holiness of heart and life . . . [and] the true boldness of faith is known by its continually working by love,"[78] themes familiar to other Pietists as well.[79]

Amidst the gossip and the derision directed at the Methodists at Oxford was the charge that they lacked balance and perspective in the area of religion. "I have been charged with being too strict," Wesley confessed to Mrs. Pendarves in 1731, "with carrying things too far in religion, and laying burthens on myself, if not on others, which were neither necessary nor possible to be borne."[80] Wesley dismissed such early criticism virtually out of hand and offered the reply, "What is this but to change holiness itself into extravagance?"[81] But censure along these lines, that the discipline and rigor of the Methodists was indeed extreme, continued apace. Matters came to a head in 1732 with the death of William Morgan, one of the original members of "The Holy Club," a death which some claimed was due to excessive fasting. Obviously, Wesley could not dismiss such a charge so easily, and so in a carefully crafted letter dated October 18, 1732, written to the deceased's father, Richard Sr., Wesley attempted to clear up any lingering misunderstandings surrounding this untimely death and in the process offered an apologetic for Oxford Methodism.

But the allegations of rigor, exactitude, and scrupulosity continued. In fact, a few years later in 1734, Richard Morgan, William's brother, complained to his father that the Methodists under Wesley's leadership "imagine they cannot be saved if they do not spend every hour, nay minute, of their lives in the service of God."[82] In an amusing coincidence in January of that same year, Wesley began what is called his "exacter" diary, in which he conscientiously recorded

> every hour in minute detail the resolutions broken and kept, his temper of devotion (on a rating scale from 1 to 9), his level of "simplicity" and "recollection," in addition to the usual record of his reading, visiting, writing, conversing, and other activities.[83]

Again, Richard Morgan bemoaned Wesley's teaching that luke-warm Christianity was the worst thing of all, worse than open sin: "There is no medium in religion," Wesley affirmed, "[and] a man that does not engage himself entirely in the practice of religion is in greater fear of damnation than a notorious sinner."[84] Even Dr. Morley, whom Wesley had described earlier as "one of the best friends I ever had in the world," cautioned Richard Morgan Jr. against "Mr. Wesley's strict notions of religion,"[85] and related that "the character of his Society prevented several from entering in the College."[86] In light of such counsel, Richard concluded in a letter to his father that if he continued under Wesley's tutoring, he would be ruined. In his own defense, Wesley wrote to Richard Morgan Sr. in 1734 and in the process articulated a well-developed, even beautiful, understanding of religion:

> I take religion to be, not the bare saying over so many prayers, morning and evening, in public or in private; not anything super-added now and then to a careless or worldly life; but a constant ruling habit of soul, a renewal of our minds in the image of God, a recovery of the divine likeness, a still-increasing conformity of heart and life to the pattern of our most holy Redeemer.[87]

Here Wesley revealed the throne room, the heart of it all, so to speak, that in the full round of activities of works of piety and of mercy, in the midst of rules and precepts, the Methodists were ever concerned with holiness, with the inculcation of holy love in both heart and life.

When Wesley included the story of the Methodists in his *Ecclesiastical History* late in his career (1781), he indicated that Methodism arose in three stages prior to 1739: first at Oxford, then in Georgia, and finally in London. Now it is precisely this first rise of Methodism at Oxford, from 1729 to 1735, that is so problematic for those scholars who maintain that historic Methodism cannot be understood apart from various practices, in particular, its class meetings, bands, and select societies. To illustrate, John Wright, who typifies this view, states,

> Wesley's thought arose within the context of Methodist practice; indeed, it *was* a central Methodist practice, in form and substance profoundly interrelated to the Methodist Societies and class meetings.[88]

Beyond this, Wright contends that the

> priority of the practice of the Methodists is evident in the relation-
> ship between the Methodist class meeting and Wesley's doctrine of
> sanctification. Both doctrine and class meetings developed into
> their classic Methodist form during the same period.[89]

The problem with this view, and others like it,[90] is that
Methodism, in terms of its basic ethos and substance, was *already* in
existence in 1729 prior to the subsequent development of its infrastructure of class meetings, bands, select societies, and the like. This
observation does not deny the importance of this infrastructure, or
the value of various Methodist practices, but is offered only to
assert that the *identity* of Methodism must lie elsewhere given the
appropriate temporal considerations and Wesley's own reckoning.
In a similar fashion, Wesley's doctrine of sanctification or holiness,
the goal of religion, was *already* in place through his reading of the
triumvirate of Kempis, Taylor, and Law. The later Methodist class
meetings, then, did not add to or alter this substance, but allowed
for its instantiation as Wesley employed suitable means "to spread
Scriptural holiness over the land."[91]

The Circumcision of the Heart

On New Year's Day, 1733, Wesley preached one of the most well-
crafted and theologically significant sermons of his career at St.
Mary's, Oxford. His text on the occasion—Romans 2:29
("Circumcision is that of the heart, in the spirit, and not in the letter")—was suggested by the celebration of the Feast of the
Circumcision of Christ as well as its Collect: "Grant us the true circumcision of the spirit that, our hearts and all our members being
mortified from all worldly and carnal lusts, we may in all things
obey thy blessed will."[92] The contents of this sermon were summarized by Wesley long afterward in a letter to John Newton on
May 14, 1765: "I preached the sermon on the Circumcision of the
Heart, which contains all that I now teach concerning salvation
from *all sin* and loving God with an *undivided heart*."[93] The following year, in his *Plain Account of Christian Perfection*, Wesley revealed
that the circumcision of the heart is nothing less than another way
of describing Christian perfection:

It is that habitual disposition of soul which, in the sacred writings, is termed holiness; and which directly implies, the being cleansed from sin, "from all filthiness both of flesh and spirit"; and, by consequence, the being endued with those virtues which were in Christ Jesus.[94]

And though Wesley actually modified this sermon—especially in the areas of justifying faith and assurance—when he published it at the beginning of his second volume of *Sermons on Several Occasions* in 1748, he nevertheless wrote in his journal many years later: "Nay, I know not that I can write a better on *The Circumcision of the Heart* than I did five and forty years ago."[95]

Just what makes this sermon so significant? For one thing, it is part of a broader genre employed by Wesley that highlights the importance of inward religion as well as the necessity of right tempers or dispositions of the heart. "The distinguishing mark of a true follower of Christ," Wesley observes, "of one who is in a state of acceptance with God, is not either outward circumcision or baptism, or any other outward form, but a right state of soul."[96] This inward work, so gracious and mysterious, what Wesley identifies as "the seal of thy calling,"[97] is considered "foolishness with the world,"[98] in its unending focus on more mundane matters and in its failure to discern the spiritual.

Second, the structure of the sermon itself, in terms of weaving an explication of the theological virtues of faith, hope, and love into the text, is conducive to Wesley's larger design of exploring Christian perfection. Indeed, each theological virtue is considered in relation to its end or goal, that is, with respect to what it means to have "the mind of Christ" and to walk according to "the royal law." In this context, then, God is rightly offered as the supreme object of our desires, affections, and intentions. However, what makes this discussion of the virtues somewhat different from other accounts in Wesley's sermons (in "The Marks of the New Birth," for example) is that, in this setting, Wesley highlights the value of humility as conducive to the reception of graces entailed in faith and in the other theological virtues implicatively related. Wesley elaborates:

This is that lowliness of mind which they have learned of Christ who follow his example and tread in his steps. And this knowledge of their disease, whereby they are more and more cleansed from one part of it, pride and vanity, disposes them to embrace with a willing mind the second thing implied in "circumcision of heart"—that faith which alone is able to make them whole, which is the one medicine given under heaven to heal their sickness.[99]

But notice that humility, though clearly valuable, is the "hand-maiden" of faith, "which alone is able to make them whole."[100] This means, of course, that the spirituality evidenced in this sermon is remarkably "Protestant" and can be distinguished, in some important respects, from Roman Catholic models that place a premium on lowliness and humility (often expressed as obedience to superiors), a point that will be developed in significant detail later.

In short, though Wesley's sermon "The Circumcision of the Heart" is both theologically significant and artfully constructed, it does not represent any significant change in Wesley's views on the salient matter of holiness. To be sure, the theological substance displayed at St. Mary's in 1733 was already well in place during the pivotal period of 1725–1729. Moreover, Wesley's views on both the cruciality of holiness and the value of inward religion (a true circumcision of the heart) are emphases that will remain throughout his lengthy career. And though such emphases will be expressed, at times, in a diversity of rhetorics (in the vocabularies of German Pietism and the Eastern Fathers, for example), they will nevertheless demonstrate not only remarkable constancy in the midst of subtle theological change, but also Wesley's lasting debt to his own Anglican tradition.

The Epworth Living

Toward the end of 1734, Samuel Wesley Sr. became concerned about the ministry at Epworth and Wroote as well as Susanna's financial condition since his health was failing. The elderly rector, therefore, made overtures to John to assume these pastoral duties, overtures that were politely refused. To illustrate, in a letter to his father in November 1734, Wesley reasoned that "wherever I can be most holy myself, there, I am assured, I can most promote holiness in others. But I am equally assured there is no place under heaven so fit for my improvement as Oxford."[101] Samuel was stunned. He had hoped that his "legacy" in the parishes of Epworth and

Wroote would continue. With a measure of frustration, Samuel replied to his reluctant son and complained that "it is not dear self, but the glory of God, and the different degrees of promoting it, which should be our main consideration and direction in the choice of any course of life."[102]

Failing here, the elderly Wesley wrote to Samuel Jr. and urged him to put some pressure on John. Like his father, Samuel Jr. accused his recalcitrant brother of self-love, of preoccupation with his own interests: "I see your love to yourself, but your love to your neighbor I do not see."[103] Beyond this, Samuel Jr. contended that Wesley had, in effect, obligated himself to undertake pastoral duties in his ordination vows. The irony—even the hypocrisy—of this argument was probably not lost on Wesley who knew that his brother Samuel had refused their father's earlier offer of pastoral duties since their assumption would mean that he would have to resign as headmaster of Tiverton Grammar School, a position he greatly cherished. Nevertheless, Wesley took this argument offered by Samuel Jr. so seriously that he actually wrote to John Potter, Bishop of Oxford, to inquire whether this was so. "It doth not seem to me that at your ordination you engaged yourself to undertake the cure of any parish," the bishop replied, "provided you can as a clergyman better serve God and the Church in your present or some other station."[104] John forwarded this answer to his brother and triumphantly observed, "Now that I can, as a clergyman, better serve God and his Church in my present station, I have all reasonable evidence."[105]

But Samuel Sr. could not be so easily turned aside. And so John Wesley wrote a letter to his father in December 1734, in which he offered more than twenty arguments as to why he should not assume the pastoral duties at Epworth and Wroote. Two points were integral to his position: First, Wesley not only repeats his claim that his own holiness (and therefore that of others) can best be promoted at Oxford, but also offers a sophisticated, even profound, definition of holiness as revealed in the following:

> By holiness I mean, not fasting, or bodily austerity, or any other external means of improvement, but that inward temper to which all these are subservient, a renewal of soul in the image of God. I mean a complex habit of lowliness, meekness, purity, faith, hope, and love of God and man. And I therefore believe

that in the state wherein I am I can most promote this holiness in myself, because I now enjoy several advantages which are almost peculiar to it.[106]

As in his apologetic to Richard Morgan Sr., Wesley reveals to his father that his one end, his ultimate purpose, must ever be holiness and that which is most conducive to it.

Second, Wesley affirms that Oxford can further his spiritual growth by providing him with freedom from trifling acquaintances as well as the opportunity to be among real Christians. He elaborates:

> And this, I bless God, I can in some measure, so long as I avoid that bane of piety, the company of good sort of men, lukewarm Christians (as they are called), persons that have a great concern for, but no sense, of religion. But these insensibly undermine all my resolutions, and quite steal from me the little fervour I have; and I never come from among these "saints of the world"... faint, dissipated, and shorn of all my strength, but I say, "God deliver me from a half-Christian."[107]

This theme of being a real Christian, so evident during this period, will continue throughout Wesley's career with some important modifications along the way. Indeed, its continuity, as well as its modifications, will provide insight into the character and purpose of this very complex and sophisticated man—a man who was governed by his heart as much as by his mind, by tempers and dispositions as much as by logic.

Samuel Wesley Sr. died a little over four months after this letter. In the interim, John reflected, hesitated, and then finally applied for the parishes. But it was too late. As he lay dying, Samuel spoke to John neither of parishes nor of legacies nor even of the obedience required of a son. Instead, he whispered, "The inward witness, son, the inward witness; that is the proof, the strongest proof of Christianity."[108] But John understood him not.

CHAPTER THREE
Georgia

The Moravians Calmly Sang On

In the closing days of his life, Samuel Wesley Sr. was anxious that a copy of his *magnum opus*, a lengthy exposition in verse on the book of Job, be presented to Queen Caroline. To that end, Samuel asked his son John to deliver the manuscript in person to the royal court. Upon arriving in London, John found that the queen was romping with her maids, but she suspended her play long enough to receive him with appropriate kindness and grace.[1] The queen noted that the book was "very prettily bound," but she quickly laid it aside without opening a page.[2] While Wesley was on this errand, he was solicited by the Reverend John Burton of Corpus Christi College, Oxford, to become a missionary to the colony of Georgia. Burton hoped that Wesley would take the Society for Promoting Christian Knowledge (SPCK) chaplaincy at Savannah and thereby further the missionary work of this important Anglican religious society. To strengthen his case, Burton also introduced Wesley to James Oglethorpe, the Governor of the Georgia colony, who made a similar engaging appeal.

With much on his mind, Wesley headed back to Epworth and laid the whole matter before his widowed mother. Without the slightest hint of reservation, Susanna exclaimed: "Had I twenty sons, I should rejoice that they were all so employed."[3] Upon further reflection and prayer, Wesley finally decided to accept the invitation to become a missionary; and in a letter to the Reverend Burton on October 10, 1735, indicated two key reasons for doing so. First of all, Wesley maintained that his chief motive for going to the colonies, to which all the rest would be subordinate, was "the hope of saving my own soul. I hope to learn the true sense of the gospel of Christ by preaching it to the heathen."[4] By employing the phrase "the true sense of the gospel" in this context, Wesley reveals that there were dimensions of the good news of salvation that were for him, even at this time, unexplored. Indeed, in this same letter, Wesley not only refers to himself as a "grievous sinner," but also points out that he is yet "laden with foolish and hurtful lusts."[5] The reply to Burton, then, demonstrates that Wesley believed the heart of the gospel, the substance of its many liberating graces, would not be actualized—instantiated in warp and woof of life—but through *mission*.

Second, the aspiring missionary furthermore declares in this letter that he could not expect to attain the same degree of holiness in England as he could in Georgia. Wesley elaborates:

> But you will perhaps ask, Can't you save your own soul in England as well as in Georgia? I answer, No, neither can I hope to attain the same degree of holiness here which I may there; neither, if I stay here knowing this, can I reasonably hope to attain any degree of holiness at all.[6]

Remarkably, Wesley had employed a similar argument earlier with respect to his father's offer of the Epworth living. Then Wesley had noted that he could be more holy at Oxford than in a parish at Epworth. Now he pointed out to the Reverend Burton that he could be more holy in Georgia than in England—and presumably at Oxford as well. The places changed, but the logic remained the same.

And to the claim that such an ambitious, even dangerous, adventure was unnecessary, since there are "heathens enough, in practice if not theory, at home," Wesley replied in a way that demonstrates, once again, not only his commitment to mission, but also—interestingly enough—his criticism of English Christianity itself. "Why then should [I] go to those in America?" he asks. "Because these heathens at home have Moses and the prophets, and those have not. Because these who *have* the gospel trample upon it, and those who have it not earnestly call for it."[7] So then, Wesley desired to preach the gospel to the heathens, as he put it, because he wanted, above all, to be a vital part of a missional setting, in which the people actually hungered for the good news of God's saving grace. In the end, he knew that he would be edified, and in a certain sense sustained, by basking in such earnest and pious desires.

The Voyage to Georgia

On October 14, 1735, John Wesley, along with his brother Charles, who was recently ordained, headed out for Gravesend to depart for Georgia. Accompanying them were Benjamin Ingham of Queen's College, Oxford, and Charles Delamotte, the son of a London merchant. At the Gravesend dock, the four boarded the *Simmonds* along with twenty-six Moravians from Herrnhut, led by their godly bishop David Nitschmann. "Our end in leaving our native country," Wesley wrote in his journal, "was not to avoid want (God having given us plenty of temporal blessings), not to gain the dung or dross of riches or honor: but singly this—to save our souls, to live wholly to the glory of God."[8]

Once the voyage was finally underway, Wesley resolved with some of his compatriots that "they would neither eat meat or drink wine but depend for sustenance on rice and biscuits."[9] And shortly thereafter, on December 7, Wesley observed: "Finding nature did not require so frequent supplies as we had been accustomed to, we agreed to leave off suppers; from doing which we have hitherto found no inconvenience."[10] This ascetic tendency with respect to sustenance was matched by Wesley's employment of time; and he quickly settled into a fixed, methodical pattern:

> Our common way of spending our time was this: from four to five we used private prayer. From five to seven we read the Holy Scriptures, adding sometimes such treatises as give an account of the sense thereof, which was once delivered to the saints. At seven we breakfasted. At eight were the public prayers, at which

were present usually between thirty and forty of our eighty passengers. From nine to twelve I commonly learned German, Mr. Delamotte Greek. My brother wrote sermons.[11]

Though the *Simmonds* was no doubt a seaworthy vessel, Atlantic crossings in the eighteenth century could be quite dangerous. The sheer length of the voyage—in this case, several months—allowed for the likelihood that the vessel would be pummeled by Atlantic storms that invariably arose during this season. On November 23, for instance, Wesley lay in his cabin only to be awakened by the tossing of the ship and the roaring of the wind, both of which showed him that he was, to use his own words, "unwilling to die."[12] A few weeks earlier, Wesley had been awakened by a great noise on the ship but soon discovered that there was no danger. "But the bare apprehension of it," he related, "gave me a lively conviction what manner of men those ought to be who are every moment on the brink of eternity."[13]

Though the voyage had been relatively smooth during December, the weather deteriorated in January 1736. Indeed, several powerful storms gathered in the Atlantic and buffeted the *Simmonds* during the period of January 17 through 25. On the first day of this ordeal, Wesley recounted in his journal that "the sea broke over us from stem to stern, burst through the windows of the state cabin where three or four of us were, and covered us all over, though a bureau sheltered me from the main shock."[14] And nature, so powerful and awesome, once again evoked a response of fear from Wesley: "[I was] very uncertain whether I should wake alive, and much ashamed of my unwillingness to die." Yet another storm appeared during the evening of January 23, and Wesley confessed in his journal: "I could not but say to myself, 'How is it that thou hast no faith?' being still unwilling to die."[15] But the most powerful and frightening of all the storms en route to Georgia did not occur until two days later. The vivid detail of Wesley's journal account, together with his several judgments, demonstrate that this storm in particular had left an indelible impression on the anxious traveler. Wesley recalls:

> In the midst of the psalm wherewith their service began the sea broke over, split the mainsail in pieces, covered the ship, and poured in between the decks, as if the great deep had already

swallowed us up. A terrible screaming began among the English. The Germans calmly sang on. I asked one of them afterwards, "Was you not afraid?" He answered, "I thank God, no." I asked, "But were not your women and children afraid?" He replied mildly, "No; our women and children are not afraid to die."[16]

So taken was Wesley with the Moravian courage and serenity in the face of such great danger that he appended to this account: "This was the most glorious day which I have ever hitherto seen."[17]

Upon later reflection, Wesley drew a connection between the powers of nature and the state of one's soul. "I can conceive no difference comparable to that between a smooth and a rough sea," he writes, "except that which is between a mind calmed by the love of God and one torn up by the storms of earthly passions. Moreover, in July 1736, when Wesley was in America, he experienced a horrific thunder and lightning storm and confessed in his journal, once again, that he was not fit to die."[18] And a couple of weeks later, while he was on a boat, crossing the neck of St. Helena Sound off the coast of South Carolina, Wesley encountered yet another ominous storm. So furious were the wind and rain at the time that they collapsed the mast of the ship, terrifying all on board. Of this incident, Wesley concluded with respect to himself, "How is it that thou hadst no faith?"[19]

The Fear of Death as a Test of Christian Experience

These dramatic narratives of Wesley's fear in the face of death illuminate not only his own spiritual experience during the Georgia period, but also some of the soteriological standards that he held throughout his life. Unfortunately, this material, so valuable in many respects, has largely been neglected by contemporary scholarship in its attempt to find the "proper Christian faith," amply (and unproblematically) evidenced while Wesley was in Savannah and Frederica. Indeed, the observation that Wesley then had "the faith of a servant" is often put forth as conclusive evidence of saving faith.[20] Such an approach, however, falls hard on the *details* of the biographical material in a number of respects.

Before the salient elements pertaining to the motif of the fear of death and their bearing on John Wesley's soteriological status can be considered, a few distinctions are in order, lest there be misunderstanding. For one thing, Wesley had maintained earlier, in a letter dated January 15, 1731, that not all fear of death is negative and that some fear is actually necessary for the continuation of life: "But if pain and the fear of death were extinguished," he observes, "no animal could long subsist."[21] In this context, then, the fear of death does not have torment or is it indicative of an existential or spiritual condition; instead, it is a remarkable and useful "intuition" to sustain and preserve life, an intuition that characterizes all believers no matter how holy. The negative senses of the fear of death, on the other hand, from which believers can rightly expect to be delivered, are expressed in Wesley's *A Farther Appeal to Men of Reason and Religion* published in 1745. Wesley notes:

> Men commonly fear death, first because of leaving their worldly goods and pleasures; [second,] for fear of the pains of death; and, [third,] for fear of perpetual damnation. But none of these causes trouble good men, because they stay themselves by *true* faith, perfect charity, and sure hope of endless joy and bliss everlasting.[22]

Though Wesley affirmed that people of true faith are not marked by the fear of death in any of these senses just enumerated, he nevertheless was sensitive enough to distinguish between fear of the prospect of physical pain in the dying process itself from the fear of perpetual damnation. Such a judgment is substantiated by Wesley's pastoral care for the sick and dying, especially in terms of the alleviation of pain, as well as his repeated—and almost exclusive—emphasis in his writings on fear in the third sense of judgment and eternal loss.[23]

Six years after his Georgia labors, Wesley preached his last sermon at St. Mary's, Oxford, in which he not only proclaimed that one who is justified and born of God is free from the fear of death, but also linked this fear, a fear that has torment, specifically with what he termed "the spirit of bondage." In his sermon "Scriptural Christianity," for example, Wesley elaborates:

> He [the Christian believer] feared not what man could do unto him, knowing "the very hairs of his head were all numbered." He feared not all the powers of darkness, whom God was daily "bruising under his feet." Least of all was he afraid to die; nay, he

"desired to depart, and be with Christ" (Phil.1.23); who, "through death had destroyed him that had the power of death, even the devil, and delivered them who through fear of death were all their lifetime," till then, "subject to bondage."[24]

And the following year, in his treatise *A Farther Appeal to Men of Reason and Religion*, Wesley associates the fear of death, the spirit of bondage, and the Jewish dispensation in a way that underscores the liberty of the gospel, especially when he points out that "the Jews were subject to the fear of death, and lived in consequence of it in a state of bondage."[25]

But perhaps the best and most lucid explication of the connection between the fear of death and the spirit of bondage is found in Wesley's sermon "The Spirit of Bondage and of Adoption," which was written the very next year, in 1746. In this sermon, Wesley explores the "legal state," that spiritual condition prior to the liberating and empowering graces of the gospel. Indeed, the one "under the law" finds that "sin let loose upon the soul . . . is perfect misery. . . . He feels . . . fear of death, as being to him the gate of hell, the entrance of death eternal."[26] Interestingly enough, Wesley explores this bondage, energized by the fear of death and the dominion of sin, in terms of the duplicity, the division of the will, which is expressed by the apostle Paul in Romans 7: "For that which I do, I allow not: for what I would, that do I not; but what I hate, that I do" (v. 15 KJV). Again, those under a spirit of bondage feel sorrow and remorse; they fear death, the devil, and humanity. They desire to break free from the chains of sin but cannot, and their cry of despair is typified by the Pauline expression: "O wretched man that I am, who shall deliver me from the body of this death?"[27] And in considering the spiritual estate of the person under such enslaving powers, Wesley affirms, "Such is the bondage under which [one] [groans]; such the tyranny of [a] hard [taskmaster]."[28]

Wesley's exploration of the theme of the fear of death, however, as well as its linkage to the spirit of bondage, was not merely an early emphasis, as is sometimes mistakenly supposed, but one that continued throughout his career. For instance, in 1750, in his sermon "The Original, Nature, Properties and Use of the Law," Wesley cautions the reader about being "entangled again with the yoke of [bondage]"; and he counsels that one should "abhor sin far more than death or hell; abhor sin itself far more than the punishment of it."[29] That same year, in his sermon "Satan's Devices," the Methodist leader reminds those who have become the sons and daughters of God that "if your eye be not steadily fixed on him who hath borne all your sins, he will bring you again under that 'fear of death' whereby you was so long 'subject unto bondage.' "[30] In fact, in his sermon "The Wilderness State," produced in 1760, Wesley chronicles the slow and subtle descent into sin and the reemergence of a spirit of fear:

> We begin to doubt whether we ever did find in our hearts the real testimony of the Spirit. Whether we did not rather deceive our own souls, and mistake the voice of nature for the voice of God. . . . And these doubts are again joined with servile fear, with that "fear" which "hath torment." We fear the wrath of God, even as before we believed; We fear lest we should be cast out of his presence; and thence sink again into that fear of death from which we were before wholly delivered.[31]

Moreover, the following decade, in 1772, Wesley dined with one who, as he put it in his journal, was "completely miserable, through 'the spirit of bondage' and in particular through the fear of death."[32]

Beyond this considerable evidence—and much more could be cited—Wesley's letter to Thomas Davenport in 1781 is especially significant because in it Wesley reveals quite clearly that the spirit of bondage—that "legal faith" that is under the power or dominion of sin and is therefore plagued by the fear of death and judgment—is not—and cannot be—justifying faith. Wesley explains:

> You are in the hands of a wise Physician, who is lancing your sores in order to heal them. He has given you now the spirit of fear. But it is in order to the spirit of love and of a sound mind. You have now received the spirit of bondage. Is it not the forerunner of the spirit of adoption? He is not afar off. Look up! And expect Him to cry in your heart, Abba, Father! He is nigh that *justifieth.*[33]

Others may have confused the spirit of bondage or the anxious fear of death with justifying faith. Clearly, Wesley did not.

So intent was Wesley in making the question of whether one had been set free from the fear of death one of his more important sote-riological standards that he specifically explored this probe in terms of his well-worked motif of real Christianity.[34] Thus, in his *Farther Appeal to Men of Reason and Religion*, produced in 1745, Wesley quotes from "Sermon Against the Fear of Death" and agrees that "a true Christian . . . is not afraid to die."[35] Elsewhere, in his "Thought on Necessity," Wesley exclaims: "O what advantage has a Christian (a real Christian) over an Infidel! He sees God! Consequently . . . he tramples on inexorable fate, and fear, and death, and hell!"[36] But perhaps the best example of the explicit association of freedom from the fear of death with the real or proper Christian faith is found in Wesley's spiritual counsel to Ms. Cummins late in his career:

> O make haste! Be a Christian, a real Bible Christian now! You may say, "Nay, I am a Christian already" I fear not. (See how freely I speak.) A Christian is not afraid to die. Are not you? Do you desire to depart and to be with Christ?[37]

So then, if the elderly Wesley affirmed in the 1770s that a real Christian is not afraid to die, then what does that make him while he was in Georgia? Indeed, fearlessness in the face of death is not only a test that Wesley applied to his own religious experience, to and from Georgia, but also one that he applied to others both early and late in his career. The continuity is striking.

The Second Rise of Methodism: The Georgia Mission

About noon on February 4, 1736, the pine trees of Georgia were visible from the mast of the *Simmonds*. A couple of days later, the party of English and Germans arrived on American soil, knelt down and prayed, and gave thanks to God for a safe voyage. The very first exercise of authority in the New World by John Wesley was to stave in the rum casks, which had been aboard the ship—an action that, though within the regulations of the trustees, was not only presumptuous, but also cost him the good will of some of the colonists.

In terms of his prospects for ministry, Wesley was set to replace Samuel Quincy, the first Anglican priest in Georgia, who had labored as the pastor of the Savannah settlement from 1732 until 1735. However, since Quincy was still living in the rectory, not quite ready to move, Wesley and Charles Delamotte had to take up quarters for the time being in the same settlement as the Moravians. Later that month, on February 25, the two began to lodge with the Germans, and such living arrangements gave them ample opportunity to observe the day-to-day behavior of this devout people, since they were all in one room from morning until night.

Deeply impressed by what he saw in the Moravian community, Wesley was emboldened to seek advice regarding his own moral and spiritual conduct from one of its leaders, August Spangenberg. Before he would answer, however, Spangenberg posed two questions to Wesley: first, "Have you the witness within yourself?" And second, "Does the Spirit of God bear witness with your spirit that you are a child of God?" Wesley was surprised by such probing questions and didn't know quite how to answer. Spangenberg nevertheless continued his queries: "Do you know Jesus Christ?" Wesley paused and said, "I know he is the Savior of the world." "True," Spangenberg replied, "But do you know he has saved you?" Wesley's response was once again both weak and indecisive: "I hope he has died to save me." The kindly Moravian leader then brought matters to a head in a very pastoral way and asked, "Do you know yourself?" Wesley responded, "I do." But he later noted in his journal that he feared these were "vain words."[38]

This interview with Spangenberg, important in many respects, revealed to Wesley that he lacked the witness of the Holy Spirit that he was a child of God. To be sure, Wesley marveled at the assurance that Spangenberg seemed to have in matters of faith. This was the same sort of steady confidence that was displayed by the broader Moravian community on board the *Simmonds*, as noted earlier. In the face of all this, Wesley was, of course, intrigued, and so he naturally wanted to learn more from this German-speaking people. To that end, Wesley continued to study German—perhaps now even more seriously—a pursuit that had actually begun at the start of the voyage.

The Salzburgers

The Moravians, however, were not the only pietistic group in Georgia with which Wesley would have cordial relations. Indeed, accompanying the *Simmonds* en route to Savannah was a sister ship, *The London Merchant*, which carried a company of two hundred refugee Salzburgers led by the Hanoverian nobleman Friedrich Von Reck. These resolute and courageous Protestants had been persecuted under the intolerant policy of Archbishop Firmian of Salzburg. Therefore, as an act of both Christian grace and charity, the SPCK sponsored the settlement of this group at New Ebenezer, near Purrysburg, twenty to thirty miles northwest of the Savannah colony.

The two Lutheran pastors in charge of this colony of Salzburgers were Johann Martin Bolzius and Israel Christian Gronau. Both men had served as teachers under August Hermann Francke in the Orphan House at Halle, and both were ordained in Germany specifically for the American mission.[39] Following the teachings of August Hermann Francke as well as those of Samuel Urlsperger, Bolzius and Gronau were naturally steeped in the tradition of Philipp Jacob Spener as well as that of the University of Halle.[40] Precursors of this theological tradition, which placed a premium on vital Christian faith, inner experience, and religious commitment, can be found in the work of Johann Arndt and in the translations of the writings of English Puritans such as L. Bayly. In time, the piety of Halle became widely known for its emphasis on grace, penance, and the necessity of regeneration—emphases that Wesley found congenial as well. And though there is no clear evidence that Wesley ever read the *Pia Desideria* of Spener, its chief affirmations, especially in terms of the importance of "real Christianity," were, no doubt, communicated to him by the Salzburg community as well as by his own reading of Arndt's classic *True Christianity*, which he mastered in about a week beginning March 24, 1736.

Immensely popular during the seventeenth and eighteenth centuries, Arndt's writings became a staple of German piety. In fact, in many German homes of this period, *True Christianity* found its place right alongside the Bible. Across the continent, in England, this work was known as early as 1648.[41] Subsequently, the Halle Pietist, Anthony William Boehm (1673–1722)—not to be confused with Jakob Boehme (1575–1624)—translated *Vier Bücher vom wahren Christentum* into English and promptly submitted a copy to the queen along with a suitable preface.[42] As with the Salzburgers, Wesley was most probably attracted to *True Christianity* because of three of its major themes: first, its soteriological thrust; second, its emphasis on genuine Christianity as embracing inward disposi- tions—as opposed to mere formal or external religion—and third, its irenic aim and tone.

Concerning the first point of soteriology, Arndt's work, like some of Wesley's later sermons,[43] was very attentive to the devel- opmental phases of the Christian life, as evidenced by the opening lines drawn from the introduction to Book Three:

> As there are different stages and degrees of age and maturity in the natural life; so there are also in the spiritual. It has its first foundation in *sincere repentance*, by which a man sets himself heartily to amend his life. This is succeeded by a *greater illumina- tion*, which is a kind of middle stage. Here, by contemplation, prayer, and bearing the cross, a man is daily improving in grace, and growing up to perfection. The last and most perfect state, is that which consists in a most *firm union*, which is founded in, and cemented by, *pure love*. This is that state which St. Paul calls, "The perfect man," and "the measure of the stature of the fullness of Christ" [Eph. 4:13].[44]

And though the typology here is clearly that of Pseudo Dionysius, with some interesting modulations, Wesley was nevertheless appreciative of the depiction of pure love as well as the importance attached to "the measure of the stature of the fullness of Christ."

Second, both Arndt and Wesley affirmed that true religion, in part, consists in inward renewal that goes far beyond mere formal change or what can be called nominal Christianity. Indeed, observe the opening lines of *True Christianity* and the emphasis placed on the practice of the Christian life:

> Dear Christian reader, that the holy Gospel is subjected, in our time, to a great and shameful abuse is fully proved by the impen- itent life of the ungodly who praise Christ and his word with their mouths and yet lead an unchristian life that is like that of persons who dwell in heathendom, not in the Christian world.[45]

Moreover, this Lutheran theologian and mystical writer, in describing the true worship of God, declared, "But that which God . . . commandeth, consisteth not barely in *external* figures, rites and ordinances: but is *inward*, requiring spirit and truth; principally demanding *faith* in Christ."[46] Elsewhere in this same work, Arndt cautions against the dangers of an inauthentic Christianity: "While every one names himself a Christian, although he do [sic] not perform the part of a Christian; by such a conversation Christ is both denied and belied."[47] Clearly, Wesley's concern with respect to dispositions, inward tempers, and a religion of the heart—a concern mediated to him by his readings of key Anglican authors and others during the period of 1725–1729—quite naturally predisposed him to a favorable reading of much of what Arndt had to offer on this score.[48]

Third, this seventeenth-century German author held that purity of doctrine is to be maintained, not by wrangling and needless dispute, but by the demonstration of a holy life. And on one occasion, Arndt even taught that "it is infinitely better to love him, than to be able to dispute and discourse about him."[49] Though Wesley probably did not go as far as this in his quest for peaceful relations (later Wesley would quip, "God made practical divinity necessary, the devil controversial," but he then immediately added, "But it is necessary: we must 'resist the devil,' or he will not 'flee from us.' "[50]), he nevertheless earnestly sought, especially after his Georgia ministry, to avoid bigotry in the holding of his opinions and desired, whenever possible, to instill a catholic spirit among the Methodists.[51] Such influence can be attributed, in part, to Wesley's reading of Arndt as well as to his several conversations with the Salzburgers.

Though the Moravians and the Salzburgers in Georgia had much in common, some strong—even passionate—tensions existed. For one thing, the Moravians had not only bishops, but also a well-worked claim to the Apostolic succession. The Salzburgers, however, as Lutherans had neither. This is perhaps why Wesley eventually came to believe that the Moravians were the more orthodox of the two groups. Sensing this negative judgment, and no doubt chafing under it, Bolzius countered that the "papistical leaven" was to be found in Wesley as well, that is, "the grounding of purity of doctrine in ecclesiastical legalism."[52] More to the point, Bolzius energetically disputed with Wesley and contended not only that Christ offered no clear teaching about ordination and succession, but also that the early Church fathers seemed to put forth "the very opposite of episcopal authority."[53]

Beyond this, Bolzius, as well as some of the other Salzburgers, complained to Wesley about the apparent antinomianism of the Moravians, that is, their slighting of the commandments of God in the name of grace. Given his own theological judgments at the time, Wesley was quite sensitive to this latter claim of "lawlessness" but not to the former one of ecclesiastical legalism. In fact, during this period, Wesley strictly adhered to the Anglican rubrics; and he, therefore, gave notice of his design beforehand to celebrate the Lord's Supper every Sunday and holiday. And though the invitation to partake of the sacrament seemed to be open to all who were heartily sorry for their sins, those who had not been episcopally baptized were simply refused admittance to the Lord's Table. Thus, the gracious and humble Bolzius was turned aside by Wesley, not because he wasn't baptized, but because the sacrament had not been performed in correct canonical fashion. The Salzburg leader took this rejection, this public humiliation, so well that it left a lasting impression on Wesley. Recalling this unfortunate incident some twenty years later, Wesley could only remark: "Can High Church bigotry go farther than this?"[54]

Wesley's Pastoral Style at Savannah and Frederica

Though Wesley often spoke of his desire to preach to the Indians, his main duty, according to the wishes of James Oglethorpe, was to serve as a pastor to the colonists at Savannah and later at Frederica as well. Ever energetic in the performance of his pastoral duties, Wesley began his ministry in Savannah on March 7, 1736, in an optimistic fashion by preaching on the text of 1 Corinthians 13. Equally sanguine about the prospects of doing good in Georgia, Charles wrote to John a few weeks later: "I see why he has brought me hither, and hope ere long to say with Ignatius, 'It is now that I *begin* to be a disciple of Christ.' "[55] This was truly a noble start for what would soon prove to be a difficult and painful ministry for both brothers. The comforts and security of Oxford were now half a world away.

Wesley's pastoral style and practices in Savannah, and later in Frederica, caused considerable resentment, even pain, among some of his flock. To illustrate, Wesley not only rebaptized the children of dissenters, but also insisted on triune immersion as the correct form of baptism. This last practice created conflict with Mrs. Parker, the wife of the Second Bailiff of Savannah, who refused to have her child dipped. Wesley, however, was equally as adamant on this point, and so the child was eventually baptized by another minister. A couple of months later, in June 1736, Mr. Horton took issue with Wesley's pastoral style and complained that his sermons were "satires on particular persons" and that the people "can't tell what religion you are of. They never heard of such a religion before."[56] Add to this Wesley's refusal to read the burial service over a dissenter and one can understand why many of the colonists were soon murmuring that their chaplain was really "a papist in disguise."[57]

Like his older brother, Charles Wesley encountered opposition to his ministry in Georgia, but it was of a very malicious kind. As secretary to the management committee of the colony and private secretary to Oglethorpe, Charles enjoyed the good will of the governor until Mrs. Hawkins and Mrs. Welch confessed to Charles that they both had sexual relations with Oglethorpe and then had the audacity to inform the governor that the Reverend Charles Wesley was spreading this particular rumor among the people! Naturally, relations between Oglethorpe and Charles Wesley were strained until the governor had the good sense to ferret out the truth and then to deal with Charles in a most kind and gracious manner. Nevertheless, because of ill health, of his inability to carry out his duties as secretary successfully, and of the lingering effects of the hateful gossip, Charles decided that it was best to return to England; and so he left Frederica, Georgia, in August 1736, having been in the colony only about six months.

Because of the sudden departure of Charles, John Wesley left his ministry at Savannah and headed for Frederica. Earlier, he had established small groups in Savannah for mutual accountability and care; and this practice constituted what Wesley himself later termed "the second rise of Methodism." Because of the beneficial nature of these little societies, Wesley brought this practice, a real means of grace, to Frederica as well. Indeed, on an earlier occasion in May 1736, when John had traded places with his brother at Frederica because Charles, as secretary to Oglethorpe, had to attend to some business in Savannah, Wesley observed in his journal:

> We began to execute at Frederica what we had before agreed to
> do at Savannah. Our design was, on Sundays in the afternoon
> and every evening after public service, to spend some time with
> the most serious of the communicants in singing, reading, and
> conversation.[58]

Unfortunately, this society in Frederica did not fare very well;
for when Wesley returned to it in October 1736, a couple of months
after Charles's departure, he learned that the public prayer services had actually been discontinued. Wanting to infuse some life
into this flagging society, Wesley held regular evening meetings for
the week of his stay, during which he supposedly read Ephrem
Syrus, "the most awakening writer . . . of all the ancients."[59] But
his final visit in January 1737 was even more discouraging, and his
diary reveals that there were "no evening meetings of the
Methodist group."[60] Wesley's despair of doing any good in this
setting is evident in the entry made on January 26:

> After having "beaten the air" in this unhappy place for twenty
> days, on January 26, I took my final leave of Frederica. It was not
> any apprehension of my own danger (though my life had been
> threatened many times) but an utter despair of doing good there,
> which made me content with the thought of seeing it no more.[61]

With the collapse of the ministry at Frederica, Wesley's efforts were
now confined to Savannah and to his hopes—vain though they
were—of being among the Indians.[62]

Before his return to Savannah, Wesley had written to the Earl of
Egmont concerning his ministry there. He observed that
"Savannah is already much too large for my care. . . . There are
more who desire and endeavour to be Christians than I ever found
in any town of the same size in England."[63] Thus, in order to meet
this pressing need, Wesley met with the society according to a
fixed pattern: after evening prayers on Wednesday and Saturday
as well as on Sunday afternoons.[64] This practice, this apportion-
ment of pastoral care, once again suggests the enduring influence
of Susanna and the Epworth rectory on her dutiful son. But
beyond this face-to-face accountability, Wesley sought to meet the
spiritual needs of his congregation in Savannah, in part, by
employing hymns in the worship service, a popular accompaniment

to Anglican style and practice. Earlier, in May 1736, Wesley had translated many Moravian hymns into English. The following year, he published several of these and some other pieces in a collection of psalms and hymns that constituted nothing less than the first English hymnbook published in America. Of the nature of this collection of hymns, one scholar observes:

> These texts, many translated from the German, express the heart of a pietism grounded in Scripture and elucidate the themes that are central to Wesley's spiritual quest—utter dependency upon grace, the centrality of love, and the desire for genuine fire to inflame his cold heart.[65]

On a more personal level, though Wesley's ascetic tendencies likely continued apace to the consternation of his brother Samuel;[66] and though his reputation for seriousness in matters of religion was quite broad, the correspondence of this period actually demonstrates that Wesley deemed religion to be "the cheerfullest thing in the world."[67] To illustrate, on March 29, 1737, in a letter to Mrs. Chapman, who was most probably the mother of the Reverend Walter Chapman, the noted evangelical cleric from Bath,[68] Wesley insists that "true religion or holiness cannot be without cheerfulness, so steady cheerfulness, on the other hand, cannot be without holiness or true religion."[69] Nevertheless, others were not so easily convinced by such affirmations. Instead, all they could see in Wesley's ministry at Savannah was neither cheerfulness nor comfort, but seriousness and repeated challenges. In fact, the following month, a "man of education" objected to Wesley's portrayal of the new birth by remarking, "Why, if this be Christianity, a Christian must have more courage than Alexander the Great."[70] What these people had failed to discern, however, was that behind this earnest and serious preacher, beyond a pastoral style that often seemed dour and rigid, lay the heart of a deeply affectionate man.

The Sophia Hopkey Relationship

Earlier, while in Savannah attending to his pastoral duties, Wesley was introduced to Sophia Hopkey, the niece of Thomas Causton, the Chief Magistrate. Almost from the start, Wesley and

Ms. Hopkey seemed to be romantically inclined toward each other. Thinking that a wife might do Wesley much good, Oglethorpe actually fostered the relationship between Wesley and this young woman—she was only eighteen at the time—by urging him to spend as much time with her as he could and by making sure that the two were placed in the same boat as they set out from Frederica to Savannah on October 25, 1736. Wesley clearly saw the danger to himself in these travel arrangements; and so the next morning, as they crossed Doboy Sound, Wesley sought reassurance from Ms. Hopkey that *her* intentions were noble and pure by posing to her the very same question, the very same standard, that he had so often applied to himself. "Miss Sophy," Wesley began, "are not you afraid to die?" "No, I don't desire to live any longer," she remarked almost without thinking: "O that God would let me go now! Then I should be at rest. In this world I expect nothing but misery."[71]

Since he was tutoring her in the areas of practical divinity and French, Wesley spent much time with Ms. Hopkey. Such close and private contact allowed him to express both kindness and affection to this young woman. The deepening intimacy of the relationship naturally encouraged Wesley, and he began to fear the prospect of inordinate affection. Put another way, Wesley was concerned he might soon love the creature more than the Creator; or perhaps Ms. Hopkey might deflect him from his high purpose and calling to preach the good news among the Indians, that is, to know the gospel in a deeper way through mission. So conflicted, torn by his devotion to this young woman and to the tasks of ministry as well, Wesley sought to manage his affections, the tempers of his heart, by means of rules and resolutions. In early November 1736, for example, Wesley resolved never to touch Ms. Hopkey again. But just ten days after this resolution was made, Wesley took Sophia by the hand and "kissed her once or twice."[72]

To strengthen his resolve against undue affection, Wesley outlined several reasons for not marrying, among which included that he didn't think himself strong enough to live in the married state; he feared it would obstruct his design to be among the Indians; and he believed Ms. Hopkey's own resolve not to marry.[73] Wesley, therefore, confided to Ms. Hopkey that he was determined not to marry until he had ministered to the Indians. This declaration of Wesley's intent apparently disturbed the young woman, for the next day she informed him in a rather cool manner that she would no longer accompany him at breakfast or come to his house alone any more. And the following day, Sophia declared that she no longer wished to study French. Despite these pronouncements, Ms. Hopkey was still emotionally tied to Wesley; for when she learned about a week later that he was planning to return to England, she "changed color several times"[74] and exclaimed "What! Are you going to England? Then I have no tie to America left."[75] When Wesley asked her about these words later, Sophia Hopkey responded in tears: "You are the best friend I ever had in the world."[76]

By early March 1737, Wesley had begun to realize that his rules, resolutions, and reasons were powerless to tame or order the affections of his heart. Indeed, one sight, one thought of Sophia, one touch of her gentle hand and all his resolutions were quickly forgotten. Failing with internal controls, Wesley sought "external" ones to manage his relationship with Sophia. Accordingly, he turned to the lot—a device of chance—of which three were made: on one was written "Marry," on the second, "Think not of it this year," and on the last (which was the one chosen), "Think of it no more."[77] Another lot was drawn on a different question, which revealed that Wesley should visit Ms. Hopkey only in the presence of Mr. Delamotte. Yet just three days later, Wesley saw his Sophia walking between the door and the garden. "The evil Soul prevailed," as Wesley put it; and he spoke with her even though Mr. Delamotte was not present. The tête-à-tête was interrupted, however, by the entrance of Mrs. Causton—an interruption Wesley later described as being once more "snatched as a brand out of the fire."[78]

So matters stood until on March 9, 1737, Ms. Hopkey informed John Wesley, to his utter bewilderment, that she had given Mr. Williamson her consent to marry—"unless you have anything to object."[79] Wesley soon thought to himself, " 'What if she mean, Unless *you* will marry me?' But I checked the thought with, 'Miss Sophy is so sincere.' "[80] The stunned pastor returned home and paced in his garden; he sought peace but found none. "From the beginning of my life to this hour," Wesley confided to his journal, "I had not known one such as this."[81] "God let loose my inordinate affection upon me," he painfully confessed, "and the poison thereof drank up my spirit. . . . 'To see her no more!' That thought was as the piercings of a sword."[82] Nevertheless, to fulfill her expressed intention, and also in part to flee the Causton home she found unbearable, Ms. Hopkey married Mr. Williamson, a man noted for neither grace nor piety, on March 12, 1737, in Purrysburg.

If Wesley saw nothing but sincerity and grace in Ms. Hopkey's character prior to her marriage, then after it he seemed to find nothing but artfulness and dissimulation. Spurned by Sophia, or at the very least misguided by her, Wesley accused the newly wed Mrs. Williamson of "insincerity before and ingratitude since her marriage."[83] Moreover, the probing and exacting pastor now discerned several ecclesiastical faults in Mrs. Williamson, the chief one being her several absences from the Lord's Supper. And on one occasion when she did receive the sacrament, on July 3, 1737, Wesley spoke with Mrs. Williamson immediately thereafter and informed her of several things that he found reprovable in her behavior, which included her neglect of half the public service, of fasting, and of almost half of the opportunities for receiving the Lord's Supper. Beyond this, Wesley disapproved of Sophia's lying and dissimulation, especially with respect to Mr. Williamson, a man whom, she had stated repeatedly, she had no design to marry. For these and other infractions, both ecclesiastical and moral, John Wesley publicly humiliated Mrs. Williamson by repelling her from communion on August 7, 1737.

Though Thomas Causton had given Wesley assurances earlier that he would take no action but that which concerned either him or his wife, the magistrate was nevertheless incensed. He, therefore, required that Wesley make known the reasons he had refused the Lord's Supper to his niece. Perhaps to protect the honor of his family, Causton floated the rumor that Wesley had denied his niece out of motives of revenge since he had made several proposals of marriage to her that were all rejected in favor of Mr. Williamson. Soon a grand jury of twenty-six people was composed, and ten indictments were posted against John Wesley in August 1737. Nothing, however, really came of this court action; and sensing that his ministry was effectively over, Wesley announced that he was returning to England, "there being no possibility as yet of instructing the Indians."[84] A halfhearted attempt was made to stop his departure until the courts were satisfied, but on December 2, 1737, Wesley, as he put it, "shook off the dust of my feet and left Georgia, after having preached the gospel (not as I ought, but as I was able) one year and nearly nine months."[85]

The Return Home

After a difficult land journey through South Carolina, Wesley boarded the *Samuel*, of which Captain Percy was the commander. On Christmas Eve the ship sailed over Charleston bar and soon lost sight of land. A few days later, Wesley experienced great anxiety and confessed that

> finding the unaccountable apprehensions of I know not what danger (the wind being small, and the sea smooth) . . . I cried earnestly for help, and it pleased God as in a moment to restore peace to my soul.[86]

After this unsettling incident, Wesley observed that "whoever is uneasy on any account (bodily pain alone excepted) carries in himself his own conviction that he is so far an unbeliever." More particularly, Wesley added: "Is he uneasy at the apprehension of *death*? Then he believeth not that 'to die is gain.' "[87]

En route to England in early January 1738, Wesley reviewed his entire ministry in Georgia, assessed his spiritual condition, and penned the following in his journal:

> By the most infallible proofs, of inward feeling, I am convinced:
> 1. Of unbelief, having no such faith in Christ as will prevent my heart from being troubled; which it could not be if I believed in God, and rightly believed also in him [i.e., Christ].
> 2. Of pride, throughout my life past, inasmuch as I thought I had what I find I have not.
> 3. Of gross irrecollection, inasmuch as in a storm I cry to God every moment, in a calm, not.
> 4. Of levity and luxuriancy of spirit, recurring whenever the pressure is taken off, and appearing by my speaking words not tending to edify; but most, by my manner of speaking of my enemies.[88]

Wesley then prayed for a faith that would entail serenity both in life and in death and for a humility that would fill his heart from that hour: "Give me faith or I die; give me a lowly spirit; otherwise *Mihi non sit suave vivere.*"[89]

Toward the end of the month, Wesley linked the issue of unbelief explicitly with the fear of death, a recurring theme during this period:

> I went to America to convert the Indians; but Oh! who shall convert me? Who, what is he that will deliver me from this evil heart of unbelief? I have a fair summer religion. I can talk well; nay, and believe myself, while no danger is near: but let death look me in the face, and my spirit is troubled. Nor can I say "To die is gain!"[90]

Shortly afterwards, Wesley, once again, associated the fear of death with painful doubt and fear as well as with the absence of peace due to sinning. He observed, "I fluctuated between obedience and disobedience: I had no heart, no vigor, no zeal in obeying; continually doubting whether I was right or wrong, and never out of perplexities and entanglements."[91] Wesley had hoped for spiritual power and victory. Instead, he was plagued by doubt and fear, and he often succumbed to the power of sin. Intuitively he knew, vaguely he sensed, that Christian liberty meant more than this.

Though Wesley was an Anglican priest, he comprehended in a very painful and honest way that he had not realized in his own life the extent of holiness that had so captured his imagination since 1725. In particular, the ghosts of Wesley's rigid and insensitive pastoral care on numerous occasions, of his public humiliation of the woman he purportedly loved, as well as of his repeated bouts with disobedience and sin, were perhaps all coming back to haunt him. Such elements would riddle his conscience and naturally undermine all sense of peace. Indeed, the disparity between the ideal of holiness and his actual practice that repeatedly unsettled Wesley, was the cause of much anxiety and fear, and made him realize his lack of crucial graces yet to be instantiated in the tempers of his heart.

But was not Wesley sincere in Georgia? Did he not intend to use all the grace of God at his disposal? Had he not communed regularly? Did he not pray and read the Scriptures on a daily basis? Had he not served his poor flock faithfully, if not prudently? Had he not *dedicated* "all [his] thoughts, and words and actions [to

God]; being thoroughly convinced, there was no medium," much earlier, upon reading the works of Jeremy Taylor?[92] Again, had he not been baptized? Was he not, after all, an earnest and virtuous missionary? What, then, could John Wesley, Anglican cleric and erstwhile leader of the Holy Club, possibly be lacking?

What makes the Georgia experience so fascinating, then, at least from a biographical perspective, is that Wesley was obviously in earnest to live the Christian life in an exemplary way, to realize holiness even to the extent of the intentions of his heart; and yet he was repeatedly frustrated in this endeavor. As noted earlier, Wesley had tried to manage his spiritual life as well as the tempers of his heart by reason, rule, and resolution; but in this he failed again and again. Like the person described by the apostle Paul in Romans 7 ("I do not understand my own actions. For I do not do what I want, but I do the very thing I hate," v. 15), Wesley was of two minds and two wills while in Georgia. His loves, in other words, were disordered, divided, often at odds with each other. Few can doubt, then, after reading the Georgia narratives, that Wesley was dissatisfied at the time, neither happy nor content with his own life and character. And if holiness and happiness are intricately related—and they clearly are—then Wesley would simply have to find other means to actualize the holy love he had so earnestly sought. The *mission* to Savannah and Frederica had begun with lofty dreams and in high hopes; it ended, however, with painful realities and in near despair.

CHAPTER FOUR
Aldersgate

Scenes from St. Mary's Church, Oxford

As the *Samuel* was pulling into Deal Harbor in England on February 1, 1738, George Whitefield was preparing to embark for Georgia, having accepted an offer from the trustees of the colony to be a minister in Savannah. The young Oxford Methodist noted the coincidence of his and Wesley's itineraries, the one departing while the other was arriving, and graciously remarked: "Anyone must needs think I should have been glad to have heard from Mr. Wesley, as he went by Deal; but I considered God ordered all things for the best."[1]

At the time of Whitefield's journey to the New World, the English colonies were already pulsing with local revivals in Northampton under the steady leadership of Jonathan Edwards; in the Raritan Valley of northern New Jersey through the labors of Theodore Frelinghuysen; and in the Presbyterian churches of the same general area through the pointed preaching of William and Gilbert Tennent. These local stirrings during the 1730s, which gave the colonies a sense of unity and purpose, would be consolidated into a Great Awakening during Whitefield's subsequent tour of 1740. Such evangelistic activity would later demonstrate, at the hands of perceptive historians, that the evangelical revival of the eighteenth century that was slowly emerging was truly a transatlantic phenomenon with both British and American phases. And though John Wesley would clearly play a significant role in the British awakening, as his ship docked in England that February morning, he was hardly ready for all that such a role would require.

Chastened by his Georgia experience, unsettled by slavish bouts of anxiety and fear, Wesley was in a pensive mood on February 1, 1738. In his journal on that day, he made four key observations, very somber in tone, about his spiritual state. Of the first, Wesley wrote:

> It is now two years and almost four months since I left my native country in order to teach the Georgian Indians the nature of Christianity. But what have I learned myself in the meantime? Why (what I the least of all suspected) that I who went to America to convert others, was never myself converted to God.[2]

Some earlier biographers have let such statements stand alone in order to underscore the gravity of Wesley's spiritual condition. However, such a device is neither fair nor accurate. For much later, in 1774 in fact, Wesley appended a "disclaimer" to this journal account, which appeared right after the comment, "I who went to America to convert others, was never myself converted to God." It read quite simply, "I am not sure of this." Accordingly, Wesley was neither sure that he wasn't converted to God while in Georgia nor quite certain that he was. His doubt, in other words, left *both* possibilities open. And though Wesley would later insist that he rarely used the term "conversion," it actually surfaced over sixty times in his writings, though admittedly more than half of these quotations were from the writings of others.

Wesley's second very humble and self-reflective observation on February 1 touched on his well-worked theme, even by this time, of what it means to be a (real) Christian. He observed in his journal:

> Or that "I know nothing of myself," that I am, as touching outward, moral righteousness, blameless? Or (to come closer yet)

the having a *rational conviction* of all the truths of Christianity? Does all this give me a claim to the holy, heavenly, divine character of a *Christian*? By no means. If the oracles of God are true, if we are still to abide by "the law and the testimony," all these things, though when ennobled by faith in Christ they are holy, and just, and good, yet without it are "dung and dross."[3]

However, in 1774, Wesley added the disclaimer, "I had even then the faith of a *servant*, though not that of a *son*," to this autobiographical material. In other words, later on—certainly not in early 1738—Wesley came to distinguish different grades or levels of faith. The retrospective in 1774, then, reveals that Wesley's spiritual condition at the beginning of 1738 was not as "dark" or as "despairing" as he had initially supposed. Wesley had, after all, a measure of both faith and grace. But was it *saving* grace and faith that he had? Indeed, as Wesley's theological journey progresses it will become evident that the faith of a servant is variously defined in his writings and does not always constitute justifying faith. This should give pause to those scholars who have assumed that the faith of a servant is unproblematically justifying faith in each and every instance, a judgment on the basis of which much of Wesley's early biography can only be misconstrued.[4]

The third observation that Wesley made in his journal at this time and that was the most despairing and therefore the most inaccurate of all simply stated, "I am 'a child of wrath, an heir of hell.' "[5] Clearly, this language was much too strong, and it called for nuances of some sort. Not surprisingly, in 1774, Wesley attached the disclaimer, "I believe not," to this entry. Indeed, this young Anglican priest in early 1738 may not have realized the full extent of holiness that he had envisioned; he may have been continually buffeted by doubt and fear; but he was hardly a "child of wrath, an heir of hell." That much, at least, was clear. In time, Wesley would come to distinguish gradations, even increments, of both grace and faith and thereby give encouragement to those who had fallen short of *regenerating, saving* grace, while at the same time he would affirm a crucial standard as to what constitutes "the proper" Christian faith.

And finally, while Wesley was at Deal Harbor, making these pointed observations in his journal, he indicated that the faith he wanted was "a sure trust and confidence in God, that through the merits of Christ my sins are forgiven, and I reconciled to the favor of God."[6] The faith he wanted, he later noted in his disclaimer of 1774, was "the faith of a son." In other words, Wesley wanted that faith, as he put it, "which none can have without knowing that he hath it. . . . For whosoever hath it is 'freed from sin.' "[7] So then, though Wesley at this time was clearly not a "child of wrath," neither was he a child of God, nor was he yet set free from the *power* or *dominion* of sin. In fact, it was precisely the later Wesley, matured and steeped in age, who noted in retrospect that at the beginning of 1738, he desired nothing less than the liberty of the "faith of a son," the freedom of a child of God.

A couple of days later, after the passengers of the *Samuel* had disembarked and Wesley was in London once more, he reflected that though the design for which he had set out to Georgia had not been realized—specifically his *mission* to the Indians—he trusted that God had "in some measure 'humbled me and proved me, and shown me what was in my heart.' "[8] So then, Wesley, the Anglican cleric and sometime missionary, not only had greater self-knowledge because of his experiences, but also was now very meek, perhaps even broken. The Georgia venture, then, clearly had not been all negative—as some have supposed—for it prepared Wesley to be open, in a very humble and teachable way, to all that God had in store for him—and there was much in store.

Peter Böhler

On February 7, 1738, Wesley had the good fortune to meet Peter Böhler, a Moravian missionary, at the house of Mr. Weinantz, a Dutch merchant. Wesley later recorded the significance of this meeting in his journal with the comment: "A day much to be remembered."[9] Born in Frankfurt am Main in 1712, Böhler grew up in Pietistic circles. In 1731, for example, he began a course of studies at Jena and joined the Herrnhut student fellowship that was under the leadership of August Spangenberg, the same Moravian divine Wesley had encountered in Georgia.[10] During his residency at the university, Böhler experienced an "instantaneous conversion" that transformed his life soon after he had met with Count Zinzendorf, principal leader of the Moravians and godson of Philipp Jacob Spener. Appreciative of Moravian piety and eager to serve, Böhler was received into this communion of faith at Herrnhut in 1737. Shortly thereafter, he made his way to England and stayed mainly in London—where he met John Wesley—and in Oxford as well.

Though this initial meeting was obviously important, Wesley did not understand all that Böhler had to relate on this occasion; and the Moravian even cautioned Wesley that his philosophy—whatever that meant—must be purged away: *Mi frater, mi frater, excoquenda est ista tua philosophia.*[11] Apparently, Wesley was intrigued by Böhler's understanding of the *nature* of faith, and so he naturally wanted to learn more. In the meantime, however, Wesley continued in his old ways—that had become a habit in Georgia—and he steered the course of his spiritual life largely by rule and resolution. (Was this what Böhler had referred to as Wesley's "philosophy"?) Later that month, for example, Wesley wrote down and renewed all of his former resolutions; and he no doubt had the desire, if not the ability, to fulfill them all.

The following month, Wesley encountered Peter Böhler again as he was visiting his brother Charles who was sick at Oxford recovering from pleurisy. On March 5, by means of his conversation with the young Moravian, Wesley was clearly convinced of unbelief, "of the want of 'that faith whereby alone we are saved.' "[12] Immediately it occurred to Wesley to leave off preaching, for how could he preach to others a faith that he, himself, lacked? Böhler reassured Wesley and counseled: "Preach faith *till* you have it, and then, *because* you have it, you *will* preach faith."[13] Accordingly, the next day, on March 6, Wesley began preaching this "new" doctrine though his heart was not fully in it. The first person he offered salvation by faith *alone* was Mr. Clifford, a prisoner under the sentence of death. Later Wesley recounted this "intellectual conversion" in his *Short History of the People Called Methodists* and noted its salutary effects upon his ministry:

> I preached in many churches, though I did not yet see the nature of saving faith. But as soon as I saw this clearly, namely on Monday, March 6, I declared it without delay. And God then began to work by my ministry as he never had done before.[14]

Much later, in 1774, Wesley deemed it appropriate to append the "disclaimer" "with the full Christian salvation," to his earlier observation on March 5 of being convinced of unbelief, "of the want of that faith whereby alone we are saved." In this context, the language of "full Christian salvation" is yet another instance of Wesley's well-worked motif of real Christianity, a motif that embraces such synonymous phrases as "real," "true," or "proper" (even "rational") Christianity. Thus, by employing such language, Wesley in retrospect indicated not only that he did, after all, have a measure of faith in March 1738, but also—and this is what has often been missed—that such faith fell short of what he termed "the full Christian salvation." In other words, in the interim, as a result of age and much pastoral experience, Wesley had grown to recognize and appreciate the faith of a servant for its measure of grace and illumination while at the same time he upheld his high standards as to what constitutes the "proper Christian faith." Both of these elements must be recognized and affirmed in order to appreciate the subtlety of Wesley's mature views.

Toward the end of the month, Peter Böhler explored the *nature* of saving faith in greater detail with Wesley by pointing out, in a very pietistic fashion, the two fruits that are inseparable from it, namely, holiness (freedom from sin) and happiness (the peace and joy that emerge from a sense of forgiveness). That is, Böhler, like Arndt, Spener, and Francke before him, connected saving faith not simply with justification and juridical change, but with regeneration and participatory change as well.[15] Wesley searched his Greek Testament to see if this doctrine was of God; and by the end of April, when he met Böhler again, he had no objection to what the young Moravian said concerning the nature of saving faith, that it is "a sure trust and confidence which a man hath in God, that through the merits of Christ *his* sins are forgiven, and *he* reconciled to the favor of God."[16] But what Wesley still could not comprehend was how could this faith be instantaneous, given in a moment, as Böhler had suggested. Again, Wesley consulted the Bible, and to his surprise he found "scarce any instances there of other than *instantaneous* conversions—scarce any other so slow as that of St. Paul."[17] But it was not until after Wesley was faced with the evidence of several living witnesses that he forthrightly confessed: "Here ended my disputing. I could now only cry out, 'Lord, help thou my unbelief!' "[18] Robert Southey, the great biographer of Wesley, was simply incredulous at this point. "Is it possible," he asked, "that a man of Wesley's acuteness should have studied the Scriptures as he had studied them, till the age of five-and-thirty, without perceiving that the conversions which they record are instantaneous?"[19]

At any rate, it is important to consider what Wesley came to mean by the instantaneous nature of saving faith, lest there be misunderstanding. Indeed, Wesley did not maintain that believers must know the exact time of salvation, the precise day or hour of redemption, or that the actualization of saving faith must always be *dramatic*. Instead, the affirmation of the instantaneous nature of redemption highlights the sheer gratuity of saving grace, that it is, to use the words of the apostle Paul, "the gift of God—not the result of works, so that no one may boast" (Eph. 2:8-9). Equally important, such grace represents not simply an incremental change, that is, one merely of *degree*, but a genuine *qualitative* change—a change that can be brought about not by human effort, desire, or will, but by God *alone*. Moreover, underscoring the instantaneous nature of saving grace is yet another way of maintaining the crucial truth that all people, whether healthy or sick souls, to use the idiom of William James, must be born again.[20] Thus, grace must become actual, not simply possible; grace must be realized, not simply imagined; and process—however long or difficult—must eventuate in the appropriation of the grace and favor of God—whether that exact moment is recognized or not. This, then, is perhaps part of the theological legacy that Böhler shared with Wesley.

On May 1, 1738, Wesley visited his brother Charles, who had relapsed and was currently resting at the house of James Hutton near Temple Bar.[21] Here, on the advice of Böhler, a little society was formed that was subsequently transferred to Fetter Lane. In theory, it was a Church of England society; but in many respects, "it was closely modeled on the Moravian system."[22] Wesley listed eleven rules of the society, which included, among other things, that members meet once a week, be divided into "bands" or small companies, and speak as "freely, plainly, and concisely" as they could concerning the real state of their hearts.[23] This society, like the Methodist ones established earlier at Oxford and in Georgia, underscored the basic truth that Christianity is a social religion and that "to turn it into a solitary [one] is indeed to destroy it."[24] So significant was the creation of the Fetter Lane meeting that Wesley, himself, later referred to it as nothing less than "the third rise of Methodism."

Schooled in a Moravian-Lutheran understanding of faith—at least for a time—proclaiming a faith that, by his own admission, he yet lacked, and no longer confining himself to the Anglican forms of prayer, but now praying "indifferently" as he put it, John Wesley was something of a puzzle, an oddity, to both friends and foes alike. Mr. Broughton, for example, upon hearing Wesley explore the nature and fruits of saving faith, objected that "he could never think that [Wesley] had not faith, who had done and suffered such things."[25] But Wesley's mood from May 10 to May 13 was very somber, even depressive. He was, to use his own words, "neither able to read nor meditate, nor sing, nor pray, nor do anything."[26] However, a letter from Böhler, who was about to set sail for the Carolinas, brought a measure of comfort. The earnest Moravian missionary counseled:

> Beware of the sin of unbelief; and if you have not conquered it yet, see that you conquer it this very day, through the blood of Jesus Christ. Delay not, I beseech you, to believe in *your* Jesus Christ; but so put him in mind of his promises to poor sinners that he may not be able to refrain from doing for you what he hath done for so many others. O how great, how inexpressible, how unexhausted is his love! Surely he is now ready to help; and nothing can offend him but our unbelief.[27]

Earlier, in an attempt to justify himself, Wesley had related to Böhler that he had "not sinned so grossly as other people."[28] But Böhler quickly replied, in a way reminiscent of both Zinzendorf and Luther, "that he had sinned enough in not believing in the Saviour."[29]

Lacking much joy, but convinced on some level of the truth of his newly found faith, Wesley encountered strong opposition in many Anglican pulpits, first at St. John the Evangelist and at St. Andrew's, Holborn, in February 1738 and then—in full tide—in May 1738 in numerous churches such as St. Katherine Cree, St. Lawrence's, St. Helen's, St. Ann's, St. John's Wapping, St. Benet's, St. Antholin's and St. George's, Bloomsbury. All these churches said in effect to Wesley, "Preach here no more!" So then, though Wesley believed he finally had a suitable message to proclaim, worth his time and energy, he was quickly losing his audience.

William Law

Wesley's relations, however, were strained, not simply with various Anglican pastors, but with William Law as well, a saintly man and something of a mystic, who had been his theological mentor up to this point. For instance, in a letter drafted on May 14, 1738, Wesley complained to Law that he had been preaching after the model of his two practical treatises (*A Practical Treatise Upon Christian Perfection* and *A Serious Call to a Devout and Holy Life*) with little effect. Wesley granted that the law of God was holy; but no sooner did he try to fulfill it than he found "it was too high for man, and that by doing the works of this law no flesh living be justified."[30] To remedy this situation, Wesley redoubled his efforts and used all the means of grace at his disposal; but still he was convinced that this was a law "whereby a man could not live, the law in our members continually warring against it, and bringing us into deeper captivity to the law of sin."[31]

Under this heavy yoke, Wesley confessed to William Law, he had continued until God directed him to a holy man (Peter Böhler) who proclaimed, "Believe, and thou shalt be saved. Believe in the Lord Jesus Christ with all thy heart and nothing shall be impossible to thee."[32] Now Wesley clearly saw, at least on a cognitive if not on an affective level, that "faith, as well as the salvation it brings, is a free gift of God."[33] Exasperated and perhaps even somewhat angry at this point, Wesley criticized Law even more pointedly and asked, "How [will you] answer it to our common Lord that you never gave me this advice?"[34] "Why did I scarce ever hear you name the name of Christ?"[35] And so the "interrogation"—and that's what it was—by the irritated protégé continued. The heart of Wesley's criticism, however, concerned the *nature* of faith itself; and he accused William Law of not having enough spiritual sensitivity and insight to realize that under his tutelage Wesley did not even have saving faith, as revealed in the following:

> If you say you advised them because you knew I had faith already, verily, you knew nothing of me, you discerned not my spirit at all. I know that I had not faith. Unless the faith of a devil, the faith of a Judas, that speculative, notional, airy shadow which lives in the head, not the heart. But what is this to the living, justifying faith in the blood of Jesus. The faith that cleanseth from all

sin, that gives us to have free access to the Father, to "rejoice in the hope of the glory of God."[36]

Here then Wesley, in an earnest and sincere fashion, distinguishes the faith that pertains to formal Christianity, "a speculative, notional, airy shadow," under which he suffered for so long, from that which pertains, more properly, to a son or daughter of God, even "the living, justifying faith in the blood of Jesus." Granted, elements of this language clearly call for more nuances as well as for a clearer articulation, especially when Wesley writes that justifying faith "cleanseth from *all* sin"; but the basic idea that justifying faith, broadly speaking, entails holiness and happiness (or power and peace) was now clearly comprehended by Wesley. And just why he had not understood all of this sooner was the substance of his complaint against William Law. Moreover, in a similar fashion, and with equal disappointment, Charles Wesley referred to William Law as "our John the Baptist." That is, he shut the Wesley brothers up under " 'the law of commandments contained in ordinances' till they groaned for deliverance."[37]

Aldersgate

Charles Wesley, like his brother John, was well acquainted with Peter Böhler and had profited much from his spiritual care and direction. By early May 1738, for instance, Charles now understood the *nature* of that "one, true, living faith, whereby alone 'through grace we are saved.' "[38] Later that month as he began to read Luther's *Commentary on Galatians* (having been introduced to this classic by William Holland, a member of the Church of England who was affiliated with the Moravians), Charles confessed with some puzzlement in his journal,

> Who would believe our Church had been founded on this important article of justification by faith alone? I am astonished I should ever think this a new doctrine; especially while our Articles and Homilies stand unrepealed, and the key of knowledge is not taken away.[39]

Again, like his older brother, Charles wanted not "an idle, dead faith, but a faith that works by love and is necessarily productive of all good works and all holiness."[40]

On Friday, May 19, while Charles was ill in bed, a certain Mrs. Turner told him that he should not rise from his sickbed until he believed. Charles, wanting to know if this woman was sincere, questioned her faith: "Has God then bestowed faith upon you?" "Yes, he has," came the reply. Not yet satisfied, and in a way reminiscent of his older brother's probing questioning, Charles continued: "Then you are willing to die?" "I am, and would be glad to die in a moment," Mrs. Turner declared. This woman's testimony, this witness to the liberating graces of redemption, no doubt, prepared Charles in some measure for what was to come. Indeed, two days later, Charles heard someone come into his room while he lay in bed and say quite distinctly, "In the name of Jesus of Nazareth, arise, and believe, and thou shalt be healed of all thy infirmities."[41] Initially, Charles had thought it was Mrs. Musgrave, a friend; but it was actually Mrs. Turner, herself, who had spoken these words. Not knowing this, Charles asked Mrs. Turner to go downstairs and get Mrs. Musgrave. While she was gone, Charles had, as he put it, "a strange palpitation of heart"; and he said, yet feared to say, "I believe, I believe!"[42] Charles now understood the graciousness and power of the gospel not simply intellectually, but also in terms of his tempers and affections. His heart as well as his mind now belonged to the Savior.

A few days later, early in the morning of May 24, 1738, John Wesley was meditating on the Scriptures and came across the following verse, which portended the events of this remarkable day: "Whereby are given unto us exceeding great and precious promises: that by these ye might be partakers of the divine nature" (2 Peter 1:4 KJV). That afternoon, Wesley attended evensong at St. Paul's in London where the choir was singing Purcell's deeply moving anthem, "Out of the deep have I called unto thee, O Lord."[43] Surely the godly yearning, mingled with heartfelt anguish, expressed in this hymn was indicative of Wesley's spiritual state as well. Later that evening, before he reluctantly went out to attend a religious society meeting in Aldersgate Street, Wesley opened his Bible once more and alighted on the passage: "Thou art not far from the kingdom of God."[44] These three elements, though commonplace occurrences in the eyes of many, were later deemed by Wesley to be revelatory of an overarching divine providence, that the Most High was somehow near and was soon to be *present* in numinous graces. In fact, so significant was the realization of grace for Wesley on this day that he placed a "narrative insert" in his journal; that is, he appended a summary of his spiritual life before, as well as a detailed account of the events that took place after, the meeting on Aldersgate Street on May 24, 1738. This literary device, as well as Wesley's specific references to his "Aldersgate experience" to his brother Samuel Jr. on October 30 and over seven years later in a letter to "John Smith" dated December 30, 1745, indicate quite clearly the crucial nature of this event.[45]

In his spiritual summary, Wesley pointed out, among other things, that while he was at Savannah he was "beating the air," being ignorant of the righteousness that comes from Christ with the result that he sought to establish his own righteousness or justification "under the law."[46] "In this . . . state," Wesley continues, "I was indeed fighting continually, but not conquering. Before, I had willingly served sin: now it was unwillingly, but still I served it." In this path marked by repeated spiritual defeat, by the continual dominance of sin, Wesley remained. In his own words, he "fell and rose and fell again."[47] Wesley, however, intuitively understood that such a condition is not what scriptural Christianity has to offer, that the proper Christian faith, to use his own idiom, is marked by a victory and a peace that he had not yet realized. Clearly, Wesley could have assured *himself* by remembering his ordination or by noting his missionary experience as well as his other works of mercy, but he refused to do so—a refusal, by the way, that brought him much criticism. Instead, in his deep humility and painful honesty, Wesley confessed to all, and to the surprise of many, that he was neither content with his own spiritual life nor willing to call it the proper Christian faith.

In light of these changes, some more telling than others, when Peter Böhler came along proclaiming a "new gospel," announcing deliverance to the captives, nothing less than freedom from the dominion of sin, Wesley eagerly embraced such a message. Remarkable as it seems, it was only then that he began to realize that there are two fruits inseparably connected with a living faith in Christ, namely, "dominion over sin, and constant peace from a sense of forgiveness."[48] Put another way, Wesley wanted nothing less than a living faith in Christ, which was "inseparable from a sense of pardon for all past, and freedom from all present sins."[49]

Twentieth-century biographers, for the most part, have focused simply on the former aspect, namely, assurance; and while this element is clearly present in the Aldersgate narrative, which will be cited below, it is the latter element, freedom from the power of sin (in conjunction with assurance), that is actually the key to all that transpired in Wesley's life at this time.

In his autobiographical account, Wesley relates that in the days just prior to May 24, 1738, his spirit was marked by "strange indifference, dullness, and coldness, and unusually frequent relapses into sin."[50] The contrast, then, which was to follow shortly by means of his Aldersgate narrative, was drawn not by nineteenth-century hagiographers, but by no one less than John Wesley himself. Just what transpired on May 24, 1738, then, is best expressed in Wesley's own words:

> In the evening I went very unwillingly to a society in Aldersgate Street, where one was reading Luther's Preface to the Epistle to the Romans. About a quarter before nine, while he was describing the change which God works in the heart through faith in Christ, I felt my heart strangely warmed. I felt I did trust in Christ, Christ alone for salvation, and an assurance was given me that he had taken away *my* sins, even *mine*, and saved *me* from the law of sin and death.[51]

Interestingly enough, Luther's Preface to the Epistle to the Romans was greatly revered by not only German Pietists but many Anglicans as well because in it they found a classic expression of the concern for a living faith as well as for the necessity of the new birth.[52] Observe the language of this sixteenth-century Preface in the following excerpt, particularly its emphasis on the extent of *unbelief* (a theme that had already been developed by Peter Böhler) and the consequent necessity of the proper Christian faith:

> As, therefore, faith alone makes a person righteous, and brings the Spirit pleasure in good outward works, so unbelief alone commits sin, and brings forth the flesh and pleasure in bad outward works, as happened to Adam and Eve in paradise, Genesis [Chapter] Three.
>
> Hence Christ calls unbelief the only sin, when he says in John 16 [:8-9], "The Spirit will convince the world of sin . . . because they

do not believe in me." . . . Unbelief is the root, the sap, and the chief prayer of all sin.[53]

And according to Martin Schmidt, it was precisely when the reader at the Aldersgate society meting came to the following words that Wesley felt his heart strangely warmed: "Faith, however, is a divine work in us which changes us and makes us to be born anew of God, John 1 [:12-13]. It kills the old Adam and makes us altogether different men, in heart and spirit and mind and powers; and it brings with it the Holy Spirit."[54] So then as Wesley was sitting in the society meeting at Aldersgate Street and hearing the words of Luther's great Reformation classic, the Methodist leader's principal organ of worship, if you will, the means by which he received comforting, saving graces, was not the *eye*, but in good Protestant fashion, the *ear*. That is, Wesley heard the words that mediated to him nothing less than the *presence* of the Holy Spirit in his heart. This paradigm of proclamation, this entrance into the deeper graces of God through feeding on words spoken in due season, the very orality of redemption, would be duplicated again and again though the preaching of the Wesley brothers, George Whitefield, John Cennick, and others in the Evangelical Revival that was soon to sweep the British Isles.

Moreover, observe once again that Wesley's own Aldersgate narrative does not simply highlight the element of assurance, but sees it in *conjuction* with the liberty of having been redeemed "from the law of sin and death," which is another way of describ ing *regeneration*. As a matter of afact, in the days that immediately followed his Aldersgate experience, Wesley—while not neglecting the importance of assurance—underscored the theme of spiritual victory in a way that he had not done before: "And herein I found the difference between this and my former state chiefly consisted" Wesley observed, "I was striving, yea fighting with all my might under the law, as well as under grace. But then I was sometimes, if not often, conquered; now, I was always conqueror."[55] Again, on May 25, Wesley exclaimed: "But this I know, I have *now peace with God, and I sin not today.*"[56] And on May 29, although feelings of joy were no longer evident, Wesley could yet profess: "I have *constant peace*, not one uneasy thought. And I have *freedom from sin*, not one unholy desire.[57]

Wesley's Western Theological Orientation

In a real sense, Peter Böhler's emphasis on the two fruits of holiness, broadly understood, and justification, which ever flow from saving faith ("freedom from sin and a constant peace from a sense of forgiveness"), fruits that Wesley had come to accept intellectually in March 1738 and that were instantiated, in some sense, in the tempers and dispositions of his heart on May 24, 1738—all of this reveals the basic western, even Protestant, orientation of much of Wesley's doctrine of salvation. And though the claim has often been made of late that Wesley's theology, especially his understanding of sanctification, both initial and entire, represents a largely eastern orientation, that claim is weakened, perhaps even undermined, by the following two considerations.

First of all, though Wesley later maintained in his writings that regeneration (freedom from the power of sin) and justification (freedom from the guilt of sin) occur simultaneously in the lives of believers—never one without the other—he did make an important *logical* distinction between these two works of grace—a distinction that was hardly found or developed in either the Eastern Orthodoxy or the Roman Catholicism of his day. Thus in his sermon "The New Birth," for example, Wesley writes, "In order of *thinking*, as it is termed, justification precedes the new birth. We first conceive his wrath to be turned away, and then his Spirit to work in our hearts."[58] Moreover, Wesley draws attention to the different natures of these works of grace by noting that "justification implies only a relative, the new birth a real, change. God in justifying us does something *for* us: in begetting us again he does the work *in* us."[59]

So understood, justification changes the relation to God such that sinners are restored to the divine favor. Regeneration, on the other hand, changes the inward nature of people such that they are restored, at least in part, to the holy image of God. Again, in his sermon "Justification by Faith," Wesley affirms that justification

> is not the being made *actually* just and righteous. This is sanctification; which is indeed in some degree the immediate fruit of justification, but nevertheless is a distinct gift of God, and of a totally different nature.[60]

By distinguishing these doctrines, then, by keeping them logically, if not temporally, separate, Wesley was able to underscore the great Pauline truth, championed by Luther, Calvin, and Cranmer in their own age, that God justifies not the righteous, but *sinners,* and that sanctification or holiness, therefore, cannot, in any sense, precede or be the basis of justification. Again, and it bears repeating, justification and sanctification remain distinct works of grace for Wesley; and it's precisely that distinctiveness that bespeaks of his basic Protestant orientation. As Albert Outler has so aptly put it, "1738 was Wesley's theological *annus mirabilis* . . . and Aldersgate was the dramatic moment in that year when he reversed the priorities between *sola fide* and holy living, never to reverse them again."[61]

Second, it is equally clear that Wesley conceived of the grace of God not in a monolithic sense, but in two key ways, as both the *favor* of the Most High and as *power* or *enabling presence*. Working with this distinction, some contemporary theologians have suggested a division of labor with respect to these graces, which, on the one hand, unduly privileges an "eastern" reading of Wesley's doctrine of salvation, whereas, on the other hand, it misses crucial Protestant emphases that were very much a part of Wesley's own theological formulations.[62] The usual form of this contemporary teaching is that grace as *favor* informs the juridical theme of justification whereas grace as *power* or *enabling presence* informs the participatory theme of sanctification, both initial and entire. However, this contemporary construction lacks sufficient explanatory power; for one of the crucial truths that was mediated to Wesley by Böhler, and one that represents the emphasis of the continental Pietists, is that grace as divine *favor* informs not simply justification, but sanctification or holiness as well.

Here, then, was Wesley's great insight; here marked his anguished breakthrough at Aldersgate, that the holiness that had so captivated his imagination since his reading of the great western sources of à Kempis, Taylor, and Law would be actualized in his life, neither by works, nor by resolve, nor by human will and effort, however well motivated or sincere, but simply and wonderfully as a result of divine graciousness and favor. Indeed, in a certain sense, Wesley continued the Reformation's clarion call of *sola gratia* by later proclaiming: "Exactly as we are justified by faith, so are we sanctified by faith. Faith is the condition, and the *only* condition of sanctification, *exactly as* it is of justification."[63] And elsewhere Wesley observed even more emphatically: "We allow, it is the work of God *alone* to justify, to sanctify, and to glorify; which three comprehend the whole of salvation."[64] So then, the sheer gratuity of grace, a Reformation insight and emphasis, informs not simply the juridical themes of Wesley's theology, but the participatory ones as well.

Now although Wesley's doctrines of justification, regeneration, as well as entire sanctification are all informed by the notion of grace as *favor*, he avoided the possible antinomian implications (we *remain* sinners while Christ's righteousness "covers" us) of this teaching by, once again, making an important distinction between justifying and sanctifying grace. In Wesley's reckoning, the former grace is (and must be) imputed simply because God justifies sinners who can have no forgiveness of sins, the very meaning of justification, apart from the atoning work of Christ. The latter grace (and its consequences), on the other hand, though it, too, represents a sheer gift, not smacking of merit in the least, is not imputed but imparted; that is, believers *actually* become holy as a result of both divine *favor* and *enabling presence*.

Salvation by Faith

On June 11, Wesley gave evidence of his newfound faith and delivered what can be called his "evangelical manifesto," as Albert Outler put it, before the venerable at St. Mary's Church, Oxford. His sermon, "Salvation by Faith," took Ephesians 2:8 as its text ("For by grace you have been saved through faith") and considered three major questions. Of the first, "What faith is it through which we are saved?" Wesley underscored the crucial truth that saving faith is "faith in Christ—Christ, and God through Christ, are the proper object of it."[65] And this orientation or disposition to Jesus Christ is precisely what distinguishes justifying faith from what Wesley termed the "faith of a heathen." Indeed, Wesley had confessed in his brief spiritual autobiography in the preface to the description of his Aldersgate experience that earlier he did not fix this faith on its proper object; then he meant only faith in God, not faith in or through Christ.[66] "Again, I knew not that I was *wholly void of this faith,"* he writes, "but only thought *I had not enough* of it."[67] Justifying faith, then, is not a matter of an increment or a *degree*, a little more of an already existing faith; on the contrary, it represents nothing less than a *qualitatively* different kind of faith. In fact, eight years later, in 1746, Wesley attributed the success of the revival, at least in part, to this new focus:

> From 1738 to this time—speaking continually of Jesus Christ; laying Him only for the foundation of the whole building, making Him all in all, the first and the last; preaching only on this plan, "The kingdom of God is at hand; repent ye, and believe the gospel,"—the "word of God ran" as fire among the stubble.[68]

Moreover, Wesley declared that justifying faith is different from the "faith of a devil" in that "it is not barely a speculative, rational thing, a cold, lifeless assent, a train of ideas in the head; but also a disposition of the heart."[69] Notice here that Wesley does not exclude an intellectual component to faith; he simply points out that this ingredient, by itself, is insufficient; it must also be joined to a disposition of the heart. That is, the mind must inform the heart, and the heart must engage the mind; it is "both/and," not "either/or." Indeed, Wesley realized that sinners respond to the justifying grace of God not merely as intellects, but as persons; they respond, in other words, with their whole being.

And last, Wesley proclaimed in St. Mary's Church, for all to hear that June morning, that justifying faith, quite remarkably, even goes beyond the faith of the apostles while Christ was on earth in that "it acknowledges the necessity and merit of his death, and the power of his resurrection."[70] This faith, then, looks to the death of Christ as the only sufficient means of redeeming humanity from eternal death, and to his resurrection as the remedy for restoring humanity to life and immortality.[71] In Wesley's own words, Christian faith is comprised of the following:

> not only an assent to the whole gospel of Christ, but also a full reliance on the blood of Christ, a trust in the merits of his life, death, and resurrection; a recumbency upon him as our atonement and our life, as *given for us*, and *living in us*. It is a sure confidence which a man hath in God, that through the merits of Christ *his* sins are forgiven, and *he* reconciled to the favour of God.[72]

Not surprisingly, after 1738, Wesley continually defined faith in terms of both assent *and* trust. Once acquired, then, this is an understanding that does not drop out. For example, in *An Earnest Appeal to Men of Reason and Religion*, written in 1743, Wesley points out that

> the right and true Christian faith is, not only to believe the Holy Scriptures and the articles of our faith are true; but also to have a sure *trust* and *confidence* . . . to be saved from everlasting damnation through Christ.[73]

And a few years later in his "Way to the Kingdom," Wesley cautions his readers against conceiving faith as a bare assent to the Bible.[74] Beyond this, in his sermon "Of the Church," produced in 1785, the elderly Wesley recounts the same *via negativa* (not the faith of a heathen, devil, the apostles, and so on) as found in his early "evangelical manifesto." The continuity is striking.

Of the second major question of the sermon "Salvation By Faith," "What is the salvation which is through faith?" Wesley proclaimed to his Oxford congregation that the salvation of which Christianity speaks is a *present* salvation and that it entails nothing less than redemption from sin here and now: "Through this faith they are saved from the *power* of sin as well as from the *guilt* of it."[75] Wesley elaborated:

> This then is the salvation which is through faith, even in the present world: a salvation from sin and the consequences of sin, both often expressed in the word "justification," which, taken in the largest sense, implies a deliverance from guilt and punishment, by the atonement of Christ actually applied to the soul of the sinner now believing on him, and a deliverance from the power of sin, through Christ "formed in his heart." So that he who is thus justified or saved by faith is indeed "born again."[76]

Much later Wesley expressed this same vital truth of a *present* appropriation of grace, actualized in the warp and woof of life, even more forcefully as revealed in his piece "A Blow at the Root; or, Christ Stabbed in the House of His Friends," produced in 1762. In it, Wesley states:

> No, it cannot be; none shall live with God, but he that now lives

to God; none shall enjoy the glory of God in heaven, but he that bears the image of God on earth; none that is not saved from sin here can be saved from hell hereafter; none can see the kingdom of God above, unless the kingdom of God be in him below. Whosoever will reign with Christ in heaven, must have Christ reigning in him on earth.[77]

And of the third major question, "How may we answer some objections?" Wesley considered many of the kinds of criticisms that might be in the minds of an eighteenth-century Anglican congregation, such as: (a) this teaching will drive people to despair, and (b) it is an "uncomfortable doctrine." Of the first objection, Wesley related that it was, after all, beneficial if the doctrine of justification by faith drove people to despair of their own efforts, their own attempts of righteousness, so that they could then receive the justification that comes from God *alone*. And though Wesley replied to the second objection, from his imagined critics, by citing a passage from the Anglican standards, the Thirty-nine Articles of Religion in particular ("that we are justified by faith only is a most wholesome doctrine and very full of comfort"), the influence of Moravianism and even of the Reformation was evident throughout this sermon. In fact, so enthusiastic was Wesley at this time, in the first flush of his Aldersgate experience, that he even referred to Martin Luther as "that glorious champion of the Lord of Hosts," language that was eventually dropped in the 1746 edition of Wesley's sermons.

But all was not well. Though Wesley had preached with great boldness at St. Mary's, he was apparently concerned with issues of doubt and fear and their place in the ongoing Christian life. And though he obviously had profited much from his acquaintance with the Moravians, some of Wesley's theological and spiritual malaise *after* his Aldersgate experience was due, in large measure, to their erroneous teaching. For one thing, the Moravians had led Wesley to believe that justification, and the new birth that necessarily accompanies it, would eliminate not simply the power of sin, which was accurate, but the *being* of sin as well, which was not. Either that or Wesley had simply misunderstood them. For example, when Wesley was en route to England on board the *Samuel*, he had written with unreasonable expectation: "The faith I want is, a sure trust and confidence in God, that through the merits of Christ my sins are forgiven, and I reconciled to the favor of God. . . . For whosoever hath it is 'freed from sin'; 'the *whole body of sin is destroyed*' in him."[78]

Moreover, in his sermon "The Almost Christian," produced a few years later in 1741, Wesley portrayed the "altogether Christian" in a way that essentially confounded regeneration with entire sanctification, a mistaken teaching mediated to him, once again, by the English Moravians. That is, Wesley portrayed the real Christian, ironically enough, in very unrealistic terms: " 'His delight is in the Lord,' *his* Lord and his all," Wesley wrote, "to whom 'in everything he giveth thanks.' *All his* 'desire is unto God.' "[79] And again,

> whosoever has this faith which "purifies the heart," by the power of God who dwelleth therein, from pride, anger, desire, "from all unrighteousness, "from all filthiness of flesh and spirit". . . is not *almost* only, but *altogether* a Christian.[80]

But the preceding characteristics are obviously apt descriptions not of the liberty of the new birth (which does indeed entail freedom from the power of sin), but that of entire sanctification. Indeed, nowhere in Scripture is it affirmed that babes in Christ (not "fathers" or "mothers") would be free from the *presence* in their hearts of such unholy tempers as pride, anger, and desire. However, it would take Wesley considerable time to work out the proper distinctions: a justified person is freed from the *guilt* of sin; a regenerated one from its *power*, and the entirely sanctified from its *being*. So then, if freedom from all sin (even its *being*) as characterizing the real or altogether Christian was the substance of the gospel that Wesley preached from March to May 1738 and following, it is little wonder that he was told by various churches to "preach here no more."

Herrnhut

Not yet realizing the full "legacy" the Moravians had bequeathed to him, both the good and the bad, Wesley desired still greater contact with this people—especially after his Aldersgate experience. To this end, Wesley, along with Benjamin Ingham and Johann Töltschig, set out for Herrnhut, a Moravian settlement about thirty miles from Dresden, in the early summer of 1738. By

July 4, Wesley had reached Marienborn, where he conversed with Count Zinzendorf, the leader of the Moravians. Wesley's reception at this community was somewhat mixed, and he was even refused permission to partake of the Lord's Supper. Of this incident, reminiscent of Wesley's own earlier ecclesiastical behavior, Benham writes:

> Ingham was admitted to . . . Holy communion. But when the congregation saw Wesley to be *homo perturbatus*, and that his head had gained an ascendancy over his heart, and being desirous not to interfere with his plan of effecting good as a clergyman of the English Church when he should become settled— for he always claimed to be a zealous English Churchman—they deemed it not prudent to admit him to that sacred service.[81]

Despite this embarrassment, a couple of days later, Wesley noted in his journal that he had encountered many living proofs of those who had been saved "from *inward as well as outward* sin."[82]

Later in the month, as Wesley and his companions came to Weimar, the gatekeeper of the city asked why they were going so far as Herrnhut. No doubt to the puzzlement of the gatekeeper, who looked at him quite hard, Wesley replied that they intended "to see the place where the Christians live." Finally, on August 1, 1738, Wesley and his friends came to Herrnhut, which was on the border of what was then known as Bohemia. At this Moravian settlement, Wesley became acquainted with the testimonies of Christian David, Michael Linner, and Arvid Gradin, among others. Christian David, for instance, pointed out that though sin still stirred in him, though it still remained, it did not reign:

> I saw not then that the first promise to the children of God is, "Sin shall no more reign over you"; but thought I was to *feel it in me* no more from the time it was forgiven. Therefore, although I had the mastery over it, yet I often feared it was not forgiven, because it still *stirred in me*, and at some times "thrust sore at me that I might fall." Because, though it did not *reign*, it did *remain* in me; and I was continually *tempted*, though not *overcome*.[83]

This distinction was very helpful to Wesley, and he would later develop it with greater care and precision. But his expectations with respect to the fruits that normally flow from justification were still unreasonable at this time, for he expected that his heart would be virtually pure. Indeed, shortly after his trip to Herrnhut, in October 1738, Wesley wrote: "I dare not say I am a new creature in this respect. For other desires *arise* in my heart. But they do not reign."[84]

Michael Linner also complicated matters for Wesley by insisting that full assurance, which excludes all doubt and fear, accompanies justification by faith. "Indeed the leading of the Spirit is different in different souls," this Moravian exclaimed. "His more usual method, I believe, is to give in one and the same moment the forgiveness of sins and a *full assurance* of that forgiveness."[85] Now Wesley had already been taught this baffling notion by the English Moravians, perhaps by Peter Böhler in particular, a notion that eventually became the occasion of much grief and anxiety. To illustrate, the day before Wesley preached the sermon "Salvation by Faith" at St. Mary's, he had received a letter that had thrown him into much perplexity. The letter maintained that whoever had *any* doubt or fear was not simply weak in faith, but "had no faith at all."[86] Deeply troubled, Wesley comforted himself with the observation that the apostle Paul referred to some in the Corinthian church as "babes in Christ" even though they were in a sense "carnal." "Surely, then these men had *some degree* of faith," Wesley insisted, "though it is plain their faith was but *weak*."[87] Nevertheless, Wesley remained troubled—and confused—for quite some time. In fact, when he was back in England during October 1738, Wesley was particularly and needlessly aggrieved because he lacked "the full assurance of faith."[88] So then, the association of full assurance with justification by faith was the second major error bequeathed to Wesley by the Moravians. This misguided notion, in conjunction with a confused doctrine of sin, which essentially confounded the liberties of regeneration and entire sanctification, help explain, in part, Wesley's troubled spirit, sadness, and lack of joy, even *after* his Aldersgate experience.

Back to England

By September 16, 1738, Wesley was in London once more, and he was pleased to learn that the society at Fetter Lane had increased from ten to thirty-two members in his absence. However, during this same month, some of Wesley's naïveté concerning the Moravians was beginning to wear off; for on September 27 or 28, Wesley drafted a letter that contained numerous criticisms in light of his recent visit. Among other things, Wesley noted the Moravian neglect of fasting, their levity in behavior, their failure to redeem the time, and their use of "cunning, guile, or dissimulation."[89] Nevertheless, because Wesley still had some doubt about the accuracy of these judgments, he quietly put this letter aside. The substance of the letter, however, eventually became a part of a later and much more lengthy one (August 8, 1740), which Wesley did indeed send and in which he criticized the Moravians for their numerous excesses.

During the latter part of October 1738 and following, Wesley also corresponded with his older brother, Samuel Jr., who had objected to his understanding of salvation and what it means to be a Christian believer. For his part, John pointed out that he had some measure of the faith that brings "salvation, or victory over sin, and which implies peace and trust in God through Christ, but the witness of the Spirit I have not, but I patiently wait for it."[90] John also reaffirmed his definition of a Christian in the following words:

> By a Christian I mean one who so believes in Christ as that sin hath no more dominion over him, and in this obvious sense of the word I was not a Christian till May 24th last past. For till then sin had the dominion over me, although I fought with it continually, but surely then, from that time to this it hath not, such is the free grace of God in Christ.[91]

Observe in this correspondence the specific reference to Wesley's Aldersgate experience of May 24, 1738, a reference that was written several months later. Once again, this is clear evidence that something vital had occurred on that date. Also note how Wesley underscores this event, this realization of grace, as the time when he became free from the power of sin, a deliverance that Wesley, himself, deemed one of the salient marks of the new birth as displayed in a later sermon by the same name. But Samuel Wesley Jr., like so many others, would have none of this. "Have you ever since continued sinless?" he asked. "Do you never, then, fall? Or do you mean no more than that you are free from presumptuous sins?"[92] After these pointed questions, Samuel drew the only conclusion he knew how: "If the former, I deny it; if the latter, who disputes?"[93]

While this disagreement with his older brother was going on— and John, by the way, was not willing to give an inch—Wesley began more narrowly "to inquire what the doctrine of the Church of England is concerning the much controverted point of justification by faith."[94] After a careful reading and editing of the Anglican homilies, Wesley published an extract, suitable for use by a wide spectrum of readers, entitled: *The Doctrine of Salvation, Faith, and Good Works Extracted from the Homilies of the Church of England.* And a few months later, Wesley published Barnes's two treatises on justification by faith alone. The motivation and purpose behind the publication of these pieces on the theme of justification by faith can be understood in a number of ways:

First of all, if Wesley had initially imbibed a Moravian/Lutheran notion of justification by faith—which, by the way, he judged to be in accord with the teaching of his own church—then it must also be noted, for the sake of accuracy, that Wesley was also in earnest that such teaching be explicated, taught, and proclaimed by means of his own Anglican tradition.

Second, Wesley knew full well that, like his brother Samuel, others would invariably take exception to the *fruits* that he maintained accompany justification and the new birth. In light of this, Wesley wanted to be able to give a reasoned defense of the liberty entailed in saving faith by appeal to the teachings of the Church of England itself. Naturally, in this endeavor, Wesley became better acquainted not only with the doctrine of the Anglican Reformation in general, but also with the work and genius of Thomas Cranmer in particular.

Third, by November 1738, the time when Wesley published his extracts, he perhaps already had some sense that his understanding of assurance and other matters pertaining to the doctrine of salvation might need revision and that study would, therefore, be appropriate. For one thing, his ongoing coldness in the midst of prayer, his lack of joy, as well as his repeated doubts and fears that he confessed to his friend Richard Viney at Oxford, reveal a problem either in Wesley's *experience* or in the *standards* he was applying to that experience, or perhaps in both. Moreover, Wesley's sadness, his heaviness, was compounded toward the end of the month when Charles Delamotte, a trusted friend who had accompanied him to Georgia, criticized him severely. Though Delamotte's judgments were much too harsh and negative, Wesley nevertheless wrote in his journal, "I was troubled."[95]

It would take Wesley much of the following year and well into the 1740s to sort all of this out: that justification, in rare instances, may occur apart from assurance, that justifying faith can indeed be marked by both doubt and fear—in other words, that there are degrees of faith as well as degrees of assurance, and that justification, and the new birth that ever accompanies it, deliver not from the *being* of sin (which pertains to entire sanctification), but only from its *power* or *dominion*. So then, it was the unreasonable expectations bequeathed to Wesley by the English Moravians that help explain the lion's share of his post-Aldersgate malaise. In spite of these expectations, Aldersgate remained significant, even crucial, for Wesley. Stripped of its excesses and mistaken notions, Aldersgate was not only the time when Wesley was set free from the *guilt* (justification) and *power* (regeneration) of sin; but it was also the occasion when he experienced a measure of assurance that he was indeed a child of God whereby he could graciously and wonderfully cry, "Abba Father." Aldersgate, then, was—and remained—a remarkable work of grace.

Field Preaching

In late fall of 1738, Wesley hastened to London to greet George Whitefield, who was just returning from Georgia. Though Whitefield was Wesley's junior by about ten years, Wesley had grown close to this one-time Oxford servitor and member of the Holy Club. Perhaps Wesley enjoyed Whitefield's ebullient spirit, his engaging style, and his easygoing manner. Like many others, Wesley was undoubtedly impressed with the preaching ability, the rhetorical powers, and grace of Whitefield, who could sway the coldest congregation and move it to tears. Benjamin Franklin's advice to those who would hear this gifted preacher was to go with empty pockets, otherwise they would give all that they had. And it was reported by some that Whitefield could bring tears to a congregation's eyes just by pronouncing the word "Mesopotamia."

Creative and unconventional in many respects, George Whitefield had already undertaken the practice of field preaching in Bristol during March 1739. At first, Wesley was horrified at such a practice—with its grass, mud, and rain—and he noted that he "could scarce reconcile [himself] at first to this strange way of preaching."[96] "I should have thought the saving of souls *almost a sin*," Wesley added, "if it had not been done *in a church*."[97] Whitefield, however, was persuasive as usual. And though we don't know the substance of all that he said on this topic, Whitefield probably convinced Wesley that he could save more souls outside a church than within it, especially since Wesley was now being excluded from so many churches. At any rate, whatever Whitefield said, it worked. For at four in the afternoon on April 2, 1739, Wesley, to use his own words, "submitted to 'be more vile' and proclaimed in the highways the glad tidings of salvation speaking from a little eminence in a ground adjoining to the city, to about three thousand people."[98] Just a few days earlier, Wesley had written to John Clayton and proclaimed that all the world was his parish: "I judge it meet, right, and my bounden duty to declare unto all that are willing to hear the glad tidings of salvation."[99] Now with the beginning of field preaching, it truly was.

Some clues as to the substance of what Wesley preached can be found in his journal of the period. On April 25, he writes that he preached to above two thousand at Baptist Mills on the topic "Ye have not received the spirit of bondage again unto fear, but ye have received the Spirit of adoption, whereby we cry Abba, Father."[100] Thus, at the very outset of the Evangelical Revival in Britain, Wesley preached freedom from the bondage or dominion of sin as part of the good news of the gospel. Whitefield, however, disagreed with Wesley on this issue—he held to more pessimistic notions—but their sharpest disagreement, theologically speaking, was yet to come.

Valuing their friendship, Wesley was undecided whether he should challenge the Calvinistic views of George Whitefield so directly as to preach on the subject of "free grace." To be sure, Whitefield would find the notion that salvation was available to all sinners very troubling. To break his indecision on this matter, Wesley cast lots on April 26, which indicated that he should "preach and print." Accordingly, a few days later, on April 29,

Wesley drafted the sermon "Free Grace" in Bristol, which, on the one hand, impugned Calvinist predestination and, on the other hand, affirmed that salvation is free for *all*, that all who are in *need* of Christ may come to the Savior. Naturally, George Whitefield was angered by this publication; and it caused a rift, not quickly healed, between the two principal leaders of the revival. Indeed, no sooner had Wesley and Whitefield joined hands than they were already beginning to go their separate ways.

Despite the difficulties between Wesley and Whitefield, by April 1739, with the employment of field preaching, all the major ingredients for a revival in Britain were in place: preachers marked by holiness and love; a message of forgiveness, liberation, and peace to proclaim; and a suitable audience. For Wesley, the first two elements were clearly in place by May 24, 1738; the last one not until April 2, 1739. However, all of these elements were necessary, none to the exclusion of the others, for promoting and sustaining the awakening that was soon to sweep across the land. Field preaching without Aldersgate, and its larger theological setting, would have been empty; Aldersgate without field preaching would have been pointless, even self-indulgent. Reluctantly, Wesley had found his calling, and grace would make his calling sure.

CHAPTER FIVE

The Form and Power of Methodism

The Foundery Chapel

That John Wesley, like George Whitefield, was a field preacher meant that he would not remain in one local church, but would travel, itinerate, throughout the British Isles. Barred from many Anglican churches, Wesley could nevertheless reach his audience by preaching in some cow pasture or in the local marketplace. But even in such untraditional settings, which allowed a measure of freedom, Wesley often encountered opposition from local leaders. To illustrate, in late spring of 1739, Beau Nash, the dandy of Bath, challenged Wesley's authority to preach; declared his meetings to be conventicles, that is, illegal and seditious assemblies; and claimed that Wesley's preaching frightened the people "out of their wits."[1]

This last charge comes as something of a surprise since Wesley's preaching style, from all reports, was calm, earnest, and sincere. His manner in the field, as in the pulpit, was hardly characterized by the antics of subsequent imitators who sought popularity far more than the kingdom of God. Nor was Wesley particularly dramatic in his preaching; shouting, stomping, the flailing of arms, and other wild gesticulations were simply not his style. And yet when Wesley preached, when he proclaimed the good news of salvation in a clear and cogent manner, people at times swooned, fell down, or cried out in heartfelt anguish as if the terrors of the Almighty were already upon them. In fact, just ten days after his encounter with Beau Nash in Bath, while Wesley was exhorting a society meeting in Wapping, some of the people collapsed; others trembled and quaked; and still others were "torn with a kind of convulsive motion in every part of their bodies, and that so violently that often four or five persons could not hold one of them."[2] Of this occurrence, Wesley remarked, "I have seen many hysterical and many epileptic fits, but none of them were like these."[3] Naturally, reports of these disturbances spread throughout the land such that even Wesley's elder brother, Samuel Jr., began to ask: "Did these agitations ever begin during the use of any collects of the Church? Or during the preaching of any sermon that had before been preached within consecrated walls?"[4] In a carefully written letter on October 1739, Wesley addressed his brother's several criticisms:

> How is it that you can't praise God for saving so many souls from death, and covering such a multitude of sins, unless he will begin this work within "consecrated walls"? . . . But I rejoice to find that God is everywhere. I love the rites and ceremonies of the Church. But I see, well-pleased, that our great Lord can work without them.[5]

So then, for the sake of giving the gospel as wide a hearing as possible, Wesley at times not only put aside the "rites and ceremonies of the church," not only preached outside consecrated walls, but also violated the parish boundaries of the Anglican Church to the annoyance and frustration of many of its clergy. Indeed, in June of this same year, Wesley wrote to his brother Charles concerning his itinerancy: "God commands me to do good unto all men, to instruct the ignorant, reform the wicked, confirm the virtuous. Man commands me not to do this in another's parish; that is, in effect, not to do it at all."[6] And a few months later, Wesley continued this theme in a letter to James Hervey:

A dispensation of the gospel is committed to me, and woe is me if I preach not the gospel. But you would have me preach it in a parish. What parish, my brother? I have none at all. Nor I believe ever shall. Must I therefore bury my talent in the earth? Then am I a wicked, unprofitable servant.[7]

Wesley had justified his "new measures," his innovative evangelistic techniques, to Charles and others earlier by making a distinction between an ordinary call and an extraordinary one:

My ordinary call is my ordination by the bishop: "Take thou authority to preach the Word of God. My extraordinary call is witnessed by the works God doth by my ministry, which prove that he is with me of a truth in the exercise of my office."[8]

To illustrate, a few years later, when Wesley, ironically enough, was barred from the pulpit at Epworth by the Reverend John Romley, who had been the amanuensis to his father in compiling his commentary on the book of Job, Wesley simply preached atop Samuel's tomb with wonderful and gracious effect: "I am well assured I did far more good to them by preaching three days on my father's tomb than I did by preaching three years in his pulpit."[9]

All during this period, then, Wesley believed he was in harmony with the Church of England. And when he was asked in September 1739 by a serious cleric in what points the Methodists differed from the Anglican Church, Wesley took this question not in terms of his "new measures" or with respect to issues of Church polity and governance, but simply in terms of doctrine: "The doctrines we preach are the doctrines of the Church of England," he replied, "Indeed, the fundamental doctrines of the Church, clearly laid down, both in her Prayers, Articles, and Homilies."[10] And the following month as Wesley preached on Acts 28:22 in Wales at Abergavenny, he related that he simply "described the plain old religion of the Church of England, which is now almost 'everywhere' spoken against, under the new name of 'Methodism.' "[11] And even Dr. Walker, canon of Exeter College, agreed that "all . . . you [Wesley] have said is true. And it is the doctrine of the Church of England."[12] But he quickly added: "It is not *guarded*. It is *dangerous*. It may lead people into *enthusiasm* or *despair*."[13]

Nevertheless, it was precisely this "plain old religion," a clear articulation of the Word enlivened by the Spirit, that was bringing both life and hope where before there was none. Little wonder then that the poor, if not his fellow clergy, often heard John Wesley gladly.

Lay Preaching

From the beginning, Wesley had understood Methodism to be very much a part of the Church of England. Like the religious society movement, the Methodist societies were an attempt to bring new life and vigor to the mother church. Given this understanding, Wesley naturally had hoped that several Anglican clergy, sensing the need for renewal, would assist him in the task of "spreading scriptural holiness across the land"; but in this hope he was greatly disappointed. To be sure, not only had the Anglican clergy, by and large, not joined his ranks, but also those few clergy who had associated with Wesley in 1738, some of whom were Oxford Methodists, quickly abandoned him for their own distinct ministries. Therefore, lacking suitable laborers to reap a burgeoning harvest, Wesley began to employ lay preachers, that is, unordained assistants whose ministries would be limited, for the most part, to the task of preaching. Wesley often spoke of these fellow laborers in the gospel as his children; and "their relationship with their leader," as Green points out, "was more paternal than anything else."[14]

Just who precisely was the first Methodist lay preacher has been much debated in Wesley studies, and the answer to this question, as Henry Rack notes, is "partly a matter of definition."[15] That is, a case can be made for more than one preacher for this distinct honor. At any rate, Wesley had asked John Cennick, the son of Quakers who had become Anglicans, to go to Bristol and Kingswood in the summer of 1739 to assist in the work of the societies. Impressed with Cennick's many talents, George Whitefield later suggested to Wesley that this lay preacher should become the first master of Kingswood, a school established for the sons of colliers near Bristol during the latter part of the 1740s. With his preaching becoming increasingly Calvinistic, Cennick eventually went over to Whitefield's connection. Wesley insisted, however, that this mutually agreeable separation was due not to any doctrinal disagreement, but to evil speaking and stubbornness on the part of Cennick since "there are several predestinarians in our societies."[16]

Later, probably sometime during the winter of 1740–1741, Thomas Maxfield, who had been converted under Wesley's ministry in Bristol in 1739, began not simply to pray, advise, and exhort—which was allowed—but also to preach in the society meeting during Wesley's absence—which was not. Upon his return, Wesley considered putting an end to this usurping practice and complained to his mother: "Thomas Maxfield has turned preacher, I find." But Susanna, surprisingly enough, urged caution: "Take care what you do with respect to that young man, for he is as surely called of God to preach, as you are. Examine what have been the fruits of his preaching, and hear him also yourself."[17]

Because of Susanna's advice and also because of the dire need of the societies themselves, Wesley eventually warmed to the idea of lay preaching and so began to employ the talents of Joseph Humphreys at the Foundery, a Methodist chapel, in September 1740. In solving one problem, however, Wesley quickly created another. For with the ministries of Cennick, Maxfield, Humphreys, and others, eighteenth-century Methodism was subjected to the same kind of criticism that was leveled against Peter Waldo and the Poor Men of Lyons in the eleventh century. Not surprisingly, many of the Anglican clergy resented—for all sorts of reasons—such irregularity on the part of the Methodists, criticized the lack of education of many of Wesley's lay preachers, and therefore did not look kindly on the movement as a whole. Much later, in 1756, Wesley became so frustrated with the ongoing criticism against his preachers that he exclaimed: "Is not a lay preacher preferable to a drunken preacher, to a cursing, swearing preacher?"[18] In fact, Wesley eventually became so committed not only to the employment of lay preachers as a suitable instrument to foster the kingdom of God, but also to a rather functional definition of ministry, that in a letter to the Reverend Samuel Walker, in 1755, he observed:

> We should judge it our bounden duty rather wholly to separate from the Church than to give up any one of these points [field preaching, praying extempore, forming societies, and lay

preaching]. Therefore if we cannot stop a separation without stopping lay preachers, the case is clear—we cannot stop it at all.[19]

The Third Rise of Methodism: Fetter Lane

As the shape, the very structure, of Methodism was slowly evolving during 1739 and the early 1740s, the theology of Methodism under Wesley's leadership was also being distinguished from various movements—Moravianism and Calvinism in particular. For example, in November 1739, Philipp Heinrich Molther, who had been introduced to the Fetter Lane Society by James Hutton, began to teach society members—Jenny Chambers among them—that until they had justifying and regenerating faith, they should be "still" and leave off the means of grace such as attendance at the Lord's Supper. Mr. John Bray, a layperson and friend of the Wesleys, added his voice to Molther's teaching such that by the time John Wesley came back to London in December 1739, he found that "scarce one in ten retained his first love."[20]

Concerned about the effect of such preaching on the Fetter Lane Society, Wesley met with Molther in late December 1739. Two issues divided these men: First, Molther contended that there are no degrees in faith and that no person has any degree of it before all things have become new. Wesley, on the other hand, maintained "that a man may have *some degree* of [faith] before all things in him are become new; before he has the full assurance of faith."[21] Second, Molther taught that the way to saving faith was to be "still," that is, not to use the means of grace such as attending church, receiving the Lord's Supper, fasting, praying, reading Scripture, and undertaking temporal and spiritual good. Wesley, on the other hand, affirmed these means of grace as conducive to the reception of (initially) sanctifying grace, that grace which makes one *holy*. In other words, he considered the means of grace to be "outward signs, words, or actions ordained of God, and appointed for this end—to be the *ordinary* channels whereby he might convey to men preventing, justifying, or sanctifying grace."[22]

Wesley developed his teaching on the necessity of instruments of spiritual growth in his *Minutes of Several Conversations* and in his subsequent sermon "The Means of Grace," produced in 1746. In this sermon, Wesley discerns two principal errors: The first, which was no doubt found among some of his Anglican colleagues, was the "abuse" of the means, that is, mistaking them for the end of religion, placing "religion rather in doing those outward works than in a heart renewed after the image of God."[23] "This is doubtless the case," Wesley warns, "with all those who rest content in the form of godliness without the power."[24] The second error, which was demonstrated in the teaching of both Molther and Bray, was the "despising" of the means, that is, contending that there were no means for conveying the grace of God or that until one received saving faith one ought to be "still." In order to correct this last teaching, Wesley delineated what he termed the "instituted" means of grace in the following fashion:

> The chief of these means are prayer, whether in secret or with the great congregation; searching the Scriptures (which implies reading, hearing, and meditating thereon) and receiving the Lord's Supper, eating bread and drinking wine in remembrance of him; and these we believe to be ordained of God as the ordinary channels of conveying his grace to the souls of men.[25]

Elsewhere in his *Minutes of Several Conversations*, Wesley added "fasting" and "Christian Conference" (meeting together for guidance, reproof, and care) to the instituted means and offered various "prudential" means (those suggested by reason, given one's circumstances), which are quite simply particular rules to foster growth in grace, reasonable arts of holy living. And so to the salient question, "Am I to wait for the grace of God which bringeth salvation by using the means, or by laying them aside?" Wesley emphatically replied: "According to the decision of Holy Writ, all who desire the grace of God are to wait for it in the means which he hath ordained; in using, not in laying them aside."[26]

In an attempt to heal the dissension at Fetter Lane, Wesley, along with his brother Charles, met with Molther on April 25, 1740. The Moravian leader, however, continued to insist that there are no degrees of faith, that no one has any faith "who has ever any doubt or fear."[27] Moreover, Molther once again misprized, even deprecated, the means of grace and insisted not only that "to those who have a clean heart the ordinances are not [a] *matter of duty*,"[28] but also that they *"ought not* to use them."[29] After this meeting, when Wesley saw the ongoing results of these teachings on the life of the society—many were indeed leaving off good works and neglecting the ordinances of the church in order "to increase faith"—he took remedial action by expounding the epistle of James, "the great antidote against this poison,"[30] but it was to little avail.

Tensions within the Fetter Lane Society increased in the months ahead. In June 1740, Mr. Simpson charged that Wesley had been "preaching up the works of the law, 'which (added Mr. V[iney]) we believers are no more bound to obey than the subjects of the King of England are bound to obey the laws of the King of France.' "[31] Finally, on July 16, 1740, Wesley was actually prohibited from preaching at this society any longer. "This place is taken for the Germans [Moravians]," it was declared.[32] Frustrated with this turn of events, as well as with the larger issues entailed, Wesley issued an ultimatum at Fetter Lane four days later, at which point he, along with eighteen or nineteen others, mostly women, left the society and began to meet at the Foundery. In his ultimatum, Wesley not only criticized the "stillness" of the society, as expected, but also impugned the notion that justifying faith excludes all doubt and fear. That is, Wesley now understood that justifying (as well as regenerating) faith does not imply the full assurance of faith as he, himself, had once mistakenly believed. This teaching, part of the inheritance that Wesley had received from the English Moravians, was appropriately put aside.

As a result of the Fetter Lane incident, Wesley's relationship with the Moravians was now marked by increasing ambiguity. On the one hand, in a letter to Charles Wesley on April 21, 1741, John listed several reasons for not joining the Moravians, among which included their tendency towards *mystical* as opposed to *scriptural* religion, their lack of self-denial, and their relative neglect of the means of grace.[33] On the other hand, when Wesley had met with Peter Böhler just a few weeks earlier, he was so impressed with the grace and witness of this young man that he remarked, "I marvel how I refrain from joining these men. I scarce ever see any of them but my heart burns within me. I long to be with them. And yet I am kept from them."[34]

Wesley's ties with the Moravians, however, soon became more tenuous—and thus less ambiguous—as a result of his meeting with Count Zinzendorf at Gray's Inn Walks on September 3, 1741. The Count, speaking in Latin, maintained that the moment a believer is justified, "he is sanctified wholly."[35] Astonished, Wesley replied, "What! Does not every believer, while he increases in love, increase equally in holiness? . . . Is not therefore a father in Christ holier than a new-born babe?"[36] The Count, who remained undisturbed, replied in such a way that Wesley could not mistake his meaning: "Our whole justification, and sanctification, are in the same instant, and [the believer] receives neither more nor less."[37] Believers, in other words, are entirely sanctified when they are justified. The Christian life, then, is not characterized by *growth* in holiness.

By this point, however, Wesley knew full well that other Moravians thought differently from Zinzendorf. In fact, when Wesley had met Peter Böhler and August Spangenburg earlier that May, they both insisted that the "old man," or carnal nature (original sin), is still present even in a child of God.[38] And though Wesley did not agree with Böhler and Spangenburg when they declared that the carnal nature remains until death, he did at least agree, certainly by the time of his conversation with Zinzendorf, that justified believers, those who are born of God, are not pure in heart, entirely sanctified. This means, of course, that Wesley was in the process of putting aside a notion to which he, himself, had once mistakenly given assent, especially when he had exclaimed on board the *Samuel*, "I want that faith which none can have without knowing that he hath it. . . . For whosoever hath it is 'freed from sin'; 'the *whole body of sin* is destroyed' in him."[39] Accordingly, the doctrine that Christian believers are freed from all sin, that they are entirely sanctified the moment they are justified, is the second principal erroneous teaching of the Moravians that Wesley eventually challenged. And by September 1741, Wesley was already accusing the Moravian community of three grand errors: "universal salvation, antinomianism, and a kind of new-reformed quietism."[40] As a consequence of this and other matters, relations with Zinzendorf were unfortunately strained, so much so that in 1745, the Count, in considering all the differences between the two communions of faith, declared that he and his people "had no connection with Mr. John and Charles Wesley."[41]

So then, these encounters with the Moravians at Fetter Lane and

Gray's Inn Walks marked a crucial transition in Wesley's theology, a time of significant clarification and adjustment. For if Wesley had continued to preach after May 1738 along the lines suggested by the English Moravians, with the unreasonable expectation that a child of God would have no doubt or fear, and if he had expected like Zinzendorf and others that "the whole body of sin" would be destroyed in a child of God, even the carnal nature, and had preached accordingly, what havoc would he have reaped not only in his own societies, but in the larger revival as well. But in the end, it was Wesley's own Anglican tradition, rich in balance and steeped in nuance, that kept him from the shoals of these errors, especially the prospect of solafidianism—an exaggeration and misunderstanding of Luther's basic teaching on justification by faith alone. Indeed, the Caroline Divines of the seventeenth century, such as Lancelot Andrews and Bishop Thomas Ken, had affirmed that teaching sinners are saved by faith is fully compatible not only with a vigorous employment of the means of grace (in response to the prevenient grace of God), but also with the necessity of works after justification as evidence of a lively faith, even of a faith that works by love.[42]

George Whitefield

During the early days of the revival, Wesley distinguished the Methodism under his leadership and care not only from Moravianism, but from Calvinism as well. As noted in the last chapter, in April 1739, Wesley had composed the sermon "Free Grace," to which his brother Charles appended a hymn on universal redemption. In these works, the Wesleys impugned the notions, so dear to Calvinists, of unconditional election, irresistible grace, and the final perseverance of the saints. Naturally, both pieces roiled Whitefield, who responded to these publications over a period of a year and a half. On September 25, 1740, for example, Whitefield wrote a letter in Boston that was eventually published in England under the title *The Perfectionist Examin'd*.[43] "I am sorry to hear, by many letters, that you seem to own a *sinless perfection* in this life attainable," Whitefield observed. "I do not expect to say indwelling sin is destroyed in me, till I bow my head and give up the ghost."[44] Copies of this letter were distributed to Wesley's congregation at the Foundery on February 1, 1741. After preaching on that day, Wesley noted from the pulpit that the letter was a private one, published without Whitefield's permission. And so Wesley told the congregation that he would do just what Mr. Whitefield, himself, would do, that is, tear up the letter, which Wesley proceeded to do; and the congregation followed suite.

Upon learning that Wesley and his congregation had torn up his letter that championed Calvinist distinctives, Whitefield decided to publish a reply that he had written earlier. The correspondence entitled *A Letter to the Rev. Mr. John Wesley in Answer to his Sermon entitled "Free Grace"* was originally written on December 24, 1740, but did not emerge publicly—Whitefield at the time had not wanted to aggravate an already difficult situation—until March 31, 1741, that is, shortly after the letter-tearing episode at the Foundery. A few days earlier, Wesley had visited Whitefield in order to see for himself if the reports of his increasingly unkind behavior were true. Sure enough, Whitefield now seemed hardened in his opposition and told Wesley quite plainly that they preached "two different gospels" and that he, therefore, would not give Wesley "the right hand of fellowship."[45] To make matters worse, Whitefield declared that he was resolved to preach against John and Charles Wesley whenever he preached at all.[46] By this time, Ann Allin and Thomas Bissicks had also entered the fray and charged that Wesley did " 'preach up man's faithfulness' and not the faithfulness of God."[47] This division, principally caused by the publication of the sermon "Free Grace," eventually led to the organization of Lady Huntingdon's Connection, an association of Calvinist preachers, as well as to the founding of the Calvinistic Methodists in Wales. In fact, the controversy surrounding Whitefield and the Wesleys became so difficult and intense at points that even some of Wesley's early lay preachers, such as John Cennick and Joseph Humphreys, were persuaded to break ranks and depart from their "father in the gospel."

Remarkably, when many biographers assess the Wesley-Whitefield relationship, they simply focus on the issues of free grace, election, and the like as if these represented the entirety of Whitefield's disagreement and censure. They do not. Indeed, a second cluster of issues highlights the important questions of just how a Christian is defined or understood in terms of sin and grace and whether or not those who are justified and born of God can expect to be cleansed from the being of sin, that is, perfected in love in this life.

Whitefield's position on these significant issues is actually difficult to assess because in corresponding with Wesley, he continually shifted from the question of "sinless perfection," that is, having a heart free from the *being* of sin, to the question of actually committing sin or being under its *power*. For example, Whitefield pointed out to Wesley in a letter drafted in September 1740 that "there must be Amalekites left in the Israelite's land to keep his soul in action,"[48] as if sin were necessary to keep one humble, as if a "heart bent towards backsliding," in opposition to and in rebellion against God, were necessary for holiness. Wesley, by the way, always deemed such reasoning to be specious and contrary to the word of God. At any rate, Whitefield furthermore maintained that the being of sin not only remains in the hearts of believers— thereby rejecting Wesley's notion of Christian perfection—but also exercises sufficient dominion over believers such that they continually commit sin. To illustrate, Whitefield wrote to Wesley on one occasion, "I differ from your notion about not committing sin."[49] And in a letter on September 25, 1740, Whitefield made his meaning even more clear: "If after conversion we can neither sin in thought, word, or deed, I do not know why our Lord taught us to pray to our heavenly Father, 'Forgive us our trespasses, etc.' "[50] Beyond this, in a letter dated March 17, 1741, Charles related to John Wesley how he had preached "on the believer's privilege, i.e. power over sin."[51] He then invited George Whitefield to the pulpit, at which point Whitefield proclaimed, once again, "the necessity of sinning."[52]

In light of these observations, some more telling than others, it is evident that John and Charles Wesley differed from George Whitefield not only in terms of Christian perfection, but also in terms of the liberty that pertains even to a son or daughter of God. That is, not only was the whole matter of heart purity at stake, but also how a Christian believer is defined in the first place. With an eye to both of these issues, Wesley published his sermon "Christian Perfection" in 1741 and affirmed that "even babes in Christ are in such a sense perfect, or 'born of God' . . . as, first, not to commit sin."[53] And again, Wesley declared, "But if you would hence infer that *all Christians do, and must commit sin, as long as they live,* this consequence we utterly deny."[54] A few years later, Wesley also published "The Marks of the New Birth," in which he stated: "An immediate and constant fruit of this faith whereby we are born of God, a fruit which can in no wise be separated from it, no, not for an hour, is power over sin."[55] Whitefield, of course, disagreed with such notions and considered Wesley to be overly optimistic, even naive.

Both Wesley and Whitefield, however, tried to put the best face on a difficult situation; and in 1742, there was some measure of reconciliation. Both men continued to respect each other, and neither doubted the sincerity or the earnestness of the other. "I spent an agreeable hour with Mr. [Whitefield]," Wesley noted in his journal in April 1742, "I believe he is sincere in all he says concerning his earnest desire of joining hand in hand with all that love the Lord Jesus Christ."[56] And in a letter to Mrs. Hutton in 1744, Wesley exclaimed, "I love Calvin a little, Luther more; the Moravians, Mr. Law, and Mr. Whitefield far more than either."[57] Whitefield, for his part, likewise expressed admiration and praise for his fellow laborer in the gospel. Indeed, Leslie Church records an expression—though possibly apocryphal—of Whitefield's ongoing affection for Wesley:

> One of the critics came to George Whitefield and said, "Sir, do you think when we get to heaven we shall see John Wesley?" "No, sir," answered George Whitefield, "I fear not, for he will be so near the Eternal Throne and we shall be at such a distance, we shall hardly get a sight of him."[58]

The Character and Principles of a Methodist

In the midst of his theological struggles with fellow Methodist George Whitefield, Wesley, in a very ironic move, published "The Character of a Methodist" in 1742 and explored this character precisely in terms of his much-disputed doctrine of Christian perfection. Indeed, in a much later work, *A Plain Account of Christian Perfection*, Wesley relates that "The Character of a Methodist" was the "first tract he ever wrote expressly on the subject of perfection."[59] Attempting to put into more biblical terms the description of the perfect Christian that he had discovered in the *Stromateis* of

Clement of Alexandria,[60] Wesley indicates that the distinguishing marks of Methodists are not their opinions, no matter how carefully crafted they may be. "As to all opinions which do not strike at the root of Christianity," Wesley explains, "we 'think and let think.' "[61] But neither do the Methodists place the whole of religion in the very elements of repentance, such as "doing no harm, or in doing good, or in using the ordinances of God," elements that formed the basic structure of the General Rules of the United Societies.[62]

On the contrary, a Methodist is one, quite simply, who has not merely the *form* of religion but also its *power*; one who has, to use Wesley's own words, " 'the love of God shed abroad in his heart by the Holy Ghost given unto him'; one who 'loves the Lord his God with all his heart, and with all his soul, and with all his mind, and with all his strength.' "[63] And when Wesley declares in this same treatise that a Methodist is entirely holy, that "the love of God has purified his heart from all revengeful passions, from envy, malice, and wrath, from every unkind temper or malign affection,"[64] could Whitefield, erstwhile Oxford Methodist, have assented to such a teaching? Given the larger theological context of this treatise, one can at least pose the question of whether Wesley was, on some level, challenging the Methodist status of Whitefield since the Calvinist leader had so vigorously denied that such a character, depicted by Wesley as integral to being a Methodist, could ever be realized in this life. Or had Wesley, once again, portrayed the attributes or traits of a Methodist in far too lofty terms, perhaps confusing the marks of a child of God with those of the entirely sanctified?

During this same year of 1742, Wesley penned another treatise, "The Principles of a Methodist," which constituted a response to Josiah Tucker's "Brief History of the Principles of Methodism." Tucker, who was the Vicar of All Saints, Bristol, and Chaplain to the Bishop of Bristol, charged Wesley with three errors: teaching justification by faith alone, believing in sinless perfection, and asserting inconsistencies. Concerning the first charge, Wesley affirmed in a way remarkably similar to his earlier sermon "Salvation by Faith" that "the true Christian faith is not only to believe the Holy Scriptures and the articles of our faith are true, but also to have 'a sure trust and confidence to be saved from everlasting damnation by Christ.' "[65] Of the second accusation, Wesley responded by citing almost all of the material from his earlier preface to *Hymns and Sacred Poems*, a writing in which he endeavored to avoid confusion by stating, among other things, precisely what Christian perfection is *not*.[66] And of the third error of inconsistency, Wesley revealed the larger logic of his teachings particularly on the matters of justification and assurance. Once again, as in the aftermath of the Fetter Lane controversy, Wesley affirmed not only that assurance *normally* accompanies justifying faith, but also that the first sense of forgiveness that pertains to a child of God is "often mixed with doubt or fear,"[67] teachings that had been misconstrued in Tucker's assessments.

Susanna's Death

Shortly after Wesley's struggles with the Moravians, Calvinists, and a few Anglicans, and while Wesley was expanding his ministry further north into Newcastle, his mother became ill. Ever since the death of her husband, Samuel, Susanna, being a poor widow, found it necessary to live with several of her children: first with Emilia, then with Samuel Jr., then with her daughter Martha and her husband Westley Hall, and finally with John Wesley at the Foundery. As she lay on her deathbed on July 30, 1742, Susanna requested that those present—John Wesley among them—sing a psalm of praise to God "as soon as I am released."[68] After her death, an epitaph was inscribed on Susanna's original gravestone as follows:

> True daughter of affliction she,
> Inured to pain and misery,
> Mourned a long night of griefs and fears,
> A legal night of seventy years,
> The Father then revealed his Son,
> Him in the broken bread made known.
> She knew and felt her sins forgiven,
> And found the earnest of her heaven.[69]

The epitaph is surprising, even odd; for it reflects an implicit criticism of Susanna's spiritual experience by her sons Charles, who wrote these words, and John, who had the gravestone placed in Bunhill Fields. The epitaph, in effect, contends that Susanna was in the "legal state" for much of her life until finally, when she was around seventy years old, she received the *assurance* of faith that her sins were forgiven. For example, in the last stanza, Charles apparently refers to the incident when Susanna received the communion cup from her son-in-law Westley Hall in January 1740. As Hall was pronouncing the words, "The blood of our Lord Jesus Christ which was given for thee," Susanna later noted that "these words struck through my heart, and I knew that God for Christ's sake had forgiven me all my sins."[70] However, had Susanna died in 1737, Charles probably would have never written such words, or would John have had such a stone placed. Perhaps the epitaph, then, tells us more about the spiritual experience of Charles and John Wesley, what they deemed to be the proper Christian faith, than it does of their mother's experience. Interestingly enough, Susanna's headstone was replaced in 1828 by the British Methodists, and the critical epitaph was replaced with a more honorific one.

The Methodist Infrastructure

During the mid-1740s, the ministry of John and Charles Wesley was beginning to bear considerable fruit. As Wesley, himself, put it, "the Word of God ran" as fire among the stubble; it was "glorified" more and more; multitudes cried out, "What must we do to be saved?"[71] Clearly, the common folk of British society from London to Bristol to Newcastle were hungry for the message of the Wesleys. Earlier, in December 1738, Wesley had drawn up the *Rules of the Band Societies* even before distinctively Methodist societies began to emerge in Bristol and London.[72] Reflecting Moravian polity and discipline to a considerable degree, the bands met weekly in order to obey the command of God: "Confess your faults one to another, and pray one for another that ye may be healed."[73] In order that its members would be able to speak freely to one another, the bands were organized in the Moravian homogeneous fashion such that men and women met in groups of their own gender. Some of the questions proposed to all aspirants before they were admitted to the bands included: "Have you the forgiveness of your sins? . . . [and] has no sin, inward or outward, dominion over you?"[74] Once admitted, however, members faced a weekly questioning that was far more sensitive and probing: "What known sins have you committed since our last meeting? ... Have you nothing you desire to keep secret?"[75] Interestingly enough, it was perhaps the very intimate and rigorously honest nature of this questioning that helps explain, in part, why the bands eventually faded away as a distinct discipline in British Methodism.

Wesley described the rise of the most general structure of Methodism, that is, the United Society, first at London, and then in other places, in the following fashion:

> In the latter end of the year 1739 eight or ten persons came to me in London who appeared to be deeply convinced of sin, and earnestly groaning for redemption. They desired (as did two or three more the next day) that I would spend some time with them in prayer, and advise them how to flee from the wrath to come, which they saw continually hanging over their heads.[76]

Beyond this, Wesley expressed the purpose of these society meetings, which were in some sense similar to the pietistic *collegia* of Spener as well as to the religious societies of the Church of England as "a company of men 'having the form, and seeking the power of godliness.' "[77] Its members, then, would be united to pray together, to receive a word of exhortation, and "to watch over one another in love, that they may help each other to work out their salvation."[78] The principal task of these meetings, as Henderson correctly points out, was one of instruction,[79] of communicating the vital truths of the Christian faith, especially to the poor and to those who had never seen the inside of an Anglican Church. This last factor of allowing all people of whatever sect or of none at all to join the societies has led Henry Rack to deem Wesley's picture of Methodism as "a mere auxiliary to the Church of England," unconvincing.[80]

In early 1742, Captain Foy suggested a solution to the payment of a debt on property that the Methodists held in Bristol; and out of his suggestion emerged what became known as the Methodist class meeting. As a subdivision of the larger Methodist society, the class meeting was composed of five to twelve members. Leadership of the classes was open to women; and Elizabeth Ritchie, Hester Ann Rogers, Agnes Balmer, as well as Mary

Bosanquet emerged as significant leaders.[81] The class meetings had something of a democratic flavor to them, at least in the sense that class distinctions were ignored and one, for example, could move into a leadership role "on the basis of faithfulness alone."[82]

Unlike that of the more general society meeting, the purpose of the Methodist class was chiefly one of discipline, to discern, as Wesley put it, "whether they [were] indeed working out their own salvation."[83] In 1743, Wesley published *The Nature and General Rules of the United Societies* that indicated the normative value of the first two precepts of the natural law (avoid evil and do good) as well as the importance of the means of grace such as praying, reading the Bible, and receiving the Lord's Supper. These same three elements (avoid evil, do good and employ the means of grace) were explored by Wesley elsewhere, not as the heart of the proper Christian faith, but as the very rudiments of *repentance*—in other words, not as the power of religion but, once again, simply as its *form*. Observe also that Wesley made a distinction between joining the United Societies and remaining therein. The former activity required only a "desire to flee the wrath to come."[84] The latter, however, necessitated both sincerity (a willingness to employ the grace of God) and repentance as evidenced by keeping the General Rules.

The disciplinary function of the class meeting, so valued by Wesley, naturally included determining whether the Methodists were walking according to the grace of God. In 1743, for example, Wesley removed several people from associating with the Methodists because it was learned (most probably in the class meetings) that they broke the rules of the United Societies by habitual Sabbath breaking, drunkenness, spouse abuse, lying, evil speaking, and the like.[85] Using quarterly examinations as well as tickets for admission, Wesley constantly pruned the Methodist vine, so to speak. On a more general level, the network of Methodist classes allowed for appropriate supervision and discipline at different levels: that is, the various classes made up a society; the societies were organized by districts; and the districts themselves were arranged by provinces or nations,[86] with Wesley, of course, as the principal overseer. In fact, so impressed was George Whitefield with this Methodist structure that in later life he attributed Wesley's greater success to it: "My Brother Wesley acted wisely," Whitefield exclaimed; "the souls that were awakened under his ministry he joined in class, and thus preserved the fruits of his labor. This I neglected, and my people are a rope of sand."[87]

In time, the Methodist infrastructure came to include "select societies" for those who walked in the light of God's countenance and were pressing toward Christian perfection, and "penitents" for those who had fallen from grace and desired renewal. In emphasizing both grace and discipline, the Methodist structure not only helped prepare its members for the kingdom of heaven by being arranged in terms of progress along the *via salutis*, but also equipped them for service to the poor. Thus, by means of the society and class meetings, Wesley and the people called Methodists ministered to both the material and the spiritual needs of the poor. Not only, for example, were the Methodists among the poor—for which they were smugly criticized by others—and not only did Wesley establish a free medical dispensary in 1746, which was the first of its kind in London, but also he and the Methodists proclaimed a gospel of liberation to the downtrodden: from the wrenching guilt of sin on the one hand, and from its crippling power on the other.

Anglican Opposition

The more Methodism grew, the more threatening it became in the eyes of some. News of civil disturbances precipitated by mobs at Wednesbury, St. Ives, Costa Green, Falmouth, and Leeds, along with reports of some of the earlier psychological responses to Wesley's preaching such as fainting, screaming, and wailing, spread throughout England during the 1740s, and several clergy, some in high office, became bitterly opposed to Methodism in general and to John Wesley in particular. William Warburton, Bishop of Gloucester, for example, complained that Wesley was an enthusiast, a fanatic, who was driving the common people mad. As a bishop steeped in Enlightenment tastes and sensibilities, Warburton considered enthusiasm to be a particular danger, a " 'kind of ebullition or critical ferment of the mind': its 'fervors . . . soon rise into madness when unchecked by reason.' "[88] In fact, so concerned was the Bishop about fanatical preaching in his parishes that he exclaimed, "The way these new prophets preached might in itself do more harm than if they revived old heresies or invented new ones."[89] In addition, Warburton, who was more than willing to engage in abusive controversy, thought that John Wesley was especially dangerous because "in parts and learning he is far superior to the rest."[90]

For his part, Edmund Gibson, Bishop of London, who had ordained Charles to the priesthood in 1735, expressed concern and consequently questioned the Wesley brothers as early as 1738 concerning their teachings on justification, assurance, and the rebaptism of dissenters. Later, as the great evangelical revival was underway, Gibson became less cautious and far more negatively disposed toward the Methodists because he now believed they actually endangered the acceptance of religious truth by "making inward, secret, and sudden impulses the guides of their actions, resolutions, and designs."[91] And Joseph Butler, Bishop of Bristol and Durham, author of the famous *Analogy of Religion,* charged specifically that Wesley's doctrine of the Holy Spirit's witness to the believer—in other words, Christian assurance—was yet another species of fanaticism. "The pretending to extraordinary revelations and gifts of the Holy Ghost is a horrid thing," Butler intoned, "a very horrid thing."[92] Discerning several "dangers" in the rise of Methodism, the Bishop requested that Wesley not preach in his diocese. Wesley, however, put aside such a request and remarked that as a fellow of an Oxford College, he enjoyed the liberty to preach anywhere in the king's realm. That the bishop took no further action against Wesley, for what many others would consider rank insubordination, indicates something of the lax ecclesiastical discipline of the Church of England at the time.[93]

Though Wesley was of the opinion that "God made practical divinity necessary; the devil, controversial,"[94] he knew quite well that he could not allow such criticism, coming from such high corners of the church, to go unanswered. "Wesley was ridiculed and abused," Cragg points out, "because the eighteenth century was not prepared to tolerate, still less to welcome, an ardent evangelical revival."[95] So then in order to offer a reasonable defense for both Methodism and the evangelical awakening itself, Wesley produced *An Earnest Appeal to Men of Reason and Religion* in 1743, *A Farther Appeal to Men of Reason and Religion* in 1744, and Parts II and III of the later work the following year. These writings, reminiscent of the work of the early church fathers, constitute an "apology," an attempt to offer a fair-minded justification for the faith and practices of the Methodists.

Operating from the basic assumption that Methodism in large measure was a revitalization of primitive Christianity and a witness to the genius of the English Reformation, Wesley proceeded to demonstrate in his *Appeals* that Methodism entails nothing less than the essential reasonableness of the love of God and neighbor, thereby uniting reason and vital piety. In his *Earnest Appeal*, Wesley explained:

> What religion do I preach? The religion of love: the law of kindness brought to light by the gospel. What is this good for? To make all who receive it enjoy God and themselves: to make them like God, lovers of all, contented in their lives, and crying out at their death, in calm assurance, "O grave, where is thy victory?"[96]

Beyond this, Wesley turned the tables, so to speak, began to critique his Anglican critics, and argued that if it is reasonable to love God and neighbor and to do good to all, "you cannot but allow that religion which we preach and live to be agreeable to the highest reason."[97]

But it was, perhaps, when Wesley explored what is actually meant by reason in these treatises that he not only offered his best apology for Methodism—and one that Bishops Butler and Gibson, at least, would be able to appreciate—but also demonstrated how sophisticated and intricate his practical theology actually was in its linking of reason and the moral law as unified and harmonious expressions of a rational, created order. Wesley observed:

> What do you mean by reason?" I suppose you mean the eternal reason, or the nature of things: the nature of God and the nature of man, with the relations necessarily subsisting between them. Why, this is the very religion *we* preach: a religion evidently founded on, and every way agreeable to, eternal reason, to the essential nature of things. Its foundation stands on the nature of God and the nature of man, together with their mutual relations.[98]

Now since Wesley elsewhere in his sermon "The Original, Nature, Properties, and Use of the Law" specifically considered the moral law, that "copy of the divine mind," *both* in terms of the love of God and neighbor *and* of "supreme, unchangeable reason," "unalterable rectitude," and "the everlasting fitness of all things that are or ever were created,"[99] it is clear that his teaching on the moral law, as an "objective" standard, actually undermines all enthusiastic excess and forms the nexus, the common element, that joins together both reasonable religion and vital piety. Wesley took such care in crafting the *Appeals*, then, precisely because he believed so much was at stake: not simply a defense of Methodism, not merely the reasonableness of the Christian faith, but also an apologetic for vital Christianity as manifested in the love of God and neighbor.

Scriptural Christianity

So often criticized by his fellow Anglican clergy, Wesley was to return the favor in kind. Since he was a university preacher, the Methodist leader was required by statute to preach at Oxford on a three-year cycle. Earlier, in 1738, in the first flush of his evangelical conversion, Wesley had preached "Salvation by Faith." In 1741, as the revival was well under way, he held forth on Acts 26:28— "Almost thou persuadest me to be a Christian"—to a very large, no doubt curious, congregation at Mary's. The theme of the sermon, the difference between a nominal and a real Christian, was not only an emphasis of Puritan piety, as found, for example in the works of William Perkins and Richard Baxter,[100] but also evident in Wesley's earlier correspondence.[101] For his Oxford congregation, Wesley portrayed the almost Christian as marked by heathen honesty, the form of godliness, having the outside of a real Christian, using all the means of grace, and by sincerity, "a real design to serve God, a hearty desire to do his will."[102] However, when Wesley proceeded to describe the traits of an "altogether Christian," a judgment that at this time still confused the graces and liberties of entire sanctification with regeneration, he likely confused, perhaps even offended, his congregation with the following words:

> Now whosoever has this faith which "purifies the heart," by the power of God who dwelleth therein, from pride, anger, desire, "from all unrighteousness," "from all filthiness of flesh and

spirit.". . . Whosoever has this faith, thus "working by love," is not *almost* only, but *altogether* a Christian.[103]

As will be apparent in the following chapter, much of what Wesley had to proclaim about "altogether Christians" in this sermon was subsequently modified. Nevertheless, the theme of real Christianity remained a vital one for Wesley during this period as demonstrated by its repeated emergence in his writings during the 1740s.[104] In fact, in 1744, in his last sermon before the university, entitled "Scriptural Christianity," Wesley developed this theme even further and actually went on the offensive. No doubt frustrated by the repeated censure from his own church, Wesley was now poised to return the criticism in this very energetic, even caustic, sermon. To illustrate, Wesley moved unswervingly to his conclusion in this sermon by posing a number of increasingly pointed questions: "Where does this Christianity now exist? Where, I pray, do the Christians live?" "Is this city a *Christian* city? Is Christianity, *scriptural* Christianity, found here?" "Are you 'filled with the Holy Ghost'? With all those 'fruits of the Spirit' which your important office so indispensably requires?" "Do ye, brethren, abound in the fruits of the Spirit. . . . Is this the general character of fellows of colleges?" "Once more: what shall we say concerning the youth of this place? Have you either the form or the power of Christian godliness?"[105] And so on and on it went, to the bemusement of some who considered such barbs sport, and to the chagrin of others who considered them offensive.

After this series of probing questions, Wesley turned up the heat, so to speak, and in a climax that was sure to roil the congregation, he referred to the youth of Oxford University as a "generation of *triflers*; triflers with God, with one another, and with your own souls."[106] The leaders of the university were naturally incensed. The vice-chancellor called for a copy of Wesley's sermon, and the bold preacher was henceforth removed from the rotation of fellows who were normally required to preach before the University. Dr. Congbeare, the Dean of Christ Church, observed on the day of the sermon: "John Wesley will always be thought a man of sound sense, though an enthusiast."[107] For his part, Wesley confessed in his journal, "I preached, I suppose, the last time at St.

Mary's. Be it so. I am now clear of the blood of these men. I have fully delivered my own soul."[108]

The content of the sermon "Scriptural Christianity," as well as the way in which it was delivered, clearly undermine the notion that John Wesley was a man who desired peace above all cost, that he was a Milquetoast cleric ever willing to gloss over the differences between the Methodists and others. Indeed, it was with boldness that Wesley had published the sermon "Free Grace" in 1739 to the dismay of the Calvinists. It was with determination in 1740 that Wesley had read a paper before the Fetter Lane Society and then walked out to the consternation of the Moravians. And it was with remarkable honesty and courage that Wesley had preached "scriptural Christianity" at St. Mary's in 1744 to the censure of his own Anglican Church. Like his father, Samuel, and his mother, Susanna, John Wesley was a deeply principled person who was willing to suffer, to be criticized, rebuked, or even outright rejected for the sake of what he believed to be preeminently important, namely, the proper or real Christian faith, what he termed "scriptural Christianity." This, indeed, was the end of Wesley's preaching career at Oxford; but it also marked an important beginning.

CHAPTER SIX
Theological Nuances and Ongoing Standards

The Study in John Wesley's House

In order to provide greater direction to the Methodist societies in terms of doctrine, discipline, and practice, John and Charles Wesley, along with four other clergy and an equal number of lay people, held the first Methodist Conference at the Foundery in London on June 25, 1744. Wesley had invited such members as John Hodges, Rector of Wenvo; Henry Piers, Vicar of Bexley; Samuel Taylor, Vicar of Quinton; as well as John Meriton, not to govern him, as he put it, but only to advise. "I myself sent for these of my own free choice," Wesley exclaimed, "Neither did I at any time divest myself of any part of the power . . . which the providence of God had cast upon me, without any design or choice of mine."[1]

In carrying out its larger purpose, the conference posed three key questions: (1) what to teach, (2) how to teach, and (3) what to do. Beyond defining the responsibilities of lay assistants, stewards, and bandleaders in significant detail, the conference considered such doctrinal matters as the relation of faith and works and the nature of justification and entire sanctification. The *Minutes* of this first Conference, as well as of subsequent ones, are remarkable in that they underscore a basic doctrinal continuity with the years 1725 and 1733, when Wesley had understood the goal of religion as holiness or entire sanctification, and with the pivotal year of 1738, when Wesley had finally comprehended aright, largely through the counsel of Peter Böhler, the *nature* of both justification and saving faith. In these areas, then, the records demonstrate a steady course marked by careful explication.

Assurance

One area of discontinuity, however, that represents the most significant ongoing modification in Wesley's doctrine of salvation concerns the whole matter of Christian assurance. Indeed, Wesley's careful reconsideration of the direct witness of the Spirit as it relates to justifying faith will later be reflected, not only in his distinction between "the faith of a servant" and "the faith of a child of God," but also in his journal emendations of 1774. And it is precisely the assessment of these changes by contemporary scholars, as well as their larger significance, that has led to very different readings of Wesley's soteriology. One school of thought, as represented by Theodore Jennings, claims that it made little difference to John Wesley whether he served God as a servant or as a son.[2] A second school, led by Randy Maddox, employs the journal material of 1774 in a way that not only attempts to diminish the significance of Aldersgate, but also contends the faith of a servant is in fact justifying faith in every instance. "Wesley revised his assumptions in the years following Aldersgate," Maddox writes, "finally coming to value the nascent faith of the 'servant of God' as justifying faith."[3] However, a careful examination of the conference *Minutes* during the 1740s will demonstrate the problematic nature of these two modern interpretations that apparently lower the redemptive bar, so to speak. Wesley linked his more nuanced views of assurance not only to the terminology of the "faith of a servant" and his journal notations in 1774, but also, and perhaps more important, to the motif of real, scriptural Christianity, a motif whereby the Methodist leader maintained his relatively high soteriological standards in the midst of much theological change.

Several years before the first Methodist Conference, in 1739, Wesley had already realized that there are degrees of both faith and assurance and that the faith of a child of God is often marked by doubt and fear. What is less known, however, is that during this same period, through the first conference, Wesley continued to insist that assurance in the form of the direct witness of the Spirit is indeed a salient mark of a child of God. In 1740, for example, Wesley observed: "I never yet knew one soul thus saved without what you call 'the faith of assurance'; I mean, a sure confidence that, by the merits of Christ, he was reconciled to the favor of God."[4] Two years later, Charles Wesley, in his sermon "Awake, Thou That Sleepest," was even more emphatic: "This experimental knowledge, and this alone, is *true* Christianity. He is a Christian who hath received the Spirit of Christ. He is not a Christian who hath not received him."[5] In a similar vein, John explored the doctrine of assurance in terms of real Christianity in a letter to John Bennett in June 1744:

> If the Bible be true, then none is a Christian who has not the marks of a Christian there laid down. One of these is the love of God, which must be felt (if it is in the soul) as much as fire upon the body. Another is the witness of God's Spirit with my spirit that I am a child of God. Till I have these marks I am not a Christian.[6]

Given these views of both John and Charles Wesley, it is not surprising to learn that the Conference in 1744 declared that "all *true* Christians have such a faith as implies an assurance of God's love, appears from [Romans 8:15; Ephesians 4:32; 2 Corinthians 8:5; Hebrews 8:10; 1 John 4:10, and 19]."[7] Beyond this, the conference queried, "Does any one believe, who has not the witness in himself, or any longer than he sees, loves, obeys God?"[8] To which it replied: "We apprehend not."[9] In this setting, then, justifying faith and assurance as the direct witness of the Holy Spirit are intricately related.

The following year, when the second annual Conference assembled at the New Room in Bristol, the topic of assurance was raised once more, but this time a slightly different answer was offered: "Is a sense of God's pardoning love absolutely necessary to our being in his favor? Or may there be some exempt cases? We dare not say there are not."[10] In other words, by 1745, Wesley and others at last understood that one may indeed be justified and yet lack the witness of the Spirit. Likewise, the conference *Minutes* of 1747 noted that there may be exceptions:

> But does not matter of fact prove, that justifying faith does not necessarily imply assurance?

> This contains the very strength of the cause; and inclines us to think that some of these may be exempt cases.[11]

Despite this affirmation, the Conference then offered this word of caution: "It is dangerous to ground a general doctrine on a *few* particular experiments."[12] Accordingly, being justified without assurance was the exception rather than the rule. In other words, assurance remained, to use Wesley's own words, "the common privilege of the children of God."[13]

Now although the 1747 Conference, like the one in 1745, recognized that there are, after all, exceptional cases, it nevertheless clarified its meaning and maintained continuity with the first Conference by underscoring the importance of real Christianity: "But this we know, if Christ is not revealed in them [by the Holy Spirit], they are not yet Christian believers."[14] In fact, though this was a period of many changes, Wesley had still not retreated from his basic and ongoing teaching that assurance is a vital ingredient of *real* Christian faith as evidenced by his following remarks made in an earlier letter to John Smith:

> No man can be a *true* Christian without such an inspiration of the Holy Ghost as fills his heart with peace and joy and love, which he who perceives not has it not. This is the point for which alone I contend; and this I take to be the very foundation of Christianity.[15]

Moreover, in 1747, Wesley continued this emphasis once again in a letter to "John Smith" and stated: "The sum of what I offered before concerning perceptible inspiration was this: '*Every* Christian believer has a perceptible testimony of God's Spirit that he is a child of God.' "[16]

In light of the preceding evidence, it is clear that even after 1745, even after he had acknowledged the exceptions to the *normal* association of justifying faith and assurance, Wesley still maintained that the witness of the Spirit is ever integral to the *proper* Christian faith. These elements, then, of both exceptional cases and the continuity of the motif of real Christianity do not contradict each other. Not surprisingly, then, in a revealing letter to his brother Charles, written a month after the 1747 Conference, John illustrates his doctrine of assurance by pointing out: "(1) that there is such an explicit assurance; (2) that it is the common privilege of *real Christians*; (3) that it is *the proper Christian faith*, which purifieth the heart and overcometh the world."[17] In other words, the observation that there are exceptions to Wesley's normal association of justification by faith and a measure of assurance is accurate; however, that he identified this faith that lacks the witness of the Spirit with real, proper Christianity is not. By 1745, then, Wesley had become much more pastorally sensitive by recognizing some important exceptions while at the same time continuing to uphold the standards of real, scriptural Christianity, the kind of serious Christianity that he had proclaimed so boldly in his last university sermon.

The Faith of a Servant

In time, Wesley would characterize those who are justified and born of God but lack the witness of the Spirit as having "the faith of a servant." This is the "narrow sense" of the phrase; and its numbers are obviously few since they are, after all, exceptional cases.[18] But during this early period of 1745 to 1747, Wesley considered the phrase "the faith of a servant" in another way, in the "broad sense." It encompasses many instances; for it corresponds not to exempt cases, but to the precursors of the proper Christian faith. In other words, the broad sense of the faith of a servant does not entail either justification or the new birth. For example, the Conference of 1746 considered the question, "Who is a Jew, inwardly?" And it replied, "A servant of God: One who sincerely obeys him out of fear. Whereas a Christian, inwardly, is a child of God: One who sincerely obeys him out of love."[19] More important for the task at hand, the Conference then went on to declare that a person can be both sincere and penitent and still not be justified, indicating that the elements most often associated with the faith of a servant in the broad sense do not necessarily issue in justification.[20]

The greatest development during this period, however, concerns not so much the direct explication of the phrase "the faith of a servant," but how Wesley linked this phrase with a key distinction that he did indeed explore in some detail at this time, namely, the distinction between "the spirit of bondage" and "the spirit of adoption." In particular, the identification of the "faith of a servant" with the "spirit of bondage" is revealed in the late sermon "The Discoveries of Faith" produced in 1788. In it, Wesley observes: "Exhort him to press on by all possible means, till he passes 'from faith to faith'; from the faith of a *servant* to the faith of a *son*; from the *spirit of bondage* unto fear, to the spirit of childlike love."[21] What, then, are the traits of the spirit of bondage displayed in the sermon "The Spirit of Bondage and of Adoption," written in 1746, and were later identified with the faith of a servant? Those under a spirit of bondage, Wesley argues, feel sorrow and remorse; they fear death, the devil, and humanity; they desire to break free from the chains of sin, but cannot, and their cry of despair is typified by the Pauline expression, "O wretched man that I am, who shall deliver me from the body of this death?"[22] In fact, in this sermon, Wesley specifically identifies "this whole struggle of one who is 'under the law' " with the spirit of bondage and with the spiritual and psychological dynamics of Romans 7.[23] More to the point, the traits just cited are hardly the attributes that constitute the proper Christian faith since Wesley defined true Christians, at the very least, as those who believe in Christ such that "sin hath no more dominion over [them]."[24]

The great difficulty, then, for those interpretations of Wesley's theology that fail to distinguish these two senses is that the negative characteristics of the faith of a servant as found, for example, in the sermon "The Spirit of Bondage and of Adoption" are then associated with justification and the new birth (since all who have the faith of a servant are "supposedly" justified), with the result that Wesley's soteriological standards have been significantly lowered. Put another way, in such views, the Christian life is understood not in terms of freedom from the power of sin, but in terms of the ongoing dominion of sin, a *plague* of sin, from which justifying and regenerating graces apparently do *not* redeem and against which believers *constantly* struggle.[25]

The Standards of Redemption

Wesley's articulation of the faith of a servant, a distinction that rendered him sensitive to a diversity of spiritual conditions that were on the way to genuine Christian faith, was not an attempt to find an easier, broader, and more inclusive path to redemption such that his *basic* soteriological standards were now much lower than they had been before. On the contrary, during this period of greater pastoral judgment and experience, Wesley actually strengthened his standards in a number of ways. First of all, during the mid-1740s, Wesley was corresponding with Thomas Church, vicar of Battersea, Prebendary of St. Paul's, and staunch critic of the Methodists. Church had charged, among other things, that Wesley was "heretical in the matter of justification, and was guilty of gross enthusiasm."[26] In his reply, "An Answer to the Rev. Mr. Church's Remarks," Wesley not only demonstrated that his teaching on justification was in full accord with the Church of England, but also pointed out, by reciting material from his earlier published *Farther Appeal*, that justification is the forgiveness or remission of sins that are *past*.[27] "I say, past," Wesley explained, "for I cannot find anything in the Bible of the remission of sins past, present, and to come."[28] By means of this temporal distinction, then, Wesley avoided the antinomian (making the moral law void) implications of an improper doctrine of justification that in its error viewed the forgiveness of the Most High not as the sheer graciousness that it is, but as indulgence, as a cover or safeguard for the ongoing practice of sin.

Second, Wesley was becoming increasingly concerned during the 1740s, as the Revival progressed, that many were mistaking the genuine liberty of the gospel for license, a license that left one undisturbed as one neglected or even repudiated the counsel of the moral law. Oddly enough, all of this was done in the name of grace and freedom; but such erroneous notions inevitably led to a slow descent into sin. The 1744 Conference explored this significant matter in the following fashion:

> Have we not also leaned towards Antinomianism?
> We are afraid we have.
> What is Antinomianism?
> The doctrine which makes void the law through faith.

What are the main pillars hereof?
That Christ abolished the moral law.
That therefore Christians are not obliged to observe it.
That one branch of Christian liberty is, liberty from obeying the commandments of God.[29]

Moreover, to correct this error, Wesley wrote two brief treatises in 1745 specifically on this head: "A Dialogue Between an Antinomian and His Friend" and "A Second Dialogue Between an Antinomian and His Friend." In these works, Wesley asserted that Christ redeemed humanity, not from the moral law itself, but from its curse;[30] that one indeed ought to obey the commandments of God, not as the basis of justification, but as the evidence of a lively faith, of "faith working by love";[31] and that real Christian liberty is "a liberty to obey God, and not to commit sin."[32]

Third, perhaps the greatest means by which Wesley upheld nothing less than gospel standards of redemption was through his consideration of the marks, privileges, and freedoms of a child of God. Indeed, for Wesley the new birth marks the beginning not simply of an incremental change, not merely one of degree, but of a qualitative change that issues in a distinct kind of life, a life that men and women cannot bring about by themselves. In fact, Wesley so emphasized this supernatural change that he maintained repeatedly throughout his writings that spiritual life itself commences when we are born again.[33] In the Conference *Minutes* of 1745, for example, Wesley and his preachers responded to the question "When does inward sanctification begin?" by pointing out that "in the moment we are justified [, the] seed of every virtue is then sown in the soul. From that time the believer gradually dies to sin, and grows in grace."[34] Again, " 'justification of *life*,' as being connected with the new birth," Wesley observed, "[is] the beginning of spiritual life, which leads us through the life of holiness to life eternal, to glory."[35] Accordingly, holiness, the presence of the Holy Spirit in the human heart, begins not at the reception of prevenient or convincing grace, but only at regeneration and justification. Prior to having sanctifying grace, then, that grace that makes one holy, believers may be many things (recipients of prevenient grace, convinced of sin, moral and virtuous), but they are not yet holy.

Moreover, in his "Marks of the New Birth," produced in 1748, Wesley gave greater precision to his understanding of the new birth and explored three marks or traits of this distinct measure of grace, namely, faith, hope, and love, which together constitute the theological virtues. Concerning faith, the first mark, Wesley reiterated the by-now-familiar theme that faith is not only an assent to divine truth, but also a confidence in the mercy of God through Jesus Christ. An equally important emphasis that emerges in this sermon is that a fruit of this faith, through which one is born again and from which one cannot be separated, is freedom from the power of sin: "power over *outward sin* of every kind; over every evil word and work; . . . And over *inward sin*."[36] In this context, then, sin is understood principally as a willful violation of a known law of God; and a Christian believer walking in the obedience of faith will be so far free as not to commit sin.[37]

When some of Wesley's peers heard of the great liberty of the children of God, as Wesley preached it, especially in terms of freedom from the power of sin, they balked and offered a number of qualifications to this teaching. One such qualification was that a Christian believer, born of God, is not one who does not commit sin, but does not commit sin *habitually*. Wesley, however, took exception to the addition of the word "habitually," which he judged to be an evasion of an important gospel promise. He, therefore, questioned his detractors, no doubt with some measure of exasperation:

> But some men will say, "True; 'whosoever is born of God doth not commit sin' *habitually*." *Habitually*! Whence is that? I read it not. It is not written in the Book. God plainly saith, he "doth not commit sin." And thou addest, "habitually!"[38]

And a few years later, in 1756, Wesley responded to his critics by considering the example of a drunkard who argued that the state of his soul was well since he was not drunk *continually*. In a letter to William Dodd, Wesley states,

> I tell my neighbor here, "William, you are a child of the devil; for you *commit sin*: you was drunk yesterday." "No, sir," says the man, "I do not *live or continue in sin*" (which Mr. Dodd says is the true meaning of the text), "I am not drunk *continually*, but only now and then, once in a fortnight or a month.". . . Shall I tell him he is in the way to heaven or to hell? I think he is in the high road

to destruction, and that if I tell him otherwise his blood will be upon my head.[39]

By the exclusion of the word "habitually" or "continually" from this context, Wesley believed he was safeguarding one of the precious promises of the gospel, namely, that so long as the children of God abide in the love of God and continue to believe, they will not commit sin. In other words, regenerating faith and willful sin are mutually exclusive in Wesley's thought: When the one appears, the other recedes. In fact, Wesley details the slow and subtle process of the loss of faith and a descent into sin—what some might call a reversal of the *via salutis*—in an important sermon during this period, "The Great Privilege of Those That Are Born of God."[40] Wesley elaborates:

> But if we do not then love him who first loved us; if we will not hearken to his voice; if we turn our eye away from him, and will not attend to the light which he pours upon us: his Spirit will not always strive; he will gradually withdraw, and leave us to the darkness of our own hearts.[41]

Notice that the grace of God in this context is not limited or restricted by human response. However, if a synergistic reading of Wesley's soteriology is offered and is drawn too tightly, neglecting the insights of the Reformation, especially in terms of the sheer gratuity of grace, then the divine freedom, itself, will at least be misunderstood and possibly eclipsed. In this reckoning, once the initial or prevenient action of the Most High occurs, then God is virtually limited to responding merely to human *response*. And this dynamic is precisely what one contemporary scholar suggests as he quotes Wesley in support of a "tight" synergism: "God does not continue to act upon the soul, *unless* the soul reacts upon God."[42] However, Wesley actually filled out his thought in this sermon, "The Great Privilege of Those Who are Born of God," and broke out of this type of restrictive synergism by underscoring divine freedom, graciousness, and mercy. Again, God gradually (and no doubt reluctantly) withdraws from the sinner, indicating, quite clearly, that the Most High *continues* to act, repeatedly woos the rebellious soul, at least for a time, though there is *no* human response at all. This is a truth that the Moravians, Lutherans, and Wesley himself understood quite well: God is remarkably gracious, and at times acts alone—sometimes in the face of human impotence and at other times in the face of human rebellion. Nevertheless, Wesley's emphasis in this sermon lies elsewhere; not on human sin and recalcitrance, but on the *sufficiency* of God's grace.

Fourth, during the 1740s, Wesley was so concerned about the ongoing slavery and deceitfulness of sin, not simply in a blatantly rebellious way, but also in a more subtle and presumptuous one, that he made it quite evident in his writings that baptism and the new birth are distinct works though they are most closely *linked* in infant baptism. That is, Wesley, being the good Anglican that he was, apparently never repudiated the teaching of his church, which moved along these lines. And so when he asserted that the new birth does not always *accompany* baptism, he immediately added: "I do not now speak with regard to infants: it is certain, our Church supposes that all who are baptized in their infancy are at the same time born again."[43] In other words, though infant baptism is not to be equated with the new birth, it is always, apparently, in some sense associated with it. And this is precisely the area in which Wesley's "sacramental" view of regeneration is strongest.

However, Wesley's relatively high estimation of infant baptism needs to be interpreted not only against the backdrop of his sacramental views, but also in terms of his own larger soteriological standards articulated during this period. And when this is done, a far more complicated picture begins to emerge. For one thing, it was Wesley himself who first raised the crucial issue of the lack of *repentance* and *faith* in infant baptism and in a way that indicates, perhaps, some hesitancy in this area. For instance, in his treatise *A Farther Appeal to Men of Reason and Religion*, written in 1745, Wesley observes, "Infants indeed our Church supposes to be justified in baptism, although they cannot then either *believe* or *repent*. [The emphasis is Wesley's.] But she expressly requires both *repentance* and *faith* in those who come to be baptized when they are of riper years."[44]

Furthermore, it should also be borne in mind that even though Wesley upheld the appropriateness and value of infant baptism, its soteriological significance was diminished somewhat by his notion of prevenient grace. In other words, because of the atonement effectuated by Jesus Christ, God the Father removes the penalty of original sin, which is eternal death, from all humanity, both Christian and non-Christian, both infant and adult alike. No one, then, is punished eternally simply on account of Adam's sin. In a letter to John Mason written much later, Wesley reasons: "Therefore no infant ever was or ever will be 'sent to hell for the guilt of Adam's sin,' seeing it is cancelled by the righteousness of Christ as soon as they are sent into the world."[45]

But what of adult baptism? Does the thing signified—the new birth—always *accompany* the sign of baptism in each instance? Remarkably, in his *Principles of a Methodist Farther Explained*, produced in 1746, Wesley associates baptism, not with being a present son or daughter of God, but with the nominal Christianity so typical of large national churches like his own:

> And, (1), none can deny that the people of England in general are *called* Christians. They are *called* so, a few only excepted, by others, as well as by themselves. But I presume no man will say that the *name* makes the *thing*, that men *are* Christians barely because they are *called* so. It must be, (2), allowed that the people of England, generally speaking, have been *christened* or baptized. But neither can we infer: these were once *baptized*, therefore they *are Christians* now.[46]

Beyond this, Wesley reveals that he was quite familiar with numerous instances of those who had been baptized in either infancy or their later years who yet had none of the characteristics of the new birth and were instead steeped in sin. This theme is developed most clearly, once again, in his "Marks of the New Birth," in which Wesley warns:

> Say not then in your heart, I *was once* baptized; therefore I *am now* a child of God. Alas, that consequence will by no means hold. How many are the baptized gluttons and drunkards, the baptized liars and common swearers, the baptized railers and evil-speakers, the baptized whoremongers, thieves, extortioners! What think you? Are these now the children of God?[47]

Such questions, of course, indicate Wesley not only maintained his considerable redemptive standards, but also simply refused to comfort these open, flagrant sinners with the notion that they were still the sons and daughters of God, heirs of the kingdom of heaven, because they had been baptized in their youth. "Say not then in your heart," Wesley reasons, "I *was once* baptized; therefore I *am now* a child of God. Alas, that consequence will by no means hold."[48] And again, "Lean no more on the staff of that broken reed, that ye *were* born again in baptism."[49] Indeed, to the mistaken claim that there is no new birth beyond baptism, a claim inimical in so many ways, Wesley energetically responds in his *Farther Appeal*:

> I tell a sinner, "You must be born again," "No," say you, "He was born again in baptism. Therefore he cannot be born again now." Alas! What trifling is this? What if he was *then* a child of God? He is *now* manifestly a "child of the devil." For the works of his father *he* doth. Therefore do not play upon words. He *must* go through an entire change of heart.[50]

Therefore, to counsel these sinners that there is no new birth but in baptism, that they can no longer be renewed and cleansed after they have succumbed to sin, is cruel indeed; it is, says Wesley, "to seal [them] all under damnation, to consign [them] to hell, without any help, without any hope."[51]

So then, Wesley's "sacramental" view of regeneration emerged in his association of the new birth with infant baptism, a legacy mediated to him through his own Anglican Church by way of Roman Catholicism. His "evangelical" view, on the other hand, arose in his differentiation of the new birth from baptism—his failure always to associate these two elements in terms of adults and his insistence that those who are born of God must evidence the *marks* of the new birth, namely, faith, hope, and love.

Inward Religion

Several well-developed themes in Wesley's writings during the 1740s demonstrate that his concern, even preoccupation, was not principally outward conformity or practice, no matter how noble or sincere, but what he termed "inward religion." In 1745, for instance, he wrote to a clerical friend as follows: "About seven years since, we began preaching inward, present salvation as attainable by faith alone. For preaching this doctrine we were forbidden to preach in the churches."[52] That same year Wesley penned a letter to "John Smith" and underscored the value of inward religion—the religion of the heart—once more:

> I would rather say, Faith is "productive of all Christian holiness" than "of all Christian practice": because men are so exceeding apt to rest in practice, so called—I mean, in outside religion; whereas *true* religion is eminently seated in the heart, renewed in the image of Him that created us.[53]

Wesley's favorite text for communicating the immense value of heart religion both as the source, the motivating factor, for external religion and as its ultimate goal was none other than Romans 14:17: "For the kingdom of God is not meat and drink; but righteousness, and peace, and joy in the Holy Ghost" (KJV). The significance of purity of intention as well as the extent of the moral law as it relates to godly motivations—truths communicated to Wesley much earlier by the triumverate of Taylor, à Kempis, and Law—were now being expressed in a public, written, and didactic manner by means of key sermons. In his "Way to the Kingdom," for example, produced in 1746, Wesley denies that the nature of religion consists in "forms of worship, or rites and ceremonies," or in any outward action whatsoever.[54] He explains:

> Yet may a man both abstain from outward evil, and do good, and still have no religion. Yea, two persons may do the same outward work—suppose feeding the hungry, or clothing the naked—and in the meantime one of these may be truly religious and the other have no religion at all; for the one may act from the love of God, and the other from the love of praise. So manifest it is that although true religion naturally leads to every good word and work, yet the real nature thereof lies deeper still, even "in the hidden man of the heart."[55]

But neither does the nature of religion consist in "orthodoxy or right opinions," Wesley cautions.[56] A believer may assent to "all the three creeds—that called the Apostles', the Nicene, and the Athanasian—and yet 'tis possible he may have no religion at all, no more than a Jew, Turk, or pagan."[57] That is, intellectual assent can never be the very essence of saving faith, but only its external form. True religion, on the other hand, is ever summed up in three particulars: "righteousness, and peace, and joy in the Holy Ghost," the very *presence* of God in the human heart.[58] Again, true religion consists in a heart right toward God and neighbor, and it implies nothing less than happiness as well as holiness.

Ever careful to communicate important soteriological truths in an *ad populum* fashion, Wesley offered perhaps the best explication of this theme of inward, true religion in his numerous discourses (thirteen in all) on the Lord's Sermon on the Mount, which were crafted in 1748 and following. Influenced by the earlier treatments of Bishop Blackall, John Norris, Henry Hammond, and others,[59] Wesley explored the substance of Matthew 5–7, the texts for these discourses, along three main lines: "(1) 'the sum of true religion'; (2) 'rules touching that right intention which we are to preserve in all our outward actions'; and (3) 'the main hindrances of this religion.' "[60]

In his "Upon our Lord's Sermon on the Mount: Discourse the Fourth," which takes Matthew 5:13-16 as its text, Wesley advocates that "Christianity is essentially a social religion, and that to turn it into a solitary [religion] is to destroy it."[61] This passage, interestingly enough, has often been cited by contemporary scholars to show that Wesley was principally, if not exclusively, concerned with public religion and the social order. However, this appears to be an anachronistic reading (confusing the twenty-first century with the eighteenth) and is *not* the meaning suggested in this sermon. For one thing, Wesley relates that Christianity is a social religion in the sense that it cannot subsist without society, without living and conversing with other people. Beyond this, he observes that a social dimension is necessary for inward religion itself, for the inculcation of such holy tempers as meekness, gentleness, and long-suffering. "But this is apparently set aside," Wesley warns, "by all who call us to the wilderness, who recommend entire solitude either to the babes, or the young men, or the fathers in Christ."[62] Thus, the chief object of Wesley's censure in this sermon is *not* inward religion, the religion of the heart, but solitary religion in the form of anchoretic monasticism, the kind of religion that leaves one *alone*. Put another way, such an isolated approach does not provide the appropriate social context for the instantiation of inward religion, for the inculcation of a diversity of virtues in the human heart. So then to those contemporary interpreters who continue to deprecate or diminish heart religion, viewing it perhaps as an extravagance, and who therefore consider social or political action to be the *chief* end of the Christian faith, Wesley offered this word of caution: "That 'the regulation of social life is the one end of religion' is a strange position indeed. I never imagined any but a Deist would affirm this."[63]

Elsewhere in this same series of sermons, Wesley points out that it was often the rich or those who considered themselves to be of the better sort who were the most presumptuous in this area and who, therefore, considered inward religion to be nothing less than "madness."[64] In fact, late in his career, even Joseph Humphreys, who was one of Wesley's early lay preachers, succumbed to various pretensions and later scoffed at inward religion: "That was one of the foolish things which I wrote in the time of my madness."[65] And in 1749, while Wesley was preaching in Ireland in the face of much opposition from local leaders, he offered the following defense or apologetic for inward religion in his *A Short Address to the Inhabitants of Ireland*:

> Religion does not consist in *negatives* only, . . . but is a *real, positive* thing; that it does not consist in *externals* only, in attending the Church and sacrament (although all these things they approve and recommend), in using all the means of grace, or in works of charity (commonly so called) superadded to works of piety; but that it is properly and strictly a principle within, seated in the inmost soul, and thence manifesting itself by these outward fruits on all suitable occasions.[66]

Again, in this same treatise, Wesley maintains that

> religion does not consist . . . either in negatives or externals, in barely doing no harm, or even doing good, but in the tempers of the heart; in right dispositions of mind towards God and man, producing all right words and actions.[67]

The Methodist way, then, from the very beginning, ever highlighted "a principle within" as the source and goal of all outward fruit and action. Consequently, the alteration of the tempers of the inmost soul was considered not a "pious indulgence" or "enthusiasm" as the spiritually dull of Wesley's own age would have it, but as nothing less than a prerequisite for godly and effective ministry.

Religious Dispositions

In the sixth discourse of the series "The Sermon on the Mount," which takes Matthew 6:1-15 as its text, Wesley defines *inward* religion in greater detail precisely in terms of those dispositions and tempers of the heart that make up *genuine* Christianity, thus linking these two important themes in his writings. He observes:

> In the preceding chapter [Matt. 5] our Lord has described inward religion in its various branches. He has laid before us those dispositions of soul which constitute real Christianity: the inward tempers contained in that holiness "without which no man shall see the Lord"—the affections which, when flowing from their proper fountain, from a living faith in God through Christ Jesus, are intrinsically and essentially good, and acceptable to God. He proceeds to show in this chapter how all our actions likewise, even those that are indifferent in their own nature, may be made holy and good and acceptable to God, by a pure and holy intention. Whatever is done without this, he largely declares, is of no value before God.[68]

In this context, the dispositions of the heart that constitute the will and make up the substance of holiness flow from a living faith in Christ. So understood, a disposition is an orientation of the human heart toward an evoking, calling God.[69] Such usage was fairly common in the eighteenth century; and the later Wesley was most probably familiar with the letter of Chatam to his nephew in 1754, which underscored the "objects" taken by, as well as the goal-directedness of, the dispositions: "Go on, my dear child," Chatam exhorted, "in the admirable dispositions you have towards all right and good."

But there is a second movement implied here as well, not simply an inclination toward diverse objects, whether good or evil, but a transformation of being, a modification of the heart, by the presence of the Holy Spirit that makes believers holy and thereby empowers them for obedience, the very heart of gospel liberty. Moreover, another clue as to what constitutes a disposition is revealed in Wesley's earlier piece *A Dialogue Between an Antinomian and His Friend*, written in 1745, in which he observes that faith cannot exist for a moment without "certain inherent qualities and dispositions (viz., the love of God and of all mankind) which make us meet for the kingdom of heaven."[70] Thus, just as faith represents a disposition for Wesley, so does love. To be sure, for Wesley, love is much more than simply a constellation of feelings or emotions, which is often fleeting. On the contrary, love is an ongoing, not easily swayed, disposition that characterizes a person over time, which is both disposing and empowering.[71] Dispositions, then, are not as ephemeral as one might initially suppose; they are more constant and enduring than the vagaries of feelings and sentiments; they are, to use Wesley's own words, "inherent qualities."[72]

In exploring the dynamics of the heart in terms of its desires, affections, and orientations, Wesley employed another term, "tempers," to describe the very same phenomena that correspond to the dispositions. That is, Wesley used the terms "disposition" and "temper" largely in an interchangeable way throughout his writings. For example, in his sermon "The Nature of Enthusiasm," written in 1750, Wesley points out with respect to evil inclinations, "No marvel then that he is daily more rooted and grounded in contempt of all mankind, in furious anger, in every unkind disposition, in every earthly and devilish temper."[73] However, in terms of frequency of occurrence, the term "tempers" appears far more often in Wesley's writings than does the term "disposition." In fact, it is used nearly six times more often.

Beyond this, Wesley utilized the term "affections" to display the "topography" of the human heart as it grows in sanctifying graces. And though the equivalence of the tempers and affections has often been asserted, such a judgment is nevertheless problematic. Indeed, the difference between these two terms, significant in some respects, can be demonstrated by an appeal to Wesley's notes on 1 Thessalonians 2:17, in which he explains:

> In this verse we have a remarkable instance, not so much of the transient affections of holy grief, desire, or joy, as of that abiding tenderness, that loving temper, which is so apparent in all St. Paul's writings toward those he styles his children in the faith. This is the more carefully to be observed, because the passions occasionally exercising themselves, and flowing like a torrent, in the apostle, are observable to every reader; whereas it requires a nicer attention to discern those calm standing tempers, that fixed

posture of his soul, from whence the others only flow out, and which peculiarly distinguish his character.[74]

Thus, Wesley's use of the term "temper" (and disposition for that matter) reveals that the temper, unlike the affections, depicts a "fixed posture of the soul." It is what the eighteenth century termed an "habituated disposition."[75] That is, the tempers are standing orientations toward behavior and are not easily shaken. The affections, on the other hand, as well as the "passions" that constitute intensified affections, are less enduring and habituated than the tempers.[76] They are, to use Wesley's own words, "transient." And though the affections are, of course, in some sense related to the will, they nevertheless can be properly distinguished from it. For instance, in his later treatise *Thoughts Upon Necessity,* Wesley maintains that to consider the will and the affections the same thing is inaccurate.[77]

What, then, are the affections? And how are they distinguished from tempers? According to Wesley, the affections, on the one hand, are simply "the will exerting itself [in] various ways."[78] In other words, they are the expressions of the will, the particular actualizations of an undergirding, predisposing reality. Tempers, on the other hand, appear to be more foundational and may even inform the affections themselves since Wesley seems to indicate in the excerpt above that the affections flow from the tempers. If such is the case, then it is the tempers and dispositions of the human heart—which in a sense constitute the will—that pose the objects of the various affections. A clear articulation of the significance of the tempers, then, was so important to Wesley simply because he identified them with the very substance of true religion. That is, they constituted the throne room, so to speak, the very heart of it all and were clearly entailed in the mission of Methodism, itself, namely, of "spreading Scriptural holiness across the land."

The Issue of Determinism

The predisposing power of the tempers, though potent and real, must be understood within the larger context of grace and freedom. Indeed, Wesley's understanding of grace not simply as divine empowerment, but also as divine favor and approval, underscoring the sheer gratuity of this gift, indicates that though the tempers predispose, one can do otherwise as a consequence of graciously restored freedom, an unmerited boon from the Most High. The stubborn sinner, for example, after years of debauchery, can yet enjoy the gift of prevenient grace and can be convicted, justified, and made holy by the *presence* of the Holy Spirit in a relatively short period of time due to the supernatural nature and efficaciousness of saving grace. Sadly, on the other hand, the entirely sanctified—those whose predisposing tempers have been restored to the image of God in all humility, patience, and love—may yet misuse their graciously restored freedom to choose evil and thereby become enslaved in unholy passions once more.

Taking into account a graciously restored liberty for *response* to God (prevenient grace) with respect to the tempers of the heart can also be expressed in terms of the process/instantaneous tension in Wesley's theology. That is, Wesley's depiction of the process, which leads up to justification and initial sanctification, underscores not only the salience of the tempers and affections of the heart, but also human cooperation with divine activity (Catholic emphasis); whereas his depiction of the instantaneous dynamic of the new birth, as expressed in his sermon by the same name,[79] highlights divine activity and approval, that it is God *alone* who justifies, regenerates, and makes holy (Protestant emphasis) and who, therefore, can do so in a relatively short period of time—despite the predisposing power and longevity of unholy tempers. Interestingly enough, the dynamics of these temporal considerations point to the larger issue of the relation of faith and works and are suggestive of both Protestant *and* Catholic conceptions of grace. By way of analogy, then, observe Wesley's language in his sermon "The Scripture Way of Salvation" as he demonstrates that the temporal elements with respect to entire sanctification are actually expressive of the relation between faith and works:

> And by this token may you surely know whether you seek it by faith or by works. If by works, you want something to be done first, before you are sanctified. You think, "I must first be or do thus or thus." Then you are seeking it by works unto this day. If you seek it by faith, you may expect it as you are: and if as you are, then expect it *now*.[80]

Temporal elements, then, not only are indicative of the relation between faith and works but also indicate soteriological roles. Indeed, the instantaneous motif in terms of justification, regeneration, and entire sanctification reveals that it is God, after all, who both forgives sins and makes one holy. Here, human cooperation and the predisposing power of the tempers and affections are at an end. That is, they are not, and cannot be, the basis upon which one is justified or regenerated. Nor is the "power" or long-lived nature of unholy tempers an impediment to being redeemed *now* as if one had to *be* or *do* something first, because of one's past history, *in order* to be forgiven and made holy. Indeed, Wesley knew full well that prostitutes and thieves sometimes entered into saving grace far more quickly than the "virtuous" or "respectable" who still suffered under some vain illusions about their own inherent goodness or of what contributions they could make to "bring about" redemption. But what is this but to make sanctification, in one form or another, the basis of justification, and thereby to be sinfully offended by the sheer gratuity of saving grace, an error from which Wesley had already been disabused several years earlier through the careful teaching of Peter Böhler. Accordingly, the *process* of sanctification cannot be the basis upon which one is justified. This, once again, would be to fall under the error of the Council of Trent and Roman Catholicism, which, in the words of Wesley, "totally confound[ed] sanctification and justification together."[81]

So then, in a theology such as Wesley's—which highlights the disposing power of the tempers and affections, a graciously restored liberty for response to God, as well as the availability of justifying and initially sanctifying grace *now*—two major interpretive errors are possible: On the one hand, to stress the process of the inculcation of tempers to the virtual neglect of the unmerited gracious activity of God may result in sinners being told that today is not, after all, the day of salvation; that they *must* be further prepared in terms of tempers and affections in order to receive the regenerating grace of God; that they, in other words, must *be* or *do* something first in order to be redeemed.[82] Worse yet, sinners may be left in a virtual state of hopelessness, in which the sins of the past and the orienting tempers left in their wake are deemed, through the specious reasoning of unbelief, to be far more potent and determinative than the present gracious, liberating activity of God.

On the other hand, though God can set the long-suffering sinner free in a "moment," without the creation and maturation of various tempers as a *prerequisite*, Wesley knew full well that it was exceedingly dangerous to continue in the practice of sin (and thereby neglect the creation of positive dispositions) due to the formative power of the tempers. Indeed, in a letter drafted in December 1747, Wesley warned his brother-in-law, the errant Westley Hall, concerning the deceitfulness of sin and recited to him the things he had done with regard to several women and then concluded:

> And now you know not that you have done anything amiss! You can eat and drink and be merry! You are every day engaged with variety of company and frequent the coffee-houses! Alas, my brother, what is this? How are you above measure hardened by the deceitfulness of sin! Do you remember the story of Santon Barsisa? I pray God your last end may not be like his! O how have you grieved the Spirit of God! Return to him with weeping, fasting, and mourning. You are in the very belly of hell, only the pit hath not yet shut its mouth upon you. Arise, thou sleeper, and call upon thy God![83]

Part of Wesley's theological genius, then, was that he held together the sheer gratuity of grace, an emphasis of Luther, Calvin, and Cranmer, as well as the formative power of the tempers—a Catholic emphasis—in a doctrine of salvation that gave the long-suffering sinner hope, but at the same time cautioned the wayward and the rebellious to beware of the deceitfulness of sin. Therefore, modern assessments of Wesley's soteriology, which seek to explore his ethic almost exclusively in terms of virtue ethics theory, without also considering Wesley's Protestant understanding of the sheer gratuity of grace, are, therefore, wide of the mark. They fail to grasp, once again, Wesley's very "conjunctive" theology. Ronald H. Stone elaborates:

> Early Methodist writers on John Wesley also study his character. Yet Wesley, familiar with the Aristotelian-Thomistic emphasis on character and virtue, as both Oxford and Anglicanism stressed it, refused to bring it into the center of his ethics. Character is too humanistic, goal-oriented, and works-oriented for Protestant ethics. To try to bring it into the center of Protestant ethics is to

overthrow the justification-sanctification dynamic of God and the human in Protestant ethics.[84]

The Church Question

Tensions between Methodism and the Church of England grew during this decade, not only because many Anglican clergy looked askance at the "enthusiasm" of the Methodists in terms of their teaching on inward religion, the direct witness of the Holy Spirit, and Christian perfection, but also because many of these same clerics contended that the Methodists disrupted church life and were creating a schism with their employment of lay preachers, their violation of parish boundaries through field preaching, and their establishment of a separate infrastructure to guide Methodist life and practice. Sensitive to these charges, the first Methodist Conference posed the question, "What then do they mean, who say, 'You separate from the Church?' " To which it replied: "We cannot certainly tell. Perhaps they have no determinate meaning; unless, by the Church they mean themselves; that is, that part of the Clergy who accuse us of preaching false doctrine."[85] And to the claim that the Methodists would leave the Church of England after the death of Wesley and other leaders, the conference noted: "But we cannot with a good conscience neglect the present opportunity of saving souls while we live, for fear of consequences which may possibly or probably happen after we are dead."[86] The following year, in his *Advice to the People Called Methodists*, Wesley reminded his flock that "you *absolutely disavow* all desire of separating from them. You openly and continually declare you have not, nor ever had, such a design."[87]

Though Wesley was doing all that he could to maintain good order within Methodism as well as to submit to the mother church, his unswerving commitment to fostering the work of the gospel was invariably pushing his polity beyond the bounds of the Anglican sense of propriety. Initially, Wesley had reaffirmed the prerogatives of the episcopacy and the importance of apostolic succession in an important letter to Westley Hall drafted in 1745. Among other things, Wesley reasoned that "it would not be right for us to administer either baptism or the Lord's Supper unless we had a commission so to do from those bishops whom we apprehend to be in a succession from the apostles."[88] But the following year, as Wesley set out for Bristol, he read Lord Peter King's account, *An Enquiry into the Constitution, Discipline, Unity, and Worship of the Primitive Church,* and it helped him begin to see that in the primitive church, bishops and presbyters were of the same order. This insight was subsequently reflected in the Conference *Minutes* of 1747 and was reinforced by Wesley's consideration of Edward Stillingfleet's *Irenicon* several years later. Indeed, Stillingfleet, the Bishop of Worcester, agreed with Lord King that bishops and presbyters in the early church were essentially the same; but he then went on to repudiate the notion that Christ had prescribed any particular form of church polity, episcopal or otherwise. Such views emboldened Wesley to respond later to the Earl of Dartmouth that Bishop Stillingfleet had convinced the Methodists that their earlier view—that none but episcopal ordination is valid—was "an entire mistake."[89]

In 1748, Mr. Swindells informed Wesley that the Reverend Thomas Ellis, an Anglican cleric, would consider it a favor if Wesley would write "some little thing to 'advise the Methodists not to leave the Church.' "[90] In response, Wesley penned *A Word to a Methodist,* which was quickly translated into Welsh by Rev. Ellis under the title *Gair i'r Methodist.* After criticizing some of the Methodists for having "forsaken the sacrament and the Church service,"[91] Wesley then laid out five reasons for not leaving the church:

> (1). Have you not received a blessing from God there more than once in times past? (2). Have not many others received the same in the prayers and the Lord's Supper? (3). If there are but two or three in the whole congregation who know God, Christ is there in their midst. And where he is, should not his servant be also? (4). Were he not there formerly, go you, who know God, and take his blessing there with you. (5). If you are Christians you are the "salt of the earth"; but how can you season others unless you move among them.[92]

Beyond this, Wesley cautioned the Methodists against scorning or belittling the Church of England; and he reminded them that as Methodists, they naturally subscribe to the doctrines of the Anglican Church, love the *Book of Common Prayer,* and have received so many blessings by participation in this broader communion of faith.[93] But the following year, as Wesley faced not his own Methodist people, but his Anglican colleagues, he wrote *A Plain Account of the People Called Methodists* at the behest of the Reverend Vincent Perronet, Vicar of Shoreham, Kent, and trusted friend, and thereby energetically repudiated the accusation that the Methodists were causing a schism. In this more polemical writing, Wesley rejects the notion that the Methodists were "gathering churches out of churches,"[94] because he now calls into question the earlier sanctity, even the soteriological status, of many within the Anglican communion who had subsequently joined the Methodists:

> For, (1), these were not Christians before they were thus joined. Most of them were barefaced heathens. (2). Neither are they Christians from whom you suppose them to be divided. You will not look at me in the face and say they are. What! Drunken Christians? Cursing and swearing Christians? Lying Christians? Cheating Christians? If these are Christians at all, they are *devil Christians*.[95]

Here, once again, Wesley links the church question to having the form of religion without its power. In other words, he sustains this engaging and, at times, contentious discussion with the standards of scriptural Christianity, the kind of Christianity that he hoped Methodism would revive in the mother church but that for want of better circumstances was being preached largely outside stained glass enclosures to people who nevertheless heard John Wesley and the Methodists gladly.

CHAPTER SEVEN
Strengthening the Foundations

The Interior of the New Room, Bristol

In traveling throughout Britain as an itinerant evangelist and in setting up class meetings in distant parts of the land, Wesley had the opportunity to be among the nation's poor. Knowing the downtrodden and their plight firsthand instead of simply by hearsay, Wesley observed, "So wickedly, devilishly false is that common objection, 'They are poor only because they are idle.' "[1] In fact, Wesley often associated many of the highest graces of the Christian faith such as humility, kindness, and patience with the poor, whereas he criticized the rich for their *idleness*, pride, and self-satisfaction. Judging from a careful reading of his journals and letters, one gets the sense that Wesley was actually uncomfortable among the rich. "There is so much paint and affectation, so many unmeaning words and senseless customs among people of rank,"[2] he observed. And yet Wesley loved to be among the poor, perhaps because he found them most open of all to the glad tidings of salvation.

To serve the needy among the Methodists, Wesley utilized the structure of the class meetings, laced throughout the realm, as appropriate vehicles to distribute such goods as food, clothing, and fuel. Especially concerned about the lack of sound medical treatment in the British Isles at the time, Wesley took it upon himself to attend medical lectures, to secure the advice of a pharmacist and physician, and to offer simple medical treatments to the indigent.[3] Moreover, in order to meet the pressing needs of those who were nearly penniless, Wesley created a free medical dispensary, the first of its kind in London, and gathered what medical knowledge he was able in the odd, though well-intentioned, manual *Primitive Physic*.[4]

Beyond these ministries, which were motivated by nothing less than Christian love and compassion, Wesley employed women who were nearly destitute in the processing of cotton at the Foundery; and he also established a lending stock for those short on funds as early as 1746. In the beginning, this loan fund had hardly amounted to more than thirty pounds; but it soon grew to such an extent that about "two hundred and fifty persons were relieved in one year."[5] Among other things, Wesley's charitable practices included collecting (or "begging") money from some of his "rich" friends and then lending it to the underprivileged in lots of twenty shillings—a sum that was then repaid within three months on a weekly basis.[6] Considering these rules of repayment, together with the structure of the Methodist class meetings, through which much of this aid was distributed, one can easily discern the accountable and responsible nature of much of Wesley's ministerial practice.

Bishop Lavington and the Nature of Enthusiasm

Through the efforts of the Wesleys, Whitefield, and others, eighteenth-century Methodism was obviously reaching a strata of society not well served by the Anglican Church. The lower and "middling" classes, for instance, often responded to the energetic appeals of these leaders. Laborers down on their luck, domestic servants, as well as a few petty merchants were often encouraged by the wider vision of the Methodists—a vision that embraced not simply mundane concerns, but spiritual ones as well. Given this ministry, one would naturally expect that Anglican clergy, bishops in particular, would have been genuinely appreciative of these labors, but such, unfortunately, was often not the case. Bishop Lavington, for example, earlier chaplain of King George I and present Bishop of Exeter, excoriated the Methodists in his *Enthusiasm of the Methodists and Papists Compar'd*, a work that appeared in three parts over the course of 1749 to 1751 and to which responses were offered by George Whitefield, Vincent Perronet, and John Wesley.

Particularly troubled by Lavington's tract, Wesley employed a rhetoric in his subsequent correspondence with the bishop that was at times unguarded. To illustrate, in a letter dated February 1, 1750, Wesley not only accuses the bishop of resolving "to throw dirt enough that some may stick,"[7] but also observes that Lavington's attempt to prove Wesley's enthusiasm, or fanaticism, from the latter's notion of conversion is an entire mistake because "you are talking of things quite out of your sphere; you are got into an unknown world!"[8] Complicating matters even further, Wesley declines a discussion of the whole matter of Christian perfection with the bishop "till you have learned a little heathen honesty"; [9] and the Methodist leader then proceeds to chide the undoubtedly stung bishop with the wry comment that the Old and New Testaments are books "which you did not seem to be much acquainted with,"[10] language that would hardly lead to mutual respect and understanding.

In the midst of this increasingly sour controversy, facing some of the same charges that he had encountered earlier at the hands of Joseph Butler and Edmund Gibson, Wesley brought forth his sermon "The Nature of Enthusiasm" in 1750, in which he challenged some of the basic assumptions of the Anglican clergy with respect to true religion and the nature of enthusiasm. Thus, in the opening paragraph of this sermon, Wesley points out that a religion of form, orthodoxy, or right opinions—what some would term nominal Christianity—does not evoke the response "much religion hath made you mad."[11] On the contrary, it is only when "you talk of righteousness and peace and joy in the Holy Ghost, [that] it will not be long before *your* sentence is passed: 'Thou art beside thyself.' "[12] To be sure, Wesley had already demonstrated the reasonableness of the religion of the Methodists, the sensibleness of holy love and heart religion, during the mid-1740s in his *Appeals*. Now he would underscore the very necessity of such religion and contend in the face of his critics, Bishop Lavington among them, that the real enthusiasts of the age were not the Methodists who championed Christian love and the witness of the Holy Spirit, but those nominal Christians, many of whom were within the Anglican church, who presumed to have what gifts and graces they so obviously lacked. Albert Outler, then, was surely correct when he described this sermon as "an exercise in irony."[13] Faced with the charge of enthusiasm, Wesley simply cast it back at the bishop and warned him to beware of the sin of presumption, the very height of enthusiasm.

The Moral Law

What perhaps lay behind Lavington's concern with respect to the Methodists was the memory of an earlier period in English history when religious and political sentiments devolved into the chaos of a civil war and regicide.[14] Several Anglican clergy, for instance, considered Methodism to be little more than a dissenting movement; and its "Puritan" and "Pietistic" elements were deemed a disruptive anomaly in a settled and reasonable age. Such concern, perhaps, would have been dispelled had Wesley's detractors considered that the Methodist movement was marked by elements that would ever keep it from the shores of fanaticism. For instance, not only had Wesley already underscored the importance of such formal elements as the means of grace (especially after the Fetter Lane incident) and the *General Rules of the United Societies* (which embraced the basic precepts of natural law to avoid evil and to do good), but also he developed his practical theology in terms of the moral law, that "transcript of the divine nature."[15]

In terms of the numerous sources that informed his understanding of the moral law, Wesley, once again, looked largely to his own Anglican tradition. Indeed, it is likely that the teachings of the Cambridge Platonists such as John Norris and John Smith informed Wesley's reflections about the moral law and helped him see it in a "platonic" sense as a "copy of the eternal mind . . . the visible beauty of the Most High."[16] For his part, Albert Outler maintained that the broader heritage of Christian Platonism was mediated to Wesley in general by "the Fathers, William of St. Thierry, the Victorines, St. Bonaventura, and the Cambridge

Platonists,"[17] and in particular by "his father's friend, John Norris, and also by Richard Lucas."[18] To be sure, Wesley read several of Norris's works at Oxford over a length of time that could only suggest both interest and influence.[19] And the mastery of John Smith was conveyed to Wesley through his reading of Henry Scougal, author of *The Life of God in the Soul of Man*, who himself freely acknowledged his debt to Smith.[20] Moreover, an examination of the works that Wesley saw fit to include in his *Christian Library*, published between 1749 and 1755, reveals that several selections from such English Platonists as Ralph Cudworth, Nathanael Culverwel, Henry More, Simon Patrick, John Smith, and John Worthington appeared in seven of the fifty volumes.[21]

It seems remarkable that Wesley, the evangelical, would have been interested in the writings of Platonists and, in some cases, Latitudinarians; but the Methodist leader was somewhat of an eclectic and was most probably attracted to the Cambridge Platonist's notion that "right and wrong are not derivative principles—that they are not established by human law . . . but exist by virtue of an eternal autonomy."[22] Indeed, "Wesley's terms 'eternal reason,' 'the essential nature of things,' or 'the fitness of things' as a basic understanding of reality, reflect the influence of Platonists such as Clarke or Norris"[23] and demonstrate what normative elements were in play and kept his theological formulations and practices, especially his understanding of grace, free from an unguarded and ill-informed "enthusiasm."

Moreover, in a way that might have surprised Bishop Lavington, given the nature of his criticism, it was John Wesley, himself, who believed it was often the particular problem of Protestants, of "gospel preachers" as he termed them, to proclaim the grace of God largely in a fanatical, antinomian fashion, that is, apart from the illuminating and guiding power of the moral law. So conceived, grace would soon become amorphous, lacking the form of "the everlasting fitness of all things that are or ever were created," and therefore would be able to support almost any self-driven or "enthusiastic" notion or practice.[24] To counter this insidious error, Wesley held that grace is most often "normed" grace. In other words, it arises and flowers in a valuational, prescriptive context and is illuminated by the moral law of God, a standard that transcends, at least in some respects, both human will and desire.

Without this other half of the *conjunction*, so to speak, grace would perhaps quickly devolve into presumption, self-will, and the antinomianism that Wesley so rightly deplored. To prevent this malady among his own preachers, Wesley issued a set of instructions in 1751, in which he made the moral law both the initial and the chief vehicle for convincing sinners:

> I think, the right method of preaching is this: At our first beginning to preach at any place, after a general declaration of the love of God to sinners, and his willingness that they should be saved, to preach the law, in the strongest, the closest, the most searching manner possible; only intermixing the gospel here and there, and showing it, as it were, afar off.[25]

And to the claim that the gospel answers all the ends of the law thereby rendering the preaching of the latter unnecessary, Wesley replied: "But this we utterly deny. It [the gospel] does not answer the very first end of the law, namely, the convincing men of sin. . . . The ordinary method of God is to convict sinners by the law, and that only."[26]

But just what did Wesley mean by "preaching the law" when he had carefully advised his preachers? For one thing, Wesley had in mind "the commands of Christ, briefly comprised in the Sermon on the Mount."[27] However, he also understood preaching the law in terms of the Ten Commandments as demonstrated in his notes on Exodus 20:1-17[28] and also in his observation that the "moral law, contained in the Ten Commandments, and enforced by the prophets, he [the Lord] did not take away."[29] In fact, Wesley draws an explicit christological link between "the commands of Christ," on the one hand, and the Decalogue, on the other, in his statement that it was none other than the Son of God who "delivered the law to Moses, under the character of Jehovah."[30] Beyond this, the Methodist evangelist declares that he "cannot believe . . . that 'the Ten Commandments were not designed for a complete rule of life and manners,' "[31] indicating that there is no contrariety between the moral law as expressed in the Decalogue *and* in the Sermon on the Mount. Indeed, the relation between the two depictions of the *same* moral law is not one of contradiction, but one of development. Remarking on the moral law, which, no doubt, finds its clearest expression in the Sermon on the Mount, Wesley writes:

Yet was it never so fully explained nor so thoroughly understood till the great Author of it himself condescended to give mankind this authentic comment on all the essential branches of it; at the same time declaring it should never be changed, but remain in force to the end of the world.[32]

Earlier, at the first Methodist Conference in 1744, Wesley had advised his helpers and assistants to preach Christ in all his offices and "to declare his law as well as his gospel, both to believers and unbelievers." In this counsel, then, the moral law holds great value not only in convicting sinners, but also in keeping believers in Christ. That is, Wesley highlighted both the *accusatory* role of the law, in a way similar to Luther, as well as the *prescriptive* role in a way similar to Calvin—the one to *bring* sinners to Christ and the other to *keep* believers alive in the Lord.

Some of the quietists in Wesley's own age, especially those who were influenced by the Lutheran tradition, took exception to Wesley's counsel just cited and maintained that believers, those justified by Christ, were free from the law and certainly from such matters as commandment keeping since they were no longer under the law but under grace. In other words, the ongoing prescriptive value of the law was either minimized or in some cases outright repudiated. Wesley, however, once again considered such views to be unbalanced and frankly antinomian; that is, they made void the law through faith or set aside some instance of obedience in the name of grace or gospel "liberty." However, "the case is not therefore, as you suppose," Wesley cautioned, "that men were *once* more obliged to obey God, or to work the works of his law, than they are *now*. This is a supposition you cannot make good."[33] In fact, so concerned was Wesley with the specter of antinomianism, of lawlessness, fanaticism, and unbridled sin, that he produced two "tracts for the times" in 1750 to warn against this despoiling error. Indeed, it is highly probable that Wesley had the teaching of such unabashed antinomians as William Cudworth and James Hervey in mind as he wrote these sermons.[34] In addition, as one scholar correctly observed, "The Law Established Through Faith, Discourse I and II," although two separate sermons, actually comprise one extended essay and should be read together.[35] Indeed, the structural relation between the two is perhaps best expressed in terms of a problem and solution model: that is, the problems raised in the first piece, the various ways of making void the law, are then countered in the second by showing how the law may yet be established by Christian faith.

For Wesley, then, obedience to the moral law *is* required in the practical Christian life, not, of course, as the condition of acceptance, but in order to *continue* in the rich grace of God.[36] And that Wesley did indeed develop a formal prescriptive use of the moral law, the *tertius usus*, is evident in his observation that "each is continually sending me to the other—the law to Christ, and Christ to the law."[37] Simply put, obedience to the moral law of God does not establish the Christian life, but it is a necessary fruit of that faith that both justifies and regenerates. If, for example, faith does not issue in obedience to the moral law of God, works of charity and mercy, and holiness, it was clear to Wesley, at least, that such is a dead, not a living, faith; it is a faith that is not being acted out in the world of God and neighbor. Bishop Lavington should have been impressed.

A Caution Against Bigotry and the Catholic Spirit

Though several Anglican clergy continued to view Methodism as either a newfangled sect or a dissenting movement, Wesley always rejected such designations. In his own estimation, Methodism, with its lay preachers, extemporary praying, and field preaching, was a reforming *movement* within the mother church to spread scriptural holiness across the land; but this movement also embraced the larger mission and context of a world parish that included ministries to Calvinists, Moravians, Lutherans, and others, as well as to the unchurched. So then, behind Wesley's ongoing fear that the Methodists would lose their purpose in forsaking the Anglican Church was his understanding that in doing so, the Methodists would descend to the form of religion without its power. That is, they would become simply another "party" or sect within the larger church and thereby surrender the very mission of Methodism itself.

To guard against this path of separation, in particular the provincialism of a party spirit, Wesley published two key sermons in 1750. In the first, "A Caution Against Bigotry," after he defines bigotry as "too strong an attachment to, or fondness for, our own party, opinion, Church, and religion,"[38] Wesley cautions his readers to beware of denying the good of other ministries and communions of faith simply because they have "no outward connection with us," they are not "of our party," or they differ from us "in our religious opinions" and "points of practice."[39] Beyond this, Wesley develops, once again, a reasoned defense for his employment of lay preachers, arguing that it would be yet another species of bigotry to hinder the good work that these humble servants do. Among the many ways that lay preachers were indirectly forbidden to do the work of God by their critics included such things as discouraging them by drawing them into needless disputes concerning their ministry, by showing unkindness toward them either in language or in behavior, and last by forbidding them "all the time you are speaking evil of [them] or making no account of [their] labors."[40] And what if lay preachers have all the gifts and graces to lead many to Christ and yet the bishop will not ordain them? "Then the bishop does 'forbid him to cast out devils,' Wesley exclaims. 'But I dare not forbid him,' he quickly adds, having already published his reasons in his *A Farther Appeal, Part III* in 1745.[41]

Wesley's other key sermon during this period, "The Catholic Spirit," is not concerned with relations *within* Methodism, as it is often interpreted today, but with relations beyond its walls, that is, with those communions of faith that differ from Methodism principally in terms of both opinions and modes of worship. Indeed, in this sermon, Wesley ever presupposes that the Methodists are united, marked by integrity of thought and practice in terms of the essentials of the Christian faith.

Taking the text "Is thine heart right, as my heart is with thy heart? . . . If it be, give me thine hand" (2 Kings 10:15) as his guide for this sermon, Wesley explicates just what is entailed in this often cited verse. A heart rightly formed includes, among other things, walking by faith, not by sight; believing in the Lord Jesus Christ and having him revealed in one's soul; having the righteousness that is by faith; and having that same saving faith filled with nothing less than the energy of love.[42] Accordingly, the standards of a heart rightly formed, which seem to be the prerequisites for fellowship in "The Catholic Spirit," are neither easily instantiated nor glib—indicative perhaps of an unthinking sentimentality or wishful thinking—but are actually quite distinct, even lofty. In fact, these standards constitute nothing less than the elements of the proper Christian faith—in all righteousness and true holiness—a faith that, though it may differ in opinions and modes of worship from other communions, should nevertheless be honored by all believers.

Moreover, in terms of the variety of opinions and modes of worship that will surely be encountered in the broader church, Wesley once again sets the standard high. That is, though these opinions and modes of worship should never preclude fellowship among those believers who evidence the marks of scriptural Christianity by having a heart rightly formed, these elements are nevertheless not a matter of indifference for both speculative latitudinarianism (opinions) and practical latitudinarianism (worship) are specifically rejected by Wesley as a curse, not a blessing. The Methodists, then, should be ever firm in their convictions, acknowledging the right of private judgment, and yet ever be open to genuine Christian fellowship—not an easy task for any communion of faith.

Ecclesiastical Developments

In 1752, John and Charles Wesley and others entered into a covenantal agreement and pledged loyalty to the Anglican Church. This covenant was reaffirmed annually, and it helped to strengthen the ties and discipline among the Methodists.[43] During this same year, Charles wrote to his brother John and emphasized that "our present call is chiefly to the members of that church wherein we have been brought up," even though Methodist ministry, from the very beginning of field preaching in 1739, had been remarkably diverse. At any rate, Charles, as well as William Grimshaw, an evangelical Anglican cleric and supporter of Methodism, were by now growing increasingly fearful that John Wesley would indeed bolt from the church. In fact, during the Conference at Leeds in 1755, Wesley posed the question whether the Methodists ought to leave the Church of England. But by the third day of this gathering, it was concluded that whether it was lawful to leave the Church or not, "it was no ways expedient"[44]— a reply that did not express the strongest of convictions.

In April 1755, Wesley and several Methodists began to read "A Gentleman's Reasons for his Dissent from the Church of England." One by one, the arguments were considered and then were quietly put aside. By October, Wesley was so strengthened in his resolve that he wrote to Thomas Adam: "We will not *go out;* if we are *thrust out,* well."[45] In this same letter, Wesley observes that the Methodists vary from the rules of the Anglican Church in terms of preaching abroad, using extemporary prayer, organizing the awakened into societies, and permitting laypeople to preach, but "no farther than we apprehend is our bounden duty."[46] Beyond this, Wesley justifies his employment of lay preachers to Mr. Adam by making a distinction between an inward and outward call to ministry. That is, though his lay preachers lack the formal, outward call, "we think they who are only called of God, and not of man, have *more* right to preach than they who are only called of man and not of God."[47]

In the face of such judgments, Frank Baker was surely correct to conclude that Wesley held two conflicting views of the church.[48] Thus, on the one hand, Wesley considered the church in an institutional way and took note of the importance of good order in terms of the episcopacy and of the prohibition of laypeople from administering the Lord's Supper, among other things. On the other hand, Wesley also viewed the church as the communion of saints, as a fellowship of believers, united corporately in the one head of the church, Jesus Christ. In this second model, Wesley reasoned that the *tasks of mission* in reaching sinners—inviting them to forgiveness and the holy love of God—must in some respects affect polity and good order. Here, once again, is Wesley's more "functional" definition of ministry; and it allowed him, without any qualms of conscience, to violate parish boundaries, to preach in the fields, to employ lay preachers, and to set up an infrastructure that, in some respects, rivaled that of the Anglican Church.

So then, if Wesley were viewed simply as a traditionalist or as a high church Tory or perhaps as one who ever affirmed the probity of the institutional church, then his comments with respect to the Donatists (He believed them to be "real Christians."),[49] the Montanists (He considered them also to be "real, scriptural Christians."),[50] as well as his pointed criticism of church Councils, ("How has one Council been perpetually cursing another, and delivering all over to Satan? . . . Surely Mahometanism was let loose to reform the Christians!"),[51] would be virtually inexplicable. If, on the other hand, Wesley were viewed simply as an innovator, as an ecclesiastical revolutionary who was ever willing to discard the old forms of a state church for the sake of present *mission*, then all of his caution, obedience, and resolve with respect to the Church of England would be missed. Put another way, just as there are many "conjunctions" in Wesley's soteriology (such as law *and* grace; faith *and* works), so too are there significant "conjunctions" in his ecclesiology as well. That is, Wesley held on to both an institutional model of the church as well as a functional one. Without the former, Methodism would have lost its form; without the latter, it would have lost its purpose.

Now one way in which Wesley could indeed connect his institutional and functional models of the church, at least in some sense, was to set high standards for his lay preachers. In March 1751, for instance, Wesley gave his brother Charles the main supervisory task of examining the preachers individually and in groups.[52] By now, there were nearly three dozen preachers in nine circuits that served about one hundred societies in England, Wales, and Ireland.[53] In terms of specific rules, John Wesley advised his assistants that "no preacher should preach above twice a day, unless on Sunday or on some extraordinary time"[54] and that none in the connection are "to preach above an hour at a time, prayer and all."[55] More important, Wesley insisted that his preachers should keep a clear focus in all their ministerial labors: "You have one business on earth," he cautioned, *"to save souls.* Give yourself wholly to this."[56]

Later, in 1756, in his "Address to the Clergy," Wesley laid out in a more formal fashion the qualifications for clergy, many of which would, of course, apply to his lay preachers as well. Ministers of the gospel ought to have, among other things, a good understanding, a clear apprehension, and sound judgment; they should possess "liveliness and readiness of thought."[57] They should evidence sound understanding and a good memory; they should have knowledge of their own office, the Scriptures, profane history, the sciences, logic, natural philosophy, geometry, patristics, as well as knowledge of the world, that is, "a knowledge of men, of their maxims, tempers, and manners such as they occur in real life."[58] In addition to these several requirements, some more valuable than others, ministers of the gospel should be characterized by prudence and "some degree of good breeding," by which Wesley meant "easiness and propriety of behavior."[59]

After exploring all of these marks or traits, however, Wesley exclaimed:

> For what are all other gifts, whether natural or acquired, when compared to the grace of God? And how ought this to animate and govern the whole intention, affection, and practice of a Minister of Christ![60]

In fact, toward the end of this essay, Wesley underscored such gracious gifts as right intention in terms of both the affections of the heart and Christian practice: "Am I, in my private life, wholly devoted to God? Am I intent upon this one thing,—to do in every point 'not my own will, but the will of Him that sent me?' "[61] Remarkably, these are some of the very same questions that Wesley had asked himself, decades earlier, as he was preparing for ministry. Clearly, questions about intentions, the affections of the heart, and various practices, tied together in a concern for saving souls, constituted much of the disciplinary intent of John Wesley as he gave guidance to his preachers.

Wesley's Marriage

Though Wesley's professional life was proceeding fairly well for the most part during the 1750s, despite the ongoing opposition from some of his peers, his personal life was quite another matter. Earlier, in August 1748, when Wesley had become ill at Newcastle, he was nursed back to health by Grace Murray, a class leader in the Methodist societies and housekeeper at the Orphan House. Impressed with the kindness and care of Ms. Murray, Wesley proposed marriage to her shortly thereafter—she was around thirty years old at the time—though his proposal was, as with his earlier Georgia initiatives, in such vague language that it could easily be misunderstood.

During the spring and early summer of 1749, Grace Murray traveled with Wesley as he labored in Ireland. In Dublin, the relationship took on a more formal and serious cast in that the couple now entered into a contract *de praesenti*. The legal status as well as the obligations incurred as a result of this agreement were often misunderstood.[62] Having entered into such an agreement, despite its ambiguity, Wesley sincerely believed that Grace Murray was betrothed to *him* and to no other; but due to a number of factors, some of which were clearly beyond Wesley's control, this agreement was never fulfilled. Indeed, the same sort of hesitancy, misdirection, and even outright confusion that played out in Georgia—a real comedy of errors—would be repeated on English soil.

Enjoying the gifts of married life since April 1749, when he took Sarah Gwynne as his bride, Charles Wesley was, surprisingly enough, strongly opposed to the possibility that his brother might marry. According to some reports, Charles believed that Ms. Murray was already engaged to John Bennet, a preacher; and he, therefore, wanted to prevent a scandal as well as eliminate the gossip that was already beginning to emerge. Whatever his motivation, Charles Wesley headed for Hineley Hill, persuaded Ms. Murray to accompany him to Newcastle, and saw to it that she married John Bennet about a week later. John Wesley was stunned. "Since I was six years old," he exclaimed, "I never met with such a severe trial as for some days past."[63]

Having failed so painfully in love on two occasions and holding some very negative views on the value of marriage itself, Wesley was contemplating marriage again shortly after the Grace Murray fiasco. Through his friendship with the Perronets, Wesley became acquainted with Mary Vazeille, a widow of a London trader and woman of considerable means. During the summer of 1750, while Wesley was, once again, in Ireland, he wrote to this middle-aged woman, although his interest at the time was clearly pastoral, not romantic. By the fall, however, Wesley began to think of Mary Vazeille as a possible wife. She impressed him by, in Wesley's own words, "your indefatigable industry, your exact frugality, your uncommon neatness and cleanness both in your person, your clothes and all things round you."[64] Beyond this, Wesley perhaps took special note that Ms. Vazeille was past child-bearing years, so his ongoing ministry would not be fettered by the demands and responsibilities of family life.

Shortly before his marriage to Ms. Vazeille, Wesley, oddly enough, had urged the preachers under his care who were single to remain so. Despite such counsel, Wesley made the claim to Vincent Perronet that his own impending marriage was appropriate, even called for, by maintaining that he could be more useful to God in a married state than in a single one. In other words, Mary Vazeille, due to her various gifts and graces, would actually aid his ministry and not detract from it. In fact, Wesley informed his wife shortly after their wedding, which took place on either February 18 or 19, 1751 (though perhaps he should have informed her *before* the wedding), not only that he wanted "to crowd all your life with the work of faith and the labour of love,"[65] but also that "if I thought I should [preach one sermon or travel one mile the less on that account] my dear, as well as I love you, I would never see your face [any]more."[66]

At first, Wesley's marriage was good, even affectionate. His letters to his wife were marked by both attentiveness and love. In March, for example, Wesley wrote: "I can imagine then I am sitting just by you, and see and hear you all the while, softly speak and sweetly smile."[67] However, as letters were the vehicles for sustaining Wesley's marriage, for expressing kindness and affection, at least early on, they were also the means that actually helped to despoil his relationship with Mary Wesley. Exercising what can best be described as poor judgment, Wesley gave his wife permission to open all of his correspondence: "If any letter comes to you, directed to the Revd. Mr. John Wesley, open it—it is for yourself."[68] Exercising this liberty, Mrs. Wesley came to realize that her husband was corresponding with several women. In 1757, for example, Wesley was writing to Dorothy Furly, Sarah Crosby, and Sarah Ryan, among others. And it was a letter to this last woman that would cause so much trouble.

As one who frequented Methodist services, Sarah Ryan was converted under John Wesley's ministry at Spitalfields in 1754 and was made the housekeeper at Kingswood a few years later. Ms. Ryan's placement in such a position drew criticism from both friends and foes alike since she had been married three times previous to this appointment—though she was currently living alone—and had not always taken the trouble to divorce one before she married another. Mrs. Wesley, undoubtedly, thought little of this housekeeper and resented the attention that her husband paid her. At a conference in Bristol where Ms. Ryan was presiding at dinner with Wesley, Mrs. Wesley, in a fit of jealous anger, burst into the room and informed the guests that "the whore now serving you has three husbands living."[69] Moreover, Mary's relationship with her husband deteriorated even further when, in searching his pockets, she discovered an endearing letter from him to Sarah

Ryan in January 1758. The language of the letter breathed an air of affection and perhaps even of deep emotional ties between the correspondents—ties that would give pause to almost any spouse:

"The conversing with you, either by speaking or writing, is an unspeakable blessing to me. I cannot think of you without thinking of God. Others often lead me to Him; but it is, as it were, going round about: you bring me straight into His presence.[70]

About a week after this discovery, Mary left John Wesley, vowing she would never return, though she came back after only a couple of days. This was to be the first of a series of departures in an increasingly sour relationship. Astonished and saddened by this turn of events, Wesley reflected over the appropriateness of his recent letter in particular, and of his correspondence with Ms. Ryan in general; and he concluded, in a rather self-assured way, that he had, after all, done well. Once this judgment was made, Wesley simply viewed this entire affair under the larger principle that he had the right, as he put it, "of conversing with whom I please." Unfortunately, such a viewpoint failed to take into account Mary Wesley's perspective or her painful estimate of things.

Just how did matters appear to Mary Wesley? For one thing, she was married to a man who often neglected her in the name of service to God: "Molly, let us make the best of life. Oh for zeal! I want to be on the full stretch for God!"[71] And though Wesley was not willing to preach one sermon less in a married state than in a single one, as noted earlier, he was apparently very willing to spend considerable time with women other than his wife—under the banner of ministry, of course—in both conversation and letter writing. Time spent, whether in ministry or not, surely bespeaks of valuation; and Mary Wesley quickly got the message.

Predestination

The same year he married Mary Vazeille, Wesley produced his "Serious Thoughts on the Perseverance of the Saints," a treatise that was certain to complicate his relations with the Calvinist Methodists, George Whitefield in particular, in the same way that his sermon "Free Grace" had done earlier. Like his father, Samuel, John Wesley was evidently not content to let sleeping dogs lie.

Given the various genres that Wesley employed in his writings, this treatise on perseverance is odd in some respects, for it does not really offer any positive statement of the Christian faith. Instead, it delineates in eight painstaking details that a child of God, "a true believer," as Wesley puts it, may make shipwreck of the Christian faith and then "he may go to hell, yea, and certainly will, if he continues in unbelief."[72] Continuing in this vein, Wesley wrote a far more extensive treatise the following year, simply entitled "Predestination Calmly Considered," in which he addresses a number of contested issues. In this work, for instance, Wesley challenges the notion that a decree of election can exist apart from a decree of reprobation. Thus, if God refuses to give the reprobate what grace they evidently need to be redeemed, then this refusal constitutes nothing less than an "active" reprobation.[73] On a more conciliatory note, Wesley does indeed define election as both "a divine appointment of some particular men, to do some particular work in the world," and as "a divine appointment of some men to eternal happiness";[74] but he insists that election, as well as reprobation, are not unconditional, as the Calvinists had claimed, but conditional. What, then, is the major condition, the decree, upon which believers are saved and the reprobate lost? Wesley answers, "He that believeth shall be saved; he that believeth not shall be damned."[75]

In Wesley's mind, then, one basic error the Calvinists had committed was to consider the sovereignty of God in an un-nuanced fashion, that is, not in concert with the other salient attributes of the Most High. "Never speak of the sovereignty of God, but in *conjunction* with his other attributes," Wesley warns. "For the Scripture nowhere speaks of this single attribute, as separate from the rest."[76] Indeed, Wesley reasons in this same treatise that if the sovereignty of God is considered in light of the divine justice, then unconditional reprobation is necessarily excluded. Put another way, if divine sovereignty is considered alone and thereby becomes the engine of unconditional reprobation, then it can surely be asked why the reprobate should be damned at all: "For their having done evil? They could not help it. There never was a time when they could have helped it."[77]

Despite such reasoning, Wesley does indeed seek some common ground with the Calvinists in his "Predestination Calmly Considered" on two key themes: First of all, he notes that at the time of conversion, it may seem *as if* believers "had no power to resist the grace of God. They were no more able to stop the course of that torrent which carried all before it."[78] How easily then may believers conclude that "the true grace of God always works irresistibly in every believer."[79] Second, Wesley comes within a hair's breadth of Calvinism[80] by ascribing to God alone the whole glory of salvation. He elaborates:

> If you add, 'Nay but we affirm, that God alone does the whole work, without man's working at all; in one sense, we allow this also. We allow it is the work of God alone to justify, to sanctify, and to glorify; which three comprehend the whole of salvation.[81]

Yet Wesley concludes, clarifying his thought, that he cannot allow that the Most High is somehow the sole worker in salvation, so "as to exclude man's working at all."[82] In other words, like the Calvinists of his own age, Wesley affirmed that justification, sanctification, and glorification are divine works, beyond the powers and abilities of sinners to effectuate. But like many Anglican clergy, Wesley insisted that we must cooperate with God, stretch out our hands, so to speak, and receive these divine and gracious gifts. Wesley develops this line of reasoning even further in his "Letter to a Gentleman at Bristol," drafted in 1758, in this pointed observation:

> Can then God give that freely, which he does not give but upon certain terms and conditions? Doubtless he can; as one may freely give you a sum of money, on condition you stretch out your hand to receive it. It is therefore no "contradiction to say, We are justified freely by grace, and yet upon certain terms or conditions.[83]

So then, Wesley embraced many of the affirmations of the evangelical Calvinists; but his own Anglican tradition that had historically avoided the excesses of both Geneva, on the one hand, and Rome, on the other, allowed him to embrace something more with the result that Wesley's doctrine of salvation was far more sophisticated and much more carefully reasoned than many of his Calvinist critics had imagined. Granted, only God's grace can forgive sinners and make them holy, but sinners must receive, in a responsible and accountable way, such grace. Simply put, justifying and regenerating graces are neither irresistible nor coerced.

Wesley's Evangelical Friends

In the face of the many trials of an evangelist, the criticism from his own peers, and even the difficulties with his wife, Wesley took comfort from several friendships with evangelical Anglican clergy who remained willingly associated with the Methodists—such people as Vincent Perronet (Shoreham), Samuel Walker (Truro), and William Grimshaw (Haworth) among others.[84] Such friendships were naturally very important to Wesley, for they provided him with opportunities for advice, support, and even correction. Therefore, the picture of a heroic Wesley who struggled alone and was dependent largely on his own resources and designs is a myth that bears little relation to the historical record. To be sure, John Wesley's evangelistic activity, in the midst of the eighteenth-century revival with all of its many obstacles and difficulties, was sustained by a network of nurturing, supportive relationships. Wesley, for example, not only sought the counsel of Vincent Perronet, but also took pride in enumerating to him the rules and discipline of Kingswood, the school that Wesley had established earlier in 1748 for the sons of colliers near Bristol.

In time, Mr. Perronet came to be one of Wesley's most trusted friends, and both John and his brother Charles were welcomed in the pulpit of the small church at Shoreham in Kent. Interested in the theology and discipline of the Methodists, Vincent Perronet had actually attended the Conference in 1747. And Wesley was so impressed with this regard that he addressed his *Plain Account of the People Called Methodists,* produced in 1749, to the vicar of Shoreham. In this piece, Wesley revealed to Perronet, as well as to a much broader audience, that his chief design—as that of his brother Charles—in embarking on a preaching career in London and elsewhere more than ten years ago was, as he put it, "to *convince* those who would hear what *true* Christianity was, and to *persuade* them to embrace it."[85] And to the charge that Wesley was dividing the Church of England by "gathering churches out of churches"[86] through the establishment of Methodist societies, Wesley responded by rejecting the very premise that the Anglican Church was simply composed of sincere and devout Christians as noted earlier.[87] And a few years later, Wesley wrote to his friend Ebenezer Blackwell, a London businessman, on the same theme and noted the gentleman's strong desire "to be, not almost only, but altogether a Christian."[88] In fact, the more intimate Wesley was with his friends, the more willing he was to discuss the important matter of the state of their souls and often in a very open and forthright manner.

A Christian Library and *Notes upon the New Testament*

By 1753, the rounds of ministerial labors were beginning to take their toll. In the fall of that year, for instance, Wesley's body was often racked with pain and fever. At first, his symptoms were so unresponsive to medication that Wesley thought he was actually going to die; and so he prepared an inscription for his tombstone in order to prevent, as he put it, "a vile panegyric." It read:

> Here lieth
> The Body of John Wesley
> A Brand plucked out of the burning
> Who died of a Consumption in the Fifty-first Year of his Age
> Not leaving, after his Debts are paid, Ten Pounds behind him
> Praying
> God be merciful to me, an unprofitable servant!
> He ordered that this, if any inscription,
> should be placed on his tombstone.[89]

Though Wesley was undoubtedly concerned during this period about his future, his journal gives no indication of the kinds of existential struggles, the anxious and tormenting fear that had marked his own brush with death several years earlier en route to Georgia. In fact, a few years later, in a letter to Elizabeth Hardy dated April 5, 1758, Wesley explains the ongoing basis for the believer's comfort and assurance:

> I am persuaded none that has faith can die before he is made ripe for glory. This is the doctrine which I continually teach, which has nothing to do with justification by works.... True believers are not distressed hereby, either in life or in death; unless in some rare instance, wherein the temptation of the devil is joined with a melancholy temper.[90]

This illness, the effects of which lingered for several months, forced Wesley to slow down, at least somewhat—something that neither his wife nor his friends were able to persuade him to do. "Having finished all the books which I designed to insert in the *Christian Library*," Wesley notes at the time, "I broke through the doctor's order not to write, and began transcribing a journal for the press."[91] In Wesley's own estimation, the writings of *A Christian Library* constituted some of the very best pieces of practical divinity gathered for the edification of English-speaking peoples. The compilation, undertaken at the request of Philip Doddridge, a pastor in Northampton,[92] was marked, interestingly enough, by a decidedly "western orientation" in its inclusion of Anglicans (Hooker, Beveridge, Taylor, and Bishop Ken)—who naturally predominated, given Wesley's theological orientation—Cambridge Platonists (Cudworth and Norris), Roman Catholics (Don Juan Avila, Brother Lawrence of the Resurrection, and Fénelon), Pietists (Arndt and Francke),[93] as well as Puritans (Baxter). And although Wesley obviously included such Eastern Fathers as Pseudo Macarius, in reprinting twenty-two of his homilies, his selection from patristic authors was not exclusively eastern, as is sometimes mistakenly supposed, but embraced the western author Clement of Rome.

While Wesley was slowly recuperating, shortly after the beginning of the new year, he sought to "redeem the time" once more by beginning work on his *Notes on the New Testament*—a work "which I should scarce ever have attempted had I not been so ill."[94] Drawing upon such diverse sources as "John Heylyn's *Theological Lectures*, John Guyse's *Practical Expositor*, Philip Doddridge's *Family Expositor*, and Johannes Bengel's *Gnomen Novi Testamenti*"[95] Wesley carefully composed notes on Scripture that, though they were far too brief by contemporary standards, were nevertheless vital in his own day as a guide for both preachers and laypeople as they grappled with basic Methodist teaching. Indeed, the careful reader will discern a number of themes that emerge in these *Notes* over the course of several books—such as the nature and extent of sin, grace as both divine favor and empowerment, the reality of Christian assurance, as well as the theme of real Christianity—themes that reflect, to a significant degree, many of Wesley's preoccupations and interests.

It is, however, the development of the theme of the kingdom of

God in the *Notes* that offers readers perhaps one of the best windows on Wesley's understanding of the nature and substance of the Christian faith. Rejecting the notion that the kingdom of God is an external or physical thing, a realm that can be readily seen with the human eye, Wesley affirms instead that it is an "inward kingdom," none other than the essence of "inward religion," that signifies the eternal glory.[96] And in explicating the meaning of Luke 17:21 ("For, behold, the kingdom of God is within [or among] you." [KJV]), Wesley observes,

> Look not for it in distant times or remote places: it is now in the midst of you: it is come: it is present in the soul of every true believer: it is a spiritual kingdom, an internal principle. Wherever it exists, it exists in the heart."[97]

Beyond this, Wesley specifically denies that the kingdom of God is to be identified with temporal, mundane existence as demonstrated in his observations on Acts 28:23:

> These were his [Paul's] two grand topics, 1. That the kingdom of the Messiah was of a spiritual, not temporal nature: 2. That Jesus of Nazareth was the very person foretold, as the Lord of that kingdom."[98]

Again, the kingdom of God

> does not consist in external observances; but in righteousness, the image of God stamped on the heart, the love of God and man, accompanied with the peace that passeth all understanding, and joy in the Holy Ghost.[99]

Thus, when Christ proclaims that his kingdom is not of this world, as in John 19:36, Wesley takes this proclamation to mean, once again, that it is "not an external but a spiritual kingdom."[100]

So then, by identifying the kingdom of God with an inward principle—whose reign occurs in the deep recesses of the soul, whereby the heart is transformed in righteousness, peace, and joy in the Holy Spirit—Wesley's unending concern with inward religion is best understood as nothing less than the inculcation of holiness. In fact, Wesley specifically links this inward kingdom with the new birth, conversion, and an array of soteriological meanings in his observation "that knowledge will not avail thee unless thou be born again—Otherwise thou canst not see, that is, experience and enjoy, either the inward or the glorious kingdom of God."[101] Accordingly, the inculcation of holy love in the human heart is not only the proper motivation for ministry, but also the point of it all—a truth that Wesley had clearly understood as early as 1725, but that was now displayed more artfully and with greater nuance in 1754. The poor and downtrodden, then, can enter into the beauty of the gospel today and know the liberation of a heart set free, despite their poverty and temporal plight, "for the kingdom of God is not meat and drink; but righteousness, and peace, and joy in the Holy Ghost" (Rom. 14:17 KJV).[102]

Assurance Revisited

Though Wesley's teaching on the kingdom of God and inward religion was remarkably consistent over time, his doctrine of assurance remained an area of important and ongoing modification. To illustrate, in his correspondence with Richard Tompson during 1755, Wesley clarifies his doctrine of assurance in two key respects: On the one hand, he argues that there is an intermediate state between a child of the devil and a child of God and that those who are not assured that their sins are forgiven may have a degree of faith and, therefore, may be admitted to the Lord's Supper.[103] On the other hand, Wesley continues to emphasize the importance of assurance for the Christian faith and asserts: "But still I believe, *the proper Christian faith* which purifies the heart implies such a conviction."[104] Indeed, in this same piece, Wesley points out with regard to assurance that "the whole Christian Church in the first centuries enjoyed it."[105] And again he exclaims, "If that knowledge were destroyed, or wholly *withdrawn*, I could not then say I had Christian faith."[106] In fact, in his summary sermon "The Scripture Way of Salvation," produced in 1765, Wesley actually links saving faith with assurance by maintaining that "it is certain this [saving] faith necessarily implies an *assurance* . . . that 'Christ loved *me*, and gave himself for *me*.' "[107]

Wesley's subsequent letters to Richard Tompson the next year contain even further clarification on this topic and one significant, though seldom understood, exception. Concerning this last point,

Wesley admits to Mr. Tompson on February 18, 1756, in a way reminiscent of the 1745 and 1747 Conferences, that one may be in a state of justification and yet lack assurance. These are the exempt cases, or exceptions, as noted earlier. Thus, when Wesley poses the question in his letter, "Can a man who has not a clear assurance that his sins are forgiven be in a state of justification?" he replies, "I believe there are *some* instances of it."[108] However, it was not until much later that Wesley indicates *the reason* for this exception. In a letter to Dr. Rutherforth in 1768, Wesley elaborates:

> Yet I do not affirm there are no exceptions to this general rule [of the association of a measure of assurance with justification]. Possibly some may be in the favor of God, and yet go mourning all the day long. But I believe this is usually owing either to disorder of body or ignorance of the gospel promises.[109]

Two issues that are often confused need to be separated here. On the one hand, the elderly Wesley still did not identify or confuse the faith of a servant, and its measure of acceptance, with the assurance that one's sins are forgiven; since being under "the spirit of bondage," a servant, properly speaking, lacks justifying faith. On the other hand, the Methodist leader recognized that in some exceptional cases, those who are justified and regenerated (and hence children of God) may lack an assurance that their sins are forgiven due to either ignorance or bodily disorder.[110] This means, then, that Wesley actually defined the faith of a servant in at least two key ways, as alluded to in chapter 6: The first, which is a broad usage and occurs repeatedly in Wesley's writings, *excludes* justification, regeneration, and assurance and corresponds to the spirit of bondage. The second, which is a narrow usage and seldom occurs, corresponds to the exempt cases and exceptions noted above and *includes* justification and regeneration but not assurance. Interestingly enough, although the faith of a servant in this second sense is obviously Christian (saving) faith, since it includes justification and regeneration, Wesley still did not refer to it as the *proper* Christian faith, since it lacks assurance. This is a subtle distinction, to be sure, but no less important for its subtlety, and it will have remarkable consequences in Wesley's subsequent theology.

CHAPTER EIGHT

The Anglican Church and Holiness

Oldham Street Methodist Chapel, Manchester

In the early days of December 1760, Wesley was once again defending himself and the Methodists, this time to the editor of the *Lloyd's Evening Post*. It was claimed, among other things, that Wesley had "apostatized from those principles of religion which [he] undertook to defend."[1] In reply, Wesley acknowledged his adherence to the three standards of the faith for all good Anglicans, namely, the Bible, the Homilies, and the *Book of Common Prayer*.[2] About a year later, Wesley faced similar criticism from the author of the *Westminster Journal;* and so he reaffirmed his theological integrity in general and his adherence to the doctrine of justification by faith in particular. Moreover, in this same response, Wesley underscored the continuity of Methodism with vital ancient religion. "We aver it [Methodism] is the one old religion," Wesley insisted, "as old as the Reformation, as old as Christianity, as old as Moses, as old as Adam."[3]

Though Wesley could make the case that Methodism was doctrinally orthodox, in step with historic Anglicanism and the broader church, it was becoming increasingly difficult during the 1760s to contend that Methodism had not departed from the ecclesiastical law of the Church of England. For one thing, some of Wesley's lay preachers were no longer content with simply preaching and took it upon themselves to administer the Lord's Supper. To illustrate, Paul Greenwood, Thomas Mitchell, and John Murlin, preachers at Norwich, all officiated at the sacrament. Upon learning of such a presumptuous action, Charles Wesley was naturally incensed and urged his brother to end this practice. John, too, was greatly concerned and took measures to reassure Charles that effective discipline would, in fact, be put into place.

Though Wesley had actually considered the idea of ordaining lay preachers to the office of priest, thereby enabling them to administer the sacraments and to foster the work of the Revival, he nevertheless hesitated during 1765 when his need of laborers was especially great. Instead, and in a highly irregular manner, Wesley sought the services of a peculiar Greek bishop, Erasmus, to solve his dilemma. After examining the bishop's credentials and being fully satisfied, Wesley allowed this Greek cleric—who, by the way, could hardly speak a word of English—to ordain John Jones and, later on, six other persons. Wesley defended his actions to the printer of *St. James Chronicle* in 1765, but eventually he had second thoughts. In his own mind, at least, the issue of legitimacy, or the lack thereof, turned not on the authority of the Greek bishop, but on the fact that the ordinations had been "procured by *money* and performed in an *unknown tongue*."[4]

As an overseer in the church, responsible for the good order of the Methodist societies throughout England and Ireland, Wesley bore the burden, heavy as it was, of seeing to it that suitable laborers would be supplied to continue the work of the gospel. And though Wesley, himself, obviously was not yet willing to ordain anyone during the mid-1760s, his commitment both to field preaching by clergy and to the employment of lay preachers was by now nonnegotiable. A letter to Charles Wesley in June 1760 had posed this basic dilemma: "Leave preaching, or leave the Church."[5] Wesley, not wishing to leave either, could only respond that "we have reason to thank God it is not come to this yet."[6] And though it may look as if Wesley were equivocating at this point, he was actually already quite firm in his views. In fact, in a letter to the Earl of Dartmouth in April 1761, Wesley reasoned that "if there is a law that a minister of Christ who is not suffered to preach the gospel in the church should not preach it elsewhere, I do judge that law to be absolutely sinful."[7] And of the value of field preaching itself, Wesley noted in 1764: "What can shake Satan's kingdom like *field-preaching*."[8] And the following year, he added with powerful effect: "So plain it is that field-preaching is the most effectual way of overturning Satan's kingdom."[9] In light of these and other pronouncements, come what may, Wesley was not about to put aside this gracious instrument of the gospel.

Bishop Warburton

Though many Anglican clergy took issue with the polity of Methodism since they deemed field preaching, the violation of parish boundaries, and the employment of lay preachers as usurpations of their duly ordered prerogatives, other clergy were far more critical of the *theology* of Methodism, which they judged to be "aberrant" and "enthusiastic." In 1762, for example, William Warburton, bishop of Gloucester, published *The Office and Operations of the Holy Spirit Vindicated from the Insults of Infidelity and the Abuses of Fanaticism*, a work that was critical of a prominent doctrinal emphasis of the Methodists. Demonstrating a measure of fair play, Warburton submitted this piece to Wesley before it was published; and the latter returned it, having corrected its false readings, improper glosses, and other errors. Once the essay was made public, however, Wesley set aside a few days, from November 26 to 29, to draft a more lengthy response.

Among other things, Warburton had maintained that the Methodists were fanatics because they claimed to enjoy operations of the Holy Spirit that were reserved, in the bishop's judgment, for the apostolic age. In his detailed reply, Wesley pointed out that he and the Methodists did not "pretend to any extraordinary measure of the Spirit," but only to what could be claimed by every Christian minister.[10] Putting aside dreams, visions, and revelations as being of a doubtful or disputable nature, Wesley instead focused on the operations of the Spirit as the "Guide of truth" who enlightens the understanding, as "the Comforter who purifies and supports the will," and as the One who now "hears and answers prayer even beyond the ordinary course of nature."[11] But Wesley also wanted to make it clear to the bishop that the ministry of the Spirit could be distinguished from the course of nature in terms of both effectiveness and time. "I have seen very many persons," Wesley stated, "changed in a moment from the spirit of fear, horror, despair, to the spirit of love, joy, and praise."[12] Indeed, it was in reality the gracious and supernatural efficacy of the Spirit, and the profession of such by the Methodists, that Warburton had found so troubling.

Sensing that Warburton's objections were actually directed not against fanaticism as such, but against real, scriptural Christianity, Wesley moved the dispute in that direction with his following observation:

> And what use is it of, what good end does it serve, to term England a Christian country? Although it is true most of the natives are called Christians, have been baptized, frequent the ordinances; and although here and there a *real* Christian is to be found, "as a light shining in a dark place,"—does it do any honor to our great Master among those who are not called by His name? Does it recommend Christianity to the Jews, the Mahometans, or the avowed heathens? Surely no one can conceive it does.[13]

To be sure, Wesley maintained that "every true Christian" receives the Holy Spirit as Paraclete or Comforter, as "the Spirit of all truth," and as the anointing mentioned in the First Epistle of John, a book of the Bible that was one of Wesley's favorites on this theme.[14] And just in case Warburton might miss the thrust of these rebuttals, Wesley offered him a question to ponder: "If men are not Christians till they are renewed after the image of Christ, and if the people of England in general are not thus renewed, why do we term them so?"[15] The original question of fanaticism had now become one of what constitutes the proper Christian faith. Wesley had indeed turned the tables on the good bishop.

James Hervey

As if the ongoing tensions between Wesley and the hierarchy of his own church were not bad enough, many Calvinist *evangelicals* took increasing offense at several of Wesley's pronouncements on the subjects of election and grace. Earlier, James Hervey, a former student of Wesley's at Oxford, had decided to be more forthright concerning the truths of predestination, election, and imputation. To that end, he drafted a work entitled *Theron and Aspasio* and asked Wesley for his comments. When Wesley returned the manuscript with his suggestions, Hervey complained, "You are not my friend if you do not take more liberty with me."[16] Wesley complied with this request, offered more serious criticisms, and thereby deeply offended his former student. Among other things, Wesley suggested that some of Hervey's notions were not scriptural; and he especially took exception to Hervey's idea of imputation since it could render believers content, even self-satisfied, without holiness. Deeply concerned, Wesley published *A Preservative Against Unsettled Notions of Religion* in 1758 as a brief rebuttal and later, after Hervey's death, *Thoughts on the Imputed Righteousness of Christ* in 1762.

Chafing under Wesley's censure, Hervey wrote a number of private letters that were critical of his former teacher's views. However, as his health began to fail in 1758, Hervey had second thoughts about publishing this material. Accordingly, on his deathbed, he specifically ordered his brother *not* to print these letters. Somehow, a copy of this material fell into the hands of William Cudworth, an unscrupulous preacher, who quickly published it. Hervey's brother, William, noticed a number of errors in the manuscript, which reflected poorly on his brother, James. Violating his previous promise not to publish, William Hervey came forward with a "corrected" edition of the work entitled *Eleven Letters from the late Rev. Mr. Hervey to the Rev. Mr. John Wesley; Containing an Answer to that Gentleman's Remarks on Theron and Aspasio.* The sermon "The Lord Our Righteousness" was Wesley's quick response. In this piece, Wesley maintained that the work of Christ was the meritorious rather than the formal cause of salvation, a view that "allowed for prevenience, free will, and 'universal redemption' and that consequently undermined the Calvinist notions of predestination and irresistible grace."[17] So significant was the publication of this sermon that Albert Outler noted, "It signals the end of Wesley's efforts to avoid an open rift with the Calvinists; it signals the beginning of that stage in his career . . . labeled 'the later Wesley.' "[18]

Though the mid-1760s do indeed mark the time Wesley could no longer avoid an open rift with the Calvinists—though the real struggle was yet to come—his relations with George Whitefield, interestingly enough, were actually improving during this period. In January 1766, for example, Whitefield visited Wesley, breathing "nothing but peace and love."[19] The following year, Wesley observed, with much gratitude, that "God has indeed effectually broken down the wall of partition which was between us."[20] Thus, though both leaders continued to articulate a very different theology, each was also fully aware of the great work of God being accomplished by the other. And in 1769, shortly before Whitefield's death, Wesley took note on more than one occasion of an agreeable and profitable time spent with this magnificent but worn-out preacher.[21]

Original Sin

Wesley's emphases on the witness of the Spirit and on initial and entire sanctification, not as natural, but as supernatural works of grace, brought him into conflict with an age steeped in the value of reason as the final arbiter of both ethical and religious sensibilities. In England, for example, Dr. John Taylor deemed the Christian doctrine of original sin to be far too pessimistic and an unwelcomed throwback to a superstitious age. In his estimation, at least, there was little in human nature that could not be improved by education and attention to virtue—in other words, by some natural course of instruction or *practice*. Consequently, the deep depravity entailed in the doctrine of original sin, as well as the call for a "supernatural," life-changing work of grace as its cure, were both deemed misguided by Taylor. In response to these "enlightened" views, which left individual reason at the center of all, Wesley complained to August Toplady in a letter composed in 1758:

> I verily believe no single person since Mahomet has given such a wound to Christianity as Dr. Taylor. They are his books, chiefly that upon Original Sin, which have poisoned so many of the clergy, and indeed the fountains themselves—the Universities in England, Scotland, Holland, and Germany.[22]

To be sure, so vital was this doctrine of original sin to John Wesley that during the year prior to his letter to Toplady, the Methodist leader crafted one of his largest theological treatises ever, *The Doctrine of Original Sin: According to Scripture, Reason, and Experience*, in response to the earlier work by Dr. Taylor, *The Scripture Doctrine of Original Sin: Proposed to Free and Candid Examination*. Distinguishing himself in many respects from Taylor and from the Deists of his own age, that is, from people like Matthew Tindal, author of *Christian as Old as Creation*, and John Toland, who penned the Deist classic *Christianity Not Mysterious*, Wesley also published a sermon on original sin, in which he declared that all who deny this vital doctrine, for whatever reason and with whatever justifications, are "but heathens still."[23] And elsewhere, in this same piece, he regarded the question (and others like it) "Is man by nature filled with all manner of evil?" as a virtual shibboleth to distinguish scriptural Christianity from paganism.[24]

In articulating a doctrine of total depravity, apart from all grace, Wesley once again displays his decidedly western orientation and, in the words of William Cannon, "goes all the way with Calvin, with Luther, and with Augustine in his insistence that man is by nature totally destitute of righteousness and subject to the judgment and wrath of God."[25] In fact, on this topic, Wesley employs what can only be described as "negative superlatives"—so foreign to eastern theologians—to display the general moral and spiritual abyss into which humanity has descended. He observes:

> Is man by nature filled with all manner of evil? Is he void of all good? Is he wholly fallen? Is his soul totally corrupted? Or, to come back to the text, is "every imagination of the thoughts of his heart evil continually"? Allow this, and you are so far a Christian. Deny it, and you are but a heathen still.[26]

Beyond this, in his treatise on original sin, Wesley considers the corruption of human nature in terms of "a want of original righteousness" and also in terms of a "natural propensity to sin," indicating that depravity, so understood, is not simply a privation, a lack of goodness, but is *also* an active power that predisposes the tempers of the human heart toward sin, disobedience, and rebellion.[27]

Now while there does indeed appear to be great similarity

between Wesley's doctrine of original sin and that of Luther and Calvin, especially in the emphasis on total depravity, upon closer examination, however, there are important differences largely due to dissimilar conceptions of grace. It must be borne in mind, for instance, that when Wesley employs the vocabulary of total depravity, he is referring to what he calls "the natural man," that is, to a person who is utterly without the grace of God. But does such a person actually exist? Not according to Wesley, for in his later sermon "On Working Out Our Own Salvation," he states:

> For allowing that all the souls of men are dead in sin by *nature*, this excuses none, seeing there is no man that is in a state of mere nature; there is no man, unless he has quenched the Spirit, that is wholly void of the grace of God. No man living is entirely destitute of what is vulgarly called "natural conscience." But this is not natural; it is more properly termed "preventing grace."[28]

And again in this same sermon, Wesley adds, drawing on John 1:9, his principal text for prevenient grace, "Everyone has some measure of that light, some faint glimmering ray, which sooner or later, more or less, enlightens every man that cometh into the world."[29] Umphrey Lee, therefore, correctly pointed out that, for Wesley, the "natural man" is a logical abstraction that does not correspond to actual men and women. "In this world," he noted, "man exists as a natural man *plus* the prevenient grace of God."[30] Simply put, the effects of original sin are still present, but they are no longer total. Human beings are fallen, but they have a measure of grace and liberty sufficient to respond to God's offer of salvation in Jesus Christ.

In its results, then, in its consequences for everyday men and women, Wesley's doctrine of original sin, understood in the context of prevenient grace, may make his theology look somewhat similar to the Eastern Orthodox notion that the Fall did not deprive humanity of all grace or of the accountability for responding to the ongoing grace of God. Nevertheless, it must be borne in mind that not only did Wesley affirm a total depravity (even if it was a "logical abstraction") that several Orthodox theologians could only find troubling, but also he developed his doctrines of original sin and prevenient grace, not so much in terms of eastern sources, but in terms of western ones, that is, in terms of Augustine and the rich resources of his own Anglican Church. To be sure,

Wesley's doctrines of original sin and prevenient grace are faithful articulations, careful amplifications, of the theology displayed in the Thirty-nine Articles of Religion.[31]

The New Birth: Sanctification Begun

Wesley's concern, even preoccupation, with the doctrine of original sin no doubt grew out of his strong soteriological interests. That is, if the problem (original sin) were repudiated or soft-pedaled—as it was by Deism and eighteenth-century rational religion—then perhaps the solution (the new birth) would be lost or misunderstood as well. And that this last point is no mere conjecture is demonstrated by an appeal to Wesley's observation: "This then is the foundation of the new birth—the *entire corruption* of our nature."[32] In fact, the doctrine of original sin, along with justification by faith, and holiness of heart and life were so crucial for Wesley that he deemed them the very essentials of religion.[33]

In eighteenth-century Anglican soteriology (that in some respects still reflected the heritage of Roman Catholicism), the basic remedy for the ills of original sin lay in the sacrament of baptism, which was most often administered to infants.[34] As the evangelical revival progressed, however, and as Wesley became increasingly concerned about the problem of nominal Christianity, he saw the need for a fresh articulation of the truths contained in the terse counsel of Christ, spoken to Nicodemus, "Ye must be born again" (John 3:7 KJV). The sermon "The New Birth," produced in 1760, was the obvious result. Influenced by the convertive piety of both Puritans (whose writings form a significant share of selections in *A Christian Library*)[35] and Pietists, especially that of August Francke and Peter Böhler, Wesley explores the *nature* of the new birth in this sermon as "that great change which God works in the soul when he brings it into life."[36] Underscoring the necessity of the new birth for present holiness and happiness as well as for future glory, Wesley challenges his readers not to rest content in mere moralism, ritual, or church custom:

> What danger, say they, can a woman be in, that is so *harmless* and so *virtuous*? What fear is there that so *honest* a man, one of so strict *morality*, should miss of heaven? Especially if over and above all this they constantly attend on church and sacrament.

One of these will ask with all assurance, "What, shall not I do as well as my neighbors?" Yes, as well as your unholy neighbors; as well as your neighbors that die in their sins.[37]

Accordingly, moral probity, education, and dependence on human resources are simply not enough. In fact, Wesley so emphasizes the supernatural change of regeneration that he maintains repeatedly throughout his writings that spiritual life itself commences when we are born again.[38]

Perhaps Wesley's favorite way of underscoring the decisive nature of the new birth was to distinguish it from the larger process of sanctification and then to demonstrate, quite clearly, the significance of the temporal elements entailed. For example, in his treatise on original sin, Wesley observed:

But regeneration is not "gaining habits of holiness"; it is quite a different thing. It is not a natural, but a supernatural, change; and is just as different from the gradual "gaining habits," as a child's being born into the world is from his growing up into a man. The new birth is not, as you suppose, the progress, or the whole, of sanctification, but the beginning of it.[39]

In a similar fashion, Wesley affirmed that regeneration is not to be confused with the ongoing *process* of holiness: "This is a part of sanctification, not the whole; it is the gate of it, the entrance into it."[40] Now since Wesley clearly distinguished the new birth from the process of sanctification, then he must have also considered, by way of corollary, the new birth itself to be a decisive, instantaneous event. And this is precisely what is found throughout his writings. Thus, in a letter to John Downes drafted earlier in 1759, Wesley not only underscores the supernatural flavor of this work, a commonplace by now, but also indicates something of the temporal elements involved:

We do believe regeneration (or, in plain English, the new birth) to be as miraculous or supernatural a work now as it was seventeen hundred years ago. We likewise believe that the spiritual life, which commences when we are born again, must in the nature of the thing have a first moment as well as the natural."[41]

The following year, Wesley depicts the instantaneousness of regeneration against the backdrop of the larger process of sanctification and indicates that the former is a crucial aspect of the latter. Drawing a by-now familiar analogy between natural birth and spiritual birth in this piece, Wesley points out that a child is born of woman "in a moment, or at least in a very short time."[42] After this, the child continues to grow until it reaches maturity. In the same way, he argues, "a child is born of God in a short time, if not in a moment. But it is by slow degrees that he afterward grows up to the measure of the full stature of Christ."[43]

The relation, then, which holds between natural birth and maturation, is similar to the relation between the new birth and sanctification. That is, Wesley is attentive to the cruciality of the new birth, the instantaneous element, *and* to the process of sanctification, the gradual element. Both aspects are acknowledged; neither, therefore, should be neglected. Moreover, this instantaneous emphasis is not simply a concern of the middle-aged Wesley, but of the elderly Wesley as well. Notice, for example, in the following selection from "The Scripture Way of Salvation," which was produced in 1765, how Wesley never repudiates the instantaneousness and therefore the discreteness of the new birth. He writes, "At the same time that we are justified, yea, in that very *moment*, sanctification begins. In that *instant* we are 'born again,' 'born from above,' 'born of the Spirit.' "[44] The key, perhaps, to unraveling Wesley's larger thought here is found in his further identification of the instantaneous element with inward religion, that is, of the association of a moment of grace, so to speak, with the activity of God. For if aspirants of God's regenerating grace are expecting that something else must be done first, then they are still expecting salvation by works. But if redemption is by the grace of God, then they can expect it as they are; and they can expect it now. That is, the instantaneous elements of Wesley's *via salutis*, once again, are his principal vehicles for underscoring the crucial truth that it is God, not humanity, who both forgives sins and makes holy. Temporal elements, in other words, indicate soteriological roles.

In light of these observations, those interpretations of Wesley's doctrine of salvation, which identify the juridical aspects of redemption (justification or forgiveness) as instantaneous and the therapeutic aspects (sanctification) as simply processive, are wide of the mark. Indeed, Wesley's doctrine of redemption is much more sophisticated than this categorization can allow. Broadly understood, sanctification is characterized by both process *and* instantaneousness, for the new birth (initial sanctification), as with justification, must, to use Wesley's own words, "have a first moment."[45] In addition, it is precisely the introduction of the instantaneous element in terms of initial sanctification that brings the notion of grace as the unmerited favor of God back into the picture where it belongs. That is, regeneration, although it represents divine empowerment, is like justification in that it too underscores the sheer gratuity of grace. Again, regeneration, as with justification, is by grace through faith.[46]

Challenges Along the Way

Part of Wesley's earlier disappointment following Aldersgate concerned his erroneous views, mediated to him by the Moravians, with respect to the degree of freedom from sin that should characterize his life. As chapter 4 has already pointed out, evidence suggests that prior to May 1738, Wesley had anticipated freedom, not simply from sin's power, but also from its very *being* or presence as revealed in his journal entry on board the *Samuel* as he was returning to England: "I want that faith which none can have without knowing that he hath it. . . . For whosoever hath it is 'freed from sin'; 'the *whole body of sin* is destroyed' in him."[47] However, unlike Wesley's erroneous views on assurance, it is difficult to determine the exact time, the precise occasion, when the Methodist leader first modified his expectations in this area as well as his basic doctrine of sin. The *terminus ad quem* appears to be 1748, the year that Wesley affirmed a believer's freedom from the *guilt* and *power* of sin in his sermons "The Marks of the New Birth" and "The Great Privilege of Those Who Are Born of God." The *terminus ad quo*, however, is far more difficult to assess and may be as early as 1741 when Wesley conversed with Count Zinzendorf at Gray's Inn Walks (in Latin) and specifically rejected the Moravian leader's notion that believers are perfected in love when they are justified, as noted earlier.[48]

Given the importance of these soteriological distinctions with respect to sin, it is surprising to learn that Wesley did not clearly articulate them, in any significant detail, until the publication of his sermons "On Sin in Believers" in 1763 and "The Repentance of

Believers" four years later. In the former sermon, for example, after Wesley affirms the universal truth, accepted by the "Greek and Romish Church [and] by every Reformed Church in Europe, of whatever denomination,"[49] that the carnal nature or original sin remains even in the hearts of those that have been born of God, he then displays what liberty from sin the children of God do indeed enjoy. Wesley elaborates:

> Christ indeed cannot *reign* where sin *reigns*; neither will he *dwell* where any sin is *allowed*. But he *is* and *dwells* in the heart of every believer who is fighting against all sin; although it be "not" yet "purified according to the purification of the sancturary."[50]

Moreover, to the distinction in this sermon between sin *remaining* though not *reigning*, Wesley adds another: "The *guilt* is one thing, the *power* another, and the *being* yet another. That believers are delivered from the *guilt* and *power* of sin we allow; that they are delivered from the *being* of it we deny."[51] This last observation succinctly summarizes Wesley's basic doctrine of sin as it relates to the theological elements of justification, regeneration, and entire sanctification. That is, justification delivers from the *guilt* of sin, regeneration from its *power* or *dominion*, and entire sanctification from its *being*. Unfortunately, these distinctions are often neglected in contemporary Methodism where a decided "shift" has taken place; that is, freedom from the *power* of committing sin is attributed not to the new birth, as it should be, but to Christian perfection, with the result that freedom from the *being* of sin is then relegated to the afterlife and glory.[52] Albert Outler, for instance, wrote in his introductory comments to Wesley's sermon "Christian Perfection" as follows:

> If, for Wesley, salvation was the total restoration of the deformed image of God in us, and if its *fullness* was the recovery of our negative *power* not to sin and our positive power to love God supremely, this denotes that furthest reach of grace and its triumphs in this life that Wesley chose to call "Christian Perfection."[53]

However, the grace of God as Wesley understood it was actually far more efficacious and liberating as it set believers free not simply from the *power* of sin, but from its very *being* or *presence* as well. Moreover, this ongoing misprizing of the reality and instantiation of the highest graces of redemption can unfortunately be found in the contemporary holiness movement as well, in which the *numerous* professions of entire sanctification are most probably indicative not of the excellency of Christian perfection as Wesley had understood it, but of the liberties entailed, once again, in the new birth, specifically freedom from the *power* of committing sin.

At any rate, given the inward corruption, the *being* of sin, that remains in the human heart, even in that of a child of God, Wesley's counsel to the spiritually earnest in his subsequent sermon "The Repentance of Believers" was naturally to repent. On the one hand, this evangelical repentance is in some respects similar to the earlier legal repentance in that it entails both contrition and considerable self-knowledge. On the other hand, it is different in that one repents not of actual sin—from which the regenerated believer has already been set free—but of inbred sin. Wesley considers the *necessity* of this second work of grace in the following fashion:

> Though we watch and pray ever so much, we cannot wholly cleanse either our hearts or hands. Most sure we cannot, till it shall please our Lord to speak to our hearts again, to "speak the second time, 'Be clean.'" And then only "the leprosy is cleansed." Then only the evil root, the carnal mind, is destroyed, and inbred sin subsists no more. But if there be no such second change, if there be no instantaneous deliverance after justification, if there be none but a gradual work of God (that there is a gradual work none denies) then we must be content, as well as we can, to remain full of sin till death.[54]

So then, redemption according to Wesley is not accomplished in one grand stroke, neither is it an uninterrupted process of gradual, barely distinguishable changes; instead, a second distinct work of grace is needed. In fact, it was Wesley himself, and not the American holiness movement, who first championed this notion of a "second" work of grace.[55]

During the same year that Wesley produced his sermon on the new birth, he wrote two others ("The Wilderness State" and "Heaviness Through Manifold Temptations") that demonstrated the importance of going on to the grace of Christian perfection—

despite numerous obstacles. In the first sermon, for example, Wesley describes the wilderness state as a loss of faith, love, joy, peace, and power brought about by temptation, ignorance, or sin. Being the adept spiritual counselor that he was, Wesley realized that one of the greatest occasions of ongoing temptation for the sons and daughters of God was the inbred sin still *present* in their hearts. Indeed, the dogs of remaining (though not reigning) pride, anger, and foolish desire may repeatedly gnaw at the soul and disrupt its peace.[56] Accordingly, as believers grow in grace, having their affections fixed on the divine glory, they will desire to be free from such filthiness of flesh and spirit in order to enjoy the love of God and neighbor in a deeper, more satisfying, way.

Moreover, in the second sermon on this broader topic, "Heaviness Through Manifold Temptations," Wesley frankly acknowledges that bodily disorders, poverty, the loss of dear friends, and the sin of loved ones, and perhaps even their apostasy, may cause a heaviness both long and severe, but that this need not result in darkness or a loss of faith. "Darkness, or the wilderness state," Wesley explains, "implies a total loss of joy in the Holy Ghost; heaviness does not; in the midst of this we may 'rejoice with joy unspeakable.' "[57] Again, God may allow heaviness for a season in order to advance believers in faith, hope, and love; but the Most High does not "[withdraw] himself because he *will*, merely because it is his good pleasure,"[58] and thereby precipitate what some might call a "dark night of the soul." In Wesley's estimation, such darkness or suffering is *not* required of the believer, as if it were an integral part or stage of the *via salutis*. Thus, when Wesley crafts the introduction to his abridgment of the *Life of Madam Guyon* late in his career, he writes:

> Hence arose that capital mistake, which runs through all her writings, that God never does, never can, purify a soul, but by inward and outward suffering. Utterly false! Never was there a more purified soul than the Apostle John. And which of the Apostles suffered less? yea, or of all the primitive Christians? Therefore all she says on this head, of "darkness, desertion, privation," and the like, is fundamentally wrong.[59]

Nevertheless, in fairness and for accuracy, it must be quickly noted that what Wesley understood by darkness and what John of the Cross intended (and those who followed in his wake) by the expression "dark night of the soul" are remarkably dissimilar. For example, in his classic text on spirituality, *Dark Night of the Soul*, John of the Cross utilizes the image of night to signify the spiritual journey of purgation and detachment as an advance in grace. He writes,

> The strait gate is this night of sense, and the soul detaches itself from sense and strips itself thereof that it may enter by this gate, and establishes itself in faith, which is a stranger to all sense, so that afterwards it may journey by the narrow way, which is the other night—that of the spirit.[60]

Put another way, the spirit and senses are freed from the specific and the knowable until they are left to encounter the darkness that is God. For Wesley, on the other hand, darkness, especially as it is employed in the sermon "The Wilderness State," does not correspond to an apophatic purgation process at all; instead it refers to ignorance, sin, and the loss of faith. However, given Wesley's larger views on suffering and the withdrawal of God as both unnecessary for spiritual maturation[61] (in the sense that one may be perfected in love without them), one may conclude that, in the end, the Methodist leader rejected the basic approach that was so dear to John of the Cross and other Christian mystics. In good Protestant fashion, for Wesley, the words "grace," "faith," and "light" were remarkably indicative of spiritual advance and maturation.

Perfect Love: Sanctification Perfected

In a real sense, the 1760s belonged to the doctrine of Christian perfection. By then, there were throughout the British Isles an increasing number of witnesses to this distinct work of grace, some of whom, no doubt, had responded to Wesley's explicit preaching on the subject as, for example, when he arrived in London in November 1761.[62] That same year, Wesley brought forth his "Farther Thoughts on Christian Perfection," the substance of which was included in his largest treatise on entire sanctification, namely, *A Plain Account of Christian Perfection*, which was penned in 1766. The composition of this work, especially its attention to chronology and sequence, suggests something of its apologetic purpose. Wesley notes, for example, the highlights of his thought in a lucid and straightforward manner: In 1725 to 1728, he read the triumvirate of Taylor, à Kempis, and Law; in 1733, he produced "The Circumcision of the Heart"; in 1739, he and his brother Charles issued the volume *Hymns and Sacred Poems*, and he produced "The Character of a Methodist"; in 1741, he wrote a sermon entitled "Christian Perfection" as well as published a second volume of hymns; and concerning the period of 1744 and thereafter, Wesley culls the insights from the various Methodist conferences on this salient theme. Indeed, the careful delineation of Wesley's views on perfect love throughout the last forty years was offered to demonstrate his remarkable consistency.[63]

The Plain Account is also valuable in that it reveals the sources—most of them western—that formed Wesley's basic understanding of sanctification or holiness. As in his autobiographical account that served as a preface to the detailed description of his evangelical conversion, and as in his letter to John Newton in May of 1765, Wesley indicates, quite clearly, that it was in the writings of Jeremy Taylor, Caroline divine; Thomas à Kempis, medieval Roman Catholic mystic; and William Law, English Nonjuror; that he found the very substance of Christian perfection. The names of Eastern Fathers such as Macarius and Ephrem Syrus, who held similar views, are not even mentioned in *The Plain Account* at all.[64]

Growing in grace on the way to perfect love is a *process* that Wesley explores in his writings in both a positive and a negative fashion. Positively speaking, the Holy Spirit becomes increasingly resident in the human heart such that the holy tempers of love are inculcated in a real and enduring way. Such a gracious activity often occurs in the communal context of the church, through the means of Word and sacrament, and is generously manifested in works of piety and mercy—in a faith, in other words, that is ever active in love. Negatively speaking, growth in holiness entails not simply the inculcation of holy love, but also the displacement of unholy tempers and affections, a radical, "cutting" work that results in nothing less than the death of the carnal nature. That is, the propensity of original sin is purged, as a consequence of efficacious grace, a heart bent toward backsliding is cleansed. In this setting Wesley deftly weaves together the temporal elements of both *process* and *instantiation*, never one to the neglect of the other, by means of an image of death that embraces *both* the process of dying as well as the actualization of death itself. Wesley elaborates:

> From the moment we are justified, there may be a gradual sanctification, a growing in grace, a daily advance in the knowledge and love of God. And if sin cease before death, there must, in the nature of the thing, be an instantaneous change; there must be a last moment wherein it does not exist, and a first moment wherein it does not.[65]

Viewed in another way, the continuity of the process of growth in grace must be matched by the discontinuity, the concluding work of actualization. That is, aspirants to God's highest graces cannot simply evolve into perfect love; they cannot simply be nurtured into entire sanctification as if it were merely a positive and open-ended process. Why is this so? It is chiefly because the entire sanctification of a soul, though marked by process, is ever preceded by the *discontinuity* of death, a death that is emblematic of the instantiation of this *quality* of love in all its purity as well as of the elimination of the carnal nature itself. Put another way, the new does not utterly appear out of the reform or the nurturing of the old; rather, the old must die. Here the twentieth-century German theologian Dietrich Bonhoeffer is both to the point and instructive: "When Christ calls a man . . . he bids him come and die."[66] All of this, then, the gentle balance of process and realization, of continuity and discontinuity, highlights the significant truth for Wesley that though entire sanctification may not be dramatic or its exact time even remembered, it is nevertheless an actualized, instantiated change that is momentous, life-changing, and in its best sense a supernatural work of God's sovereign grace.

The Myth of John Wesley and Eastern Orthodoxy

Though recent scholarship in Wesley studies suggests a strong relationship between Eastern Orthodoxy and the theology of John Wesley,[67] especially on the subject of Christian perfection, the claim is actually based on an anachronistic reading of history and a confused employment of tradition. First of all, in Wesley's usual list of the early church Fathers, as seen in his sermon "On Laying the Foundation of the New Chapel, near City Road, London," Wesley does not specifically single out Eastern Fathers for any special attention, but rather gives a general listing that includes both Latin and Greek authors:

> This is the *religion of the primitive church*, of the whole church in the purest ages. It is clearly expressed, even in the small remains of Clemens Romanus, Ignatius, and Polycarp. It is seen more at large in the writings of Tertullian, Origen, Clemens Alexandrinus, and Cyprian. And even in the fourth century it was found in the works of Chrysostom, Basil, Ephrem Syrus, and Macarius.[68]

Second, it is anachronistic, and therefore inappropriate, to refer to early Eastern Fathers such as Origen (185–254), Clement of Alexandria (150–215), Chrysostom (374–407), Basil (329–379), Ephrem Syrus (306–373), and Macarius (380–430) as constituting Eastern Orthodoxy, a tradition that is actually a later historical development. To be sure, the second, third, and fourth centuries of Christianity are best described not as the period of "Eastern Orthodoxy" or of "The Roman Catholic Church" for that matter, but as the period of "The Ancient Catholic Church," out of which the great theological traditions were yet to emerge. In this early period, then, a catholic or universal church arose and distinguished itself from Gnostic and other heresies. The fragmentation of Christendom into discreet theological traditions, then, did not actually begin until later, that is, in the fifth and sixth centuries. Simply put, for the sake of accuracy, a distinction must be made between the *tradition* of Eastern Orthodoxy and the early Eastern Fathers.

Third, with this distinction in place, it can be affirmed that Wesley did indeed appeal to the writings of Eastern Fathers such as Clement of Alexandria and Ephrem Syrus in his explication of Christian perfection, but it is also equally clear that Wesley did not, as is mistakenly supposed, appeal to Eastern Orthodoxy in the sense that this *tradition itself* provided the salient cues for his theological understanding. In fact, whenever Wesley considered the Greek tradition as a discreet *tradition*, his observations were most often *negative*. For example, in his treatise *The Doctrine of Original Sin*, produced in 1756, Wesley notes:

> The gross, barbarous ignorance, the deep, stupid superstition, the blind and bitter zeal, and the endless thirst after vain jangling

and strife of words, which have reigned for many ages in the Greek Church, and well-nigh banished true religion from among them, make these scarce worthy of the Christian name, and lay an insuperable stumbling-block before the Mahometans.[69]

Moreover, in his sermon "The General Spread of the Gospel," produced much later in 1783, Wesley criticizes those churches under the jurisdiction of the Patriarch of Moscow as having little knowledge of true religion. "The western churches," Wesley maintains, "seem to have the pre-eminence over all these in many respects. They have abundantly more knowledge; they have more scriptural and more rational modes of worship."[70] And a few years later, in 1789, Wesley once again found much in the Eastern Orthodoxy troubling:

What do the Christians, so called, of the Eastern Church, dispersed throughout the Turkish dominions, know of genuine Christianity? Those of the Morea, of Circassia, Mingrelia, Georgia? Are they not the very dregs of mankind?[71]

Beyond this, there is little evidence to suggest that Wesley had much contact with eighteenth-century Eastern Orthodoxy, other than the fiasco of having the Greek bishop Erasmus, as noted earlier, ordain some of Wesley's lay preachers. Such limited contact between Wesley and the Eastern Orthodoxy of his own age is surely a troubling fact for those contemporary interpreters who would like to maintain that the Methodist leader looked quite favorably upon this tradition. Wesley had traveled to Herrnhut, so to speak; he never went to Constantinople.

Given the paradigm shift that has taken place in Wesley studies in the later part of the twentieth century, in which "Eastern Orthodoxy" has been deemed perhaps the most important theological tradition upon which Wesley drew in his own theology of sanctification, one is actually surprised to learn of the relative paucity of references to the Eastern Fathers in a very large Wesleyan corpus, though numerous citations and allusions to Scripture can be found throughout. To illustrate, the references to eastern authors found in Wesley's published works have been carefully gathered and listed by Ted Campbell (in an appendix) in his book *John Wesley and Christian Antiquity*.[72] When each reference in the Wesleyan corpus is considered against the larger stream of traditional sources (Anglican, Puritan, Moravian, Pietist, Lutheran, and so on) that fed into Wesley's theology, one can only conclude that the recent paradigm shift in Wesley studies, especially when those studies ignore the contributions of other significant traditions, not only is based on an exaggerated estimation of the influence of eastern writings on Wesley's thought, but also, and perhaps more important, fails to distinguish between the *similarity* of ideas and the more difficult-to-prove matter of their direct *causation*. To be sure, that Wesley's views on entire sanctification were *similar* to those of the Eastern Fathers is readily conceded and affirmed. However, that these same fathers were the *source*, the direct cause, of Wesley's key insights in this area is energetically denied. Here, Wesley's own reckoning on the matter, offered on at least three occasions in his writings, must be considered decisive.

Moreover, though much has been made of Wesley's inclusion of the Pseudo-Macarian homilies[73] in his *Christian Library*, there are problems here as well. For one thing, Wesley had probably been introduced to this literature, interestingly enough, by some of his pietist friends (in a German translation) while he was in Georgia. However, not only are the references to this literature in Wesley's own writings scarce, but also the Methodist leader's principal citation of the Macarian literature is not even on the much-discussed contemporary topic of *theosis* or sanctification, but on that of *sin*. In other words, the Pseudo-Macarian homilies served to substantiate for Wesley the important truth, affirmed by the church from the earliest of times, that sin remains in the believer, that the carnal nature yet troubles a son or daughter of God. To illustrate, in his sermon "The Scripture Way of Salvation," produced in 1765, Wesley states:

> How exactly did Macarius, fourteen hundred years ago, describe the present experience of the children of God! "The unskillful (or inexperienced), when grace operates, presently imagine they have no more sin. Whereas they that have discretion cannot deny that even we who have the grace of God may be molested again."[74]

This is not to deny, of course, that Wesley most probably valued these homilies for their clear presentation of the holy life; and several modern scholars have made this claim, Albert Outler chief among them. In at least one place in this literature, for instance, Pseudo-Macarius employs the image of the "circumcision of the heart" as one that adequately depicts the work of perfection in the soul.[75] But it must also be borne in mind that Wesley's editing of these homilies was done both carefully and intentionally, no doubt reflecting some of his own eighteenth-century Anglican judgments. Not surprisingly then, Wesley painstakingly omitted each and every reference to the ascetic life in these homilies; and whenever he encountered the term *theosis* (divinization), a favorite of the Eastern Orthodox, he simply removed it and substituted his more easily understood (and western) term *sanctification*.[76] Add to this Kurowski's recent work, which has underscored several key theological differences between Pseudo-Macarius and Wesley (especially in the areas of grace, the image of God, and human freedom),[77] and the picture that is beginning to emerge is that although Wesley clearly appreciated some of the insights of Pseudo-Macarius, especially in the area of *hamartiology*, he nevertheless remained quite critical of some aspects of this Syrian monk's theology. As with the work of other Fathers, here was a critical appropriation, one that was informed not only by a larger theological vision, a real concert of voices, in which Anglican, Moravian, and Lutheran notions were in the mix, but also one that in its criticism was ever attentive to a biblical idiom.[78]

The Importance of the Anglican and Pietist Traditions

Though many theological streams clearly fed into Wesley's sophisticated and well-nuanced thought, he often explicated the insights so acquired from the resources of his own Anglican tradition. For example, earlier, with respect to the teaching of justification by faith alone, Wesley had comprehended the necessarily *instantaneous* nature of this work of grace (as a reflection of the larger issue of faith and works) through the able teaching of the pietist leader Peter Böhler.[79] But afterward, Wesley articulated the substance of this teaching by means of the Anglican Homilies, especially after he had begun more narrowly to inquire what the doctrine of the Church of England is concerning the much controverted point of justification by faith.[80]

In a similar fashion, the substance of Wesley's deepest insights concerning Christian perfection came from Anglican sources[81] (Taylor and Law) as well as from medieval mysticism (à Kempis), as noted earlier; even though Moravian pietism, reflecting the genius of the Continental Reformation, once again, made an important and lasting contribution. And though Wesley took pride in *A Plain Account* in not having changed his views over the last forty years— a boast that, once again, highlights the initial and ongoing significance of the western triumvirate—he actually made a crucial change in 1741, as Luke Tyerman has noted.[82] At that time, Wesley took the key insight of the instantaneous nature of justification as that which held in place the sheer gratuity of grace, a truth that he had learned from Böhler; and he then applied it, remarkably enough, to his understanding of Christian perfection. In other words, entire sanctification, like justification, occurs in a moment simply because this *supernatural* work of grace represents the utter *favor* of God and is nothing less than a sheer *gift*. For example, in his sermon "The Scripture Way of Salvation," produced in 1765, Wesley reflects on the larger issue of faith and works as they pertain to entire sanctification: "Look for it [entire sanctification] then every day, every hour, every moment. Why not this hour, this moment? Certainly you may look for it *now*, if you believe it is by faith."[83]

This means, then, that for Wesley, not only was the substance of entire sanctification informed largely by Western sources, but also the manner of its actualization, its instantiation. To be sure, the reformation emphasis of *sola gratia*, developed by Continental Protestants and Pietists, streamed into Wesley's understanding of Christian Perfection where it took shape in his instantaneous motif, apart from which his teaching cannot be properly understood. In this way, Wesley continued the Reformation in his insistence that transformation, the very heart of sanctification, represents grace not simply as divine empowerment, but as divine favor as well. Here, in other words, the usual division of labor, so to speak, between the juridical and the therapeutic aspects of redemption, once again, breaks down; for grace as divine favor informs both justification and entire sanctification. Wesley states, "Exactly as we are justified by faith, so are we sanctified by faith. Faith is the condition, and the *only* condition of sanctification, *exactly as* it is of justification."[84]

This largely Protestant theological context that marked an earnestness to recover the gracious truths of the gospel—some of which had been rendered opaque by the theological obfuscations of the Middle Ages—is hardly characteristic of Eastern Orthodox notions of sanctification even today—notions that, because of their unswerving emphasis on *process*, are unable to include, in a conjunctive way, the broader theological significance of Wesley's instantaneous motif, *especially as it relates to entire sanctification*. Indeed, the catholicity that Wesley sought in his own theological understanding never repudiated the considerable value of his own Anglican Church or its sufficiency as a "catholic" communion of faith that not only was enormously rich in theological resources, but also rightly avoided the excesses of both Rome and Geneva.[85] And if Wesley's conceptions of *both* justifying *and* sanctifying graces were rightly informed by key Reformation insights, apart from which they cannot be properly understood, then it should also be noted that these same insights, once again, had hardly made their way to Constantinople.

The Witnesses to Perfect Love

Though Charles Wesley, like his brother John, affirmed throughout the 1760s the importance of going on to perfection, there nevertheless were some noteworthy differences in their respective doctrines. For one thing, Charles apparently afforded a greater place for suffering on the road to perfect love than did John; and during the summer of 1766, Wesley, for his part, implied that his younger brother had set perfection so high that there could hardly be any witnesses to it. In terms of his own teaching, however, John declared: "One word more, concerning setting perfection too high. *That perfection* which I believe, I can boldly preach, because I think I see five hundred witnesses of it."[86] Observe here the proper relation between Scripture and experience for Wesley: Experience is not the source of doctrine, but its confirmation. In other words, experience cannot create a doctrine absent from—or contradictory to—the biblical witness. Nevertheless, if a supposed biblical teaching had no living witnesses to attest to its truth, then Wesley, as others, could only conclude that this particular *interpretation* of Scripture was in error. To illustrate, on the topic of Christian perfection, Wesley exclaimed, "For if there be *no living witness* of what we have preached for twenty years, I cannot, dare not preach it any longer."[87] Experience, then, held great hermeneutical power for Wesley, and it was one of the principal reasons he believed Charles's views, at least in some respects, called for modification.

Some wondered, however, like George Whitefield, if Wesley was somewhat naive in receiving so many testimonies to perfect love: "If a man says, 'I now feel nothing but love,' and I know him to be an honest man, I believe him," Wesley opined.[88] Actually, many of these professors were well known to Wesley, for they were a part of the Methodist societies and participated in either bands or select societies where their behavior could be readily assessed. On one occasion, for instance, Wesley wrote, "I believe within five weeks six in one class have received remission of sins and five in one band received a second blessing."[89] So then, it was often in a communal setting, in the context of a band or select society meeting, that many of the Methodists awaited the second work of grace. It was here, in other words, that the Lord would often speak to their hearts a second time, "Be thou clean."

Forthright and honest as he was, Wesley realized that some who testified to the reality of perfect love would eventually lose such grace and that still others would descend so low as to be under the power or dominion of sin once more. Nevertheless, in good Arminian fashion, Wesley was clearly unwilling to deny the earlier *reality* of entirely sanctifying grace, despite its subsequent loss. In June 1763, for instance, Wesley elaborates in his journal:

> A little after preaching, one came to me who believed God had just set her soul at full liberty. She had been clearly justified long before but said the change she now experienced was "extremely different" from what she experienced then, "as different as the noonday light from that of daybreak"; that she now "felt her soul all love and quite swallowed up in God." Now suppose, ten weeks or ten months hence, this person should be cold or dead; shall I say, "She *deceived* herself; this was merely the work of her own *imagination*"? Not at all; I have no right so to judge, nor authority to speak. I will rather say, "She was *unfaithful* to the grace of God, and so *cast away* what was *really given.*"[90]

Though Wesley obviously took great pains to affirm the reality of entirely sanctifying grace wherever it was to be found, he nevertheless rejected some testimonies he judged to be ill conceived or misguided: "I spent the greatest part of this day in examining them one by one. The testimony of some I could not receive."[91] And then there were those odd professions of faith—some of them made repeatedly and with much energy—that Wesley believed to be evidence not of perfect love, but of fanaticism—and that of the rankest sort.

The Bell and Maxfield Fiasco

Wesley's example of preaching the doctrine of Christian perfection in a balanced, tempered, and judicious way was unfortunately not followed by all of his preachers. George Bell, for instance, who had been converted in 1758 and was subsequently associated with Thomas Maxfield and John Wesley at the Foundery, preached Christian perfection in London and peppered his sermons with screaming and with wild gesticulations from the pulpit. His "perfection," if that's even the proper term, was frankly antinomian: free from rule, precept, and good judgment. Indeed, so fanatical was Bell that he actually believed he had a miraculous power to discern the spirits, and he sharply condemned his opponents—mistaking them for the enemies of God—on this basis.[92] Hearing several disturbing reports, Wesley investigated the whole matter; and after meeting with Bell in December 1762 and realizing that there would be no change in his behavior, Wesley expelled this ranting preacher from his leadership role in the London societies of West Street and the Foundery. The following month, Wesley met with Bell and tried to convince him, in a very pastoral way, of his numerous mistakes, the latest one being the teaching that the world would end on February 28 of that same year. After this meeting, which by the way did not go well, George Bell and those associated with him, such as John Dixon, Joseph Calvert, and Benjamin Biggs, quit the Methodist society and renounced all fellowship with John Wesley.

Thomas Maxfield, a friend of George Bell's, was similarly caught up in this controversy. This is the same preacher, it will be recalled, whom Susanna Wesley had recommended to her son in 1740. Now, more then twenty years later, Wesley was no longer satisfied with Maxfield's ministry, in particular with his deprecation of justification (teaching a justified person is not born of God) and his repudiation of instantaneous entire sanctification. In a stinging letter, drafted in October 1762, Wesley rebuked his erring disciple: "You have over and over denied instantaneous sanctification to *me*. But I have known and taught it (and so has my brother, as our writings show) above these twenty years."[93] And some scholars believe that two of Wesley's publications in 1762, that is, "Cautions and Directions Given to the Greatest Professors in the Methodist Societies" as well as "A Blow at the Root; or, Christ Stabbed in the House of His Friends," were both written with an eye to Maxfield.[94]

So disruptive was the ministry of Maxfield that a division emerged in some of the London societies. Mrs. Coventry, for example, threw down her class ticket and those of her husband, daughters, and servants and proclaimed that she would " 'hear *two doctrines* no longer.' . . . Mr. Maxfield preached *perfection*, but Mr. Wesley pulled it down."[95] John Wesley's reply to this criticism was quick and to the point: "So I did; that perfection of Benjamin Harris, G. Bell, and all who abetted them."[96] By March 1763, Maxfield had actually excluded himself from the Methodist pulpit by refusing to preach at the Foundery. "[And] so the breach is made," Wesley declared.[97] But the damage had already been done. "They [Bell and Maxfield] made the very name of Perfection stink in the nostrils," Wesley wrote, "even of those who loved and honored it before."[98] That same year, Maxfield became an independent minister in London, severing all connection with John Wesley.

The Bell-Maxfield fiasco convinced Wesley that greater care and discipline had to be exercised in terms of *what* was preached from a Methodist pulpit. To that end, the Methodist Conference that met in 1763 adopted the Model Deed and inserted it into the *Minutes*.[99] This document was important for two reasons: First, it established a standard of doctrine for preachers in accordance with John Wesley's *Explanatory Notes upon the New Testament* and his four volumes of *Sermons*. Second, the Deed created a line of succession, so to speak. That is, the right to appoint preachers after the deaths of John and Charles Wesley and William Grimshaw, a trusted associate, was guaranteed to the Conference. In this way, Wesley hoped to bring greater order and stability to the ongoing life of Methodism.

CHAPTER NINE
A Contentious Decade

The Methodist Chapel at Oxford as It Appeared in Wesley's Time

Throughout the second half of the eighteenth century, England was growing along numerous lines. In terms of population, her numbers swelled from roughly 5.8 million in 1750 to nearly nine million by the end of the century; and the cities, especially London, Manchester, and Birmingham, felt the impact.[1] Despite this increase, English society, for the most part, remained something of a pyramid with very few at the top and all too many at the bottom. Earlier in the century, Daniel Defoe, the noted author, had suggested a seven-fold division of the English people along the following lines:

1. The great, who live profusely
2. The rich, who live plentifully
3. The middle sort, who live well
4. The working trades, who labor hard, but feel no want
5. The country people, farmers, etc., who fare indifferently
6. The poor, who fare hard
7. The miserable, who really pinch and suffer want.[2]

This stratification of society over the course of the eighteenth century was affected by a number of social, economic, and scientific changes known collectively as the Industrial Revolution. Among other things, James Watt's perfection of his steam engine in 1775; Arkwright's frame (1769), Hargreaves's jenny (1770), and Crompton's mule (1779), which helped advance the textile industry; as well as technical advances in the smelting of iron with coal, which made the production of cast iron both rapid and cheap, all helped pave the way to a new world.[3] As a consequence of these and other changes, labor was slowly transferred from primary goods to the production of manufactured ones; technical efficiency rose dramatically due to the increased use of machines; and tasks became increasingly routine and specialized with the result that significantly more manufactured goods were produced than ever before. Moreover, since manufacturing on such a scale also demanded large investments of capital, new class distinctions as well as the rise of the urban poor were left in the wake of such industrialization.

Though Wesley was often adept at pointing out the inconsistencies of his theological opponents, he nevertheless struggled, at times, to understand in a penetrating way some of the more systemic social and economic evils of the day. As his nation was making this transition from a mercantilist economy to a capitalist one (Adam Smith's *An Inquiry into the Nature and Causes of the Wealth of Nations* was published in 1776), Wesley plodded along in his *Thoughts on the Present Scarcity of Provisions*, produced in 1773, and reduced the stubborn complexities of unemployment, a lack of food, and inflation to his own personal moral concerns with respect to the liquor industry, taxes, and luxury. Indeed, Wesley's ongoing fear of wealth—as well as the corruption it can bring to the human heart—is actually the lodestar of much of his economic analysis. And while such a vantage point can, no doubt, reveal some of the faults of eighteenth-century England, it nevertheless offers little footing for a convincing and judicious prescription for the way ahead.

Wesley and British Politics

The politics of this period, especially during the 1760s and thereafter, were equally complicated and at times turbulent. In the eyes of some, the Hanoverian monarchs would always lack legitimacy; but George III, who could at least speak English, had the added misfortune of alienating the colorful and oddly popular figure John Wilkes. Criticizing an earlier speech of the king in the anti-Tory journal *The North Briton* in April 1763, Wilkes was arrested, imprisoned, and charged with seditious libel. The opposition leader was soon released, however, on the basis that he had not been given due process and that his parliamentary privilege had been violated. A salacious and vulgar piece, "An Essay on Woman," that surfaced this same year was associated with Wilkes's name (though he was most likely not the author of it); and he was, therefore, expelled from Parliament. Not willing to face these new charges of libel and blasphemy, Wilkes fled to France for a season but returned to England in 1768 to be elected to Parliament once more. His base of support in Middlesex elected him on three occasions, but the House of Commons invalidated the election each time. And when the seat of Wilkes was eventually offered to his defeated opponent, Luttrell, the lower and middle classes of London erupted in riots. Wilkes had become by this time a *cause célèbre*, the emblem of free speech and liberty.

While the Wilkes affair was still in full flush, Wesley was entreated by a friend to respond to this political controversy. The Methodist leader entered the fray quite reluctantly and noted in the opening paragraph of his essay *Free Thoughts on the Present State of Public Affairs*, "I am no politician; politics lie quite out of my province."[4] Enlarging on this theme, Wesley wryly noted: "I grant every cobbler, tinker, porter, and hackney-coachman can do this; but I am not so deep learned: while they are sure of everything, I am in a manner sure of nothing."[5]

For many English as well as for some Americans, the name Wilkes stood for liberty and for protection against what they perceived to be an increasingly tyrannical Parliament. In fact, Virginia sent tobacco and Boston shipped turtles to Wilkes while he was in prison, and the government of South Carolina offered him 1,500 pounds to pay his debts.[6] Wesley, however, was not so taken in by the likes of Wilkes and considered him to be something of a rabble-rouser who misprized English liberties and thereby misled the people. In his essay, for example, Wesley distinguishes between civil and religious liberty and maintains, in contrast to the radicals, that the English never enjoyed such liberty as they do today. Fearful that some were even then "sowing the seeds of rebellion," Wesley cautions against the willful disobedience and rebellion that give life to tyranny in the form of "king mob."

A few years after the riots in London had occurred, in 1772, Wesley penned his *Thoughts Upon Liberty* and developed some of the same themes of his earlier essay. "Religious liberty is a liberty to choose our own religion to worship God according to our own conscience," Wesley reasons.[7] And "every man living, as man, has a right to this, as he is a rational creature."[8] Did England, then, lack such liberty as some political malcontents had maintained? Wesley replies,

> His late Majesty was desired, about thirty years ago, to take a step of this kind. But his answer was worthy of a King, yea, the King of a free people: "I tell you, while I set on the English throne, no man shall be persecuted for conscience' sake."[9]

And when Wesley explores the nature and extent of civil liberty in the realm, the other half of the equation, so to speak, he likewise finds it everywhere abundant:

> What is civil liberty? A liberty to enjoy our lives and fortunes in our own way; to use our property, whatever is legally our own according to our own choice. And can you deny, "that we are robbed of this liberty?" Who are? Certainly I am not . . . I still enjoy full civil liberty. I am free to live, in every respect, according to my own choice. My life, my person, my property, are safe.[10]

A few years later in his *Calm Address to the Inhabitants of England*, Wesley distinguishes his Tory sentiments from all notions of Jacobitism, the ill-founded and often-leveled charge of the Whigs; and he affirms that "English liberty commenced at the [Glorious] Revolution. And how entire is it at this day."[11] Elsewhere in this same treatise, Wesley elaborates:

> Every man says what he will, writes what he will, prints what he will. Every man worships God, if he worships him at all, as he is persuaded in his own mind. Every man enjoys his own property; nor can the King himself take a shilling of it but according to law. . . . So that it is impossible to conceive a fuller liberty than we enjoy both as to religion, life, body and goods.[12]

Wesley not only disagreed with the increasingly popular political rhetoric in England, but also thought that its first principles, its foundational presuppositions and assumptions, were often badly flawed. To address these basic issues, Wesley published his *Thoughts on the Origin of Power* in 1772 and thereby displayed, once again, his traditional "High Church Tory thinking."[13] In this essay, after Wesley contends that the supreme power, "the power over life and death, and consequently over our liberty,"[14] comes from above such that the powers that reign in the nation are "ordained of God," he demonstrates the inconsistency, if not the hypocrisy, of those political leaders who championed the notion that all power comes from the people when these very same leaders excluded, for no good reason, over half of the population; that is, women, young men, and those who lacked forty shillings a year.

Wesley and American Politics: Slavery

Some of Wesley's other political writings of the time greatly offended not so much the English, but the Americans, especially when he considered the basic liberty and dignity that pertains to all human beings. To illustrate, Wesley strongly criticized American slavery, which denied slaves their basic human rights; and he denounced this practice late in his career in a letter to Wilberforce in the following fashion: "Go on, in the name of God and in the power of his might, till even American slavery (the vilest that ever saw the sun) shall vanish away before it."[15]

Earlier, in 1774, Wesley had produced his essay *Thoughts Upon Slavery*, in which he impugned the logic that kept this vicious practice in place. The grand plea of American slaveholders was that this practice, though controversial, was *legal*. Drawing from some of the insights expressed in his earlier sermon "The Original, Nature, Properties and Use of the Law," Wesley reasons that a human or positive law cannot overturn natural law; it cannot, as he puts it, "change the nature of things."[16] In other words, not only are matters that pertain to the basic rights of humans, as beings created in the image of God, not subject to the whims of the crowd or to the vagaries of their *votes* but also laws that express the popular will are valid *only* to the extent that they are in harmony with natural or moral law, with "the everlasting fitness of all things that are or ever were created."[17] Wesley elaborates:

> If neither captivity nor contract can, by the plain law of nature and reason, reduce the parent to a state of slavery, much less can they reduce the offspring. It clearly follows that all slavery is as irreconcilable to justice as to mercy.[18]

And with respect to the evasion of some American slaveholders that they did not buy their slaves, but simply inherited them, Wesley was both adamant and consistent: "Is it enough to satisfy your own conscience? Had your father, have you, has any man living, a right to use another as a slave?"[19] Liberty, both civil and religious, is the right of every human being "as soon as he breathes the vital air."[20] The taskmasters of slavery, therefore, had no basis to deny their slaves the very rights that they so zealously protected for themselves. This inconsistency, even hypocrisy, cannot bear the weight of either reasoned argument or the requirements of the love of God and neighbor. "Give liberty to whom liberty is due," Wesley insists, "that is, to every child of man, to every partaker of human nature."[21]

The American Revolution

In the middle of the eighteenth century, England and France vied for power in North America during the French and Indian War (1754–1763), a struggle that resulted in a complete victory for the British, though the toll in both human lives and expenditures had been great. To alleviate some of the economic burden of the war—the national debt had risen from 70 million to 130 million pounds[22]—England taxed the colonies in light of the counsel of George Grenville, the prime minister: "Limit the expense and make the Americans pay a share."[23] The Americans suffered under this added burden, and in time, the rallying cry among the colonists became, "Taxation without representation is tyranny."

Interestingly enough, Wesley's early views toward the American colonists had actually been sympathetic, and he, too, was apparently troubled by some of the policies of Grenville. For example, in his *Free Thoughts on the Present State of Public Affairs*, drafted in 1768, Wesley exclaims: "I do not defend the measures which have been taken with regard to America: I doubt whether any man can defend them, either on the foot of law, equity or prudence."[24] But much had changed by 1775 (the Boston Massacre as well as the Boston Tea Party had taken place, for instance); and in that year, Wesley wrote to Lord North as follows:

> I do not intend to enter upon the question [of] whether the Americans are in the right or in the wrong. Here all my prejudices are against the Americans; for I am an High Churchman, the son of an High Churchman, bred up from my childhood in the highest notions of passive obedience and non-resistance.[25]

These comments to North are intriguing in the sense that Wesley had connected the temporal and spiritual realms, that is, the political order with an ecclesiastical one. Such linkage was standard fare for many of England's eighteenth-century Tories, having been schooled on such notions since the Anglican Reformation. "There is the closest connexion . . . between my religious and my political conduct." Wesley later wrote, "the selfsame authority enjoining me to 'fear God' and to 'honor the King.' "[26] That Wesley had actually drunk deeply from the wells of this long-standing tradition is also evidenced by his tying together favor for his doctrine of Christian perfection with obedience to the king: "Those who are the avowed enemies of Christian Perfection," Wesley observed, "are in general the warmest enemies of King George and of all that are in authority under him."[27]

The year 1775 is again an important window on Wesley's changing political views because during this time, he also read Samuel Johnson's *Taxation No Tyranny*, a work Wesley subsequently edited and then published under the title *A Calm Address to Our American Colonies*. Johnson, the noted English writer and lexicographer, was grateful that his ideas were receiving a broader hearing, despite the apparent plagiarism. However, as Henry Rack has noted, "Even allowing for relaxed contemporary standards in this matter, Wesley was remarkably cavalier in his borrowings."[28]

At any rate, with the publication of *A Calm Address*, Wesley demonstrated that he was in many respects "a true-blue Anglican . . . a paladin of the Crown and the law."[29] Exploring the grand question that preoccupied the journals of the day, "Has the English Parliament a right to tax the American colonies?"[30] Wesley reaffirms that nothing could be more plain than "that the supreme power in England has a legal right of laying any tax upon them [the American colonists] for any end beneficial to the whole empire."[31] Indeed, Wesley reasons that whoever denies the English Parliament the power to tax also denies it the right to make any laws at all. Beyond this, Wesley carefully reminds the American colonists that they are in a "state of nature," that they have "sunk down into colonists, governed by a charter," and that, perhaps more important, their ancestors had ceded to the king and Parliament, "the power of disposing, without their consent, of both their lives, liberties, and properties."[32] Moreover, as if these views were not difficult enough, the political judgments expressed toward the end of this treatise would certainly give pause to many American Methodists in the days ahead, especially when their "father in the gospel" exclaims, "No governments under heaven are so despotic as the republican; no subjects are governed in so arbitrary a manner as those of a commonwealth."[33] And in language that went beyond Johnson's original work, Wesley concludes that the real ground of our calamities is sin, "which never will or can be thoroughly removed, till we fear God and honor the King!"[34]

The following year, Richard Price, the noted Unitarian, published *Observations on the Nature of Civil Liberty, the Principles of Government and the Justice and Policy of the War with America*, in which he championed many of the arguments of the American colonists with respect to liberty. So popular was this work that it quickly sold sixty thousand copies and about double that number shortly thereafter in a less expensive edition.[35] Wesley's *Some Observations on Liberty Occasioned by a Late Tract* was his quick response. Drawing on some of the elements of his earlier writings—*Thoughts Upon Liberty*, for instance—Wesley once again distinguishes religious and civil liberty in this present essay and, in contrast to Dr. Price, contends that the colonists, as British subjects, richly enjoy both freedoms. Wesley observes:

> There is unquestionably such a thing as the forfeiting of a charter: Whether the colonies have forfeited theirs or not, I leave others to determine. Whether they have or have not, there can be no reason for making the least doubt but, upon their laying down their arms, the Government will still permit them to enjoy both their civil and religious liberty in as ample a manner as ever their ancestors did, and as the English do at this day.[36]

Apparently, Wesley was hardly taken in by the language of liberty and freedom bandied about in many of the American political tracts. Behind such calls, he discerned in a careful and judicious way, not the cry for liberty, but the cry for *independency*.

As the father of Methodism, Wesley clearly had both an interest and a stake in the politics of the colonies even though Methodism in America during the 1770s was largely a lay movement. To illustrate, around 1760, Robert Strawbridge, an immigrant farmer, had organized meetings in Maryland and Virginia. Farther north, Philip Embury and his cousin, Barbara Heck, began a successful lay ministry in New York in 1766; and a year later, Captain Thomas Webb (whose highest military rank was actually that of Lieutenant) labored in Philadelphia. To aid these plantings of American Methodism, Wesley sent two of his more gifted lay preachers to the colonies in 1769, Richard Boardman and Joseph Pilmore. Two years later, Francis Asbury as well as Richard Wright joined their numbers.

As the tensions between the colonies and England grew worse, all of the preachers whom Wesley had sent to America returned home by 1777, with the exception of Francis Asbury, who, because of his talents and deep commitments, emerged as Wesley's counterpart in the New World, the father of American Methodism.[37] Deeply committed to American democracy, Asbury often found Wesley's political views disappointing ("The greater share the people have in Government the less liberty, either civil or religious, does the nation in general enjoy.");[38] and such views naturally posed problems for the American Methodists from time to time that Congregationalists and Presbyterians hardly suffered at all. Moreover, Wesley complicated matters even further the following year by publishing the sermon "The Late Work of God in North America," a work that explored the decline of *true religion* in the New World not only in terms of the corrosive power of wealth as it led to the "complication of pride, luxury, sloth, and wantonness,"[39] a favorite theme of Wesley's, but also in terms of the "spirit of independency diffusing itself from north to south."[40]

Though Wesley freely expressed his own political views in essays, tracts, and published sermons, he nevertheless maintained that all political speech against the king should be strictly avoided in the pulpit. "There is a plain command in the Bible, 'Thou shalt not speak evil of the ruler of the people,' " Wesley cautioned.[41] Indeed, since it is the main duty of gospel preachers to "preach Jesus Christ, and him crucified,"[42] the only kind of political preaching that Wesley tolerated in a Methodist pulpit was the refutation of the evil speaking and the vile aspersions cast against the king. And the Methodist leader substantiated this counsel in the following way:

> It is always difficult and frequently impossible for private men to judge of the measures taken by men in public offices.... Generally, therefore, it behooves us to be silent, as we may suppose they know their own business best.[43]

Again, Wesley insists, "it [is] our main business to preach 'repentance towards God, and faith in our Lord Jesus Christ.' "[44] It is the proclamation of the gospel, the glad tidings of salvation, not divisive ideology, that must ever resound in the church.

Domestic Affairs

It is quite ironic that shortly before Wesley began discoursing on justice on a grand scale—that is, on the political level in terms of both Britain and her American colonies—his personal life was deeply troubled. His wife, Mary, for instance, pained by the ongoing inattention, finally left Wesley in September 1774. Thus, the earlier cycle of leaving and returning—played out most notably in 1758, 1768, and 1771—had finally been broken.

A month before Mary left, Wesley had imprudently decided to draft a letter rehashing nearly all of his wife's faults from the time of their wedding some twenty-three years earlier to the present. Naturally, the incidents surrounding Sarah Ryan were recounted in some detail as was Mary's practice of opening her husband's correspondence. Perhaps Wesley reopened these old wounds because he wanted to give added force to the letter's conclusion that a wife should be utterly humble, insignificant, and governed by her husband—the only solution to his marital discord that this erring husband was apparently willing to recognize. As in the past, Wesley cautioned his wife:

> Do not any longer contend for mastery, for power, money, or praise. Be content to be a private, insignificant person, known

and loved by God and me. Attempt no more to abridge me of the liberty which I claim by the laws of God and man. Leave *me* to be governed by God and my own conscience. Then shall I govern *you* with gentle sway.[45]

This was hardly a prescription for reconciliation. Such appeals had not worked in the past; they would not work now or in the future.

Though the couple was irrevocably separated in 1774—an arrangement that was apparently mutually satisfying—this by no means put an end to relationship. Indeed, John and Mary Wesley continued to correspond at least until October 1778. One issue that surfaced in this late correspondence was Mary's poor judgment in relating some of her husband's incautious remarks to his opponents, namely, the Calvinistic Methodists—a group that had already become estranged from Wesley earlier in the decade. And though this particular incident actually began in 1775, it does not appear in the extant correspondence until 1777, at which time Wesley complained:

> Likewise you have spoken all manner of evil against me, particularly to my enemies and the enemies of the cause I live to support. Hereby many bad men have triumphed and been confirmed in their evil ways. . . . A sword has been put into the hands of the enemies of God, and the children of God have been armed against one another.[46]

In past separations, when Mary had fled the Wesley home, John was willing to allow her to return whenever she pleased and without stipulation; but this was no longer the case. Indeed, in the same letter that Wesley criticized his wife's actions, he also laid down three conditions that had to be met before she could return: (1) restore his papers, (2) promise to take no more, and (3) retract what she had said against him.[47] Mary had left easily in the past; she could no longer easily return. Forgiveness was now laden with conditions.

With the deterioration of the relationship, the very last letter Wesley wrote to his wife was by no means conciliatory. Wesley saw too clearly the injustices done to him to be well aware of his wife's own justified grievances. Sadly, the letter is composed of little more than a repetition of past charges and concludes with an even larger condition for return: "If you were to live a thousand years," Wesley declared to his wife, "you could not undo the mischief that you have done. And till you have done all you can towards it, I bid you farewell."[48] Conditions or not, Mary was not about to return. The years of travel, relative neglect, and life with an authoritarian—and at times self-righteous—husband had taken their toll.

When Mary Wesley died a few years later on October 8, 1781, John was not immediately informed; and he, consequently, did not attend her funeral. But one suspects that even if Wesley had been aware of the time and place of the service, he would not have attended anyway—a suspicion strengthened by the observation that his wife's death left "no ripple on the correspondence."[49] The last breach, regrettably, had been that wide.

The Calvinist Controversy

As difficult as the breakup of Wesley's marriage was during the 1770s, yet another relationship that had turned remarkably sour was with the Calvinist Methodists. As with his marriage, the relationship with the Calvinists was complicated, leaving room for much misunderstanding; and it was worsened by Wesley's own actions. For instance, wanting to spark a conversation with the Calvinists over some key theological issues, Wesley crudely summarized what he took to be the teachings of Augustus M. Toplady, curate at Broad Hembury and author of the hymn "Rock of Ages." Not content with this, Wesley then had the audacity to affix Toplady's initials, without his permission, to the oddly drawn document:

> One in twenty (suppose) of mankind are elected; nineteen in twenty are reprobated. The elect shall be saved, do what they will; the reprobate shall be damned, do what they can. Reader, believe this, or be damned. Witness my hand, A_____ T_____.[50]

Naturally, Toplady was incensed and wanted to engage his detractor in dialogue, but Wesley simply refused: "Mr. Augustus Toplady I know well," Wesley opined, "But I do not fight with chimney-sweepers. He is too dirty a writer for me to meddle with. I should only foul my fingers."[51]

By the fall of 1770, George Whitefield, the gifted orator and Calvinist leader, had died at Newburyport, Massachusetts, on his seventh preaching tour of America. The trustees of the Tabernacle at Greenwich in England invited Wesley to preach the funeral sermon there on November 23. Accepting this opportunity to praise his colleague in ministry, and perhaps also to put a good face on what had been at times a difficult relationship, Wesley chose as his text Numbers 23:10: "Let me die the death of the righteous, and let my last end be like his!" (KJV). In the third part of his sermon, Wesley underscored the fundamental doctrines that Whitefield had proclaimed, namely, justification by faith and the new birth, never once mentioning the "eternal covenant" or absolute predestination. This omission, naturally, roiled Whitefield's Calvinist friends, and thus the seeds were planted for the fierce controversy that was soon to come.

Earlier, at the Methodist Conference in August 1770, Wesley and his preachers concluded that they had leaned too much toward Calvinism. This observation had already been made in 1744, but now it was offered with more force and with even less guarded language in eight propositions. Upon reading these Conference *Minutes,* Lady Huntingdon, who had been associated with the Wesleys from the earliest days of the Revival, was greatly disturbed. This is the same woman who had walked out in protest with Wesley in the midst of the Fetter Lane controversy in 1740. But in the meantime much had changed. Now the Countess had become the patron of many of the Calvinist Methodists, having embraced their views after corresponding with Howell Harris; and she subsequently founded a college at Trevecca in 1768 for the training of preachers. From her new theological vantage point, this Calvinist benefactor referred to the *Minutes* of the 1770 Conference as nothing less than "popery unmasked."[52] Accordingly, in January 1771, Lady Huntingdon dismissed Joseph Benson from Trevecca for what amounted to adherence to Wesley's "popish" views. The saintly John Fletcher, confidant of Wesley's and president of the college, resigned in support of Benson, his gifted protégé.

Somewhat surprised by the energy of the Calvinist reaction, in particular to the criticism that he had received in the first half of 1771 at the hands of William Romaine in the *Gospel Magazine,* Wesley reviewed the whole affair in a letter to Mary Bishop that same year and concluded with respect to the "infamous" eight propositions:

The more I consider them, the more I like them, the more fully I am convinced, not only that they are true, agreeable both to Scripture and to sound experience, but that they contain truths of the deepest importance.[53]

Moreover, in an earlier letter to John Fletcher, dated March 22, 1771, Wesley affirmed that the blood and righteousness of Christ are the sole meritorious cause of our salvation and then inquired, "Who is there in England that has asserted these things more strongly and steadily than I have done?"[54]

Walter Shirley, the cousin of Selina Lady Huntingdon, however, was not convinced. Sensing that the Conference *Minutes* of 1770 contained a "dreadful heresy," Shirley issued a "circular letter" that proposed a rival conference be held in August 1771, the same time as Wesley's upcoming meeting in Bristol. In addition, the letter recommended that the rival conference go as a body to Wesley's assembly and insist on a formal recantation of the *Minutes* of the previous year. The wide circulation of this letter, whose language in several places was unguarded, polarized the theological parties for a time; and Lady Glenorchy, for example, dismissed Wesley's preachers from her chapel shortly after its publication. This letter also created significant interest in the 1771 Conference, and Wesley, himself, noted in his journal that "we had more preachers than usual at the Conference in consequence of Mr. Shirley's circular letter."[55]

As promised, on August 8, 1771, Shirley and nine or ten others attended the conference at Bristol. After much discussion, Wesley concluded that "they were satisfied that we were not so dreadful heretics as they imagined, but were tolerably sound in the faith."[56] In an irenic move, Wesley and his preachers issued what in Wesley's eyes was simply a clarifying statement, but in Shirley's eyes constituted a retraction of the earlier minutes. The statement is worth quoting at length:

Whereas the doctrinal points in the Minutes of a Conference held in London, August 7th, 1770, have been understood to favor justification by works—Now, we, the Rev. John Wesley and others assembled in Conference, do declare that we had no such meaning, and that we abhor the doctrine of justification by works as a most perilous and abominable doctrine. And as the said Minutes are not sufficiently guarded in the way they are expressed, we hereby solemnly declare, in the sight of God, that we have no trust or confidence but in the alone merits of our Lord and Savior, Jesus Christ, for justification or salvation, either in life, death or the day of judgment. And though no one is a *real Christian* believer (and consequently cannot be saved) who doth not good works when there is time and opportunity, yet our works have no part in meriting or purchasing our justification, from first to last, either in whole or in part.[57]

Such a declaration quelled the flames of controversy at least for a time; and a letter, supposedly in Shirley's own writing, acknowledged that he had been too hasty in his judgment of Wesley's sentiments.[58]

But all was not well. For even before the ink had fully dried on Wesley's declaration, he sent off John Fletcher's *Vindication* of the Minutes of 1770 for publication (*First Check to Antinomianism*), notwithstanding Walter Shirley's earnest request not to do so. Fletcher, who at times was referred to as Wesley's "Vindicator," had been associated with the father of Methodism for several years. Born in Switzerland of a distinguished family, Fletcher refused to subscribe to some of the teachings of Calvinism, and he thus declined Swiss ordination as a young man. Emigrating to England in 1752, Fletcher served as a capable tutor and was soon attracted by the piety and earnestness of the Methodists. In 1757, after consultation with Wesley, Fletcher was ordained deacon in the Church of England on March 6 and a priest the following Sunday. A man not only of deep piety, Fletcher also possessed great intellectual skills—skills that Wesley clearly wanted to utilize given his current predicament. In fact, so confident was Wesley in Fletcher's ability, in his carefully reasoned arguments, that he wrote to the Countess of Huntingdon less than a week after the 1771 Conference:

"The principles established in the *Minutes*" I apprehend to be no way contrary to this, or to that faith, that consistent plan of doctrine, which was once delivered to the saints. I believe, whoever calmly considers Mr. Fletcher's Letters will be convinced of this. I fear, therefore, "zeal against those principles" is no less than zeal against the truth and against the honor of our Lord. "The preservation of His honor appears so sacred" to *me*, and has done for above these forty years.[59]

And then in what looked like a retraction of his earlier conciliatory declaration, Wesley was now so emboldened by his colleague's work as to declare to the Countess:

> But till Mr. Fletcher's printed letters are answered, I must think everything spoke against those *Minutes* is totally destructive of His honor, and a palpable affront to Him both as our Prophet and Priest, but more especially as King of His people.[60]

Encouraged by the reception of his *Vindication* and also by Wesley, John Fletcher published his *Second Check to Antinomianism* the following month. Wesley especially liked the title of this apologetic work since he believed that Calvinism could easily become "a deadly enemy to all Christian tempers."[61] Not surprisingly, the publication of the *Checks* brought the controversy to a new level of intensity. Rowland Hill, who preached for the Countess in her chapels, joined the fracas in the middle of 1772 with his *Friendly Remarks upon Fletcher's Checks*. Indeed, it was Fletcher's *Second Check* that had convinced Hill that he could no longer remain silent. And a few years later, in 1777, Hill published his *Imposture Detected*, a work whose tone left much to be desired. In fact, Richard Green described it as "a miserable piece of writing, marked by the lowest degree of rude abuse, fitter for Billingsgate than for the pen of a Christian minister."[62] Of this piece, Wesley related: "I read the truly wonderful performance of Mr. Rowland Hill. I stood amazed! Compared to him Mr. Toplady himself is a very civil, fair-spoken gentleman."[63]

Richard Hill, the brother of Rowland, picked up his pen in opposition after the publication of Fletcher's *Third Check to Antinomianism*. One of his more important works, "Review of all the Doctrines Taught by Mr. John Wesley," so irked Wesley, who accused Hill of throwing enough dirt with the hopes that some would stick,[64] that he decided to take time out of his busy schedule in order to offer a detailed reply. Accordingly, in his piece "Some Remarks on Mr. Hill's 'Review of all the Doctrines Taught by Mr. John Wesley,' " published in September 1772, Wesley pointed out the logical inconsistencies in Hill's own argument, its erroneous presuppositions and assumptions, as well as Hill's annoying habit of quoting the language of *A Christian Library* as if it were Wesley's own. "Observe," Wesley cautioned, "the question is, whether I contradict myself; not whether I contradict somebody else; be it Mr. Baxter, Goodwin, Fletcher, the 'Christian Library,' or even my own brother: These are not myself."[65] And of the term "Arminian" that had surfaced in Mr. Hill's *Review* as one of derision, Wesley observed:

> But so long as he remains in that sentiment, what peace am I or Mr. F., or indeed any *Arminian*, to expect from him? since any agreement with us would be "a covenant with death, and a conspiracy against the kingdom of Christ." I therefore give up all hope of peace with him, and with all that are thus minded. For I do not believe what he terms "the truths of God," the doctrine of absolute predestination.[66]

In his *Finishing Stroke*, published the following year, Richard Hill turned his attention not so much toward Wesley as toward Fletcher and accused him of caricaturing the Calvinist position. Fletcher's reply in this particular instance as well as his general comportment throughout the entire controversy convinced Wesley that he had finally found a suitable successor, a champion even, to lead the Methodists after he was gone. "But has God provided one so qualified? Who is he? Thou art the man!" Wesley declared to Fletcher in January 1773. But such an honor was not to be, for John Fletcher, who had suffered ill health from time to time, died about six years prior to John Wesley.

The Theology of the *Minutes*

What was it about the Conference *Minutes* of 1770 that had so disturbed the Calvinists? For one thing, this theological document was characterized by an imperative mood that employed such language as "work, labor, and obedience," which some thought undermined the doctrine of justification by faith alone. For example, the *Minutes* reiterated several judgments from the first Methodist Conference with respect to the place of works prior to justification and in a way that some could only find troubling:

> We have received it as a maxim, that "a man is to do nothing in order to justification." Nothing can be more false. Whoever desires to find favor with God, should "cease from evil, and learn

221

to do well." So God himself teaches by the Prophet Isaiah. Whoever repents, should "do works meet for repentance." And if this is not in order to find favor, what does he do them for.[67]

Because they were not privy to the intricacies of Wesley's doctrine of prevenient grace, the Calvinists of 1770 could only conclude, just as Lord Acton had done much later, that not only was Wesley teaching salvation by works, but also he had undermined the doctrine of justification by faith by allowing his theology to devolve into moralism, self-effort, and pious platitudes. The reality of Wesley's theology, however, was quite otherwise. Indeed, Wesley had other vocabularies, other rhetorics, in his theological repertoire, especially the distinction between "not in the same sense" and "not in the same degree," as these phrases pertained to the place of works *prior* to justification. To illustrate, these distinctions were not only employed in Wesley's early work *A Farther Appeal*, but also surfaced much later in the summary sermon "The Scripture Way of Salvation," produced in 1765. In the former work, for example, Wesley reasons:

> And yet I allow you this, that although both repentance and the fruits thereof are in *some sense* necessary before justification, yet neither the one nor the other is necessary in the *same sense* or in the *same degree* with faith. Not in the *same degree*: for in whatever moment a man believes (in the Christian sense of the word) he is justified, his sins are blotted out, "his faith is counted to him for righteousness.". . . Faith alone therefore justifies, which repentance alone does not, much less any outward work. And consequently none of these are necessary to justification in the *same degree* with faith.
>
> Nor in the *same sense*: for none of these has so direct, immediate a relation to justification as faith. This is *proximately* necessary thereto; repentance, *remotely*, as it is necessary to the increase or continuance of faith: and the fruits of repentance still more remotely, as they are necessary to repentance.[68]

The distinctions "not in the same sense" and "not in the same degree" noted above carry many of the nuances utilized by Wesley to articulate, on the one hand, the *necessity* of repentance and its fruits prior to justification—that made him look like a Roman Catholic in the eyes of the Calvinists—and, on the other hand, that repentance and its fruits do *not* justify—that made him look like the Evangelical Anglican that he actually was.

Again, by the first phrase, "not in the same sense," Wesley affirms that repentance is remotely *necessary* for justification, and its fruits are even more remotely so. "I cannot therefore agree, that 'we are accepted without any terms previously performed to qualify us for acceptance,' " Wesley exclaims, "For we are not accepted, nor are we qualified for, or capable of, acceptance, without repentance and faith."[69] Elsewhere, in his *Farther Appeal*, Wesley is even more emphatic and writes, "Repentance *absolutely* must go before faith; fruits meet for it, if there be opportunity."[70] Observe that the temporal element, that is, the condition "if there be time and opportunity for them," pertains only to works suitable for repentance and not to repentance itself. Repentance, though still only remotely or indirectly necessary to justifying faith, is apparently *always* necessary. In fact, when Wesley considers the case of the thief on the cross, he concludes that this abject criminal likewise came to faith in Christ through no other way than the path of repentance. "Even in the thief upon the cross," Wesley observes, "faith was attended by repentance, piety, and charity. . . . Repentance went before his faith."[71] Thus, by designating repentance as the free gift of God, Wesley underscored human inability apart from convincing grace; by designating repentance as the condition of justification, he pointed to the responsibilities entailed in the reception of such grace. Once again, grace-assisted cooperation, and not human merit or works righteousness, is the chord struck here.

Now if the phrase "not in the same sense" (or "in some sense") allows Wesley to affirm the *necessity* of repentance prior to justifying faith, then the second phrase, "not in the same degree," makes it clear that repentance and its fruits *do not justify*. To illustrate, in 1765, in his sermon "The Scripture Way of Salvation," which contains many of the same theological subtleties of the earlier *A Farther Appeal*, Wesley points out:

> But they [repentance and its fruits] are not necessary in the *same sense* with faith, nor in the *same degree*. Not in the *same degree*; for those fruits are only necessary *conditionally*, if there be time and opportunity for them. Otherwise a man may be justified without them, as was the "thief" upon the cross. . . . But he cannot be

justified without faith: this is impossible. Likewise let a man have ever so much repentance, or ever so many of the fruits meet for repentance, yet all this does not at all avail: he is not justified till he believes. But the moment he believes, with or without those fruits, yea, with more or less repentance, he is justified.[72]

So then, with this distinction "not in the same degree" in his theological repertoire, the elderly Wesley was able to declare that repentance and its works, though now in some sense necessary to justification, *do not justify*. Faith *alone* justifies. In fact, so insistent was Wesley concerning his teaching of *sola fide* that in the same year he wrote "The Scripture Way of Salvation," he also remarked to John Newton, "I think on Justification just as I have done any time these seven-and-twenty years, and just as Mr. Calvin does. In this respect I do not differ from him an hair's breadth."[73] Indeed, Wesley's claim of *sola fide* is actually a credible one, but only when it is considered not in terms of the first distinction, "not in the same sense," but in terms of the second distinction, "not in the same degree." Indeed, it is the confusion or the neglect of these two senses that led some to argue that Wesley had retreated from the notion of *sola fide*.

Wesley, no doubt, had compounded the problem with his Calvinistic critics, the Countess of Huntingdon[74] and Walter Shirley among them, because he had resorted to a single vocabulary (that works are in some sense necessary prior to justification) in the Conference *Minutes* to explicate a complex theological problem. However, even in the 1770s, Wesley had another theological vocabulary available to him, namely, the language of "not in the same degree," the language of *sola fide*. Such language, perhaps, would have demonstrated to and convinced some of the Calvinist Methodists that, for Wesley, repentance and its fruits, though indirectly necessary to justification, could *never* justify. But so much was lost in the heat of the polemics.

A second set of equally troubling issues explored by the 1770 Conference concerned the theological content of the eight freshly crafted theses that were offered as a review of the whole affair, the first four of which read as follows:

(1.) Who of us is now accepted of God?
He that now believes in Christ with a loving, obedient heart.

(2.) But who among those that never heard of Christ?
He that, according to the light he has, "feareth God and worketh righteousness."
(3.) Is this the same with "he that is sincere?" Nearly, if not quite.
(4.) Is not this salvation by works?
Not by the merit of works, but by works as a condition.[75]

Such language, without qualification, was unguarded and no doubt led to Wesley's earlier conciliatory tone. Indeed, this phrasing could easily lead to the conclusion that all that was required for redemption for those who did not know Christ was sincerity, or simply doing the best that they were able *(facere quod in se est)*. If that were the case, then the Calvinists did indeed have substantial grounds for complaint.

But as it was, the Calvinists had missed key theological distinctions—and once again Wesley didn't help them much at the time—that were the required background for a proper interpretation of the statement "fearing God and working righteousness." To illustrate, for Wesley, there were *degrees* of acceptance (due to prevenient grace); but not all degrees *necessarily* entailed justifying, regenerating faith, that distinct faith, which in delivering from both the guilt and power of sin makes one *holy*.

Viewed another way, many Calvinists had failed to comprehend how Wesley, due to his different understanding of (prevenient) grace, could *affirm* the faith of those who "feared God and worketh righteousness," in the broad sense even though they had never heard the name of Christ.[76] Wesley's theological opponents, perhaps, had immediately concluded that any such affirmation necessarily implied justification; but the Methodist leader had asserted no such thing. In fact, much earlier, in 1754, for instance, in his *Explanatory Notes upon the New Testament*, Wesley defines the faith of a servant in terms of the spirit of bondage and fear that cleaved to the old covenant.[77] Elsewhere, he associates the phrase with those who "fear God and worketh righteousness" as in his commentary on Acts 10:35.[78] However, this latter usage makes clear that the faith of a servant, at times, was conceived in a very broad way by the English leader and included all those believers of *whatever religious tradition* who endeavored to worship God according to the light and grace that they had. Wesley explains:

> But in every nation he that *feareth God and worketh righteousness* . . .
> is *accepted of him*—through Christ, though he knows him not. . . .
> He is in the favor of God, whether enjoying his written word and
> ordinances or not.[79]

Since those who fear God and work righteousness are accepted even though they may be ignorant of Christ, the Holy Scriptures, and the sacraments, this demonstrates that such acceptance is not indicative of justification or of the real, proper Christian faith, as some of the Calvinists may have surmised, but instead is an important implication, once again, of Wesley's doctrine of prevenient grace, which is both universal and christologically based.[80]

Accordingly, when the Conference *Minutes* of 1770 are critically examined in terms of the language of those who "fear God and work righteousness," it must be borne in mind that Wesley never employs the word "justified" or its cognates with respect to this material. The "acceptance," then, of those who have never heard of Christ or who have encountered the gospel but are not yet the children of God may mean that such people are *in process*, so to speak, that they are on *the way* of salvation and are, therefore, not to be discouraged. That is, these believers have received a degree of (prevenient) grace and so will be responsible for more. But they are not yet justified and born of God.

So then, Wesley's deft handling of the ongoing pastoral problem as to how to minister most effectively to those who have the faith of a servant, who "fear God and work righteousness," demonstrates, once again, not only the *conjunctive* nature of his theology, but also his sophisticated, and inclusive, understanding of grace. Put another way, Wesley held two things together, and in tension, not simply one: on the one hand, great pastoral sensitivity and care towards the aspirants of the redeeming graces of God, and on the other hand, the maintenance of the proper standards of the Christian faith. Again, if people were discouraged, condemned, or rejected while under the convincing grace of God, they might despair of God's justifying and regenerating grace and thereby be lost to the kingdom. However, if acceptance in this context were simply equated with justification, such that the faith of one who "fears God and works righteousness" was in turn identified with the proper Christian faith *in every instance*, then this would have the unfortunate effect of lowering the standards of redemption, of leaving people in their sins, and of allowing enslaving powers to continue unabated. As a good pastor, Wesley, despite much criticism from the Calvinists, acknowledged every degree of grace, every glimmer of light; but he also urged people to go forward, to enjoy the liberties of grace for which Christ died, even the holiness without which no one will see the Lord which has its beginning, its instantiation, not in the spirit of bondage unto fear, but in the new birth.

The Upshot of It All

The energetic criticism of the Calvinist controversy, of course, flowed in both directions. To be sure, the *Minutes* of 1770 contained an explicit critique of Calvinism. As in 1739 with the publication of the sermon "Free Grace," in 1740 before the Fetter Lane Society, and in 1744 before Oxford University, Wesley hoped to foster a lively debate with the publication of the *Minutes* of 1770 concerning theological matters that he deemed particularly important. Clearly, both Wesley and Fletcher had come to believe that Calvinism could, at times, foster antinomianism; that is, Reformed theological teachings, oddly enough, could undermine the importance of being *holy*. "I am afraid Lady Huntingdon's preachers will do little good wherever they go," Wesley wrote to Mrs. Woodhouse in 1773, "They are wholly swallowed up in that detestable doctrine of predestination, and can talk of nothing else."[81] A year later, Wesley wrote to Fletcher concerning the truth that after justification, God is pleased or displeased with believers according to the actual tempers of their hearts and according to their works. "I see more and more clearly," Wesley observed, "that 'there is a great gulf fixed' between us and all those who, by denying this, sap the very foundation both of inward and outward holiness."[82] And Wesley's tone became even more serious when in 1777, he cautioned Francis Wolfe: "O beware of Calvinism and everything that has the least tendency thereto. Let a burnt child dread the fire!"[83] And the following year, in a letter to Mary Bishop, Wesley—probably thinking of the work of Calvinist "gospel" preachers—made it abundantly clear what was at the heart of salvation in his following observation:

> Let but a pert, self-sufficient animal, that has neither sense nor grace, bawl out something about Christ and His blood or justification by faith, and his hearers cry out, "What a fine gospel sermon!" Surely the Methodists have not so learnt Christ. We know of no gospel without salvation from sin.[84]

One of the great attractions of Calvinist theology, of course, was the comfort it could bring believers in knowing that their redemption was utterly in the hands of God through the inscrutable decrees. As such, the elect would not, indeed, could not, be lost. In a real sense, Wesley's doctrine of Christian assurance—an assurance that develops as one grows in grace and becomes *increasingly* holy—was an answer, in part, to the comfort that Calvinist notions of predestination and election could afford. By 1771, for example, Wesley had distinguished full assurance, which excludes doubt and fear, from initial assurance, which does not; he had come to a greater appreciation of the faith of a servant and its degree of acceptance; and he had realized that in exceptional cases, one may even be justified and yet lack assurance due to either ignorance of the gospel promises or bodily disorder. Nevertheless, the theme that Wesley chose to develop during this late period of his life, in the midst of the Calvinist controversy, was none other than a strong identification of assurance with the proper (real) Christian faith. To illustrate, in his sermon "On the Trinity," produced in 1775, Wesley declared:

> But I know not how *anyone* can be a Christian believer till "he hath (as St. John speaks) the witness in himself"; till "the Spirit of God witnesses with his spirit that he is a child of God"—that is, in effect, till God the Holy Ghost witnesses that God the Father has accepted him through the merits of God the Son.[85]

Here there would be no consolation from decrees or from doctrinal teaching and the like. Instead, assurance would be given to the soul *directly* by the presence of the Spirit who makes the believer holy.

In 1778, Wesley continued his critique of Calvinism by publishing the first edition of the *Arminian Magazine*, a journal that printed "Extracts and Original Treaties on Universal Redemption."[86] As Wesley's answer to the Calvinist *Gospel Magazine*, the *Arminian*

Magazine brought forth "some of the most remarkable tracts on the universal love of God and on His willingness to save all men from all sin."[87] A few years earlier, Wesley had expressed similar sentiments when he wrote, "Nothing will so effectually stop the plague of Calvinism as the preaching salvation from all sin and exhorting all to expect it now by naked faith."[88]

By the end of the decade, the Calvinist controversy had basically run its course, not because the two parties had come to some sort of an agreement—indeed they were as far apart as ever—but because many involved were simply tired of the polemics. In the meantime, Wesley's ministry in London was prospering; and so he turned his attention to other matters—plans for replacing the Foundery, a building that had served the Methodists so well in the past. The new structure, which became known variously as "Wesley's Chapel," the "New Chapel," or simply "City Road Chapel," was built not far from the old Foundery, directly across from Bunhill Fields where Susanna Wesley had been buried. The foundation stone for the chapel was laid, with some celebration, on April 21, 1777, and the building was formally opened by Wesley on November 1, 1778. Of its design, Wesley noted in his journal, "It is perfectly neat, but not fine"[89]—architecture, in other words, well suited to the Methodists.

It is fitting that Wesley continually paid attention to the institutional needs of Methodism in order to ensure that its genius, especially its emphasis on holy love, would be passed from generation to generation. This task became increasingly important toward the end of the decade and into the next simply because Wesley would soon take action, which, despite his own protests to the contrary, would move Methodism beyond the ecclesiastical parameters of the Church of England. In other words, what Charles Wesley had feared all along was about to take place.

CHAPTER TEN

A Church Established

Ebenezer Blackwell's Home at Lewisham

Recognizing that the work of Methodism in America was in great need of suitable laborers, Wesley entreated Dr. Lowth, the Bishop of London, to that end in August 1780. "There are three ministers in that country already," the bishop exclaimed.[1] "True, my Lord," Wesley replied, "but what are three to watch over all the souls in that extensive country?"[2] Realizing that his powers of persuasion had failed, Wesley became increasingly critical of the bishop's ordination practices. Wesley's words are worth quoting at length because they not only express his frustration with respect to furthering the work of God in America, but also give evidence of his conception of vital gospel ministry. Wesley observed:

> I have heard that your Lordship is unfashionably diligent in examining the candidates for Holy Orders—yea, that your Lordship is generally at the pains of examining them *yourself*. Examining them! In what respects? Why, whether they understand a little *Latin* and *Greek* and can answer a few trite questions in the science of divinity! Alas, how little does this avail! Does

your Lordship examine whether they serve *Christ* or *Belial*? whether they love God or the world? whether they ever had any serious thoughts about heaven or hell? whether they have any real desire to save their own souls or the souls of others? If not, what have they to do with Holy Orders? and what will become of the souls committed to their care?[3]

In his reply, Wesley by no means deprecated the importance of learning for vital ministry as his earlier treatise on this topic, *An Address to the Clergy*, produced in 1756, clearly demonstrated. Rather, in his current response to Lowth, Wesley underscored the importance *also* of the knowledge of practical divinity, specifically the wisdom and grace required in saving souls. "My Lord, I do by no means despise learning," Wesley noted, "I know the value of it too well. But what is this, particularly in a Christian minister, compared to piety? What is it in a man that has no religion? 'As a jewel in a swine's snout.' "[4] Expressing his frustration in a way that was sure to irritate the bishop, Wesley added, "Your Lordship did see good to ordain and send into America other persons who knew something of Greek and Latin, but who knew no more of saving souls than of catching whales."[5]

But perhaps Wesley's conversation with the bishop was nearly moot by this point, for the political and religious situation in America was changing rapidly. For example, in 1780, the British army was soundly defeated at King's Mountain, South Carolina. The following year, the British troops, nearly exhausted, were again defeated at the battle in Cowpens, South Carolina; and the French fleet not only conquered the British naval force at Hampton Roads, but also soon blockaded the Chesapeake Bay. Finally, all land operations on American soil ceased with the British capitulation at Yorktown, at which point Charleston and Savannah were soon evacuated. Thus, the very places the Wesleys had begun their ministry in America during the 1730s now showed the signs of the British retreat.

Since in Wesley's mind the Church of England was in some sense tied to the temporal order, that is, to the British nation and its colonies, any change in that order would necessitate a change in the religious one as well. Accordingly, reflecting on the American situation a few years later, in 1784, Wesley reasoned in his treatise *To Our Brethren in America* as follows:

As our American brethren are now totally disentangled both from the State and from the English hierarchy, we dare not entangle them again either with the one or the other. They are now at full liberty simply to follow the Scriptures and the Primitive Church.[6]

The American Ordinations

Emboldened by his earlier readings of Lord Peter King and Edward Stillingfleet, as noted in chapter 6, and encouraged by the changed American political situation, Wesley was determined to act decisively in the face of both the great need in America and the ongoing indifference on the part of the Anglican hierarchy. Exercising the role of a bishop at the 1784 Conference, Wesley set apart Thomas Coke as superintendent by the imposition of hands and by prayer. Wesley's diary referred to this event using the language of "ordained." The journal, however, stated that Dr. Coke was "appointed," though the actual certificate given to the new superintendent employed the words, "set apart." Once in America, Thomas Coke had instructions to consecrate Francis Asbury as General Superintendent, a ceremony that took place at the founding Christmas Conference of 1784.[7] Beyond this, Wesley ordained Richard Whatcoat and Thomas Vasey as elders in order to foster the work of the Methodists in America.

Wesley justified such irregular actions—at least by Anglican standards—by noting that "the case is widely different between England and North America. . . . Here, therefore, my scruples are at an end."[8] And in a letter to Barnabas Thomas in March 1785, Wesley made his case along the following lines: "I am now as firmly attached to the Church of England as I ever was since you knew me. But meantime I know myself to be as real a Christian bishop as the Archbishop of Canterbury."[9] Charles Wesley, however, was not convinced. Indeed, the ordinations for America had caused a ripple in the relationship, which John quickly sought to repair. After posting several letters that insisted he had not separated from the Church of England by his recent actions, Wesley finally came to realize that the rift between him and his brother Charles was not to be so easily managed: "I see no use of you and me disputing together; for neither of us is likely to convince the other. You say I separate from the Church; I say I do not. Then let it stand."[10]

Though Wesley professed one thing to his brother, his ongoing actions suggested otherwise. For the Methodist leader had not only ordained for the American work, but also crafted *The Sunday Service*, an edited form of *The Book of Common Prayer*, that was brought over to the New World by Dr. Coke. This liturgical manual, in its emphases and omissions, reflected Wesley's seasoned theological judgments and what reforms he deemed necessary. Indeed, according to Frank Baker, "Wesley was carrying out most of the reforms desired by Puritans more than a century earlier."[11] Beyond this, Wesley included with *The Sunday Service* his own editing of the Anglican Thirty-nine Articles that were now reduced to just twenty four.[12] Wesley justified his excisions on the basis of the touchstone of Scripture; but the practical theology that had emerged in the ongoing tasks of ministry, that is, in fostering and sustaining the evangelical revival, no doubt, played a role as well. At any rate, though *The Sunday Service* was embraced by the Americans, at least initially, it was flatly rejected by the Methodists in Scotland. Moreover, when Wesley tried to introduce this work to the English Methodists in 1786, they reacted quite strongly to his omissions and much preferred the traditional Anglican resources. Fatigued by this struggle, Wesley, himself, employed *The Book of Common Prayer* at the City Road Chapel and counseled: "Wherever the people make an objection, let the matter drop."[13]

Though Wesley appeared to be at the peak of his power in terms of the American Methodists with his ordinations of 1784, that power, ironically enough, was soon dissipated—at least to a certain extent—and was eventually shared by others, by the very American leaders whom Wesley had appointed. For example, in September 1786, Wesley stated that the American Methodists should meet in a general conference at Baltimore on May 1, 1787. In addition, Wesley desired that Richard Whatcoat be appointed Superintendent to assist Francis Asbury. Both counsels, however, were quietly put aside by the American Methodists to Wesley's considerable dismay. Indeed, relations between Wesley and the American church, in general, and Francis Asbury, in particular, became so difficult at times that, in September 1788, Wesley felt compelled to remind Asbury that

there is, indeed, a wide difference between the relation wherein

233

you stand to the Americans and the relation wherein I stand to all . . . American Methodists: I am under God the father of the whole family.[14]

And Wesley soon became angry when he learned that Asbury, not content with the title of superintendent, was now being referred to by his American colleagues as "bishop." Wesley cautioned Asbury (and Thomas Coke, for that matter) in the following way:

> I study to be little: you study to be great. I creep: you strut along. I found a school: you a college! nay, and call it after your own names! O beware, do not seek to be something! Let me be nothing, and "Christ be all in all.". . . How can you, how dare you suffer yourself to be called Bishop? I shudder, I start at the very thought! Men may call me a knave or a fool, a rascal, a scoundrel, and I am content; but they shall never by my consent call me Bishop! For my sake, for God's sake, for Christ's sake put a full end to this![15]

Despite Wesley's energetic protestations, this counsel, too, was quietly put aside. For his part, Asbury maintained that no person in Europe knew how to direct those in America, and he told George Shadford, "Mr. Wesley and I are like Caesar and Pompey: he will bear no equal, and I will bear no superior."[16] Wesley was honest and realistic enough, however, to know what lay ahead for in this same year he wrote to Richard Whatcoat:

> It is truly probable the disavowing *me* will, as soon as my head is laid, occasion a total breach between the English and American Methodists. They will naturally say, "If they can do without us, we can do without *them*."[17]

Preparing for a British Church

To ensure that his contribution to the British evangelical revival would not be seen as a competitor to the Anglican Church, Wesley insisted during the early part of the 1780s that Methodist preaching services not be held at the same time as Anglican worship. Indeed, so concerned was Wesley about this issue that he wrote several letters to this effect. And though Wesley cautioned in 1786 that "to fix it [Methodist preaching] at the same hour is obliging them to separate, either from the Church or us," by 1789 he was apparently already beginning to make allowances for such over-lap;[18] and he now became unwilling to call it leaving the church. To the printer of the *Dublin Chronicle*, for example, he wrote, "Could I even then deny that I had service in church hours? No; but I denied, and do deny still, that this is leaving the Church."[19]

Many of the Methodists in Britain during the 1780s, of course, attended both Methodist and Anglican services, and it was, there-fore, only natural to compare the two. Discerning a significant dif-ference between these settings, some Methodists complained to Wesley that Anglican worship was, at times, led by priests who did not preach the liberty of the gospel, and whose very lives also failed to give witness to the bountiful grace of God. So concerned was Wesley about fostering scriptural Christianity—as opposed to a dead formalistic faith—that he advised those under his spiritual care even to the point of forsaking Anglican services:

> Those ministers (so called) who neither live nor preach the gospel I dare not say are sent of God. Where one of these is set-tled, many of the Methodists dare not attend his ministry; so, if there be no other church in that neighbourhood, they go to church no more.[20]

Here nothing less than the integrity of the gospel and the care of souls was at stake. Such matters, therefore, required *exceptional* action.

Though Wesley repeatedly affirmed on an institutional level that he had no desire for Methodism to leave the Church of England, he was realistic enough to prepare for just such a possibility. In fact, at the Conference of 1784, Wesley promulgated the Deed of Declaration, which provided for the structure of Methodism beyond his death. To illustrate, the Deed articulated fifteen regula-tions for the conduct of the Conference that included, among other things: defining the Methodist Conference for the Trust Deeds; establishing a connection throughout Britain; stipulating that the Conference is to meet annually in London, Bristol, or Newcastle; laying down guidelines for the reception of preachers into full con-nection; establishing a President and a Secretary of the Conference who are to be elected annually; maintaining that forty members constitute a quorum; and, last, affirming that all decisions are to be made by majority vote.

Though the Deed of Declaration appears to be somewhat "democratic" in its prescriptions, it also reveals Wesley's tendency, on occasion, toward autocracy in that he made allowance for only one hundred of his preachers to be a part of the legal governing body of the Conference. Thomas Coke was strongly opposed to this action and believed that "all preachers in full connection should be members, as had been the case for over a dozen years before 1780."[21] At the time of the Deed's composition in 1784, there were about two hundred preachers; and it made little sense that about half of them, many of whom had sacrificed much for the gospel, should be dishonored by exclusion—and in such an arbitrary manner. John Hampson Sr., for instance, who was utterly devoted to Wesley, was not among the legal hundred—to his great dismay. Such a fanciful figure, then, was an *inevitable* prescription for bad feelings, resentment, and for the spawning of many unholy tempers. And yet Wesley took no responsibility for this.

At any rate, this elaborate and well-crafted infrastructure must not be viewed simply as the way in which Wesley provided for the institutional life of Methodism beyond his death, but also be seen as a means that could, if necessary, provide order for Methodism independent of the mother church. More to the point, if several of the members of the Conference were fully ordained and thereby able to administer the sacraments, the Church of England would hardly be needed at all. To be sure, the decrees of this pivotal British Conference, in conjunction with Wesley's actions with respect to the American Methodists (in preparing *The Sunday Service* and ordaining Coke, Whatcoat, and Vasey), have led John Whitehead and others to consider 1784 as the "grand climacteric year of Methodism."[22] Acknowledged or not, Wesley was actually preparing for a separation from the Church of England.

Such a severance became increasingly evident, even likely, as a result of Wesley's subsequent actions in ordaining for the work in Britain. For example, in 1785, Wesley repeated his earlier claim that though he had never exercised in *England* the power that he believed God had given him—though, of course, he had already done so in America—he firmly believed himself to be a "scriptural [episcopos] as much as any man in England or in Europe."[23]

However, shortly after this most recent pronouncement, Wesley ordained John Pawson, Thomas Hanby, and Joseph Taylor as ministers for Scotland. Wesley justified this action by noting that the Church of England was not the established church in that land. "The alteration which has been made in America and Scotland has nothing to do with our kingdom," he exclaimed.[24] Nevertheless, Wesley's hesitancy in this area is reflected not only in his observation to Joshua Keighley in May 1787, that "I know not but I have already gone too far,"[25] but also in his requirement that those who were ordained for work in Scotland must abandon their orders once they crossed the border into England. But as V. H. H. Green aptly points out, "If ordination meant anything at all this was indefensible. If it was valid then it must be indelible."[26]

But Wesley did not stop there. Having ordained for America and now for Scotland, he finally crossed the Rubicon, so to speak, in 1788 and set apart ministers for work in England. Thus, Alexander Mather was ordained deacon and presbyter on August 6 and August 7, respectively. And in a similar fashion, Henry Moore and Thomas Rankin were ordained the following year on February 26 and 27. Indeed, by the end of his career, Wesley had actually ordained more than twenty-five ministers for work in Scotland, England, America, and even in such places as Nova Scotia, Newfoundland, and the West Indies. That Wesley was not censured for such action by his own church indicates something of the lax and indulgent standards of the time. However, if he had been called to task, Wesley would have likely replied that the work of the gospel *necessitated* such actions, that it was far better to send in laborers to the field than to watch the harvest rot on the ground. Accordingly, in his sermon "Prophets and Priests," produced in May 1789, Wesley justified his rather functional definition of ministry in the following manner:

> I say, put these two principles together—first, I will not separate from the Church; yet, secondly, in cases of *necessity,* I will vary from it (both of which I have constantly and openly avowed for upwards of fifty years)—and inconsistency vanishes away. I have been true to my profession from 1730 to this day."[27]

Remarkably enough, shortly after the beginning of his ordinations, Wesley had remarked to Barnabas Thomas that "I am now as firmly attached to the Church of England as I ever was since you knew me."[28] And in a letter to Henry Moore, drafted in 1788, Wesley affirmed: "I am a Church-of-England man; and, as I said fifty years ago so I say still, in the Church I will live and die, unless I am thrust out."[29] Moreover, during this same year, Wesley wrote to Dr. Coke, no doubt with a good measure of energy: "As I said before, so I say still, I cannot, I dare not, leave the Church, for the reasons we all agreed to thirty years ago in the conference at Leeds."[30]

Robert Southey, one of the more able biographers of the nineteenth century, took issue with Wesley's repeated claims of allegiance to the Church of England in the wake of his several ordinations:

> He [Wesley] had been led toward a separation imperceptibly, step by step; but it is not to his honour that he affected to deprecate it to the last, while he was evidently bringing it about by the measures which he pursued."[31]

The Danger of Riches

In his later years, Wesley was not only concerned with the ongoing infrastructure of both British and American Methodism, but also preoccupied with the vitality, the very substance, of the Methodist faith. Wesley's principal fear in this area was that Methodism would soon devolve into a dead faith, having the outward form of religion but lacking the power thereof. Such decline, Wesley believed, would be brought about by none other than the specter of riches. Indeed, precisely due to their diligence and frugality, qualities quite valuable in themselves, the Methodists ran the risk of becoming rich. Wesley observed,

> Does it not seem (and yet this cannot be!) that Christianity, true scriptural, Christianity has a tendency in process of time to undermine and destroy itself? For wherever true Christianity spreads it must cause diligence and frugality, which, in the natural course of things, must beget riches. And riches naturally beget pride, love of the world, and every temper that is destructive of Christianity.[32]

To caution against this calamity, Wesley wrote two key sermons during the 1780s, one at the beginning of the decade and the other toward the end.

In his sermon "The Danger of Riches," produced in 1780, Wesley warned those under his direction that riches (whatever is above the plain necessities or—at most—the conveniences of life) "naturally lead to some or other . . . foolish and hurtful desires," such as the desire of the flesh, the desire of the eyes, and the pride of life.[33] Moreover, Wesley discerned a close connection between the accumulation of wealth, on the one hand, and the inculcation of unholy tempers in the human heart, on the other. Though Wesley did not draw an exact equation in this area—for he taught not only that "before the end even the rich shall enter into the kingdom of God,"[34] but also that "it is no more sinful to be rich than to be poor,"[35]—he nevertheless did indeed associate the graces of humility, meekness, and kindness with the poor; and pride, haughtiness, and arrogance with the rich. "Oh what advantage have the poor over the rich!" Wesley remarked in 1788, "These are not wise in their own eyes, but all receive with meekness the ingrafted word which is able to save their souls."[36] Interestingly enough, Rattenbury contends that behind all these religious sentiments and justifications Wesley had "a mediaeval dread of riches,"[37] and J. H. Plumb, the noted historian, goes ever further to claim that among the Methodists, "there was a rabid envy of luxury and elegance, of the aristocratic and libertarian attitude to life."[38]

In his other major sermon on this theme, during this period, simply entitled "On Riches," Wesley tied this whole discussion of wealth and the inculcation of holy tempers in the heart not with envy or a fear of elegance but with his ongoing concern, once again, for being a real Christian:

> But it would not be strange if rich men were in general void of all good dispositions, and an easy prey to all evil ones, since so few of them pay any regard to that solemn declaration of our Lord, without observing which we cannot be his disciples. . . . "If any man will come after me," will be a *real* Christian, "let him deny himself, and take up his cross daily, and follow me."[39]

In denying themselves, in being among the less fortunate, earnest Christians availed themselves of the very settings that would be most conducive to spiritual growth. For Wesley, then, it was not sufficient simply to send money to the poor. Instead, one must actually visit the poor and be among them. "O how much better is it to go to the poor than to the rich," Wesley declared earlier in the decade, "And to the house of mourning, than to the house of feasting."[40]

Precisely in order to foster fellowship between the poor and those who had more of life's means, Wesley wrote an important sermon in 1786 entitled "On Visiting the Sick." In this sermon, Wesley, in a very pastoral fashion, advised the Methodists just how to be among the sick and poor, how to bring about the amelioration of their condition:

> But it may not be amiss usually to begin with inquiring into their outward condition. You may ask whether they have the necessaries of life. Whether they have sufficient food and raiment. If the weather be cold, whether they have fuel.[41]

But after this, Wesley asserted, the visitor is to proceed to things of *greater* value. "These little labours of love," he wrote, "will pave your way to things of *greater* importance. Having shown that you have a regard for their bodies you may proceed to inquire concerning their souls."[42] And Wesley repeated this judgment, no doubt for emphasis, but this time he clearly displayed the goal of all gospel ministry:

> While you are as eyes to the blind and feet to the lame, a husband to the widow and a father to the fatherless, see that you still keep *a higher end in view*, even the saving of souls from death, and that you labour to make all you say and do subservient *to that great end*.[43]

These value judgments expressed in the sermon are by no means idiosyncratic but represent Wesley's own best thinking throughout his career. For example, much earlier, in 1748, Wesley had written concerning those engaged in ministry that "he doth good, to the uttermost of his power, even to the bodies of all men. . . . How much more does he rejoice if he can do any good to the soul of any man!"[44] And two years later, Wesley continued this theme in his sermon "Upon Our Lord's Sermon on the Mount, Discourse the Thirteenth" and wrote:

Over and above all this, are you zealous of good works? Do you, as you have time, do good to all men? Do you feed the hungry and clothe the naked, and visit the fatherless and widow in their affliction? Do you visit those that are sick? Relieve them that are in prison? Is any a stranger and you take him in? Friend, *come up higher. . . .* Does he enable you to bring sinners from darkness to light, from the power of Satan unto God?[45]

So then, for Wesley at least, a part of what it meant to love your neighbor as yourself always involved the exercise of both material gifts and spiritual talents; it entailed the employment of all those gifts and graces that would enhance the physical well-being of the poor *and* their spiritual character. Second, and perhaps more important, though the material needs of the neighbor had chronological priority (in the sense that they were the very first things to be done), they clearly did not have valuational priority in Wesley's thought,[46] for their fulfillment prepared the way, to use Wesley's own words, for things of *greater importance.*

In a characteristic fashion, Wesley's own life clearly matched his teachings on this important issue of poverty and wealth because not only did he go about begging for the poor on several occasions, most notably among his "rich" friends in London in 1785 and in 1787, but also he died with little more than a teapot to his name—despite the large sum of money that had flowed through his hands. Where had all the money gone? Wesley quite simply distributed it among the poor and his preachers and thereby helped bring about, at least in a small way, the kingdom of God on earth.

Loss and Decline

Though Wesley was obviously quite energetic in ministry during the 1780s, this was actually a very difficult decade for him. For one thing, he was shorn of two of his dearest friends and fellow laborers. In August 1785, for instance, Wesley's designated successor, John Fletcher, died and was entombed in the churchyard in Madeley where he had labored for so many years. Wesley naturally offered much praise in remembrance of this godly soul and even wrote a brief account of Fletcher's life. A few years later, in 1788, Charles Wesley, brother, fellow laborer in the gospel, and dear friend, someone who had been with John from the very beginning of the great evangelical revival, passed away into glory. Upon learning of his brother's death, Wesley remarked, "The Lord gave, and the Lord hath taken away; blessed be the name of the Lord!"[47]

Before his death, Charles Wesley, holding the notion of consecrated ground dear, left instructions that he was not to be buried at City Road Chapel, or in the Dissenters cemetery across the way, that is, in Bunhill Fields where his mother, Susanna, had been laid to rest. Instead, he was to be interred in Marylebone churchyard in the northwest part of London. Of this request, John remarked: " 'Tis pity but the remains of my brother had been deposited with me. Certainly that *ground* is *holy* [the City Road Chapel] as any in England, and it contains a large quantity of 'bonny dust.' "[48] In death, then, as in life, Charles Wesley yet distinguished himself from his elder brother.

Of his own health, Wesley had often boasted just how good it was. Indeed, the birthday pages of his journal are filled with such material. On one such occasion, late in his career, Wesley remarked, "By the blessing of God I am just the same as when I entered the twenty-eighth [year]. This hath God wrought, chiefly by my constant exercise, my rising early, and preaching morning and evening."[49] In fact, so vigorous was Wesley at the time that he decided to take an excursion in June 1783 to Holland—one of Wesley's few respites from his ongoing labors—a place to which he returned in 1786. The trip went well, by all reports, but shortly after Wesley's return to England in August 1783, he was seized with "a most impetuous flux."[50] A grain and a half of opium was administered to him in three doses to bring about some relief. This narcotic naturally stopped the cramps that Wesley had been suffering, but it also, to use his own words, "took away my speech, hearing and power of motion, and locked me up from head to foot, so that I lay a mere log."[51]

Wesley soon recovered from his "flux," but the sanguine observations on his health that had marked the beginning of the decade evaporated as he approached its end. In October 1789, for instance, Wesley noted that his sight was decayed, his strength decreased, and "I cannot easily preach above twice a day."[52] On January 1, 1790, the elderly preacher detailed how age was now taking its toll:

I am now an old man, decayed from hand to foot. My eyes are dim; my right hand shakes much; my mouth is hot and dry every morning; I have a lingering fever almost every day; my motion is weak and slow. However, blessed by God, I do not slack my labour. I can preach and write still.[53]

Real Christianity

Though Wesley was obviously in decline, it is truly remarkable that he was yet preoccupied with the theme that had surfaced so many times in his writings throughout the years, namely, the importance of being a real Christian. Such a concern had not only remained with Wesley in the midst of all his labors, but also intensified as he began to count the days that remained. In fact, the 1780s mark Wesley's greatest interest in this theme, judging from the number of times it appeared in the more than sixty sermons of this very productive period. In 1785, for example, Wesley continued to highlight the distinction between nominal and real Christians and pointed out in his sermon "The New Creation," employing a familiar rhetoric by now, that the former "have the form of godliness without the power."[54] Clues, by the way, as to when Wesley himself determined in his own mind to be a real Christian are found in the late sermon "In What Sense We are to Leave the World," in which he indicated, once again, the significance of the year 1725: "When it pleased God to give *me* a settled resolution to be not a *nominal* but a *real* Christian (being then about two and twenty years of age) my acquaintance were as ignorant of God as myself."[55]

As in an earlier period, Wesley reflected back on the Oxford Methodists, but this time in a letter to Henry Brooke in 1786, in which he avowed that their original design was nothing less than to be "Bible Christians."[56] Moreover, the following year, in his sermon "Of Former Times," Wesley revealed that the goal of "the Holy Club" was above all to help each other be "real Christians."[57] But perhaps the most noteworthy accent during this late interval of Wesley's life was his strong identification of real, scriptural Christianity with the new birth and, therefore, with all the marks of the new birth, such as faith, hope, and love. For example, in a pastoral letter to his nephew Samuel Wesley, who had converted to Roman Catholicism (though he later renounced this move), Wesley cautioned: "Except a man be born again . . . he cannot see the kingdom of heaven except he experience that inward change of the earthly, sensual mind for the mind which was in Christ Jesus."[58] Furthermore, in his sermon "Walking by Sight and Walking by Faith," produced in 1788, Wesley proclaimed,

> How short is this description of real Christians! And yet how exceeding full! It comprehends, it sums up, the whole experience of those that are truly such, from the time they are born of God till they remove into Abraham's bosom. For who are the "we" that are here spoken of? All that are true Christian believers. I say "Christian," not "Jewish" believers. All that are not only *servants* but *children* of God.[59]

And a year later, Wesley's strong identification of real Christianity with regeneration, with the children of God, was again unmistakable. "How great a thing it is to be a Christian," he declares in his sermon "On a Single Eye," "to be a real, inward, scriptural Christian! Conformed in heart and life to the will of God! Who is sufficient for these things? None, unless he be born of God."[60]

It was also during the decade of the 1780s—when Wesley became an octogenarian—that he began to elaborate further and then to summarize some of his more important distinctions between the faith of a servant and the faith of a child of God. For example, in his sermon "On Faith," written in 1788, Wesley revealed, in part, the difference between a servant and a child of God: " 'He that believeth,' as a child of God, 'hath the witness in himself.' This the servant hath not."[61] Beyond this, Wesley maintained that one who is a servant of God, who "feareth God and worketh righteousness," enjoys the favor of God and is, therefore, accepted "to a degree" as illustrated in his sermon "On Friendship with the World": "Those on the contrary 'are of God' who love God, or at least fear him, and keep his commandments." This is the lowest character of those that "are of God," who are not properly sons, but servants.[62]

Unfortunately, early in his ministry, John Wesley had not fully appreciated the notion that those who "fear God and work righteousness" are indeed accepted of him, and because of this failure, he and his brother Charles caused great harm among those who were attentive to early Methodist preaching. In 1788, reflecting on this regrettable situation, Wesley confessed:

> Indeed nearly fifty years ago, when the preachers commonly called Methodists began to preach that grand scriptural doctrine, salvation by faith, they were not sufficiently apprised of the difference between a servant and a child of God. They did not clearly understand that even one "who feared God, and worketh righteousness, is accepted of him."[63]

Observe in these preceding reflections, then, that Wesley held two ideas together, both important elements of his "conjunctive" theology: On the one hand, he or she who fears God and works righteousness is not a rank unbeliever; but on the other hand, "one that fears God is [still] waiting for His salvation."[64] Indeed, late in his career, Wesley continued to associate the faith of a servant, in a broad sense, not with justification, but with the spirit of bondage. Additional evidence of this linkage is found in a letter to Thomas Davenport drafted in 1781, in which Wesley counseled as follows:

> You are in the hands of a wise Physician, who is lancing your sores in order to heal them. He has *given* you now *the spirit of fear*. But it is in order to *the spirit of love and of a sound mind*. You have now *received the spirit of bondage*. Is it not the forerunner of the spirit of adoption? He is not afar off. Look up! And expect Him to cry in your heart, Abba, Father! He is nigh that justifieth![65]

Accordingly, this preceding excerpt demonstrates, quite clearly, that in this late period, Wesley still did not confuse the issue of "acceptance" (for the light and grace that they have) with justification, for those under "the spirit of fear" are still waiting for the One who justifies. This means, of course, that these believers are in the way of salvation; consequently, if they continue in this grace—and unfortunately some will not—then the One "who is nigh" will justify. Moreover, in a similar fashion, Wesley distinguishes properly saving faith from that which, though it constitutes a degree of acceptance, nevertheless remains, to use Wesley's own words, "only" the faith of a servant. To illustrate, in his sermon "On Faith," written in 1788, Wesley observes,

> But what is the faith which is properly saving? Which brings eternal salvation to all those that keep it to the end? It is such a

divine conviction of God and of the things of God as even in its infant state enables everyone that possesses it to "fear God and work righteousness." And whosoever in every nation believes thus far the Apostle declares is "accepted of him." He actually is at that very moment in a state of acceptance. But he is at present *only* a servant of God, not properly a son. Meantime let it be well observed that "the wrath of God" no longer "abideth on him."[66]

And again in this same sermon Wesley cautions, "There is no reason why you should be satisfied with the faith of a materialist, a heathen, or a deist; nor indeed with that of a servant."[67]

For Wesley, then, the servants of God, in a broad sense, obviously lack what he termed "the proper Christian faith" and hence cannot enjoy the privileges of the sons and daughters of God; yet they have a measure of faith that arises from the prevenient and convincing grace, which precedes it, and are *for that reason* not to be discouraged. Thus, Wesley's seasoned and relatively favorable estimation of the faith of a servant in this sense probably emerged from his consideration that such a faith, in the normal course of spiritual development, would in time become the faith of a child of God. In fact, in his sermon "On Faith," written in 1788, Wesley highlighted just such a consideration:

> And, indeed, unless the servants of God halt by the way, they will receive the adoption of sons. They will receive the *faith* of the children of God by his *revealing* his only-begotten Son in their hearts. . . . And whosoever hath this, "the Spirit of God witnesseth with his spirit that he is a child of God."[68]

Likewise, Wesley's appreciation of a degree of acceptance and his exhortation to servants to improve the rich grace of God is revealed in a sermon produced in 1788, "On the Discoveries of Faith," in which he observed,

> Whoever has attained this, the faith of a servant . . . in consequence of which he is in a degree (as the Apostle observes), "accepted with him.". . . Nevertheless he should be exhorted not to stop there; not to rest till he attains the adoption of sons; till he obeys out of love, which is the privilege of all the children of God.[69]

Simply put, the faith of a servant of God is valued not only for the measure of faith that it is, but also for what it will soon become: the qualitatively different faith of a child of God, where faith will be filled not with the energy of fear, but with the energy of love.

Beyond this, in January 1787, Wesley acknowledged that "to believe Christ gave Himself for me is the faith of a Christian,"[70] and a year later he not only once again clarified the distinction between the faith of a servant and of a son, but also maintained that assurance is an integral component of the proper Christian faith. In his sermon "On Faith", for example, Wesley reasons:

> Thus the faith of a child is *properly and directly* a divine conviction whereby every child of God is enabled to testify, "The life that I now live, I live by faith in the Son of God, who loved me, and gave himself for me." And *whosoever hath this*, "the Spirit of God witnesseth with his spirit that he is a child of God."[71]

Even more significantly, there is nothing in Wesley's often-quoted 1788 letter to Melville Horne that detracts from this identification and emphasis. Thus, in this correspondence, Wesley maintains that the servants of God who lack assurance are not thereby condemned, a commonplace by now, but he then goes on to assert—and this is what has often been missed—that "we preach assurance as we always did, as a *common* privilege of the children of God."[72]

Wesley's Protestant Spiritual Orientation

Wesley's ongoing attentiveness to real, proper scriptural Christianity can be expressed in a contemporary idiom with the term "spirituality" and its cognates. And although this exact term rarely surfaced in Wesley's writings—he much preferred the word "sanctification"—the Methodist leader nevertheless developed many of the themes that make up the current discipline of spirituality.[73] There are, of course, many kinds of Christian spiritualities,[74] and their differences can best be explored in terms of not only distinct traditions such as Anglicanism, Roman Catholicism, Lutheranism, and Eastern Orthodoxy, but also four principal axes, namely, (1) apophatic/kataphatic, (2) cognitive/affective, (3) personal/social, and (4) ascetic/incarnational.

In terms of the first axis, Wesley's spirituality can be suitably described as "kataphatic" in that he sought God not in the "negative way" of mystical darkness, devoid of sensate content, but in the "affirmative way" of mediation; that is, divine grace and presence, for Wesley, were communicated through various *means*, whether they were Scripture, prayer, the sacraments, Christian conference, or fasting. Here the emphasis was on light, not darkness, and on the *presence* of God graciously mediated to the community of faith, rather than on the hidden One of apophatic mystery. And though Wesley did indeed place a premium on reason and its powers—so typical of his enlightened age—and even used the term "rational Christian" synonymously with a [real] scriptural Christian,[75] he nevertheless articulated his own spiritual emphases along very affective lines. That is, spiritual growth, for Wesley, was principally, though not exclusively, a matter of the will and the various tempers or dispositions that constitute it. Put another way, spiritual progress consisted in orienting the various tempers and affections of the heart, through sanctifying grace, to the highest and most worthy loves—in particular, the love of God and neighbor. Indeed, the principal question for Wesley, from his earliest days at Oxford to the preaching of his final sermon, had always been, not "What can I know?" but "How can I love?"[76]

It is precisely Wesley's strong affective spirituality that serves as a clue to the personal/social axis. Since the process of redemption alters the dispositions of the heart, not in a superficial, but in a decisive way, in a real circumcision so to speak, then the life of the soul, what Wesley often termed inward religion, must form, at least to some extent, the basis of the social axis in terms of both motivation and ultimate purpose. That is, social ministry not only must be motivated by the gentle graces of holy love rather than by such unholy tempers as envy or class animosity, but also must see its highest end not in the satisfaction of maintenance needs, though clearly important as noted earlier, but in the inculcation of the holy tempers of love in ever-broadening circles until the kingdom of God reigns in body *and* soul and over house, city, nation, and world.

Now in order to meet both the material and spiritual needs of the poor, Wesley exercised a rigorous asceticism, a thoroughgoing self-denial, so that he would be not only a proper steward of all God's gifts, but also a blessing to the poor, especially to those in the greatest need. "No man living can 'afford' to waste any part of what God has committed to his trust" he cautions, "None can 'afford' to throw any part of that food and raiment into the sea which was lodged with him on purpose to feed the hungry and clothe the naked."[77] Wesley's ascetic spirituality, then, was never an end in itself nor was it dark or morbid; but it always had a larger purpose in view. Indeed, it was a salient means employed in order to do the greatest good to the very least of all. And like so much of Wesley's life, it was motivated by love, by nothing other than holy love.

So then, Wesley's spirituality can suitably be described as kataphatic, affective, both personal and social, and somewhat ascetic. And when the contemporary scholar Sager considers various types of spirituality in terms of their basic orientation, he lists the kataphatic and affective orientation, so emblematic of Wesley, under the heading of "Personal Renewal," in which the key descriptive phrases "born again," "holiness of life," "feeling in worship," and "prayer leading to presence" all come into play.[78] Yet another axis that must be considered, however, and one that some believe to be far more basic, runs along a problem/solution continuum and distinguishes, at least in some respects, Protestant spiritualities from Catholic ones.

Though there is obviously great diversity with respect to Catholic spiritualities, there is nevertheless a basic paradigm that is able to illuminate and explain much of this richness.[79] Understanding the root human problem in a largely Augustinian way as self-curving, sinful pride and its solution, therefore, as some form of ongoing humility, many Catholic spiritualities develop this paradigm in terms of a leading motif. *The Rule of Saint Benedict*, for example, utilizes the paradigm of pride/humility throughout its many counsels and views humility as principally informed and energized by the motif of *obedience*. Put another way, the solution to sinful pride that plagues the life of the monk is gracious humility, a humility that is fleshed out and actualized in ongoing obedience to the abbot. As such, one can never err in obeying the abbot who represents no one less than Jesus Christ. Accordingly, among the more than seventy "instruments" of good works, *The Rule* advises: "To obey the abbot's commands in all things, even if he strays from his own path."[80]

In a similar fashion, the works of Catherine of Genoa, medieval saint and mystic, explore a life of humility as a response to God's grace; but this time not so much in terms of the motif of obedience, but in terms of an unassuming and sacrificial *service* to one's neighbor. To illustrate, as a female tertiary lay dying of the plague, which was still taking its toll in fifteenth-century Europe, Catherine simply would not let this infectious disease and the danger it posed bar the way to love, ministry, and compassion. And so with great humility, and even self-forgetfulness, Catherine bent over and kissed the lips of "this poor soul tenderly and encouraged her to 'call Jesus.' "[81] Here, loving, humble service became the very staple of the holy life, leading not only to further appropriations of grace, but also to greater conformity to Christ.

The genius of this Catholic spiritual tradition was mediated to Wesley, in part, through Thomas à Kempis, who had been deeply influenced by the Brethren of the Common Life—as noted in chapter 2—and who had developed the basic Catholic paradigm in his work *The Imitation of Christ*. In this spiritual classic, for instance, humility is, once again, offered as the way ahead, though this time it is informed not so much by the motifs of obedience or service—though they, too, are clearly important—but by that of patient *suffering*. A Kempis observes, "Progress in the spiritual life does not consist so much in the possession of the grace of consolation as it does in the following: being able, with humility and patient resignation, to live without it."[82] Indeed, in this setting, to embrace desolation and suffering, without immediately seeking succor or consolation, marks the way toward spiritual growth and maturity; it is nothing less than the pathway to having the mind of Christ.

The basic spiritual paradigm of the Protestant Reformers, and the one that most influenced Wesley in his own reflections, is somewhat different and in a certain sense is even more radical than the Catholic one just considered. While not neglecting the importance of self-curving sinful pride, both Luther and Calvin maintained that the far more basic evil of *unbelief* was actually the root of all. Thus, Martin Luther in his *Lectures on Genesis* concludes that Eve was urged on by the serpent to commit the sin of all sins, the one from which all other sins arise: namely, to doubt the Word and thereby forfeit trust in God. "Unbelief is the source of all sins," Luther exclaims, "when Satan brought about this unbelief by driving out or corrupting the Word, the rest was easy for him."[83] Moreover, this German Reformer underscores this motif once again in his observation on Genesis 3 that "all evils result from unbelief or doubt of the Word and of God. For what can be worse than to disobey God and to obey Satan."[84]

Likewise, John Calvin, Genevan leader and Protestant Reformer, rejected the well-worked Augustinian notion that pride was the root of evil and focused instead on the whole question of faithlessness. Examining the text of Genesis 3, Calvin reasons, "Since the woman through *unfaithfulness* was led away from God's Word by the serpent's deceit, it is already clear that disobedience was the beginning of the Fall."[85] And again, "Adam would never have dared oppose God's authority unless he had disbelieved in God's Word."[86] Even more emphatically, Calvin declares in his *Institutes of the Christian Religion*:

> Unfaithfulness, then, was the root of the Fall. But thereafter ambition and pride, together with ungratefulness, arose, because Adam by seeking more than was granted him shamefully spurned God's great bounty.[87]

Like his Protestant predecessors, John Wesley took great care to come to his own understanding of these matters in light of the biblical accounts. Beginning with Genesis 3, a familiar text by now, Wesley describes the fall of Eve in his sermon "The End of Christ's Coming," produced in January 1781, and maintains that Satan, as an external foil, mingled truth with falsehood so that "unbelief begot pride . . . it begot self-will."[88] Elsewhere, in his sermon "On the Fall of Man," penned the following year, Wesley again underscores unbelief as the primal factor and exclaims, "Here sin began, namely, unbelief. 'The woman was deceived,' says the Apostle. She believed a lie: she gave more credit to the word of the devil than to the word of God."[89] For Wesley, then, as for his fellow Protestant leaders, the nature of human sin, its irreducible essence, is not pride, but, once again, unbelief. A lack of faith in God (and the alienation left in its wake) is the true foundation for the *subsequent* evils of pride and self-will. Here, then, we encounter an unbelief/faith axis rather than a pride/humility one. Salvation, then, is ever by grace through faith.

This Protestant orientation of Wesley's spirituality is evident not only in his claim, as noted in chapter 4, that "exactly as we are justified by faith, so are we sanctified by faith. Faith is the condition, and the *only* condition of sanctification, *exactly as* it is of justification,"[90] in which key Reformation insights with respect to grace and faith feed into both juridical *and* participatory themes, but also in the rhetoric employed during the 1780s to underscore the utter graciousness of entire sanctification, that it is a sheer unmerited gift that is, therefore, to be received *now* by *naked faith*. Interestingly enough, earlier Wesley had been reluctant to employ this language of "naked faith" and viewed it largely in a negative way.[91] But toward the end of his career, he actually began to embrace this vocabulary, though he invested it with his own very Protestant meanings. That is, "naked faith" was no longer understood negatively in an apophatic way as indicative of the quintessential darkness of the spirituality of John of the Cross and others—a usage that brought forth Wesley's earlier criticisms both in his journal and in his sermon "The Wilderness State"[92]—but it was conceived in the 1780s as highlighting the gracious divine soteriological *role* in entire sanctification itself. To illustrate, Wesley cautions Robert Carr Brackenbury in a letter drafted on September 18, 1780, as follows:

> You must not set the great blessing afar off, because you find much war within. Perhaps this will not abate, but rather increase, till the moment your heart is set at liberty. The war will not cease before you attain, but by your attaining, the promise. And if you look for it by *naked faith*, why may you not receive it now?[93]

Moreover, Wesley counsels Ann Loxdale in a letter written on March 4, 1786, in a similar fashion:

> You unquestionably did enjoy a measure of His pure and perfect love. And as you received it at first by *naked faith*, just so you may receive it again; and who knows how soon? May you not say,
> > If Thou canst so greatly bow,
> > Friend of sinners, why not now?[94]

And the following year, Wesley highlights entirely sanctifying grace, once again, not simply as empowerment, but also as the utter *favor* of the Most High, demonstrating the cruciality of such faith. He then goes on to connect the issue of "nakedness" to the immediate availability of this highest grace—an immediacy that must be understood not simply temporally, but also, and perhaps more important, soteriologically, that is, as indicative of divine gracious activity. In a letter to Mrs. Bowman, for example, Wesley notes:

> You have only one thing to do—leaving the first principles of the doctrine of Christ, go on to perfection. Expect continually the end of your faith, the full salvation of your soul. You know, whenever it is given, it is to be received only by *naked faith*. Therefore who knows but you may receive it *now*?[95]

The legacy of the Protestant Reformation mediated to Wesley, in part, by Moravian and Salzburger Pietists had already borne such remarkable fruit in Wesley's life. This rich and vital tradition had taught the Methodist leader, among other things, the sufficiency of God's grace for all human need whether it be for forgiveness, favor, empowerment, or cleansing. To be sure, Wesley knew full well that a loving and merciful God was ever ready to lavish such gracious gifts upon all in need. The way forward, then, at every step along the way, from the first flush of repentance to the utter cleansing of the heart, was ever by grace through faith.

Unfortunately, some of the sons and daughters of the revival would not go on to perfect love—even though they continually employed the means of grace—not because divine grace was either insufficient or lacking, but simply because fear and willful unbelief barred the way. And when Wesley had earlier explored that faith "whereby we are sanctified, saved from sin and perfected in love," as in his sermon "The Scripture Way of Salvation," he noted it is a divine evidence and conviction: first of all, that "God hath promised it in the Holy Scripture"; second, "that what God hath promised he is *able* to perform"; third, "that he is able and willing to do it *now*"; and finally, "that *he doth it*."[96] So then, for those who resisted the highest graces of God in an ongoing manner, and sometimes in some very subtle ways, the eighteenth century was hardly different from the first: "And he [Jesus] did not do many deeds of power there, because of their unbelief" (Matt. 13:58).

CONCLUSION
"The Best of All"

Wesley's Bible and Case

There are few people in the history of the church who ministered over a longer period of time or who were more indefatigable in their labors than John Wesley. Indeed, with the exceptions of his visit to Herrnhut, shortly after his evangelical conversion, as well as his trips to Holland, Wesley was continually preoccupied with the rounds of ministry. Preaching, meeting the societies, crafting sermons and letters, as well as ameliorating the plight of the poor were the principal staples of this well-focused and remarkably dedicated life. And during the last few years of his witness, as Wesley's health began to deteriorate, his principal fear was neither pain nor death, but that he would no longer be able to serve the church he so loved. "I hope I shall not live to be useless," he remarked to Thomas Taylor.

The Wedding Garment

As Wesley looked out from the vantage point of a life well lived and nearly over, he took note of those things that were necessary for the ongoing vitality of Methodism. Accordingly, in the early part of 1790 Wesley wrote a sermon entitled "The Wedding Garment," which epitomized some of the leading themes of Methodism throughout the years. For one thing, this sermon underscored the necessity of personal holiness to qualify believers for heaven and to make them fit for glory. Thus, even at this late date, Wesley yet feared that an erroneous and superficial notion of faith might make the law of love void among some of his people, that the "righteousness of Christ," which entitles believers to heaven, might be misunderstood as a substitute for personal holiness. In this sermon, then, Wesley makes clear that the righteousness of the saints, though derived from Christ, is both real and imparted. Therefore the notion that justified believers remain under the power of sin while clothed with the righteousness of Christ is simply rejected. Wesley elaborates:

> In the Revelation we find mention made of "linen white and clean, which is the righteousness of the saints." And this too many vehemently contend means the righteousness of Christ. But how then are we to reconcile this with that passage in the seventh chapter, "They have washed their robes, and made them white in the blood of the Lamb"? Will they say, "The righteousness of Christ was washed and made white in the blood of Christ"? Away with such antinomian jargon. Is not the plain meaning this?—it was from the atoning blood that the very righteousness of the saints derived its value and acceptableness to God.[1]

In addition, Wesley points out, once again, that orthodoxy is a small part of religion and must not be mistaken for the very substance of the Christian faith, which is not a string of ideas or speculation of any sort, but holy love reigning in the heart.

Remarkably, Wesley distinguished holiness, which is itself the wedding garment, even from some of the General Rules of the United Societies, lest the Methodists be content with the mere form, or the shell, of the Christian faith. Thus, Wesley underscored a difference between, first, holiness and "avoiding evil" and then, second, between holiness and "doing good." Concerning the former, Wesley pointed out: "How many take holiness and harmlessness to mean one and the same thing! Whereas were a man as harmless as a post he might be as far from holiness as heaven from earth."[2] And with respect to the latter, Wesley reasoned:

> Yea, suppose a person of this amiable character to do much good wherever he is, to feed the hungry, clothe the naked, relieve the stranger, the sick, the prisoner, yea, and to save many souls from death: it is possible he may still fall far short of that holiness without which he cannot see the Lord.[3]

Clearly, then, the imagination that any work, however noble, supersedes the necessity of holiness is the "very marrow of antinomianism," the substance of that which makes void the holy law of love.

Inward Religion Revisited

Beyond Wesley's emphasis on holiness as imparted and instantiated in the warp and woof of life, his reading of à Kempis, Pascal, and Fenelon—judging from his comments in April of this same year[4]—convinced him of the inestimable value of the soul. To illustrate, in a letter to William Black a few months later, Wesley noted that "one soul is worth all the merchandise in the world."[5] This accent on the vitality of the soul and the significance of inward religion continued in Wesley's ministry though he was, from time to time, criticized sharply for precisely these themes by those who were either outright ignorant of such matters or thought all of this to be irrelevant, extravagant, and at best a pious indulgence.

Unperturbed by such criticism, Wesley continued to highlight the value of inward religion in his later years in two key ways: first, by emphasizing his well-worked theme of real Christianity, and second, by showing the necessity of "going on to perfection." Concerning the first emphasis, in writing to his niece Sarah in August 1790, Wesley linked "perpetual cheerfulness" with the "temper of a Christian."[6] "Real Christians know it is their duty to maintain this," Wesley observed, "which is in our sense to rejoice evermore."[7] Moreover, the previous month Wesley had affirmed that unless believers have "new senses, ideas, passions, [and] tempers, they are no Christians! However just, true, or merciful they may be, they are but atheists still."[8] And when Wesley preached his very last open-air sermon in the fields at Winchelsea in October 1790, it was the none other than the words of real Christianity on his lips:

> I went over to that poor skeleton of ancient Winchelsea. . . . I stood under a large tree, on the side of it, and called to most of the inhabitants of the town, "The kingdom of heaven is at hand; repent, and believe the gospel." It seemed as if all that heard were, for the present, almost persuaded to be Christians.[9]

Earlier that summer Wesley had composed the sermon "On Living Without God," which proved to be something of a puzzle to those who had utterly identified Christianity with ethics. In this sermon, Wesley revealed that the proper Christian faith ever goes beyond simply becoming more moral or ethical to nothing less than participating in the very life of God through inward sanctifying grace, that grace which makes one holy:

> From hence we may clearly perceive the wide difference there is between Christianity and morality. Indeed nothing can be more sure than that *true* Christianity cannot exist without both the inward experience and outward practice of justice, mercy, and truth; and this alone is given in morality. But it is equally certain that all morality, all the justice, mercy, and truth which can possibly exist without Christianity, profiteth nothing at all, is of no value in the sight of God, to those that are under the Christian dispensation.[10]

Concerning the second emphasis, that is, Christian perfection, Wesley continued to underscore its salience in his later years; for in his estimation it was a doctrine pivotal to growth in grace, a lure to spiritual betterment. And though Wesley, for example, had affirmed earlier to Robert Hopkins that "you will never find more life in your own soul than when you are earnestly exhorting others to go on to perfection,"[11] Wesley, himself, was apparently very guarded concerning his own experience: "I speak of myself very little," he wrote to Sarah Crosby a decade earlier, "were it only for fear of hurting *them*. I have found exceeding few that could bear it; so I am constrained to repress my natural openness."[12] Was this an allusion to Wesley's own perfection of love? Was this a hint at his entire sanctification? The reference is not at all clear.

In September 1790, Wesley had referred to Christian perfection as "the grand depositum which God has lodged with the people called Methodists"; and he maintained, furthermore, that "for the sake of propagating this chiefly He appeared to have raised us up."[13] But this forthright assertion must not be taken to mean that Wesley viewed Christian perfection as a Methodist distinctive as if it were a denominational marker. Such a provincial view would have invariably marked defeat for Methodism—and Wesley clearly knew this. Indeed, the doctrine of perfect love belonged not simply to the Methodists but to the whole church, to the universal community of faith. A few months earlier, for example, in April 1790, Wesley had cautioned that "the Methodists are to spread life among *all* denominations; which they will do till they form a separate sect."[14] Thus, the ecclesiastical question of whether Methodism would remain in the Anglican Church, which had preoccupied Wesley throughout the years, was actually connected to the very purpose of Methodism in the first place: namely, to spread scriptural holiness across the land, to be a witness to all people—to Anglicans, Moravians, Calvinists, Roman Catholics, and others—of the remarkable value of holy love. It was, therefore, to maintain the *universality* of this witness that Wesley had urged his people not to depart from the Church of England. Little wonder that he (and his brother) had been so concerned about this issue.

But Wesley was also concerned with the other half of the equation, so to speak, not that the Methodists would leave the Church, but that they would be cast out or at least frustrated in their ongoing mission by a hostile or indifferent clergy. In June, for example, Wesley asked the Bishop of Lincoln, Dr. Pretyman Tomline, "For what reasonable end would your Lordship drive these people out of the Church?"[15] "And is it a Christian, yea a Protestant bishop," Wesley continued, "that so persecutes his own flock."[16] The following month, a few days after Wesley's last Conference which was held in Bristol, he wrote to William Wilberforce, reformer and statesman: "Now sir, what can the Methodists do? They are liable to be ruined by the Conventicle Act, and they have no relief from the Act of Toleration! If this is not oppression, what is?"[17]

The Ongoing Danger of Riches

Yet another ingredient for the ongoing vitality of Methodism was the care that Wesley took to warn his people of the danger of wealth.

He had already developed this theme much earlier, especially during the 1780s; but now as he approached his own demise, Wesley penned yet two more sermons on this head entitled "On Worldly Folly" and "The Danger of Increasing Riches." In the former sermon, Wesley cautions against setting one's heart on the ephemeral, the fleeting, that is, on anything that is less that God: "Whoever is seeking happiness in the things that perish is laying up treasure for himself. This is absolutely inconsistent with *being rich* (or rather, *growing* toward God)."[18] Beyond this, Wesley observes in a summary and poetic fashion: "He who is a child of God can truly say: All my riches are above! All my treasure is thy love."[19] Beyond this, in the latter sermon, "The Danger of Increasing Riches," Wesley allows an exception to his earlier, rather medieval and "ecclesiastical" definition of wealth by noting that one's debts must also be taken into account in any reckoning. He states:

> But here an exception may be made. A person may have more than necessaries and conveniencies for his family, and yet not be rich. For he may be in debt; and his debts may amount to more than he is worth. But if this be the case he is not a rich man, how much money soever he has in his hands.[20]

And this exception should have given pause to all those who were ever quick to judge their neighbors merely with respect to their outward conditions. Wesley cautions in this same sermon, "And beware of forming a hasty judgment concerning the fortune of others. There may be secrets in the situation of a person which few but God are acquainted with."[21]

But what is perhaps most remarkable in "The Danger of Increasing Riches" is its broad recognition of distinct kinds of ministry, a recognition that had already been developed in Wesley's sermon "On Visiting the Sick." Indeed, the value judgments in "The Danger of Increasing Riches" are remarkably similar to those expressed years earlier by the Methodist leader. To illustrate, in this sermon Wesley reasons as follows:

> Ye angels of God, ye servants of his, that continually do his pleasure, our common Lord hath entrusted you also with talents *far more precious* than gold and silver, that you may minister in your various offices to the heirs of salvation."[22]

Accordingly, ministering to both body and soul in a very holistic way was ever Wesley's goal in his many labors.

The Letters to Wilberforce and Sharp

The accumulation of wealth—an affront to Christian integrity—was bad enough, but when it was done at the expense of one's neighbor, in trading and keeping slaves, it became simply intolerable, a clear violation of both good sense and the basic human right of liberty. Thus, shortly before his death, Wesley wrote to Wilberforce, who was a member of Parliament at the time, and urged him to continue his reforming, abolitionist efforts: "O be not weary of well doing! Go on, in the name of God and in the power of His might, till even American slavery (the vilest that ever saw the sun) shall vanish away before it."[23] A few years earlier, Wesley had corresponded with Granville Sharp, who had founded a society for the abolition of slavery in 1787, and noted that "ever since I heard of it . . . I felt a perfect detestation of the horrid slave trade, but more particularly since I had the pleasure of reading what you have published upon the subject."[24] Beyond this, a month later in November 1787, Wesley revealed similar sentiments to Thomas Funnell: "Whatever assistance I can give those generous men who join to oppose that execrable trade I certainly shall give. I have printed a large edition on the *Thoughts on Slavery.*"[25] Clearly, then, in Wesley's eyes, the ongoing practice of slavery was nothing less than a scandal, "not only to Christianity but [to] humanity [as well]."[26]

It was not really any political philosophy, however, that had led Wesley to such judgments on slavery. Rather, it was some of Wesley's own theological concerns expressed in his attentiveness to moral law, that "copy of the divine mind," that actually confirmed his views. Put another way, the moral law, which expresses the "fitness of relations" between God and humanity, was an "objective" standard that Wesley could appeal to, above the pull and tug of unjust laws and political pressures, to ensure that all human beings, ever created in the image and likeness of God, were not denied precisely what belonged to them *as* human beings—the right of liberty among them. Wesley's life and witness, then, informed by sophisticated theological reasoning, was surely an encouragement to Wilberforce, Shaftsbury, and others as they helped to turn back this "execrable trade" in Britain.

Wesley's Health

Though Wesley was characteristically concerned with the plight of others in the early days of 1790, his own physical need was great. By now his strength had nearly abated, the optimistic references to his health in the journal were all gone, and he slowed down considerably. He was, quite simply, an old man on the doors of eternity, his strength spent in the rounds of ministry. "Time has shaken me by the hand," Wesley wrote to Freeborn Garrettson in February 1790, "and death is not far behind."[27] The nearly worn-out preacher had actually noted a sudden change in his condition earlier in August 1789 when his eyes became dim and his strength left him.[28] In 1791, Wesley wrote to Thomas Greathead, "I am half blind and half lame"; but he took some comfort in adding, "but by the help of God I creep on still."[29] The following month, Wesley knew the end was approaching; and so he wrote to Ezekiel Cooper that "those [who] desire to write or say anything to me have no time to lose."[30] Wesley preached his last sermon, at Leatherhead, towards the end of February with a disposition marked by seasoned grace. It had been a long career, spanning much of the eighteenth century, and it was now drawing to a close.

The Enduring Theological Themes

Wesley's journey had clearly been a remarkable one. It is therefore appropriate to note at this point, and in a summary fashion, the salient theological avenues that flowed into the thoroughfare of this long and rich life.

Growing up in a pious rectory, in which a curious mix of Puritan discipline and Anglican sensibilities held sway, Wesley was prepared to appreciate later the holy living tradition in Catholicism as well as in his own Church of England. The names à Kempis, Taylor, and Law marked his awakening to the proper Christian faith though Wesley struggled for years to actualize the graces that had so captivated his vision and purpose. His early numerous soteriological missteps, especially while he was in Georgia, held great teaching power for the Methodists and for subsequent generations. And it was, remarkably enough, his own Anglican tradition that had, in part, misled him where there were not a few contemporary examples of those who had inadvertently made sanctification, in some form or other, the basis of justification.

En route to Georgia, aboard the *Simmonds*, Wesley encountered several Moravian Pietists. The Methodist leader was so captivated by the godliness and fearlessness of these Germans, especially in the face of death, that he had several important conversations with them, in particular with August Spangenburg, their much beloved leader. Beyond this, the genius of the Pietism of Halle was communicated to Wesley by the Salzburgers who likewise were on a mission in Georgia—a mission sponsored, in part, by the SPCK. Bolzius and Gronau, for example, two of the Salzburger leaders, left a lasting impression on Wesley due to their sanctity, deep humility, and gracious spirit. And it was precisely this Moravian and Salzburger influence, in conjunction with the collapse of his own ministry in Georgia, that prepared Wesley, now broken, humble, and teachable, for all that lay ahead.

Back in England in 1738, Wesley had the good fortune to meet Peter Böhler at the home of Mr. Weinantz, a Dutch merchant. Disabusing Wesley of his contrived "philosophy," marked principally by works and resolutions, Böhler introduced him to a Lutheran Pietist understanding of grace that underscored the sheer gratuity of the divine favor with respect to *both* justification *and* regeneration. Stunned by this simple teaching that the peace and power of the gospel are sheer, unmerited gifts to be received by grace *alone* and therefore *now*, Wesley quickly scrambled through the Scriptures, the touchstone of his faith, and found "scarce any instances there of other than *instantaneous* conversions—scarce any other so slow as that of St. Paul."[31]

By March of this same year, Wesley was thoroughly convinced of the truth of Böhler's teaching and that it was in accordance not only with Scripture, but also with the doctrine of the Church of England. These precious promises, to be received by faith, had by now conquered Wesley's mind but not yet his heart, that complex of dispositions that should be ever oriented toward God. And it was not until May 24, 1738, a decisive date in Wesley's spiritual journey and one specifically remembered over seven years later, that Wesley finally entered in. Attending a religious meeting in Aldersgate Street in London and listening to *Luther's Preface to the Epistle to the Romans*, Wesley received the graces of justification, regeneration, and a measure of assurance, now instantiated, emblazoned on his heart, the total effect of which led him to write in his journal, "I felt my heart strangely warmed."[32]

So then Wesley had received forgiveness, the empowering presence of the Holy Spirit, and a measure of assurance by *hearing* Luther's classic *Preface* read. In this setting, the Holy Spirit took the very *words* of the reader that evening and burned them into Wesley's heart. These gifts of grace, therefore, were mediated to Wesley, a real conjunction of Word and Spirit, such that the whole was simply greater than the sum of the parts. Undoubtedly, Wesley heard clear and distinct words that evening, as would anyone else at this religious meeting; but the point is that he had received far more than words, for the transcendence of the Spirit, present to the hearing *ear* of faith, was communicated to him, made immanent in his heart, through the instruments, the very human vessels, of speech. This was a Protestant conversion, to be sure, in its very orality. Not surprisingly, shortly thereafter, in April 1739, Wesley was determined to continue to *proclaim* the glad tidings of salvation to the middling classes of Britain and, of course, to the poor.

By 1741, as the great Evangelical Revival was underway, Wesley took the next step, so to speak, and continued the genius of the Protestant Reformation by conceiving the sheer gratuity of grace not simply in terms of justification and regeneration, as Böhler had taught him, but in terms of entire sanctification as well. Simply put, just as justification (peace) and regeneration (power) constituted the gracious *gifts* of God, to be received now by faith *alone*, so too was the highest of graces, even the entire sanctification of the heart (being), to be likewise received. In short, Wesley now connected key Reformation insights, with respect to grace and faith, with the full scope of the holy living tradition he so loved. Recall Wesley's own language in terms of the approach toward entire sanctification:

And by this token may you surely know whether you seek it by faith or by works. If by works, you want something to be done first, before you are sanctified. You think, "I must first be or do thus or thus." Then you are seeking it by works unto this day. If you seek it by faith, you may expect it as you are: and if as you are, then expect it *now*.[33]

Indeed, the graciousness of these unmerited gifts was underscored by Wesley in his observation, made in 1752, that "we allow it is the work of God *alone* to justify, to sanctify, and to glorify; which three comprehend the whole of salvation."[34] Such a judgment, of course, does not exclude divine/human cooperation so long as such working together (or synergism as it is often called) is understood in a conjunctive way, that is, not as constituting the entirety of the flow of redemption, but as a *process* caught up in the *even larger* conjunction that embraces and holds in tension the *cruciality* and sheer gratuity of divine instantiating action. Therefore, an unswervingly "Catholic" reading of Wesley in its nearly exclusive emphasis on the processes of redemption (and sometimes in a very open ended way) is unable to account for the decisive, qualitatively distinct actualizations of grace that occur at definite points along the way (whether recalled or not, whether dramatic or not) in the ongoing lives of believers.

For Wesley, then, the transitions from sinner to justified believer, as well as from being initially holy as a child of God to becoming entirely so were each, for want of better language, "threshold" changes, changes that were distinct and, therefore, in some sense set apart from earlier growth in grace.[35] Put another way, justification (broadly understood) and entire sanctification were the two principal foci of the Wesleyan way of salvation; and their integrity was held in place precisely by the language of *sola gratia, sola fide*.

However, if these Reformation insights were neglected and Wesley's doctrine of Christian perfection were viewed simply through his "Catholic" paradigm of processive growth, then the qualitative difference that characterizes entire sanctification would be missed because it would be viewed simply as the last increment of a long and ongoing process. So understood, the change entailed in perfection would be like all other prior incremental changes of heart cleansing, except that it would be the "last" one. However, such a view misprizes the transition from impurity to *being* pure in heart, which, in some sense, is unlike all other incremental changes with the exception of justification and the new birth. Indeed, the transition from a heart not quite perfected in love to heart purity is actually similar to the transition from being unholy to becoming a child of God in that both of these foci mark *crucial* receptions of grace, significant qualitative modulations, the very graciousness of which is properly comprehended only through Wesley's "Protestant" paradigm of *sola* language.

Moreover, Wesley affirmed that the process of divine/human cooperation can, after all, be cut short when grace as sheer unmerited favor comes into prominence, since the new birth for sinners, as well as entire sanctification for believers, can ever be realized *now*. In other words, so much growth and change can happen in a relatively short period of time, a truth that perplexed all those who were more inclined toward some form of self-justification and sanctification or who had affirmed, sometimes in subtle ways, that their own working in the process of redemption was in fact—if not fully acknowledged or even recognized—*absolutely* required for entire sanctification, a sanctification that because of these misunderstandings was unswervingly equated with chronological maturity and adult Christian states.

But this "Protestant" side of Wesley that highlights the divine gracious activity at every step along the way must, of course, be seen in *conjunction* with his "Catholic" side (drawn in part from the Eastern Fathers mediated to him by his own Anglican tradition) that does indeed highlight divine/human cooperation as aspirants await the further instantiation of grace in works of piety, charity, and the like, and, of course, in the means of grace. Wesley parsed these distinctions very carefully in 1765 for his Calvinist detractors in his summary sermon "The Scripture Way of Salvation," in which the Methodist leader employed the language of "not in the same sense," or "not in the same degree," to affirm, on the one hand, the sheer graciousness of God's gifts, but, on the other hand, the importance of responding to such divine initiatives, a response itself ever enabled by grace. Despite these efforts, many of the evangelical Calvinists simply could not comprehend the imperative mood in Wesley's theology ("God works; therefore you can work; God works; therefore you must work") and how it could possibly be in harmony with *sola gratia* and *sola fide*. Wesley, for his part, actually held these "Catholic" and "Protestant" emphases together in a large and intricate tension, in which the sheer gratuity of grace was not undermined by the importance of responding to divine initiatives and thereby growing in holiness. Moreover, Wesley repeatedly maintained that such cooperation with God's gracious overtures to the soul, though in some sense necessary if there be time and opportunity, can never be the *basis* upon which one is converted or subsequently cleansed from the *being* of sin; for it is ever upon the merits of Christ alone that these salvific boons, these wonderful gifts, are graciously given.

So then, it is almost as if grace as divine/human cooperation in Wesley's theology marks the "normal" processes in which aspirants wait and grow in the means of grace until they receive the "extraordinary," qualitatively distinct "threshold" graces of justification, broadly understood, and entire sanctification—graces that are not only the two well-articulated foci of the Wesleyan *via salutis*, but also, in a real sense, the works of God *alone*. What then, according to Wesley, actually occurs in the interim between the new birth and entire sanctification? For one thing, believers are growing in holy tempers, which are sheer gifts of grace, as they participate in the life of the church and are formed through works of piety and mercy until they receive that remarkable *faith*, again a gift of grace, that sanctifies entirely. Such a conjunction of graces, carefully nuanced, marks a real soteriological calculus, with greater approximations and instantiated increments along the way; and yet not all growth in grace is incremental, simply a matter of *degree*, for qualitatively distinct actualizations occur in the hearts of believers and are nothing less than the sole handiwork of God—for only the Most High can bring a soul to life, spiritually speaking, make it holy, and sanctify it entirely.

The importance and necessity of the instantiation, or *realization* of graces (in space and time), was also borne out in one of the cherished emphases of the Methodists, namely, the doctrine of Christian assurance. Unlike Roman Catholicism, which deemed such knowledge by and large presumptive and therefore directed its members to a priestly hierarchy who offered the comfort of the sacraments, Methodism remained firm in its teaching that Christian assurance is a *common* privilege of the sons and daughters of God and that it may occur in a diversity of settings, that is, within the walls of the church, through preaching and the sacraments, and beyond them. This *direct* witness of the Holy Spirit to redeemed souls, which went beyond conscience and a recognition of the fruits of the Spirit, smacked of "mysticism" to Rome especially since this witness sometimes skirted the *mediation* of priestly administrations. Moreover, some in the Anglican Church held similar reservations, although far too many, such as Bishop Butler, simply rejected the direct witness of the Holy Spirit outright as yet another species of Methodist fanaticism.[36] The *definite* and direct instantiations along the way of salvation, from no assurance at all (a state of abject sin) to the full assurance of faith that accompanies Christian perfection, were written off as instances of a practical theology gone terribly wrong. Indeed, Gibson and others much preferred the "normal" cycles and routines of Christian nurture, in which grace was understood as reason, good churchmanship, and common virtue, all of which ever marked the way forward. And it was perhaps the very supernatural flavor of the Spirit's witness that was so offensive, a reality that underscored not only the limits of human power, but also humanity's utter dependence on a God of Holy Love.

Wesley's Last Days

By Friday, February 25, 1791, Wesley was back in City Road London, and Elizabeth Ritchie, a friend, was concerned as she watched the elderly gentleman step down from his coach. Being ill from a fever that arose a day earlier, Wesley immediately went to bed and asked to be left alone for a half hour. He remained bedridden over the weekend. By Monday his weakness had increased, and his friends became alarmed. That evening, Wesley had a restless night, but when asked whether he was in pain, he replied, "No." The next day, Tuesday, March 1, Wesley was sinking. He called on Mr. Bradford to give him a pen and ink but could no longer write. Elizabeth Ritchie, who was at his side, replied, "Let me write for you, sir; tell me what you would say."[37] "Nothing," Wesley spoke, "but that God is with us."[38] In the afternoon, Wesley got up, and to the astonishment of all, given his condition, he broke out in the words of a hymn by Isaac Watts:

> I'll praise my Maker while I've breath;
> and when my voice is lost in death,
> praise shall employ my nobler powers.

My days of praise shall ne'er be past,
while life, and thought, and being last,
or immortality endures.

Happy the man whose hopes rely
On Israel's God; He made the sky,
And earth, and seas with all their train;
His truth for ever stands secure,
He saves the oppressed, he feeds the poor,
And none shall find His promise vain.[39]

Dr. Whitehead, Elizabeth Ritchie, Charles Wesley's widow and daughter, as well as nine others were present in the little room. Wesley gathered his strength once more and cried out, "The best of all, God is with us!" The dying leader lingered throughout the night often repeating the lines from Watts's hymn, "I'll praise; I'll praise." The following morning, March 2, Wesley uttered his last word, "Farewell!" and died "without a struggle or a groan" at about 10:00 A.M.

As Wesley closed his eyes that March morning, there were nearly three hundred preachers in Britain alone, and over seventy thousand Methodists. The classes, bands, and the select societies would soon meet; the poor would receive both spiritual and material care, and the common people would hear the glad tidings of salvation in chapels as in the fields. Lending stocks, loans, a medical dispensary, and even a stranger's society that ministered to the forgotten of England were a part of this considerable legacy. Penny tracts and the publication of Wesley's sermons made their contribution as well. And though Wesley offered no profession of perfect love, not even on his deathbed, who could doubt that he died in the highest graces as evidenced in a life well lived in service to both God and neighbor. This had been an exemplary Christian life; and those present that morning, no doubt, sensed something of the awe, sanctity, and even sweetness of this passing: "Precious in the sight of the Lord is the death of his faithful ones" (Psalm 116:15).

And though Wesley lived and died as a good son of the Church of England, faithful to her doctrines, mindful of her catholicity and her rich Reformation traditions, ever careful to reach the poor in service marked by energy, passion, and love, he had hardly been recognized—much less appreciated—by many of his Anglican peers then as now. But Wesley's legacy remains, his work endures, and the witness to holy, sacrificial love goes forward among a rich diversity of people—a people who not only have come to know Jesus Christ in a deep, satisfying, and redemptive way, fortified by grace and empowered by love, but who also, in their quiet moments, have come to realize, that recognized or not, appreciated or not, on that March morning in 1791 had died one of England's greatest saints.

Notes

1. The Puritan and Anglican Heritage

1. Anthony Armstrong, *The Church of England, the Methodists, and Society, 1700–1850* (Totowa, N.J.: Rowman and Littlefield, 1973), 46.

2. Ibid.

3. Ibid., 35.

4. John White was also appointed the chairperson of the Committee for Scandalous Ministers, an appointment that involved him in the examination and ejection of many Anglican clergy. For more on this topic, see Robert C. Monk, *John Wesley: His Puritan Heritage* (Nashville: Abingdon Press, 1966), 20.

5. There is evidence to suggest that Dr. Samuel Annesley had been ordained episcopally even earlier in 1639, probably as a deacon. See Frank Baker, "Wesley's Puritan Ancestry," *London Quarterly & Holborn Review* 187 (July 1962): 183.

6. Ibid. Frank Baker maintains that in this latter setting, in 1694, Dr. Annesley conducted the first public ordination held by the Presbyterians after the ejections of 1662 and that one of the ordinands was none other than Edmund Calamy, a Puritan divine who was prominent in the Westminster Assembly and in the Savoy Conference. But Calamy's presence in 1694 is not possible since he had been dead for years, having expired in 1666. One suspects that the date for the ordination ceremony is not accurate, a fact that would, then, allow for Calamy's presence.

7. John A. Newton, *Methodism and the Puritans* (London: Dr. Williams's Trust, 1964), 19.

8. Charles Wallace Jr., ed., *Susanna Wesley: The Complete Writings* (New York: Oxford University Press, 1997), 70.

9. Rupert E. Davies, *The Works of John Wesley*, Bicentennial ed., vol. 9, *The Methodist Societies: History, Nature, and Design* (Nashville: Abingdon Press, 1989), 231. Emphasis is mine. R. Ellis Roberts is critical of the

"Puritan Sabbath," especially in his observation: "It is indeed puzzling by what logic the Puritan divines defended the observance of Sunday; it was true they kept it as a day of mourning, much less joyful than the Jewish Sabbath they imitated." Cf. R. Ellis Roberts, *The Church of England* (London: Francis Griffiths, 1908), 144.

10. Southey makes the claim that Susanna Wesley had reasoned her way to Socinianism, from which she was rescued by her husband, Samuel. This is a claim, not an argument, since Southey does not offer sufficient, substantiating reasons for such a judgment. See Robert Southey, *The Life of Wesley; and Rise and Progress of Methodism*, vol. 1 (London: Longman, Brown, Green, and Longmans, 1846), 9-10.

11. Though this indeed was a serious dispute between Susanna and Samuel on political matters, Heitzenrater is correct to point out that this couple actually "held very similar theological and political views and were of a mind in the methods of raising their children." See Richard P. Heitzenrater, *Wesley and the People Called Methodists* (Nashville: Abingdon Press, 1995), 26.

12. Rebecca Lamar Harmon, *Susanna, Mother of the Wesleys* (Nashville: Abingdon Press, 1968), 47.

13. See Francis J. McConnell, *John Wesley* (New York: Abingdon Press, 1939), 12.

14. Edwards suggests that Samuel returned perhaps because he realized that though Susanna had strong Jacobite sympathies, she nevertheless accepted *de facto* but not *de jure* the accession of William and Mary. See Maldwyn Edwards, *Family Circle: A Study of the Epworth Household in Relation to John and Charles Wesley* (London: The Epworth Press, 1961), 47.

15. Some well-known biographies insist that Wesley was born on June 17, 1703, whereas others maintain a date of June 28, 1703. Why is there this discrepancy? The answer has to do with an emperor, a pope, and the British sense of what's appropriate.

The first reform of the Western calendar was effected by Julius Caesar in 45 B.C. An improvement over the previous reckoning, this calendar determined the year to be 365¼ days and, therefore, added an additional day every four years (a leap year). The problem with this "Julian" calendar, however, is that the earth actually takes a little less than 365¼ days to revolve around the sun. Though this difference seems small, the calendar actually shifts seven days every thousand years, and so by the sixteenth century, Pope Gregory XIII was faced with a considerable problem (a difference of ten days by that point) in reckoning the date of Easter.

Pope Gregory set up a commission that arrived at a new formula, a formula otherwise known as the Gregorian calendar. Like the Julian calendar, a day would be added every fourth year, with an important exception: Leap years would be removed at century boundaries (1700, 1800, 1900, etc.), but would be put back at century boundaries divisible by 400 (1200, 1600, 2000, etc.). Thus, this reform made an adjustment to the Julian calendar by dropping three days every four centuries and is accurate to the tune of one day every 2,800 years. This means that in the year 4382, the calendar will have to be corrected by one day. (Be sure not to lose any sleep over this.)

So with this reform in place, why should there still have been a discrepancy of eleven days in the British calendar in the eighteenth century? The answer lies in the recognition that the British did not adopt the Gregorian calendar—a popish plot for sure!—until 1752. By this time, the discrepancy was up to eleven days, and so Parliament corrected the calendar by that amount in the same year. Wesley's birthday then emerged as June 28 and not June 17. So in later life, Wesley celebrated his birthday (usually with boastful comments about his excellent health) on June 28. For more on the differences between the Julian and Gregorian calendars, see Stephen Jay Gould, *Questioning the Millennium: A Rationalist's Guide to a Precisely Arbitrary Countdown* (New York: Harmony Books, 1997), 141-49.

16. Newton, *Methodism and the Puritans*, 6.

17. Leslie F. Church, *Knight of the Burning Heart: The Story of John Wesley* (London: The Epworth Press, 1938), 15-16.

18. W. Reginald Ward and Richard P. Heitzenrater, eds., *The Works of John Wesley*, Bicentennial ed., vol. 19, *Journals and Diaries II* (Nashville: Abingdon Press, 1990), 286-87.

19. Ibid., 19:286.

20. Frank Baker, ed., *The Works of John Wesley*, Bicentennial ed., vol. 25, *Letters I* (New York: Oxford University Press, 1980), 330-31.

21. Ward and Heitzenrater, *Journals and Diaries*, 19:290-91.

22. Baker, *Letters*, 25:329.

23. John Telford, *The Life of John Wesley* (New York: Methodist Book Concern, 1899), 19-20. Emphasis is mine.

24. Frank Baker, *John Wesley and the Church of England* (Nashville: Abingdon Press, 1970), 9.

25. Harmon, *Susanna*, 80.

26. Monk, *Puritan Heritage*, 182.

27. Telford, *Life of John Wesley*, 5.

28. John Telford, ed., *The Letters of the Rev. John Wesley, A.M.* (London: The Epworth Press, 1931), 5:76.

29. Baker, "Puritan Ancestry," 183.

30. Gordon Rupp, *Religion in England, 1688–1791* (Oxford: Clarendon Press, 1986), 173.

31. Ibid.

32. Southey, *Life of Wesley*, 7.

33. Armstrong, *Church of England*, 51.

34. Heitzenrater, *Wesley and the People*, 24.

35. Ibid., 30.

36. Ibid., 27-28.

37. Ibid., 30-31.

38. Ward and Heitzenrater, *Journals and Diaries*, 18:243 (May 24, 1738).

39. The point, however, of this autobiographical narrative is not to display the sharpest contrast possible between Wesley's life at Epworth and later at Charterhouse. The work of Luke Tyerman, a nineteenth-century biographer, is already well known—and criticized—for its claim that "Wesley entered the Charterhouse a saint, and left it a sinner." See Luke Tyerman, *The Life and Times of the Rev. John Wesley, M.A., Founder of the Methodists* (New York: Harper & Bros., 1872), 1:22.

40. Telford, *Life of John Wesley*, 30.

41. Ibid.

42. Church, *Burning Heart*, 31.

43. Baker, *Letters*, 25:148 (from Susanna Wesley, August 19, 1724).

44. Indeed, Albert C. Outler maintains that Wesley "had grown up with a gospel of moral rectitude and then had been converted (in 1725) to the 'holy living' tradition of Jeremy Taylor, William Law, Thomas à Kempis, and the Eastern Fathers." See Thomas C. Oden and Leicester R. Longden, eds., *The Wesleyan Theological Heritage: Essays of Albert C. Outler* (Grand Rapids, Mich.: Zondervan Publishing House, 1991), 64.

45. Baker, *Wesley and the Church*, 12.

2. The End of Religion

1. Luke Tyerman, *The Life and Times of the Rev. John Wesley, M.A, Founder of the Methodists* (New York: Harper & Bros., 1872), 1:33.

2. Frank Baker, ed., *The Works of John Wesley*, Bicentennial ed., vol. 25, *Letters I* (Nashville: Abingdon Press, 1980), 149.

3. Ibid., 25:160.

4. Ibid.

5. Ibid.

6. Ibid.

7. Ibid., 25:158.

8. Ibid., 25:160.

9. Ibid., 25:157. Italics are mine.

10. Ibid., 25:160.

11. W. Reginald Ward and Richard P. Heitzenrater, eds., *The Works of John Wesley*, Bicentennial ed., vol. 18, *Journals and Diaries I* (Nashville: Abingdon Press, 1988), 244 (May 24, 1738).

12. Ibid., 18:244, n. 37.

13. Ibid., 18:212.

14. Ibid.

15. Ibid.

16. Baker, *Letters*, 25:162.

17. Ibid. 25:163. Susanna had raised the question that if all mirth is "vain and useless" as à Kempis had suggested, "why then does the Psalmist so often exhort us to rejoice in the Lord?"

18. Ibid., 25:166.

19. Ibid. In *A Plain Account of the People Called Methodists*, produced in 1749, Wesley indicates to Vincent Perronet the ongoing importance of prudential rules, especially when he states, "That with regard to these little prudential helps we are continually changing one thing after another, it is not a weakness or fault (as you imagine) but a peculiar advantage which we enjoy. By this means we declare them all to be merely prudential, not essential, not of divine institution. We prevent, so far as in us lies, their growing formal and dead. We are always open to instruction, willing to be wiser every day than we were before, and to change whatever we can change for the better." Cf. Rupert E. Davies, ed., *The Works of John Wesley*, Bicentennial ed., vol. 9, *The Methodist Societies: History, Nature, and Design* (Nashville: Abingdon Press, 1989), 262-63.

20. Baker, *Letters*, 25:171.

21. Ibid.

22. Thomas Jackson, ed., *The Works of John Wesley* (Grand Rapids, Mich.: Baker Book House, 1978), 11:366-67.

23. Ibid., 11:366.

24. Baker, *Letters*, 25:168.

25. Richard P. Heitzenrater, *Wesley and the People Called Methodists* (Nashville: Abingdon Press, 1995), 35.

26. Baker, *Letters*, 25:169.

27. Ibid., 25:170.

28. Ibid.

29. Ibid., 25:174-75.

30. See Heitzenrater, *Wesley and the People*, 35.

31. Albert C. Outler, ed., *The Works of John Wesley*, Bicentennial ed., vols. 1-4. *Sermons* (Nashville: Abingdon Press, 1984–87), 3:152, "In What Sense We Are to Leave the World."

32. Baker, *Letters*, 25:175.

33. Ibid.

34. Ibid., 25:175-76. For an interesting treatment of the Cambridge Platonist John Norris, see John C. English, "John Wesley's Indebtedness to John Norris [epistemology and education]," *Church History* 60 (March 1991): 55-69.

35. Baker, *Letters*, 25:179.

36. Ibid., 25:188. Susanna also recommended the writings of Pearson. In her estimation, his definition of faith was in no way defective. See Baker, *Letters*, 25:183.

37. Richard P. Heitzenrater, "John Wesley and the Oxford Methodists" (Ph.D. diss., Duke University, 1972), 59.

38. Ibid.

39. Ibid.

40. Baker, *Letters*, 25:194.

41. Henry D. Rack, *Reasonable Enthusiast: John Wesley and the Rise of Methodism*, 2nd ed. (Nashville: Abingdon Press, 1992), 63.

42. Ibid.

43. Ibid., 68.

44. Gerald R. Cragg, ed., *The Works of John Wesley*, Bicentennial ed., vol. 11, *The Appeals to Men of Reason and Religion* (Nashville: Abingdon Press, 1989), 183.

45. Baker, *Letters*, 25:208.

46. Ibid., 25:215. Emphasis is mine.

47. Jackson, *Works*, 12:20.

48. Baker, *Letters*, 25:208-9.

49. Ward and Heitzenrater, *Journals and Diaries*, 18:244.

50. Ibid., 244-45. For an evenhanded study of William Law and his relationship to John Wesley, see J. Brazier Green, *John Wesley and William Law* (London: The Epworth Press, 1945); see also Eric W. Baker, *A Herald of the Evangelical Revival: A Critical Inquiry into the Relation of William Law and John Wesley and the Beginnings of Methodism* (London: The Epworth Press, 1948).

51. Jackson, *Works*, 11:367.

52. Gordon Rupp, *Religion in England, 1688–1791* (Oxford: Clarendon Press, 1986), 224. In his sermon "The Use of Money," produced in 1760, Wesley states, "So I am convinced, from many experiments, I could not study to any degree of perfection either mathematics, arithmetic, or algebra, without being a deist, if not an atheist. And yet others may study them all their lives without sustaining any inconvenience. None therefore can here determine for another, but every man must judge for himself, and abstain from whatever he in particular finds to be hurtful to his soul." Cf. Outler, *Sermons*, 2:270.

53. Although Outler makes the claim that Wesley "had been converted (in 1725) to the 'holy living' tradition of Jeremy Taylor, William Law,

Thomas à Kempis, and the Eastern Fathers, when Wesley, himself, recounts his theological journey during this period, he mentions only the western contributions of à Kempis, Taylor, and Law." See Albert C. Outler, "John Wesley as a Theologian: Then as Now," in *The Wesleyan Theological Heritage: Essays of Albert C. Outler*, ed. Thomas C. Oden and Leicester R. Longden (Grand Rapids, Mich.: Zondervan Publishing House, 1991), 64.

54. V. H. H. Green, *The Young Mr. Wesley: A Study of John Wesley and Oxford* (New York: St. Martin's Press, 1961), 305-10.

55. For an example of this equivalence, see Hoo-Jung Lee, "Experiencing the Spirit in Wesley and Macarius," in *Rethinking Wesley's Theology for Contemporary Methodism*, ed. Randy L. Maddox (Nashville: Kingswood Books, 1998), 197-212.

56. Baker, *Letters*, 25:235.

57. Ibid. 25:240.

58. Outler, *Sermons*, 3:581.

59. John Telford, *The Life of John Wesley* (New York: Methodist Book Concern, 1899), 58-59.

60. Ibid., 59.

61. Heitzenrater, *Wesley and the People*, 45-46.

62. J. H. Overton, *John Wesley* (Boston: Houghton, Mifflin, 1891), 28, n. 1. Heitzenrater points out that "the first contemporary reference to the term comes in a letter from John Clayton, at Oxford, to John Wesley, visiting London in August 1732." See Heitzenrater, *Wesley and the People*, 45-46.

63. Tyerman points out that several of these Methodists did not remain with the society: "Clayton shunned the Wesleys; Broughton opposed them; Ingham left them; Hervey, though with Christian courtesy, wrote against them; Gambold, at one period, hesitated not to say that he was ashamed of them; and even Whitefield, for a little while, was alienated from them"; see Tyerman, *Life and Times*, 1:68.

64. Rack, *Reasonable Enthusiast*, 90.

65. Ibid.

66. See Heitzenrater, "Oxford Methodists," 143.

67. V. H. H. Green, *John Wesley* (London: Thomas Nelson, 1964), 29.

68. Outler, *Sermons*, 3:275-76.

69. Jackson, *Works*, 11:367.

70. Outler, *Sermons*, 3:504.

71. Martin Schmidt, *John Wesley: A Theological Biography*, 3 vols., trans. Norman R. Goldhawk (Nashville: Abingdon Press, 1962), 1:140. And observe that Anton Wilhelm Böhme is the same person who translated Arndt's *True Christianity* into English.

72. August H. Francke, *A Christian Library*, vol. 29, *Nicodemus*, ed. John Wesley (London: J. Kershaw, 1826), 468.

73. Ibid., 29:479.

74. Ibid., 29:473.

75. Ibid., 29:483. Wesley also reveals the ongoing influence of Puritanism on his life and thought in the production of the sermon "On the Sabbath," written in 1730. Cf. Outler, *Sermons*, 4:268-78.

76. Francke, *Nicodemus*, 29:482.

77. Ibid.

78. Ibid., 29:492.

79. Outler maintains that "the term 'pietism' had pejorative overtones in the rhetoric of both orthodox and liberals who have served as our chief arbiters of theological fashions now for four centuries; this is apparent in any standard church history or history of Christian thought." See Albert C. Outler, "Pietism and Enlightenment: Alternatives to Tradition," in *Christian Spirituality III*, ed. Louis Dupre and Don Saliers (New York: Crossroad, 1989), 242.

80. Baker, *Letters*, 25:293.

81. Ibid.

82. Ibid., 25:365.

83. Heitzenrater, *Wesley and the People*, 52.

84. Baker, *Letters*, 25:365-66.

85. Rack, *Reasonable Enthusiast*, 76.

86. Baker, *Letters*, 25:366.

87. Ibid., 25:369.

88. John W. Wright, "Wesley's Theology as Methodist Practice: Postmodern Retrieval of the Wesleyan Tradition," *Wesleyan Theological Journal* 35, no. 2 (Fall 2000): 9.

89. Ibid., 21.

90. David Lowes Watson, for example, contends that "the form and power of early Methodist discipleship lay in its methods." However, it is perhaps more accurate to state that the form did, indeed, lay in its methods, but the power in the *presence* of the Holy Spirit. See David L. Watson, "Aldersgate Street and the General Rules: The Form and the Power of Methodist Discipleship," in *Aldersgate Reconsidered*, ed. Randy L. Maddox (Nashville: Kingswood Books, 1990), 45.

91. Jackson, *Works*, 8:299.

92. Outler, *Sermons*, 1:399.

93. John Telford, ed., *The Letters of the Rev. John Wesley, A.M.* (London: The Epworth Press, 1931), 4:299.

94. Jackson, *Works*, 11:367.

95. Ward and Heitzenrater, *Journals and Diaries*, 23:105.

96. Outler, *Sermons*, 1:402.

97. Ibid.

98. Ibid.

99. Ibid., 1:404.

100. In a letter to Susanna, written a year before "The Circumcision of the Heart" was preached, Wesley again underscores the value of humility: "That is the very thing I want to do; to draw off my affections from this world, and fix them upon a better world. But how? What is the surest and the shortest way? Is it not to be humble? Surely this is a large step in that way." See Baker, *Letters*, 25:329.

101. Baker, *Letters*, 25:395.

102. Ibid., 25:396.

103. Ibid., 25:411.

104. Ibid., 25:420.

105. Ibid., 25:421.

106. Ibid., 25:399.

107. Ibid., 25:400.

108. See Richard P. Heitzenrater, "Great Expectations: Aldersgate and the Evidences of Genuine Christianity," in Maddox, *Aldersgate Reconsidered*, 61.

3. Georgia

1. Maldwyn Edwards, *Family Circle: A Study of the Epworth Household in Relation to John and Charles Wesley* (London: The Epworth Press, 1961), 32.

2. Ibid., 31.

3. Martin Schmidt, *John Wesley: A Theological Biography* (Nashville: Abingdon Press, 1962–1973), 1:131.

4. Frank Baker, *The Works of John Wesley*, Bicentennial ed., vol. 25, *Letters I* (Nashville: Abingdon Press, 1980), 439.

5. Ibid., 25:441.

6. Ibid.

7. Ibid., 25:442.

8. W. Reginald Ward and Richard P. Heitzenrater, eds., *The Works of John Wesley*, Bicentennial ed., vol. 18, *Journals and Diaries I* (Nashville: Abingdon Press, 1988), 136-37.

9. V. H. H. Green, *John Wesley* (London: Thomas Nelson, 1964), 41.

10. Ward and Heitzenrater, *Journals and Diaries*, 18:140.

11. Ibid., 18:314.

12. Ibid., 18:140.

13. Ibid., 18:139.

14. Ibid., 18:141.

15. Ibid., 18:142.

16. Ibid., 18:143.

17. Ibid.

18. Ibid., 18:165.

19. Ibid., 18:169.

20. In a rather interesting move, Theodore Jennings actually obviates the whole question of Wesley's soteriological status by claiming that it made little difference to him whether he served God as a servant or as a son. See Theodore W. Jennings, "John Wesley Against Aldersgate," *Quarterly Review* 8, no. 3 (Fall 1988): 16.

21. Baker, *Letters*, 25:265.

22. Gerald R. Cragg, ed., *The Works of John Wesley*, Bicentennial ed., vol. 11, *The Appeals to Men of Reason and Religion* (Nashville: Abingdon Press, 1989), 136. Emphasis is mine.

23. Shortly after Wesley's return to England from Holland in August 1783, he was seized with "a most impetuous flux." A grain and a half of opium was administered to him in three doses to bring about some relief. This narcotic naturally stopped the cramps that Wesley had been suffering from, but it also, to use his own words, "took away my speech, hearing, and power of motion, and locked me up from head to foot, so that I lay a mere log." See Ward and Heitzenrater, *Journals and Diaries*, 23:287.

24. Albert C. Outler, ed., *The Works of John Wesley*, Bicentennial ed., vol. 1, *Sermons* (Nashville: Abingdon Press, 1984), 162. Though one might suspect that Wesley would have linked freedom from the fear of death with Christian perfection, the evidence clearly indicates that he most often associated it with both justification and the new birth. Such a liberty, in Wesley's mind, is entailed in the graces of a child of God and is implied in Paul's observation, "There is therefore now no condemnation for those who are in Christ Jesus" (Rom. 8:1). In other words, with no condemnation, there is no anxious fear of death and judgment. Moreover, Wesley's later statement (on February 3, 1738), "Hereby I am delivered from the fear of the sea, which I had both dreaded and abhorred from my youth," does not necessarily indicate that he was free from all fear of death at this time. Indeed, one can overcome a fear of water or heights, for example, and still have a fear of death, hell, and judgment due to one's spiritual condition.

25. Cragg, *Appeals*, 11:146.

26. Outler, *Sermons*, 1:257. For more on Wesley's understanding of eternal loss, see "Of Hell," Outler, *Sermons*, 3:31ff. Indeed, the word "hell" appears over five hundred times in Wesley's writings, a fact that has proved troubling to those modern scholars who hold what can only be termed "sentimental" and therefore unrealistic understandings of "holy love."

27. Ibid., 1:258.

28. Ibid., 1:259. Bracketed material has been inserted to indicate that the context of this sermon clearly indicates that this material is not auto-biographical for John Wesley. The "I," in other words, is a literary device employed to engage the reader and to give existential force to this material.

29. Ibid., 2:19. For more on Wesley's understanding of the moral law and its role in spiritual life in convincing sinners, leading them to Christ, and in offering guidance for growth in grace, see Kenneth J. Collins, "John Wesley's Theology of Law" (Ph.D. diss., Drew University, 1984).

30. Outler, *Sermons*, 2:142. Wesley's own fear of death dissipated after his evangelical conversion, and never surfaced again in his journal. And Wesley's letter to Elizabeth Hardy in May 1758 does not contradict this affirmation. In this correspondence, Wesley wrote: "I myself was so a few years ago. I felt the wrath of God abiding on me. I was afraid every hour of dropping into hell. I knew myself to be the chief of sinners. Though I had been very innocent in the account of others, I saw my heart to be all sin and corruption." Interestingly, this excerpt reveals the Methodist leader's "quaint," not literal, use of the phrase "a few years ago." Indeed, when one pays attention to Wesley's rhetoric, his use of language, it becomes clear that, as he got older and looked back on important periods of his life, Wesley often became sentimental; and his use of time sequence was neither literal nor exact.

In terms of this Hardy letter, for instance, consider the following: First of all, if "a few years ago" were to be interpreted literally, then this should refer to the period, five years earlier, when Wesley thought that death was near and so composed his epitaph on November 26, 1753 (see John Telford, *The Letters of the Rev. John Wesley, A.M.* [London: The Epworth Press, 1931], 4:20; and Ward and Heitzenrater, *Journals and Diaries*, 20:482). The problem, however, is that there is no evidence of the fear of death in his journal at this time. On the contrary, although Wesley had been quite ill earlier that summer, he yet displayed remarkable faith and confidence in God, exclaiming: "I had now, with the flux, a continual headache, violent vomitings, and, several times in an hour, the cramp in my feet or legs. . . . But God enabled me to be *thoroughly content and thankfully resigned to him*" (Ward and Heitzenrater, *Journals and Diaries*, 20:469). Second, the phrase "Though I had been very innocent in the account of others," in the Hardy letter is actually a clue and most likely refers to Mr. Broughton's positive assessment of Wesley's faith in April 1738 even though Wesley had known himself to be a sinner (Ward and Heitzenrater, *Journal and Diaries*, 18: 234-35).

At any rate, the larger point remains: If a proper, scriptural Christian is not afraid to die, a soteriological standard that Wesley repeatedly affirmed, then what does that make him en route to Georgia? Again, the key issue here has to do with the *standards* of redemption. Wesley may not have always lived up to those standards throughout his life, but the period of 1753 to 1758 offers no evidence of the fear of death that was so typical of the younger Wesley. The Hardy reference, indeed, is "quaint" not literal; it points to an earlier, crucial period of Wesley's life.

31. Outler, *Sermons*, 2:207. A descent once more into sin, to be ensnared yet again, and possibly to one's eternal loss, is a sobering element of Wesley's Arminian theology.

32. Ward and Heitzenrater, *Journals and Diaries*, 22:357. In this context, Wesley notes that it would be well if this person were attentive to the convincing grace of the Holy Spirit until "he receives the Spirit of adoption."

33. Telford, *Letters*, 5:95.

34. For more on the motif of real Christianity and its significance in Wesley's soteriology, see Kenneth J. Collins, *A Real Christian: The Life of John Wesley* (Nashville: Abingdon Press, 1999); and Kenneth J. Collins, "Real Christianity as Integrating Theme in Wesley's Soteriology: The Critique of a Modern Myth," *The Asbury Theological Journal* 51, no. 2 (Fall 1996): 15-45.

35. Cragg, *Appeals*, 135-136. Though the fear of death was no longer an issue for Wesley after Aldersgate, he nevertheless grappled, at least on one occasion, with the prospect of death as oblivion or as extinction. In a letter to his brother Charles, for example, in 1766, Wesley wrote: "I have no more fear than love. Or if I have [any fear, it is not that of falling] into hell but of falling into nothing." See Telford, *Letters*, 5:16.

36. Thomas Jackson, ed., *The Works of John Wesley* (Grand Rapids, Mich.: Baker Book House, 1978), 10:479-80.

37. Telford, *Letters*, 6:31. As is also characteristic of this period, Wesley asked Ms. Cummins if she had "power over all sin." See also Wesley's journal of March 17, 1772 for an example of his ongoing use of the distinction almost/altogether Christians; his entry of August 12, 1772 for the use of the term "notional" believers; and his letter to Patience Ellison in 1777 where he links the distinction between almost/altogether Christian with being an outside/inside Christian. Cf. Ward, *Journals*, 22:311 and 22:345, and Telford, *Letters*, 6:274.

38. Ward and Heitzenrater, *Journals and Diaries*, 18:146.

39. Baker, *Letters*, 25:448, n. 3.

40. Richard P. Heitzenrater, *Wesley and the People Called Methodists* (Nashville: Abingdon Press, 1995), 60.

41. Arthur Wilford Nagler, *Pietism and Methodism, Or, The Significance of German Pietism in the Origin and Early Development of Methodism* (Nashville: Publishing House M.E. Church, South, 1918), 143.

42. Johann Arndt, *A Christian Library*, vol. 1, *True Christianity* (London: T. Blanshard, 1819), 1:137-39.

43. See "The Spirit of Bondage and of Adoption," in Outler, *Sermons*, 1:248-66; and "The Scripture Way of Salvation," in Outler, *Sermons*, 2:153-69.

44. Arndt, *True Christianity* in *A Christian Library*, 1:355. Moreover, this German pastor's soteriological concerns can also be seen in the following topics treated in *True Christianity*: repentance, 277; self-denial, 168; justification by faith 172, 173, 265, 381; faith and love 170, 240, 241; humility, 305-6; hope, 343; regeneration by faith, 267; new birth, 153; faith delivers from the guilt and power of sin, 177, 367-68; restoration of the *imago dei*, 135-43; holiness and happiness, 173, 203; Christ is our wisdom, righteousness, sanctification, and redemption, 208, 274; love of God and neighbor 217-219, 221, 313; redemption is a narrow path, 250; and Christian perfection, 355, 358. See also Wilhelm Koepp, *Johann Arndt* (Berlin: *Protestantischer Schriftenvertrieb*, 1912), 73ff.

45. Johann Arndt, *True Christianity*, trans. Peter Erb (New York: Paulist Press, 1979), 21.

46. Arndt, *True Christianity*, in *A Christian Library*, 1:207; see also pp. 211, 213, 270, and 356.

47. Ibid., 1:177, see also p. 269. Note that the opposite of inward religion for both Arndt and Wesley is not social action and relevance—a contemporary judgment—but formal, orthodox (consisting in correct opinions), impersonal, lifeless religion. Moreover, notice how Wesley aptly ties together inward religion, the religion of the heart, with good works in the following comment: "So manifest it is that although true religion naturally leads to every good word and work, yet the real nature thereof lies deeper still, even in 'the hidden man of the heart.' " Cf. "The Way to the Kingdom" in Outler, *Sermons*, 1:220, and 3:313, 3:320, 3:496, and 3:523.

48. Further evidence of inward religion in Wesley's thought can be found in the following: in the sermon "The Marks of the New Birth," in which he states, "The true living, Christian faith, which whosoever hath is 'born of God,' is not only an assent, an act of understanding, but a *disposition* which God hath wrought in his heart" (Outler, *Sermons*, 1:418, emphasis is mine); and in "The Great Privilege of Those That Are Born of God," in which Wesley affirms, "we may learn that it [being born of God] implies not barely the being baptized, ... but a vast inward change; a change wrought in the soul by the operation of the Holy Ghost" (Ibid.,

432). And see also Outler, *Sermons*, 2:117 ("Christian Perfection") and 2:195 ("The New Birth").

49. Arndt, *True Christianity*, in *A Christian Library*, 1:356.

50. Nehemiah Curnock, *The Journal of the Rev. John Wesley, A.M.* (London: The Epworth Press, 1938), 4:4.

51. See Outler, *Sermons*, 2:61-78 ("A Caution Against Bigotry") and 2:79-95 ("Catholic Spirit").

52. Schmidt, *Theological Biography*, 1:180.

53. Ibid., 181.

54. W. H. Fitchett, *Wesley and His Century: A Study in Spiritual Forces* (New York: Abingdon Press, 1922), 104.

55. Baker, *Letters*, 25:455.

56. Ward and Heitzenrater, *Journals and Diaries*, 18:161-62.

57. Green, *John Wesley*, 45. Wesley seemed to be self-assured with little doubt about the appropriateness of his ministerial style. And in one case in particular, concerning the death of an only child, Wesley could even appear outright cold and unthinking, especially when he noted in his journal that this event was a "happy misfortune" for the father and that "the punishment was just." See Ward and Heitzenrater, *Journals and Diaries*, 18:516.

58. Ward and Heitzenrater, *Journals and Diaries*, 18:160.

59. Ibid., 18:172. See also Heitzenrater, *Wesley and the People*, 66ff. There is considerable doubt among scholars that Wesley was reading the actual Ephrem while he was in Georgia. Cf. Randy L. Maddox, "John Wesley and Eastern Orthodoxy: Influences, Convergences, and Differences," *The Asbury Theological Journal* 45, no. 2 (Fall 1990): 45, n. 19.

60. Heitzenrater, *Wesley and the People*, 66.

61. Ward and Heitzenrater, *Journals and Diaries*, 18:175.

62. Earlier, in June 1736, Wesley had hoped that a "door [would be] opened for going up immediately to the Choctaws, the least polished, i.e., the least corrupted of all the Indian nations." But this plan was frustrated by Oglethorpe, himself, who believed not only that Wesley ran the danger of being intercepted or killed by the French there, but also that this would leave Savannah "destitute of a minister." See Ward and Heitzenrater, *Journals and Diaries*, 18:163.

63. Baker, *Letters*, 25:486.

64. Heitzenrater, *Wesley and the People*, 66.

65. Ibid., 69.

66. Earlier, around March 1736, John and Charles became vegetarians—at least for a time. Samuel Jr. was annoyed and remarked the following month: "You cannot imagine you have the same call to it that Daniel had to refuse the king's provision. It cannot be religion, for

abstaining from meats is a doctrine of devils." See Baker, *Letters*, 25:458 and Ward and Heitzenrater, *Journals and Diaries*, 18:155.

67. Baker, *Letters*, 25:500. Baker indicates that William Wogan was the devout London layman who published several works, at least one of which Wesley read at Oxford, his *Right Use of Lent* (1732). His most famous work, however, was *An Essay on the Proper Lessons of the Church of England.* See Baker, *Letters*, 25:499, n. 1.

68. Ibid., 25:502, n. 1.

69. Ibid., 25:502.

70. Ward and Heitzenrater, *Journals and Diaries*, 18:179.

71. Ibid., 18:436.

72. Ibid., 18:442.

73. Ibid., 18:469. For a lively, and in some parts controversial, account of Wesley's views on human sexuality, see Willie Snow Ethridge, *Strange Fires: The True Story of John Wesley's Love Affair in Georgia* (New York: Vanguard, 1971).

74. Ward and Heitzenrater, *Journals and Diaries*, 18:476.

75. Ibid.

76. Ibid., 18:477.

77. Ibid., 18:480.

78. Ibid., 18:482.

79. Ibid., 18:485.

80. Ibid.

81. Ibid., 18:486.

82. Ibid.

83. Ibid., 18:490. For more on Wesley's relationship with women, cf. John P. Briggs, "Unholy Desires, Inordinate Affections: A Psychodynamic Inquiry into John Wesley's Relationship with Women," *Connecticut Review* 13 (Spring 1991): 1-18; Henry Abelove, *The Evangelist of Desire: John Wesley and the Methodists* (Stanford, Calif.: Stanford University Press, 1990); Earl Kent Brown, *Women in Mr. Wesley's Methodism* (Lewiston, N.Y.: Edwin Mellon, 1983); John C. English, " 'Dear Sister': John Wesley and the Women of Early Methodism," *Methodist History* 33, no. 1 (October 1994): 26-33.

84. Ward and Heitzenrater, *Journals and Diaries*, 18:193.

85. Ibid., 18:195.

86. Ibid., 18:207.

87. Ibid. Emphasis is mine.

88. Ibid., 18:208-9.

89. Ibid., 18:209. "Let life be a burden to me."

90. Ibid., 18:211.

91. Ibid., 18:213.

92. Jackson, *Works*, 11:366.

4. Aldersgate

1. W. Reginald Ward and Richard P. Heitzenrater, eds., *The Works of John Wesley*, Bicentennial ed., vol. 18, *Journals and Diaries I* (Nashville: Abingdon Press, 1988), 213.

2. Ibid., 18:214.

3. Ibid., 18:214-15. Overton writes: "If John Wesley was not a true Christian in Georgia, God help millions of those who profess and call themselves Christians!" Cf. J. H. Overton, *John Wesley* (Boston: Houghton, Mifflin, 1891), 58.

4. Randy L. Maddox, who is typical of this view and has criticized evangelical understandings of conversion in his *Aldersgate Reconsidered*, writes elsewhere: "Wesley revised his assumptions . . . finally coming to value the nascent faith of the 'servant of God' as justifying faith. With each of these concessions it became more difficult to assert an exclusive twice-born model [of conversion]." See Randy L. Maddox, *Responsible Grace: John Wesley's Practical Theology* (Nashville: Kingswood Books, 1994), 155.

5. Ward and Heitzenrater, *Journals and Diaries*, 18:215.

6. Ibid., 18:215-16.

7. Ibid., 18:216. Wesley's desire to be free from the enslaving powers of sin is crucial to a proper interpretation of his early, pre-Aldersgate biography. For a view that discounts this material and maintains that whether Wesley served the Most High as a servant or as a child of God made little difference, see Theodore W. Jennings Jr., "John Wesley Against Aldersgate," *Quarterly Review* 8 (Fall 1988): 3-22.

8. Ward and Heitzenrater, *Journals and Diaries*, 18:221.

9. Ibid., 18:223.

10. Martin Schmidt, *John Wesley: A Theological Biography* (New York: Abingdon Press, 1962), 1:225.

11. Ward and Heitzenrater, *Journals and Diaries*, 18:226. "My brother, my brother, that philosophy of yours must be purged away."

12. Ibid., 18:228.

13. Ibid.

14. Rupert E. Davies, ed., *The Works of John Wesley*, Bicentennial ed., vol. 9, *The Methodist Societies: History, Nature, and Design* (Nashville: Abingdon Press, 1989), 430.

15. For more on the influence of Pietism on the life and thought of John Wesley, see F. Ernest Stoeffler, "Pietism, the Wesleys and Methodist Beginnings in America," in *Continental Pietism and Early American Christianity*, ed. F. Ernest Stoeffler (Grand Rapids, Mich.: William. B. Eerdmans, 1976), 184-221; Kenneth J. Collins, "The Influence of Early

German Pietism on John Wesley [Arndt and Francke]," *The Covenant Quarterly* 48 (November 1990): 23-42; Dale W. Brown, "The Wesleyan Revival from a Pietist Perspective," *Wesleyan Theological Journal* 24 (1989): 7-17. Sir Percy Scott, *John Wesleys Lehre von der Heiligung vergleichen mit einen lutherish-pietistischen Beispel* [John Wesley's doctrine of salvation compared with a Lutheran-pietistic example] (Berlin: Alfred Topelman, 1939).

16. Ward and Heitzenrater, *Journals and Diaries*, 18:233-34. On April 1, 1738, while Wesley was at Mr. Fox's society, his heart was "so full," as he put it, that he could not "confine [himself] to the forms of prayer, which we were accustomed to use there. Neither do I purpose to be confined to them any more, but to pray indifferently, with a form or without, as I may find suitable to particular occasions." Cf. Ward and Heitzenrater, *Journals and Diaries*, 18:233.

17. Ibid., 18:234. Wesley heard the experiences of Mrs. Fox and Mr. Hutchins (of Pembroke College), "two living witnesses that God *can* (at least, if he *does* not always) give that faith whereof cometh salvation in a moment, as lightning falling from heaven." See Ward and Heitzenrater, *Journals and Diaries*, 18:235.

18. Ibid. At the time Böhler wrote of Wesley: "He is a poor sinner, who has a broken heart and who hungers after a better righteousness than that which he has had up till now, namely after the righteousness which is in the blood of Jesus Christ." See Schmidt, *Theological Biography*, 1:243.

19. Robert Southey, *The Life of Wesley; and Rise and Progress of Methodism* (London: Longman, Brown, Green, and Longmans, 1846), 1:134.

20. William James, *The Varieties of Religious Experience: A Study in Human Nature* (New York: Modern Library, 1929), 78ff.

21. John Telford, *The Life of John Wesley* (London: Methodist Book Concern, 1899), 99.

22. Arnold Lunn, *John Wesley* (New York: The Dial Press, 1929), 109.

23. Ward and Heitzenrater, *Journals and Diaries*, 18:236.

24. Albert C. Outler, ed., *The Works of John Wesley*, Bicentennial ed., vols., 1-4, *Sermons* (Nashville: Abingdon Press, 1984–87), 1:533, "Upon Our Lord's Sermon on the Mount, Discourse IV."

25. Ward and Heitzenrater, *Journals and Diaries*, 18:235.

26. Ibid., 18:238.

27. Ibid., 18:239. As Böhler was getting ready to embark for America, Wesley wrote the following, indicating in what high esteem he held this young man: "O what a work hath God begun since his coming into England! Such an one as shall never come to an end till heaven and earth pass away." See Ward and Heitzenrater, *Journals and Diaries*, 18:237.

28. Schmidt, *Theological Biography*, 1:240.

29. Ibid. Indeed, as Schmidt so aptly points out, Böhler directed Wesley to Luther's deep insight that "lack of [saving] faith is the most serious sin."

30. Frank Baker, ed., *The Works of John Wesley*, Bicentennial ed., vol. 25, *Letters I* (New York: Oxford University Press, 1982), 540-41.

31. Ibid., 25:541.

32. Ibid.

33. Ibid. For some helpful explorations of the complicated relationship between William Law and John Wesley, cf. K. Harper, "[William] Law and [John] Wesley," *Church Quarterly Review* 163 (January-March 1982): 61-71; John R. Tyson, "John Wesley and William Law: A Reappraisal [Appendices]," *The Wesleyan Theological Journal* 17, no. 2 (Fall 1982): 58-78.

34. Baker, *Letters*, 25:541.

35. Ibid. See also J. Brazier Green, *John Wesley and William Law* (London: The Epworth Press, 1945); and Eric W. Baker, *A Herald of the Evangelical Revival: A Critical Inquiry into the Relationship Between William Law and John Wesley and the Beginnings of Methodism* (London: The Epworth Press, 1948).

36. Baker, *Letters*, 541-42.

37. Telford, *Life of John Wesley*, 108.

38. Ward and Heitzenrater, *Journals and Diaries*, 18:237.

39. Thomas Jackson, ed., *The Journals of Rev. Charles Wesley* (May 17, 1738) (London: John Mason, 1849), reprinted (Grand Rapids, Mich.: Baker Book House 1980), 1:88.

40. Ibid.

41. Ibid., 1:90. For helpful studies on the conversion of Charles Wesley, see Franz Hildebrandt, *Christianity According to the Wesleys* (London: The Epworth Press, 1956); Bernard G. Holland, "The Conversions of John and Charles Wesley and Their Place in Methodist Tradition," *The Proceedings of the Wesley Historical Society* 38 (1971): 45-53, 65-71; and Barbara Ann Welch, "Charles Wesley and the Celebration of the Evangelical Experience" (Ph.D. diss., University of Michigan, 1971).

42. Ibid., 1:91.

43. V. H. H. Green, *John Wesley* (London: Thomas Nelson, 1964), 59.

44. Ibid. Wesley did, indeed, practice what is called "bibliomancy," that is, he would often open the Bible to a random selection and then consider the text especially meant for him at that particular moment.

45. Baker, *Letters*, 25:575 and 26:183.

46. Ward and Heitzenrater, *Journals and Diaries*, 18:246.

47. Ibid., 18:247.

48. Ibid., 18:247-48.

49. Ibid., 18:248. For works which unduly minimize the significance of

Aldersgate in a way that does not take into account Wesley's standard of the new birth as freedom from the *power* of sin as well as his important distinction between the faith of a servant and the faith of a child of God, especially as it bears on the proper interpretation of May 24, 1738, and the Methodist leader's earlier theological journey, cf. Theodore W. Jennings Jr., "John Wesley Against Aldersgate," *Quarterly Review* 8 (Fall 1988): 3-22; Randy L. Maddox, "Celebrating Wesley—When?" *Methodist History* 29, no. 2 (January 1991): 63-75; Randy L. Maddox, "Aldersgate: A Tradition History," in *Aldersgate Reconsidered*, ed. Randy L. Maddox (Nashville: Kingswood Books, 1990), 133-46.

50. Word and Heitzenrater, Journals and Diaries, 18:249.

51. Ibid., 18:249-50.

52. Schmidt, *Theological Biography*, 1:263.

53. E. Theodore Bachmann, ed., *Luther's Works: Word and Sacrament I* (Philadelphia: Fortress Press, 1960), 35:369.

54. Ibid., 35:370.

55. Ward and Heitzenrater, *Journals and Diaries*, 18:250.

56. Ibid., 18:251. For more on Wesley's hamartiology, see John Chongnahm Cho, "Adam's Fall and God's Grace: John Wesley's Theological Anthropology," *Evangelical Review of Theology* 10, no. 3 (July 1986): 202-13; John R. Tyson, "Sin, Self and Society: John Wesley's Hamartiology Reconsidered [his Sermons on several occasions]," *The Asbury Theological Journal* 44, no. 2 (Fall 1989): 77-89.

57. Ward and Heitzenrater, *Journals and Diaries*, 18:253.

58. Outler, *Works*, 2:187. Emphasis is mine.

59. Ibid., 1:431-32. Works that explore the pietistic emphasis on regeneration and its possible influence on Wesley's own theological formulations are the following: J. Steven O'Malley, "Pietistic Influence on John Wesley: Wesley and Gerhard Tersteegen," *Wesleyan Theological Journal* 31, no. 2 (Fall 1996): 48-70; Geoffrey F. Nutall, "Continental Pietism and the Evangelical Movement in Britain," in *Pietismus und Reveil: Referate der internationalen Tagung der Pietismus in der Niederlanden und seiner internationalen Beziehungen* [Pietism and awakening: Papers of the International Congress of Pietism in the Netherlands and its international relationships], ed. J. Van den Berg and J. P. Van Doreen (Zist Verlag, 1987), 74ff.; and Sir Percy Scott, *John Wesleys Lehre von der Heiligung vergleichen mit einen lutherish-pietistischen Beispel* [John Wesley's doctrine of salvation compared with a Lutheran-pietistic example] (Berlin: Alfred Topelman, 1939).

60. Outler, *Sermons*, 1:187. Emphasis is mine.

61. Albert C. Outler, "The Place of Wesley in the Christian Tradition," in *The Wesleyan Theological Heritage: Essays of Albert C. Outler*, ed. Thomas

C. Oden and Leicester R. Longden (Grand Rapids, Mich.: Zondervan Publishing House, 1991), 84.

62. See Maddox, *Responsible Grace*, 151ff.

63. Outler, *Sermons*, 2:163. Emphasis is mine.

64. Jackson, *Works*, 10:230. Emphasis is mine.

65. Outler, *Sermons*, 1:120.

66. Ward and Heitzenrater, *Journals and Diaries*, 18:247.

67. Ibid.

68. John Telford, ed., *The Letters of John Wesley, A.M.* (London: The Epworth Press, 1931), 2:264.

69. Outler, *Sermons*, 1:120. For an interesting autobiographical reference concerning the faith of a devil and Wesley's own early faith, see Telford, *Letters*, 4:219.

70. Outler, *Sermons*, 1:121. Since Wesley affirms that saving faith goes beyond that which the apostles had before Christ's death and resurrection, this means that the disciples were not born of God, in the proper sense, prior to Pentecost. The birthday of the Church, then, cannot be the time when the apostles were "entirely sanctified" as some holiness works erroneously maintain.

71. Ibid.

72. Ibid. For similar descriptions of this kind of faith see ("Justification by Faith") 1:193ff., and ("The Scripture Way of Salvation") 2:160ff.

73. Cragg, *Appeals*, 11:69.

74. Outler, *Sermons*, 1:230.

75. Ibid., 1:123. Emphasis is mine.

76. Ibid., 1:124. Wesley explores the distinctions between the guilt, power, and being of sin in his sermons "On Sin in Believers" and "The Repentance of Believers." See Outler, *Sermons*, 1:314-53.

77. Jackson, *Works*, 10:364.

78. Ward and Heitzenrater, *Journals and Diaries*, 18:215-16.

79. Outler, *Sermons*, 1:137.

80. Ibid., 1:139.

81. Clifford W. Towlson, *Moravian and Methodist: Relationships and Influences in the Eighteenth Century* (London: The Epworth Press, 1957), 69.

82. Ward and Heitzenrater, *Journals and Diaries*, 18:260.

83. Ibid., 18:274. Christian David also indicated that there was an "intermediate state" between the bondage described in the seventh chapter of the Epistle to the Romans and the liberty of the children of God portrayed in the eighth chapter. See ibid., 18:270ff.

84. Ibid., 19:18.

85. Ibid., 18:281-82. Emphasis is mine.

86. Ibid., 18:254. Beyond Towlson's important work on the Moravians

and the Methodists, the following should be consulted in order to acquire the proper interpretive context for this, at times, complicated relationship: Leon O. Hynson, "John Wesley and the 'Unitas Fratrum': A Theological Analysis," *Methodist History* 18 (October 1979): 26-60; F. Ernest Stoeffler, "Religious Roots of the Early Moravian and Methodist Movements," *Methodist History* 24, no. 3 (April 1986): 132-40; W. P. Stephens, "Wesley and the Moravians," in *John Wesley: Contemporary Perspectives*, ed. John Stacey (London: The Epworth Press, 1988), 23-36.

87. Ward and Heitzenrater, *Journals and Diaries*, 18:254.

88. Ibid., 19:19.

89. Telford, *Letters*, 1:258.

90. Baker, *Letters*, 25:576-77. This observation of Wesley's proves difficult for those interpreters who maintain that Aldersgate simply represents the time of the Methodist leader's assurance. For more on this vital topic, see Arthur S. Yates, *The Doctrine of Assurance: with Special Reference to John Wesley* (London: The Epworth Press, 1952); Mark A. Noll, "John Wesley and the Doctrine of Assurance," *Bibliotheca Sacra* 132 (April-June 1975): 161-77; and Michael E. Lodahl, " 'The Witness of the Spirit': Questions of Clarification for Wesley's Doctrine of Assurance," *Wesleyan Theological Journal* 23, nos. 1 and 2 (Spring-Fall 1988): 188-97.

91. Baker, *Letters*, 25:575.

92. Ibid., 25:598.

93. Ibid.

94. Ward and Heitzenrater, *Journals and Diaries*, 19:21.

95. Ibid., 19:22.

96. Ibid., 19:46.

97. Ibid. It is clear that Wesley's "churchmanship" was changing at this point. In time, he would "violate parish boundaries" in his field preaching, a practice which roiled many of the Anglican clergy. For the best treatment of Wesley's relationship with the Church of England, see Frank Baker, *John Wesley and the Church of England* (Nashville: Abingdon Press, 1970).

98. Ward and Heitzenrater, *Journals and Diaries*, 19:46.

99. Baker, *Letters*, 25:616.

100. Ward and Heitzenrater, *Journals and Diaries*, 19:51.

5. The Form and Power of Methodism

1. W. Reginald Ward and Richard P. Heitzenrater, *The Works of John Wesley*, Bicentennial ed., vol. 19, *Journals and Diaries II* (Nashville: Abingdon Press, 1990), 64 (June 5, 1739).

2. Ibid., 19:70. Such responses hardly surprised some of the more reserved at the university, for it was reported by one disputant of Wesley's that "they always took [Wesley] to be a little crack-brained at Oxford." See Ward and Heitzenrater, *Journals and Diaries*, 19:81.

3. Ibid.

4. Frank Baker, ed., *The Works of John Wesley*, Bicentennial ed., vol. 25, *Letters I* (Oxford: Clarendon Press, 1980), 682.

5. Ibid., 25:694-95.

6. Ibid., 25:660. In an interesting twist, despite many favorable responses to his preaching in June 1739, Wesley began to doubt "whether God would not lay me aside and send other labourers into his harvest." See Ward and Heitzenrater, *Journals and Diaries*, 19:73.

7. Baker, *Letters*, 25:692.

8. Ibid., 25:660. Elsewhere, in a letter to Mrs. Crosby, Wesley writes: "I think the strength of the cause rests there; on your having an extraordinary call. So I am persuaded has every one of our lay Preachers: Otherwise, I could not countenance his preaching at all. It is plain to me, that the whole work of God termed Methodism is an extraordinary dispensation of his providence." See Thomas Jackson, ed., *The Works of John Wesley*, 14 vols. (Grand Rapids, Mich.: Baker Book House, 1978), 12:356.

9. Baker, *Letters*, 26:237.

10. Ward and Heitzenrater, *Journals and Diaries*, 19:96.

11. Ibid., 19:106.

12. Ibid., 19:123.

13. Ibid. Something of the substance of *what* Wesley was preaching can be found in his comments in September of this same year: "Thence I went to Lambeth and showed (to the amazement, it seemed, of many who were present) how 'he that is born of God doth not commit sin.' " See Ward and Heitzenrater, *Journals and Diaries*, 19:99.

14. V. H. H. Green, *John Wesley* (London: Thomas Nelson, 1964), 130.

15. Henry D. Rack, *Reasonable Enthusiast: John Wesley and the Rise of Methodism*, 2nd ed. (Nashville: Abingdon Press, 1992), 210.

16. Ward and Heitzenrater, *Journals and Diaries*, 19:185.

17. Jackson, *Works*, 5:516. See also Richard P. Heitzenrater, *Wesley and the People Called Methodists* (Nashville: Abingdon Press, 1995), 115.

18. Gerald R. Cragg, ed., *The Works of John Wesley*, Bicentennial ed., vol. 11, *The Appeals to Men of Reason and Religion and Certain Related Open Letters* (Nashville: Abingdon Press, 1989), 29.

19. Baker, *Letters*, 26:595.

20. Ward and Heitzenrater, *Journals and Diaries*, 19:130 (December 19, 1739).

21. Ibid., 19:132. See also Arthur S. Yates, *The Doctrine of Assurance:*

With Special Reference to John Wesley (London: The Epworth Press, 1952), 128 ff. for more on the question of "full assurance."

22. Albert C. Outler, *The Works of John Wesley,* Bicentennial ed., vols. 1-4, *Sermons* (Nashville: Abingdon Press, 1984–87), 1:381.

23. Ibid., 1:378.

24. Ibid., 1:383. See the extensive treatment of Wesley's doctrine of the means of grace in Henry H. Knight III, *The Presence of God in the Christian Life: John Wesley and the Means of Grace* (Metuchen, N.J.: Scarecrow Press, 1992).

25. Outler, *Sermons,* 1:381.

26. Ibid., 1:384. Outler indicates that Professor Massey Shepherd, an eminent Anglican liturgiologist, maintained that Wesley's threefold means of grace "have a sound basis in the official Anglican formularies: Prayer Book, Ordinal, Homilies, Catechism." See ibid., 1:377.

27. Ward and Heitzenrater, *Journals and Diaries,* 19:147.

28. Ibid.

29. Ibid. The great danger in Molther's position is one of fanaticism, for if neither those who lack faith nor those whose hearts are pure should use the means of grace, then it is virtually inevitable that something other than the Word of God, received in word and sacrament, will soon constitute the substance of this way.

30. Ibid., 19:151. Unlike Luther, who had referred to the Epistle of James as one of "straw," Wesley looked favorably on this writing and saw it as a principal means to impugn the error of solafidianism.

31. Ibid., 19:159.

32. Ibid., 19:161. It was James Hutton who had acquired a chapel for the Fetter Lane Society to use, and they promptly refused to let Wesley preach there. See Heitzenrater, *Wesley and the People,* 112.

33. Ward and Heitzenrater, *Journals and Diaries,* 19:191.

34. Ibid., 19:190.

35. Ibid., 19:213. In holding such a view, Zinzendorf basically contends that not only is the righteousness of Christ imputed to believers with respect to justification, but with respect to sanctification as well. Wesley, on the other hand, made a distinction between the juridical and the participatory and taught that imputation is limited to the former. Again, for Wesley, imputation does not apply to the participatory themes of sanctification, both initial and entire, themes which are characterized by imparted, not imputed, grace. That is, believers actually become holy and grow in holiness.

36. Ibid.

37. Ibid., 19:214.

38. Ibid., 19:195. The summary form of this insight that the carnal

nature remains even in a child of God can be found in two key sermons of Wesley: "On Sin in Believers," and "The Repentance of Believers." See Outler, *Sermons,* 1:314-34 and 1:335-52.

39. Ward and Heitzenrater, *Journals and Diaries,* 18:216. Emphasis is mine.

40. Ibid., 19:222.

41. Ibid., 20:88.

42. Henry R. McAdoo, *The Spirit of Anglicanism: A Survey of Anglican Theological Method in the Seventeenth Century* (London: A. & C. Black, 1965), 320-36. See also P. E. More and F. L. Cross, *Anglicanism: The Thought and Practice of the Church of England,* illustrated from the Religious Literature of the Seventeenth Century (London : S.P.C.K., 1957).

43. Ward and Heitzenrater, *Journals and Diaries,* 19:180.

44. Luke L. Tyerman, *The Life and Times of the Rev. John Wesley, M.A., Founder of the Methodists,* 3 vols. (New York: Harper & Bros., 1872), 1:316.

45. Ward and Heitzenrater, *Journals and Diaries,* 19:188.

46. Ibid., 188-89.

47. Ibid., 19:182. John Cennick had made such criticisms as well. For Wesley's response to Whitefield and others, see ibid., 19:182-83.

48. Baker, *Letters,* 26:32.

49. Robert Southey, *The Life of Wesley; and the Rise and Progress of Methodism* (London: Longman, Brown, Green, and Longmans, 1846), 1:314.

50. Baker, *Letters,* 26:32.

51. Ibid., 26:54. For studies that explore Wesley's doctrine of sin and offer both clarity and accuracy, see Richard S. Taylor, *A Right Conception of Sin: Its Importance to Right Thinking and Right Living* (Kansas City, Mo.: Nazarene Publishing House, 1939); John R. Tyson, "Sin, Self and Society: John Wesley's Hamartiology Reconsidered [his Sermons on several occasions]," *The Asbury Theological Journal* 44, no. 2 (Fall 1989): 77-89; Gordon Stanley Dicker, "The Concept 'Simul Justus et Peccator' in Relation to the Thought of Luther, Wesley and Bonhoeffer, and Its Significance for a Doctrine of the Christian Life" (Th.D thesis, Union Seminary, 1971).

52. Baker, *Sermons,* 26:54.

53. Outler, *Sermons,* 2:105.

54. Ibid., 2:107.

55. Ibid., 1:419. For a good study that compares Wesley's understanding of sin with nineteenth-century American formulations, see Paul M. Bassett, "Wesleyan Words in the Nineteenth-Century World: 'Sin,' a Case Study," *Evangelical Journal* 8 (Spring 1990): 15-40.

56. Ward and Heitzenrater, *Journals and Diaries,* 19:260.

57. Baker, *Letters,* 26:113-14.

58. Leslie F. Church, *Knight of the Burning Heart: The Story of John Wesley* (London: The Epworth Press, 1938), 126.

59. Rupert E. Davies, *The Works of John Wesley*, Bicentennial ed., vol. 9, *The Methodist Societies: History, Nature, and Design* (Nashville: Abingdon Press, 1989), 31.

60. Ibid.

61. Ibid., 9:34.

62. Ibid., 9:35.

63. Ibid. Here, Wesley, in underscoring the great twofold commandment, considers Methodism to be nothing less than genuine or scriptural Christianity.

64. Ibid., 9:38.

65. Ibid., 9:53. For more on the topic of damnation, see Wesley's sermon "Of Hell," Outler, *Sermons*, 3:30-44.

66. Davies, *Methodist Societies*, 9:53, n. 28.

67. Ibid., 9:61. Of the matter of assurance being a "common" privilege of a child of God, Wesley wrote to Tucker: " 'Yet I believe he may not know that he has it till long after.' This I deny; I believe no such thing. 'I believe, the moment a man is justified he has peace with God.' " See ibid.

68. Ward and Heitzenrater, *Journals and Diaries*, 19:283.

69. Ibid., 19:283-84.

70. Arnold A. Dallimore, *Susanna Wesley: The Mother of John and Charles Wesley* (Grand Rapids, Mich.: Baker Book House, 1993), 162.

71. Davies, *Methodist Societies*, 9:222-23. Giving evidence of his determination, Wesley observed in 1743: "I am more and more convinced that the devil himself desires nothing more than this, that the people of any place should be half-awakened and then left to themselves to fall asleep again. Therefore, I determine, by the grace of God, not to strike one stroke in any place where I cannot follow the blow." See Ward and Heitzenrater, *Journals and Diaries*, 19:318.

72. Davies, *Methodist Societies*, 9:67.

73. Ibid., 9:77.

74. Ibid. The bands were distinct from the classes in that they were generally smaller and were not geographically oriented. Instead, its members were separated according to age, sex, and marital status. See Heitzenrater, *Wesley and the People*, 119.

75. Davies, *Methodist Societies*, 9:78.

76. Ibid., 9:69.

77. Ibid. Heitzenrater points out that "although there is no evidence of John or Charles Wesley having had any contact with the Epworth religious society as such when they were children, their parents' concern for

the family was certainly of a piece with their nurture of the congregation." See Heitzenrater, *Wesley and the People*, 30-31.

78. Davies, *Methodist Societies*, 9:69.

79. D. Michael Henderson, *John Wesley's Class Meeting: A Model for Making Disciples* (Nappanee, Ind.: Francis Asbury Press, 1997), 83.

80. Rack, *Reasonable Enthusiast*, 279.

81. Ibid., 97-98.

82. Henderson, *John Wesley's Class Meeting*, 47.

83. Davies, *Methodist Societies*, 9:69.

84. Ibid., 9:256.

85. Ward and Heitzenrater, *Journals and Diaries*, 19:318 (March 12, 1743).

86. Maximin Piette, *John Wesley in the Evolution of Protestantism* (London: Sheed & Ward, 1937), 464.

87. Henderson, *Class Meeting*, 30.

88. Cragg, *Appeals*, 11:25-26.

89. Ibid., 11:25.

90. Ibid., 11:33. Wesley later accused both Bishop Warburton and Lavington of drawing "caricatures" of the Methodists. See Ward and Heitzenrater, *Journals and Diaries*, 22:246.

91. Cragg, *Appeals*, 11:14.

92. Ibid., 11:30.

93. For a study that explores Wesley's relationship with the Anglican bishops of his day, see Frank Baker, *John Wesley and the Church of England* (Nashville: Abingdon Press, 1970), 58-73.

94. Ward and Heitzenrater, *Journals and Diaries*, 20:407.

95. Cragg, *Appeals*, 11:5.

96. Ibid., 11:51.

97. Ibid., 11:53. Wesley's appeal to reason in this context is not limited to "theoretical reason" but embraces practical, moral elements as well. It is similar in some respects to the medieval "intellectus" rather than "ratio."

98. Ibid., 11:55.

99. Outler, *Sermons*, 2:10.

100. Cf. William Perkins, *The Works of William Perkins*, ed. Ian Breward (Abingdon, Berkshire: Sutton Courtenay Press, 1970); and Richard Baxter, *A Call of the Unconverted, to Turn and Live* (New York: American Tract Society, 1833).

101. See Wesley's earlier letter to his brother Samuel Jr. on October 30, 1738 (Baker, *Letters*, 25:575).

102. Outler, *Sermons*, 1:136.

103. Ibid., 1:139.

104. In 1746, for example, in his *Principles of a Methodist Farther Explained*, Wesley rejects the argument that because the English were baptized as infants that they were all, therefore, Christians now. And in a somewhat caustic vein, giving some indication of his sentiments on this subject, Wesley adds: "Consequently, [they] are no more *scriptural Christians* than the open drunkard or common swearer." The next year, Wesley continues this theme and cautions against "that abundance of those who bear the name of Christians [who] put a part of religion for the whole, generally some outward work or form of worship." See Davies, *Methodist Societies*, 9:225; and Baker, *Letters*, 26:229. For other references to real Christianity during this period, see Ward and Heitzenrater, *Journals and Diaries*, 19:198, 19:318; John Telford, ed., *The Letters of the Rev. John Wesley*, 8 vols. (London: The Epworth Press, 1931), 2:267; and Davies, *Methodist Societies*, 9:228.

105. Outler, *Sermons*, 1:178.

106. Ibid., 1:179.

107. John Telford, *The Life of John Wesley* (New York: Methodist Book Concern, 1899), 172.

108. Ward and Heitzenrater, *Journals and Diaries*, 20:36-37.

6. Theological Nuances and Ongoing Standards

1. Thomas Jackson, ed., *The Works of John Wesley*, 14 vols. (Grand Rapids, Mich.: Zondervan Publishing House, 1959), 8:312.

2. Theodore W. Jennings, "John Wesley *Against* Aldersgate," *Quarterly Review* 8, no. 3 (Fall 1988): 16.

3. Randy L. Maddox, *Responsible Grace: John Wesley's Practical Theology* (Nashville: Kingswood Books, 1994), 155.

4. W. Reginald Ward and Richard P. Heitzenrater, eds., *The Works of John Wesley*, Bicentennial ed., vol. 19, *Journals and Diaries II* (Nashville: Abingdon Press, 1990), 136.

5. Albert C. Outler, ed., *The Works of John Wesley*, Bicentennial ed., vols. 1-4, *Sermons* (Nashville: Abingdon Press, 1984–87), 1:154. Emphasis is mine.

6. Frank Baker, ed., *The Works of John Wesley*, Bicentennial ed., vol. 26, *Letters I* (Oxford: Clarendon Press, 1980), 107-8.

7. Jackson, *Works*, 8:276. Emphasis is mine.

8. Ibid.

9. Ibid. A few months later, Wesley noted that a little child of four years old had the full assurance of faith and thus was entirely sanctified, indicating quite clearly that this highest grace was not reserved simply for *adults*. See Ward and Heitzenrater, *Journals and Diaries*, 20:39.

10. Jackson, *Works*, 8:282.

11. Ibid., 8:293.

12. Ibid. Emphasis is mine. For a contemporary treatment of the Methodist doctrine of assurance, see Geoffrey Wainwright, "The Assurance of Faith: A Methodist Approach to the Question Raised by the Roman Catholic Doctrine of Infallibility," *One in Christ: A Catholic Ecumenical Review* 22, no. 1 (1986): 44-61.

13. Robert Southey, *The Life of John Wesley; and Rise and Progress of Methodism* (London: Longman, Brown, Green, and Longmans, 1846), 1:258. That Wesley maintains assurance is the *common* privilege of the sons and daughters of God suggests that it is rare when assurance, marked by doubt and fear, does not soon follow the new birth.

14. Jackson, *Works*, 8:293.

15. Baker, *Letters*, 26:182. Emphasis is mine. The following year Wesley again wrote to "John Smith" and maintained: "I suppose that every Christian believer, over and above that imperceptible influence, hath a direct perceptible testimony of the Spirit that he is a child of God." See ibid., 26:203.

16. Ibid., 26:246. Emphasis is mine. In an earlier letter to "John Smith," Wesley had maintained that "everyone that is born of God, and doth not commit sin, by his very actions saith, 'Our Father which art in heaven,' 'the Spirit itself bearing witness with their spirit that they are the children of God. . . .' " See ibid., 26:232.

17. Ibid., 26:254-55. Emphasis is mine. Notice that Wesley, in commenting on Acts 1:5, reveals that all true believers, not simply the entirely sanctified, have been baptized with the Spirit: "Ye shall be baptized with the Holy Ghost—And so are all true believers to the end of the world." See John Wesley, *Explanatory Notes Upon the New Testament* (Salem, Ohio: Schmul Publishers), 275.

18. I have reversed the terminology used in my earlier book, *The Scripture Way of Salvation*. In that setting, the terms "broad" and "narrow" referred to whether the position included justification; that is, the terms did *not* refer to the *numbers* entailed. Though this was an apt distinction, I have reversed it in the present work simply because most people invariably think of the *numbers* of people entailed—and not whether the position *includes* or excludes justification—when the language of broad and narrow is used. Now the term "broad" means it includes many people; "narrow" means it doesn't. Such usage is present in *A Real Christian: The Life of John Wesley* by Kenneth J. Collins (Nashville: Abingdon Press, 1999). This should bring greater clarity to the discussion.

19. Jackson, *Works*, 8:287-88.

20. Ibid., 8:288-89. In this setting, the Conference defined sincerity as "a constant disposition to use all the grace given."

21. Outler, *Sermons*, 4:35. Emphasis is mine.

22. Ibid., 1:258.

23. Ibid. Observe that the servants of God are awakened, but they see not a God of love, but One of wrath. It is, therefore, important not to confuse the issue of awakening with regeneration (and conversion).

24. Baker, *Letters*, 25:575. Also note that although Wesley eventually made distinctions among freedom from the guilt (justification), power (regeneration), and the being (entire sanctification) of sin, as evidenced in his sermon "On Sin in Believers," he continually maintained that even a babe in Christ has freedom from the power of sin. See Outler, *Sermons*, 1:314-34.

25. Observe that Maddox has substituted the terminology of "penalty, plague, and presence" for Wesley's language of being free from the "guilt, power, and being of sin," with the result that the cruciality of deliverance has been lost: "Wesley understood human salvation in its fullest sense to include deliverance (1) immediately from the *penalty* of sin, (2) progressively from the *plague* of sin, and (3) eschatologically from the very *presence* of sin and its effects." Also, note that deliverance from the "presence" of sin has been relegated not to this life, but to the eschaton. See Maddox, *Responsible Grace*, 143-44.

26. Rupert E. Davies, *The Works of John Wesley*, Bicentennial ed., vol. 9, *The Methodist Societies: History, Nature, and Design* (Nashville: Abingdon Press, 1989), 80.

27. John Telford, ed., *The Letters of the Rev. John Wesley, A.M.*, 8 vols. (London: The Epworth Press, 1931), 2:224.

28. Ibid.

29. Jackson, *Works*, 8:278.

30. Ibid., 10:271. Wesley's whole approach to the moral law, which includes its ongoing normative value in the life of the believer, is much more similar to that of Calvin than Luther. See Paul Scott Wilson, "Wesley's Homiletic: Law and Gospel for Preaching," *Toronto Journal of Theology* 10 (1994): 215-25.

31. Jackson, *Works*, 10:270, 279.

32. Ibid., 10:281.

33. Telford, *Letters*, 4:332. Compare this letter to Wesley's sermon "On Working Out Our Own Salvation," in which he notes that "salvation begins with what is usually termed (and very properly) "preventing grace. . . ." This, however, does not contradict his earlier statements so long as it is realized that in the former, Wesley is referring to salvation, properly speaking, which always includes holiness; but in the latter, he is

simply highlighting a "degree" of salvation in that the sinner is at least on the way to holiness. In short, in no sense was Wesley arguing in this sermon that those who merely have prevenient grace are in fact holy and are therefore redeemed, properly speaking. See Outler, *Sermons*, 3:203.

34. Jackson, *Works*, 8:285.

35. Outler, *Sermons*, 2:411. Emphasis is mine. Interestingly enough, in his sermon "On Living Without God," Wesley indicates that at regeneration, the spiritual senses of the believer come alive to discern the love of God. In this context, he employs such sensory language as "tasting" "feeling" and so on to make his point. See Outler, *Sermons*, 4:173.

36. Ibid., 1:419. Emphasis is mine. Later, Wesley will clarify his teaching here and distinguish freedom from the guilt, power, and being of sin, especially in his sermons "Sin in Believers" and "Repentance of Believers." See Outler, *Sermons*, 1:327.

37. Wesley expresses this distinction later in a letter to Mrs. Bennis though such an understanding is clearly supposed in this sermon. See Telford, *Letters*, 5:322.

38. Outler, *Sermons*, 1:420.

39. Telford, *Letters*, 3:169.

40. Outler, *Sermons*, 1:439ff. Though the claim has at times been made that the standards reflected in this mid-career sermon are not those of the later Wesley, such a claim is actually impugned by a comparison of this sermon, written in 1748, with Wesley's subsequent sermons "On Sin in Believers" and "The Repentance of Believers," written during the 1760s. See Outler, *Sermons*, 1:314-53.

41. Ibid., 1:442.

42. See Randy L. Maddox, "Responsible Grace: The Systematic Perspective of Wesleyan Theology," *Wesleyan Theological Journal* 19, no. 2 (Fall 1984): 13. Emphasis is mine. For more on the implications of Maddox's position, see Kenneth J. Collins, "Recent Trends in Wesley Studies and Wesleyan Holiness Scholarship," *The Wesleyan Theological Journal* 35, no. 1 (Spring 2000): 67-86.

43. Outler, *Sermons*, 2:197.

44. Cragg, *Appeals*, 11:111. See also p. 135. Wesley's Catholic/Anglican heritage, with its association of regeneration and infant baptism, pulls his theology toward both sacerdotalism and, ironically enough, the irresistibility of grace. Knight, in trying to avoid this predicament, draws a distinction between irresistible grace and the inability to resist grace, a distinction that seems artificial to say the least. "The reason infants are invariably born again," Knight explains, "is not that baptismal grace is irresistible for them, but, unlike adults, they are unable to resist it." See Henry H. Knight III, *The Presence of God in the*

Christian Life: John Wesley and the Means of Grace (Metuchen, N.J.: Scarecrow Press, 1992), 180.

45. Telford, *Letters*, 6:239-40.

46. Davies, *Methodist Societies*, 225.

47. Outler, *Sermons*, 1:428-29. In a later letter to William Green, Wesley maintains that "nine-tenths of men in England have no more religion than horses, and perish through the contempt of it." See Telford, *Letters*, 8:179.

48. Outler, *Sermons*, 1:428-29.

49. Ibid., 1:430. Wesley's language here is strong, "Lean no more on the staff of that broken reed"; nevertheless, his point is to underscore the importance of real, vital, inward change, a change without which one would not be fit for the kingdom of heaven.

50. Cragg, *Appeals*, 11:107.

51. Outler, *Sermons*, 1:429.

52. Baker, *Letters*, 26:125.

53. Ibid., 26:179. Emphasis is mine. There are over one hundred references to "true religion" in Wesley's writings, which range from the 1730s to the 1790s, and this indicates that this theme, like the motif of real Christianity, is marked not by its discontinuity or extinction, but by its continuity and significance.

54. Outler, *Sermons*, 1:219.

55. Ibid., 1:219-20.

56. Ibid., 1:220. See also Wesley's letter to Vincent Perronet in 1748, in which he relates that orthodoxy, or right opinions, is "at best but a very slender part of religion, if it can be allowed to be any part of it at all." See Telford, *Letters*, 2:293.

57. Outler, *Sermons*, 1:220. Outler maintains that in this sermon, Wesley denies that religion consists in either correct praxis or doctrine. See Outler, *Sermons*, 1:217.

58. Ibid., 1:221.

59. Ibid., 1:466-67.

60. Ibid., 1:467. It was, of course, Thomas à Kempis who had first revealed to Wesley the significance of inward religion, the religion of the heart, as noted in Wesley's later comments in his *Plain Account of Christian Perfection*. See Jackson, *Works*, 11:366.

61. Outler, *Sermons*, 1:533.

62. Ibid. 1:535.

63. Telford, *Letters*, 6:205.

64. Outler, *Sermons*, 1:673. See also Wesley's comments on inward religion in *A Farther Appeal to Men of Reason and Religion*, in Cragg, *Appeals*, 11:275.

65. See Jackson, *Works*, 4:493.

66. Davies, *Methodist Societies*, 9:283.

67. Ibid., 9:284. Wesley was not surprised that many Irish remained in the Roman Catholic faith since "Protestants can find no better ways to convert them than penal laws and Acts of Parliament." See Ward and Heitzenrater, *Journals and Diaries*, 20:189.

68. Outler, *Sermons*, 1:572-73.

69. Clapper expresses this dynamic by noting that dispositions (and affections for that matter) are transitive, that is, they take "objects." See Gregory S. Clapper, *John Wesley on Religious Affections: His Views on Experience and Emotion and Their Role in the Christian Life and Theology* (Metuchen, N.J.: Scarecrow Press, 1989), 163ff.

70. Jackson, *Works*, 10:274.

71. Clapper, *Religious Affections*, 163.

72. Jackson, *Works*, 10:273.

73. Outler, *Sermons*, 2:58. Maddox also believes Wesley used the terms "disposition" and "temper" in an equivalent way as revealed in his following observation: "He was using 'temper' in this connection in a characteristic eighteenth-century sense of an enduring or *habitual* disposition of a person." See Maddox, *Responsible Grace*, 69. For other examples of Wesley's interchangeable use of "disposition" and "temper," see Jackson, *Works*, 5:176, 325, and 459.

74. John Wesley, *Explanatory Notes upon the New Testament* (London: William Bowyer, 1755), most recent reprint, Grand Rapids, Mich.: Baker Book House, 1987 (1 Thess. 2:17).

75. Maddox, *Responsible Grace*, 69.

76. Clapper, interestingly enough, argues that a person is more in control of an affection than a passion. See Clapper, *Religious Affections*, 69. For his part, Richard Steele contends that there is no "hard-and-fast dividing line, however, between the passions and the affections." See Richard B. Steele, *"Gracious Affection" and "True Virtue" According to Jonathan Edwards and John Wesley* (Metuchen, N.J.: Scarecrow, 1994), 208.

77. Jackson, *Works*, 10:468.

78. Outler, *Sermons*, 2:474.

79. Ibid., 2:198. For a series of essays that helps place Wesley in the broader context of various theological traditions, see Kenneth E. Rowe, ed., *The Place of Wesley in the Christian Tradition*, rev. ed. (Metuchen, N.J.: Scarecrow Press, 1980).

80. Outler, *Sermons*, 2:169. Emphasis is mine.

81. Ibid., 3:506.

82. See also Wesley's comments, by way of analogy, with respect to the approach to entire sanctification in Outler, *Sermons*, 2:169.

83. Ward and Heitzenrater, *Journals and Diaries*, 20:203. Westley Hall was something of a scoundrel: He jilted one of the Wesley sisters, Kezia, in order to marry another; he apparently had many illicit love affairs and actually preached and practiced polygamy. There is evidence, however, that shortly before he died, he was in a state of repentance.

84. Ronald H. Stone, *John Wesley's Life and Ethics* (Nashville: Abingdon Press, 2001), 217.

85. Jackson, *Works*, 8:280.

86. Ibid., 8:281.

87. Davies, *Methodist Societies*, 9:127. Later in his career, Wesley feared that if the Methodists left the Church of England, they would only have the "form" of religion without its power: " 'But whenever the Methodists leave the Church, God will leave them." Lord, what is man! In a few months after, Mr. Ingham himself left the Church, and turned all the societies under his care into congregations of Independents. And what was the event? The same that he had foretold. They swiftly mouldered into nothing." See Outler, *Sermons*, 3:589-90.

88. Ward and Heitzenrater, *Journals and Diaries*, 20:110.

89. Telford, *Letters*, 4:150.

90. Ward and Heitzenrater, *Journals and Diaries*, 20:210.

91. Davies, *Methodist Societies*, 9:244.

92. Ibid. In this fifth reason, Wesley once again indicates the importance of social intercourse for the flowering of the Christian faith. For a treatment of this dynamic in a nineteenth-century American context, see A. Gregory Schneider, *The Way of the Cross Leads Home: The Domestication of American Methodism* (Bloomington: Indiana University Press, 1993).

93. Davies, *Methodist Societies*, 9:245.

94. Ibid., 9:258.

95. Ibid. And to the question: "But there are some true Christians in the parish, and you destroy the Christian fellowship between these and them'; Wesley replied: "That which never existed cannot be destroyed. But the fellowship you speak of never existed. Therefore it cannot be destroyed." See Davies, *Methodist Societies*, 9:258-59.

7. Strengthening the Foundations

1. W. Reginald Ward and Richard P. Heitzenrater, eds., *The Works of John Wesley*, Bicentennial ed., vol. 20, *Journals and Diaries III* (Nashville: Abingdon Press, 1991), 445.

2. Ibid., 21:156.

3. Manfred Marquardt, *John Wesley's Social Ethics: Praxis and Principles* (Nashville: Abingdon Press, 1992), 28.

4. Ward and Heitzenrater, *Journals and Diaries*, 20:151, n. 6.

5. Ibid., 20:125.

6. Ibid., 20:204.

7. John Telford, ed., *The Letters of John Wesley, A.M.*, 8 vols. (London: The Epworth Press, 1931), 3:262.

8. Ibid., 3:265.

9. Ibid., 3:266.

10. Ibid., 3:267.

11. Albert C. Outler, ed., *The Works of John Wesley*, Bicentennial ed., vols. 1-4, *Sermons* (Nashville: Abingdon Press, 1984–87), 2:46.

12. Ibid.

13. Ibid., 2:45. Outler points out that "Wesley does not propose to rehabilitate the term, nor defend himself. Instead, he chooses to take his critics' own premise that enthusiasm is 'false confidence' and argue from that to a different conclusion."

14. J. R. H. Moorman, *A History of the Church in England*, 2nd ed. (New York: Morehouse-Barlow Co., 1967), 237ff.

15. Outler, *Sermons*, 2:10.

16. Ibid.

17. Ibid., 1:59. Outler also notes that "Norris was the chief English disciple of the French Cartesian, Nicholas Malebranche, and Wesley was more heavily influenced by Malebranche's 'occasionalism' than was any other eighteenth-century British theologian."

18. Ibid.

19. V. H. H. Green, *The Young Mr. Wesley* (New York: St. Martin's Press, 1961), 305-19.

20. Gerald R. Cragg, ed., *The Cambridge Platonists* (New York: Oxford University Press, 1968), 30.

21. John C. English, "The Cambridge Platonists in Wesley's 'Christian Library,'" *Proceedings of the Wesley Historical Society* 36 (October 1968): 161-62.

22. Cragg, *Cambridge Platonists*, 26.

23. Mitsuo Shimizu, "Epistemology in the Thought of John Wesley" (Ph.D. diss., Drew University, 1980), p. 29.

24. Outler, *Sermons*, 2:10.

25. Thomas Jackson, ed., *The Works of John Wesley*, 14 vols. (Grand Rapids, Mich.: Baker Book House, 1978), 11:486. Nevertheless, God can send not only terror, but also comfort by means of the law. Commenting on a watch-night service held in April 1761, Wesley writes, "Though I preached the law from the beginning of my sermon to the end, yet many

were exceedingly comforted—so plain it is that God can send either terror or comfort to the heart, by whatever means it pleaseth him." See Ward and Heitzenrater, *Journals and Diaries*, 21:301.

26. Outler, *Sermons*, 2:22. For additional references in Wesley's writings that indicate the error of only preaching the gospel to unawakened sinners, see Frank Baker, ed., *The Works of John Wesley*, vol. 26. *Letters* (New York: Oxford University Press, 1982), 418, 483, and 485-87.

27. Baker, *Letters*, 26:482.

28. See John Wesley, *Explanatory Notes Upon the Old Testament* (Salem, Ohio: Schmul Publishers, n.d.).

29. Outler, *Sermons*, 1:551.

30. Wesley, *NT Notes*, 294 (Acts 7:35).

31. Ward and Heitzenrater, *Journals and Diaries*, 20:366. Interestingly enough, Wesley also links the moral law as expressed in the Ten Commandments with natural law as evidenced in his following observation: "He now speaks directly of the heathens, in order to convince the heathens . . . [to] *Do by nature*—That is, without an outward rule; though this also, strictly speaking, is by preventing grace. *The things contained in the law*—The ten commandments being only the substance of the law of nature." See Wesley, *NT Notes*, 366 (Rom. 2:14).

32. Outler, *Sermons*, 1:553. Compare Wesley's functions of the moral law in his sermon "The Original, Nature, Properties and Use of the Law," with that of Luther and Calvin. Cf. Outler, *Sermons*, 2:15-16; Jaroslav Pelikan, ed., *Luther's Works: Lectures on Galatians, 1535*, vol. 26 (St. Louis: Concordia Publishing House, 1963), 308-9; John T. McNeill, ed., *Calvin: Institutes of the Christian Religion*, vol. 1 (Philadelphia: The Westminster Press, 1960), 360.

33. Outler, *Sermons*, 2:27.

34. Ibid., 2:1.

35. Ibid., 2:3.

36. This distinction is also apparent in Wesley's reply to his Calvinist detractors who accused him of moralism—and other things—in the wake of the Conference *Minutes* of 1770. Wesley responds that "the lines in question do not refer to the condition of obtaining, but of continuing in, the favour of God." See Telford, *Letters*, 5:259.

37. Outler, *Sermons*, 2:18. It is interesting to note that all the uses of the law for Wesley are theological. Thus, the political use of the law, *politicus usus*, as found, for example, in the theologies of both Luther and Calvin, is not evident in Wesley's articulation of the functions of law.

38. Ibid., 2:76.

39. Ibid., 2:69-70.

40. Ibid., 2:76. James Rigg underscores the value of Wesley's employment of lay preachers by making a distinction between a sacramental and an evangelical understanding of redemption. "The High Churchman," he writes, "makes salvation to be directly dependent on sacramental grace and apostolical succession. Whereas the evangelical believer, the man who has received the doctrine of salvation by faith, as it was taught by Peter Böhler, and as it is understood by the Reformed Churches in general, learns from St. Paul that 'faith cometh by hearing, and hearing by the Word of God. . . .' See James Harrison Rigg, *The Churchmanship of John Wesley and the Relations of Wesleyan Methodism to the Church of England* (London: Wesleyan Conference Office, 1878), 58.

41. Outler, *Sermons*, 2:75.

42. Ibid., 2:88.

43. Richard P. Heitzenrater, *Wesley and the People Called Methodists* (Nashville: Abingdon Press, 1995), 188.

44. Ward and Heitzenrater, *Journals and Diaries*, 21:10.

45. Baker, *Letters*, 26:609.

46. Ibid.

47. Ibid., 26:610.

48. Frank Baker, *John Wesley and the Church of England* (London: The Epworth Press, 1970), 137ff. For one of the more important nineteenth-century answers to the question whether John Wesley was a high churchman, see James Harrison Rigg, *John Wesley, The Church of England and Wesleyan Methodism* (London: The Wesley-Methodist Book Room, 1883).

49. Telford, *Letters*, 3:170-71.

50. Ward and Heitzenrater, *Journals and Diaries*, 20:356.

51. Ibid., 20:489.

52. Heitzenrater, *Wesley and the People*, 181.

53. Ibid. Interestingly enough, Rupp maintains that "the relations between Wesley's movement and the Church of England might have been different, had the original members of the Holy Club or the new evangelical clergy been prepared to share in the itinerancy. In default of such a company of ordained clergy, John Wesley had no option but to rely on laymen." See E. Gordon Rupp, *Religion in England, 1688–1791* (Oxford: Clarendon Press, 1986), 391.

54. Baker, *Letters*, 26:500.

55. Ibid.

56. Ibid., 26:601. In a letter to Ebenezer Blackwell in December 1751, Wesley indicates what he means by "preaching the gospel." He writes: "Some think, preaching the law only; others, preaching the gospel only. I

think, neither the one nor the other, but duly mixing both, in every place, if not in every sermon." See ibid., 26:483.

57. Jackson, *Works*, 10:482.

58. Ibid., 10:484.

59. Ibid., 10:485.

60. Ibid., 10:486. For a work that affirms Wesley's employment of lay preachers was an important window on his broader understanding of the church, see James L. Garlow, "John Wesley's Understanding of the Laity as Demonstrated By His Use of the Lay Preachers" (Ph.D. diss., Drew University, 1979).

61. Jackson, *Works*, 10:499.

62. Hardwicke's Act was passed a few years later in 1753 in order to rectify these problems. This Act declared, quite simply, that henceforth "no marriage was valid unless performed after banns or by licence." See John Pollock, *John Wesley* (Oxford, England: Lion Publishing, 1989), 193.

63. Baker, *Letters*, 26:388-89.

64. Pollock, *John Wesley*, 193.

65. Baker, *Letters*, 26:451.

66. Ward and Heitzenrater, *Journals and Diaries*, 20:378, n. 51.

67. Baker, *Letters*, 26:455. For further evidence of Wesley's endearing letters to his wife, Mary, ("I had the pleasure of receiving two letters from my dearest earthly friend"), see Baker, *Letters*, 16:456, 457, and 462.

68. Ibid., 26:454.

69. Stanley Ayling, *John Wesley* (New York: William Collins Publishers, 1979), 224.

70. Telford, *Letters*, 4:4.

71. Ibid., 3:180.

72. Jackson, *Works*, 10:297.

73. Ibid., 10:206-7.

74. Ibid., 10:210.

75. Ibid. Compare this with Calvin's observation: "As Scripture, then, clearly shows, we say that God once established by his eternal and unchangeable plan those whom he long before determined once for all to receive into salvation, and those whom, on the other hand, he would devote to destruction. . . . By his just and irreprehensible but incomprehensible judgment he has barred the door of life to those whom he has given over to damnation." McNeill, *Calvin*, 2:931.

76. Jackson, *Works*, 10:220.

77. Ibid., 10:221.

78. Ibid., 10:204. A related issue, and one in which Wesley would be in agreement with Calvin, is that regeneration is not a natural work but a supernatural one. That is, the new birth is utterly beyond the ability of

human nature to effectuate and therefore must graciously and freely be received from a beneficent and loving God. See Outler, *Sermons*, 1:179; and Jackson, *Works*, 9:92.

79. Jackson, *Works*, 10:204.

80. See Telford, *Letters*, 4:298.

81. Jackson, *Works*, 10:230.

82. Ibid., 10:231.

83. Ibid., 10:306.

84. See Heitzenrater, *Wesley and the People*, 203.

85. Rupert E. Davies, *The Works of John Wesley*, Bicentennial ed., vol. 9, *The Methodist Societies: History, Nature, and Design* (Nashville: Abingdon Press, 1989), 254 ("A Plain Account of the People Called Methodists").

86. Ibid., 9:258.

87. Ibid.

88. Frank Baker, ed., *The Works of John Wesley*, Bicentennial ed., vol. 26, *Letters II* (New York: Oxford University Press, 1982), 505.

89. Ward and Heitzenrater, *Journals and Diaries*, 20:482.

90. Telford, *Letters*, 4:13. The following month, again in a letter to Elizabeth Hardy, Wesley describes his fearful period, "a few years ago," prior to Aldersgate when he felt the wrath of God on him "though I had been very innocent in the account of others," a likely reference to Mr. Broughton's earlier objection that "he could never think I [Wesley] had not faith, who had done and suffered such things." In this context, then, Wesley's use of the term "a few years ago," as is sometimes his literary style, is quaint and not literal. Indeed, Wesley's spiritual condition depicted in this May letter to Elizabeth Hardy is obviously not a contemporary reference in light of the substance of Wesley's earlier letter to this same woman in April, where he maintains that true believers are not distressed "either in life or in death," and also in light of the absence of any mention of the fear of death whatsoever in his journal accounts, where one would most likely expect them; that is, when Wesley had actually thought he was going to die a few years earlier, in the fall of 1753. Moreover, in Wesley's very depressing letter to his brother, Charles, in 1766 even then John Wesley has no fear of death or punishment, but wonders if his demise will result in oblivion, "of falling into nothing." Cf. Telford, *Letters*, 4:20, 5:16, and Ward and Heitzenrater, *Journals and Diaries*, 18:235.

91. Ward and Heitzenrater, *Journals and Diaries*, 20:483.

92. Baker, *Letters*, 26:190. See Baker's note number ten, in which he maintains that Wesley wrote to Doddridge (though the letters have been lost) asking his advice on "an anthology of evangelical theology."

93. Though Arndt is not, technically speaking, a pietist, his writings— in particular, *Wahres Christentum*—had such an impact on Francke and

Spener that Arndt is best listed as a "pietist," or at least as an important forerunner of this movement.

94. Baker, *Letters*, 20:483.

95. Heitzenrater, *Wesley and the People*, 188.

96. Wesley, *NT Notes*, 48, 107 (Matt. 13:24 and Mark 4:26).

97. Ibid., 188 (Luke 17:21).

98. Ibid., 357 (Acts 28:23).

99. Ibid., 401 (Rom. 14:17).

100. Ibid., 266 (John 19:36).

101. Ibid., 218 (John 3:3).

102. This observation does not deny the importance of ministering to the temporal needs of the poor. It only demonstrates that such temporal needs can never be the believer's ultimate concern as if "what we shall eat and drink" were the most important concern of all.

103. Baker, *Letters*, 26:575. Observe, however, that Wesley slipped back into his all-or-nothing language a few years later in 1759 when he wrote: "Is He not still striving with you? striving to make you not almost but altogether a Christian? Indeed, you must be all or nothing—a saint or a devil, eminent in sin or holiness!" See Telford, *Letters*, 4:52.

104. Baker, *Letters*, 26:575. Emphasis is mine.

105. Ibid.

106. Ibid.

107. Outler, *Sermons*, 2:161. Bracketed material is drawn from the immediate context. Notice that, in this setting, there are echoes of Luther's *pro me* description of his own faith. For evidence concerning the several distinctions that Wesley made in terms of assurance (full assurance of faith, full assurance of hope, and so on), see Telford, *Letters*, 2:385, 3:161; Wesley *NT Notes*, 575, 632, and 638; Jackson, *Works*, 9:32; and Davies, *Methodist Societies*, 9:375-76.

108. Telford, *Letters*, 3:163. Emphasis is mine. Nevertheless, not even this significant exception undermined Wesley's strong association of real Christianity and assurance. Indeed, a month later, in March 1756, Wesley wrote to Richard Tompson: "My belief in general is this—that every Christian believer has a divine conviction of his reconciliation with God." See Telford, *Letters*, 3:174. See also Wesley's letter to Mr. Tompson on February 6, 1756.

109. Ibid., 5:358.

110. In addition, Wesley wrote to Dr. Rutherforth in 1768: "Therefore I have not for many years thought a consciousness of acceptance to be essential to justifying faith." See Telford, *Letters*, 5:359. See also Lycurgus M. Starkey Jr., *The Work of the Holy Spirit: A Study in Wesleyan Theology* (Nashville: Abingdon Press, 1962), 68-69.

8. The Anglican Church and Holiness

1. John Telford, ed., *The Letters of the Rev. John Wesley, A.M.*, 8 vols. (London: The Epworth Press, 1931), 4:115.

2. Ibid.

3. Ibid., 4:131.

4. Ibid., 4:290. For some of Wesley's observations on the Greek church, see Thomas Jackson, ed., *The Works of John Wesley*, 14 vols. (Grand Rapids, Mich.: Zondervan Publishing House, 1959), 9:217, 274.

5. Telford, *Letters*, 4:100.

6. Ibid.

7. Ibid., 4:147.

8. W. Reginald Ward and Richard P. Heitzenrater, eds., *The Works of John Wesley*, Bicentennial ed., vol. 21, *Journals and Diaries IV* (Nashville: Abingdon Press, 1992), 479.

9. Ibid., 22:8.

10. Telford, *Letters*, 4:339.

11. Ibid., 4:344.

12. Ibid., 4:342. For a work that explores the topic of conversion in the broader Wesleyan tradition, see Kenneth J. Collins and John H. Tyson, eds., *Conversion in the Wesleyan Tradition* (Nashville: Abingdon Press, 2001).

13. Ibid., 4:375. In the heat of the polemics with the bishop, Wesley's tone once again turns, as is evident in the following: "I was a little surprised to find Bishop Warburton so entirely unacquainted with the New Testament; and, notwithstanding all his parade of learning, I believe he is no critic in Greek." See Telford, *Letters*, 4:199.

14. Telford, *Letters*, 4:380.

15. Ibid., 4:376.

16. John S. Simon, *John Wesley, the Master-Builder* (London: The Epworth Press, 1927), 166.

17. Albert C. Outler, ed., *The Works of John Wesley*, Bicentennial ed., vols. 1-4, *Sermons* (Nashville: Abingdon Press, 1984–87), 1:445.

18. Ibid., 1:446.

19. Ward and Heitzenrater, *Journals and Diaries*, 22:29.

20. Telford, *Letters*, 5:69.

21. Ward and Heitzenrater, *Journals and Diaries*, 22:168, 172.

22. Telford, *Letters*, 4:48.

23. Outler, *Sermons*, 2:183. Notice that the language used by Wesley in this sermon to describe the carnal nature, such terms as "total corruption," "empty of all good," "filled with all manner of evil," and the like, reveals the basis for his criticism of classical pagan anthropologies as those of Horace and Seneca. See Burton Raffel, trans., *The Essential Horace:*

Odes, Epodes, Satires and Epistles (San Francisco: North Point Press, 1983); and Seneca, *Moral Essays*, 3 vols. (Cambridge, Mass.: Harvard University Press, 1935), vol 1.

24. Ibid. Wesley's thought on the doctrine of original sin remained constant throughout his life. Compare, for example, the sermon "Original Sin," written in 1759, with "The Image of God," written twenty-nine years earlier: "Because if man be not naturally corrupt, then all religion, Jewish and Christian is vain, seeing it is all built on this—all method[s] of cure presupposing the disease." The continuity is striking.

25. William Ragsdale Cannon, *The Theology of John Wesley: With Special Reference to the Doctrine of Justification* (Nashville: Abingdon Press, 1946), 200.

26. Outler, *Sermons*, 2:183-84.

27. Jackson, *Works*, 9:407. Wesley is careful, however, to indicate that total depravity does not undermine human freedom in terms of things of "an indifferent nature," as he puts it; instead, it affects our freedom for righteousness in the sight of God. See Wesley's *Remarks on a Defence of Aspasio Vindicated* in Jackson, *Works*, 10:350. For other references to "total depravity" in this treatise, see Jackson, *Works*, 9:197, 237, and 273.

28. Outler, *Sermons*, 3:207.

29. Ibid.

30. Umphrey Lee, *John Wesley and Modern Religion* (Nashville: Cokesbury Press, 1936), 124-25. Emphasis is mine. And it should also be noted that Wesley used the phrases "natural man" and "natural state" in two distinct senses. This has led to much confusion in Wesley studies among those scholars who have failed to appreciate the difference. On the one hand, in the sermon "Original Sin," the natural state is depicted as exclusive of the grace of God. But as has been indicated above, such a person does not exist, for there are no people without divine prevenient grace. On the other hand, the phrases "natural man" and "natural state," which appear in the sermons *Awake, Thou That Sleepest*, preached by Charles in 1742, and *The Spirit of Bondage and of Adoption*, preached by John in 1746, correspond to real flesh and blood individuals, not to theoretical constructs.

31. See Philip Schaff, *The Creeds of Christendom with a History and Critical Notes*, vol. 3, 6th ed. (Grand Rapids, Mich.: Baker Book House, 1983), 492-94. Note especially the language of Articles IX (Of Original or Birth-Sin) and X (Of Free-Will).

32. Outler, *Sermons*, 2:190. Emphasis is mine.

33. Ward and Heitzenrater, *Journals and Diaries*, 21:456.

34. See Outler, *Sermons*, 2:186.

35. Robert C. Monk, *John Wesley: His Puritan Heritage* (Nashville: Abingdon Press, 1966), 249-52.

36. Outler, *Sermons,* 2:193. See also Monk, *Puritan Heritage,* 43; and F. Ernest Stoeffler, "Tradition and Renewal in the Ecclesiology of John Wesley," in *Traditio-Krisis-Renovatio aus theologische Sicht* [Tradition, crisis, and renewal from a theological point of view], ed. B. Jasper and R. Mohr (Marburg, Germany: N. G. Elwert, 1976), 305.

37. Outler, *Sermons,* 2:195.

38. Telford, *Letters,* 4:332. Compare this letter to Wesley's sermon "On Working Out Our Own Salvation," in which he notes that "salvation begins with what is usually termed (and very properly) 'preventing grace.' " This, however, does not contradict his earlier statements so long as it is realized that in the former, Wesley is referring to salvation, properly speaking, which always includes holiness; but in the latter, he is simply highlighting a "degree" of salvation in that the sinner is at least on the way to holiness. In short, in no sense was Wesley arguing in this sermon that those who merely have prevenient grace are in fact holy and are therefore redeemed, properly speaking. See Outler, *Sermons,* 3:203.

39. Jackson, *Works,* 9:310.

40. Outler, *Sermons,* 2:198.

41. Telford, *Letters,* 4:332. Wesley's additional comment, "Let it be wrought at all, and we will not contend whether it be wrought gradually or instantaneously," does not detract from his basic position that the new birth is instantaneous; instead, it serves to highlight the importance of real transformation, a favorite theme of Wesley's.

42. Outler, *Sermons,* 2:198. Lindstrom notes that it is "this combination of the gradual and instantaneous that particularly distinguishes Wesley's conception of the process of salvation." See Lindstrom, *Sanctification: A Study in the Doctrine of Salvation* (Grand Rapids, Mich.: Francis Asbury Press, 1982), 121.

43. Outler, *Sermons,* 2:198.

44. Ibid., 2:158. I have underscored the words "moment" and "instant." The other emphasis is Wesley's own.

45. Telford, *Letters,* 4:332.

46. Outler, *Sermons,* 2:163. The instantaneous motif, for Wesley, functions not simply in a chronological way, but also in a soteriological way. Viewing it exclusively in terms of the former can only fail to discern the diversity of traditions that actually fed into Wesley's understandings. For more on the significance of these temporal issues, see Kenneth J. Collins, *The Scripture Way of Salvation: The Heart of John Wesley's Theology* (Nashville: Abingdon Press, 1997), 114-17.

47. Ward and Heitzenrater, *Journals and Diaries*, 18:216. Emphasis is mine.

48. Ibid., 19:214.

49. Outler, *Sermons*, 1:318.

50. Ibid. 1:323.

51. Ibid., 1:328. Wesley, at times, employs a slightly different terminology and describes the liberty entailed in entire sanctification as being cleansed of the *root* of sin—another way of referring to sin's *being* or *presence*. See Outler, *Sermons*, 3:204; 4:26.

52. See Randy L. Maddox, *Responsible Grace: John Wesley's Practical Theology* (Nashville: Kingswood Books, 1994), 143.

53. Outler, *Sermons*, 2:97. Emphasis is mine. Outler's soteriological pessimism is also reflected in his wry comment that serves as part of the introduction to "The Marks of the New Birth" (and "The Great Privilege of Those That Are Born of God"): "Here Wesley comes as close as he ever will to an unnuanced notion of Christian existence as sinless; he even goes on to denounce those who try to qualify this with the more modest claim that the regenerate "do not commit sin *habitually*. . . ." See Outler, *Sermons*, 1:416.

54. Ibid., 1:346.

55. Wesley writes to Thomas Olivers: "We should neither be forward nor backward in believing those who think they have attained the *second blessing*"; to Mrs. Crosby, "I believe within five weeks six in one class have received remission of sins and five in one band received a *second blessing*"; to Samuel Bardsley, "Never be ashamed of the Old Methodist doctrine. Press all believers to go on to perfection. Insist everywhere on the *second blessing* as receivable in a moment, and receivable now, by simple faith"; to Jane Salkeld, "Exhort all the little ones that believe to make haste and not delay the time of receiving the *second blessing*; and be not backward to declare what God has done for your soul to any that truly fear Him"; to Mrs. Barton, "It is exceeding certain that God did give you the *second blessing*, properly so called. He delivered you from the root of bitterness, from inbred as well as actual sin"; and to Ann Bolton, "Certainly till persons experience something of the *second awakening*, till they are feelingly convinced of inbred sin so as earnestly to groan for deliverance from it, we need not speak to them of *present* sanctification." See Telford, *Letters*, 3:212; 4:133; 5:315; 5:333; 6:116; and 6:144-45. Emphasis is mine.

56. Outler, *Sermons*, 2:210.

57. Ibid., 2:234.

58. Ibid., 2:229.

59. Jackson, *Works*, 14:277. See also the able discussion on John of the Cross in Robert G. Tuttle Jr., *Mysticism in the Wesleyan Tradition* (Grand Rapids, Mich.: Francis Asbury Press of Zondervan Publishing House, 1989), 31-38.

60. St. John of the Cross, *Dark Night of the Soul,* trans. and ed. E. Allison Peers (New York: Doubleday, 1990), 75.

61. Wesley writes, for example, "From the Apostle's manner of speaking we may gather, thirdly, that even heaviness is not *always* needful." See Outler, *Sermons,* 2:234.

62. Ward and Heitzenrater, *Journals and Diaries,* 21:343.

63. Wesley also offered a briefer history of his views in a letter to John Newton, the year preceding. See Ward and Heitzenrater, *Journals and Diaries,* 21:510-11.

64. Outler's comment, "He [Wesley] carefully records his readings in the theology of holiness: Kempis, William Law, the French and Spanish mystics, Juan de Castaniza [Lorenzo Scupoli], Macarius the Egyptian," which serves as the introduction to the material drawn from the *Plain Account* in Outler's own edited work, *John Wesley,* is somewhat misleading for it suggests that all were "sources" for Wesley and were therefore "included" in the *Plain Account.* However, as was Wesley's custom in delineating the *sources* of his historic insight concerning Christian perfection, only western authors are actually mentioned in this treatise. See Albert C. Outler, ed., *John Wesley, The Library of Protestant Thought* (New York: Oxford University Press, 1964), 251-52.

65. Jackson, *Works,* 8:329.

66. Dietrich Bonhoeffer, *The Cost of Discipleship,* 2nd ed. (New York: Macmillan Publishing Co., 1960), 7.

67. Cf. Randy L. Maddox, "John Wesley and Eastern Orthodoxy: Influences, Convergences and Differences," *The Asbury Theological Journal* 45, no. 2 (Fall 1990): 29-53; and Brian Frost, "Orthodoxy and Methodism," *London Quarterly & Holborn Review* 189 (1964): 13-22.

68. Outler, *Sermons,* 3:586. Notice the omission of Irenaeus, a name found in other lists. See Wesley's letter to Dr. Middleton on January 24, 1748/9 in Jackson, *Works,* 10:79.

69. Jackson, *Works,* 9:217.

70. Outler, *Sermons,* 2:487.

71. Ibid., 4:88. For more negative observations on Greek Orthodoxy, see Outler, *Sermons,* 2:580-81; and Jackson, *Works,* 9:216-17.

72. Ted A. Campbell, *John Wesley and Christian Antiquity: Religious Vision and Cultural Changes* (Nashville: Kingswood Books, 1991), 125-34.

73. Pseudo-Macarius was probably a monk who lived in Syria or Asia Minor from 380–430 (whom Wesley, by the way, thought to be Macarius the Great, an Egyptian monk).

74. Outler, *Sermons,* 2:159. For more on Wesley and Macarius, cf. John C. English, "The Path to Perfection in Pseudo-Macarius and John Wesley," *Pacifica,* 11, no. 1 (February 1998): 54-62.

75. For an interesting study on Wesley's employment of the work of Macarius, see Howard A. Snyder, "John Wesley and Macarius the Egyptian," *The Asbury Theological Journal* 45, no. 2 (Fall 1990): 55-60.

76. Cf. Macarius, *Primitive Morality: Or, the Spiritual Homilies of St. Macarius the Egyptian* (London: W. Taylor and J. Innys, 1721) with John Wesley, *A Christian Library, Consisting of Extracts from and Abridgements of the Choicest Pieces of Practical Divinity which have been published in the English Tongue*, 30 vols. (London: T. Blanshard, 1819–27), 1:72ff.

77. Mark T. Kurowski, "The First Step Toward Grace: John Wesley's Use of the Spiritual Homilies of Macarius the Great," *Methodist History* 36, no. 2 (January 1998): 113-24.

78. For example, in his work *The Character of a Methodist*, produced in 1742, Wesley was dependent on Clement of Alexandria's description of the "perfect Christian" as found in the *Stromateis*. However, what is less known is that in an important letter written several years later in 1774, Wesley is sharply critical of how the Christian character was depicted by Clement in some of his writings. Wesley elaborates, "Many years ago I might have said, but I do not now, 'Give me a woman made of stone, A widow of Pygmalion' And just such a Christian, one of the Fathers, Clemens Alexandrinius, describes: But I do not admire that description now as I did formerly. I now see a Stoic and a Christian are different characters." See Jackson, *Works*, 12:297-98.

79. For a good study of the influence of German pietism on the life and thought of John Wesley, see Arthur Wilford Nagler, "Pietism and Methodism: A Comparative Study," in *Pietism and Methodism, Or, The Significance of German Pietism in the Origin and Early Development of Methodism* (Nashville: Publishing House M.E. Church, South, 1918), 120-41.

80. Ward and Heitzenrater, *Journals and Diaries*, 19:21. The homilies that Wesley chose to extract for publication and edification indicate the salient influence of Cranmer and the English Reformation on much of his thought. See *Certain Sermons or Homilies, Appointed to Be Read in Churches* (Oxford, 1683). And for an account of the history and theology of the Homilies and Articles of Religion, see J. T. Tomlinson, *The Prayer Book, Articles and Homilies* (London, 1897).

81. See More's discussion of the saintliness of Jeremy Taylor as an example of "Caroline piety" in Paul Elmore More, *The Spirit of Anglicanism* (London: S.P.C.K, 1957), 740-42.

82. Luke Tyerman, The Life and Times of the Rev. John Wesley, M.A., Founder of the Methodists, 3 vols. (New York: Harper & Bros., 1872), 2:593.

83. Outler, *Sermons*, 2:169.

84. Ibid., 2:163. Emphasis is mine. In this context, by the term "sanctification," Wesley clearly means "entire sanctification."

85. See Ted A. Campbell, "Christian Tradition, John Wesley, and Evangelicalism [his view of apostolic and Anglican traditions]," *Anglican Theological Review* 74 (Winter 1992): 54-67; and Ernest Gordon Rupp, "Son to Samuel: John Wesley, Church of England Man," in *The Place of Wesley in the Christian Tradition*, ed. Kenneth E. Rowe (Metuchen, N.J.: Scarecrow Press, 1976), 39-66.

86. Telford, *Letters*, 5:20.

87. Ibid., 5:41. Wesley goes on to chide his younger brother in this same letter: "Is there or is there not any instantaneous sanctification between justification and death? I say, Yes; you *(often seem to)* say, No."

88. Ward and Heitzenrater, *Journals and Diaries*, 21:415.

89. Telford, *Letters*, 4:133.

90. Ward and Heitzenrater, *Journals and Diaries*, 21:414-15.

91. Ibid., 21:247.

92. Ibid., 21:398-99.

93. Ibid., 21:394.

94. Cf. J. Brazier Green, *John Wesley and William Law* (London: The Epworth Press, 1945), 207; and Outler, *John Wesley*, 299-304.

95. Ward and Heitzenrater, *Journals and Diaries*, 21:403.

96. Ibid.

97. Ibid., 21:408.

98. Telford, *Letters*, 5:38.

99. For a different account of Wesley's earlier reluctance to accept Maxfield as a preacher, see Frank Baker, *John Wesley and the Church of England* (Nashville: Abingdon Press, 1970), 83-84.

9. A Contentious Decade

1. Henry D. Rack, *Reasonable Enthusiast: John Wesley and the Rise of Methodism*, 2nd ed. (Nashville: Abingdon Press, 1992).

2. Roy Porter, *A History of England* (London: The Folio Society, 1982), 53.

3. J. H. Plumb, *England in the Eighteenth Century* (Baltimore: Penguin Books, 1950), 78-79.

4. Thomas Jackson, ed., *The Works of John Wesley*, 14 vols. (Grand Rapids, Mich.: Baker Book House, 1978), 11:14.

5. Ibid., 11:15.

6. Plumb, *England*, 122, 125.

7. Jackson, *Works*, 11:37.

8. Ibid.

9. Ibid., 11:40. Wesley revealed his strong support of the legitimacy of the Hanoverian monarchy in his *Concise History of England*, in which, as Clark points out, the Methodist leader argued, in effect, as follows: "The marriage in 1209 between King John and Isabella was not 'lawful; their children were illegitimate, and the Stuarts' title' 'by birth' unfounded; King George I was 'lineally descended' from Matilda, who [therefore] had a 'prior right.'" See J. C. D. Clark, *English Society 1660–1832* (Cambridge: Cambridge University Press, 2000), 287.

10. Jackson, *Works*, 11:42.

11. Ibid., 11:137.

12. Ibid.

13. Rack, *Reasonable Enthusiast*, 378. For a view that attempts to make Wesley a political radical (even arguing against the right of private property) in light of a Marxist critique and analysis, see Theodore W. Jennings Jr., *Good News to the Poor: John Wesley's Evangelical Economics* (Nashville: Abingdon Press, 1990). See also *The Thirty-nine Articles of the Church of England*, in which the right of private property is affirmed (in Article XXXVIII) in Philip Schaff, *The Creeds of Christendom*, vol. 3 (Grand Rapids, Mich.: Baker Book House, 1983), 493.

14. Jackson, *Works*, 11:46.

15. Ibid., 13:153. See also Frank Baker, "The Origins, Character, and Influence of John Wesley's Thoughts Upon Slavery," *Methodist History* 22, no. 2 (January 1984): 75-86.

16. Jackson, *Works*, 11:70.

17. Albert C. Outler, ed., *The Works of John Wesley*, Bicentennial ed., vols. 1-4, *Sermons* (Nashville: Abingdon Press, 1984–87), 2:10. In this setting Wesley also describes the law in very "platonic" language: "The law of God . . . is a copy of the eternal mind, a transcript of the divine nature; yea, it is the fairest offspring of the everlasting Father, the brightest efflux of his essential wisdom, the visible beauty of the Most High."

18. Jackson, *Works*, 11:79.

19. Ibid. Bishop Andrew of the Methodist Episcopal Church inherited several slaves upon marriage to his second wife. The bishop, sensing the moral difficulty, renounced all ownership of his slaves and executed legal papers that transferred them to his wife. Tensions over this and other matters strained relations between Northern and Southern delegates until a Plan of Separation provided for what was soon to be the two distinct branches of the Methodist Episcopal Church in America. See Frederick Norwood, *The Story of American Methodism: A History of the United Methodists and Their Relations* (Nashville: Abingdon Press, 1974).

20. Jackson, *Works*, 11:79.

21. Ibid. Leon O. Hynson also underscores the importance of human

rights for Wesley in his "Wesley's 'Thoughts Upon Slavery': A Declaration of Human Rights," *Methodist History* 33, no. 1 (October 1994): 46-57.

22. Plumb, *England*, 126. See also John Wesley Bready, *England before and after Wesley: The Evangelical Revival and Social Reform* (London: Hodder and Stoughton, 1938).

23. Plumb, *England*, 126.

24. Jackson, *Works*, 11:24.

25. John Telford, ed., *The Letters of the Rev. John Wesley, A.M.*, 8 vols. (London: The Epworth Press, 1931), 6:161.

26. Ibid., 6:267.

27. Ibid., 6:192. For a discussion of the character of King George, see Roy Porter, *England in the Eighteenth Century* (London: The Folio Society, 1998), 426, 431-32.

28. Rack, *Reasonable Enthusiast*, 346.

29. Porter, *England in the Eighteenth Century*, 165.

30. Jackson, *Works*, 11:82.

31. Ibid.

32. Ibid., 11:83. For helpful discussions on Wesley's at times strained relations with the American Methodists, cf. L. M. Holland, "John Wesley and the American Revolution," *Journal of Church and State* 5 (November 1963): 199-213; David T. Morgan, "Dupes of Designing Men: John Wesley and the American Revolution," *Historical Magazine of the Protestant Episcopal Church* 44 (June 1975): 121-131; and Allan Raymond, "I Fear God and Honour the King: John Wesley and the American Revolution," *Church History* 45 (September 1976): 316-28.

33. Jackson, *Works*, 11:87.

34. Ibid., 11:88.

35. Plumb, *England*, 135. Plumb points out that although both Price and Priestley were very much pro-American and deemed the success of the colonies in terms of a grand script of the triumph of virtue over sin, and though they, as a consequence, supported Wilkes, they nevertheless detested his morals.

36. Jackson, *Works*, 11:18.

37. Richard P. Heitzenrater, *Wesley and the People Called Methodists* (Nashville: Abingdon Press, 1995), 264.

38. Jackson, *Works*, 11:105.

39. Outler, *Sermons*, 3:601.

40. Ibid. Wesley also makes this same claim in his *A Calm Address to the Inhabitants of England,* in which he states: "Almost from their settlement in the country, but more especially from this time, the people of this as well as the other provinces, multiplied exceedingly. This was the natural

effect of the unparalleled lenity of the Government they were under, and the perfect liberty they enjoyed, civil as well as religious. Through the same causes, from the smallness of their taxes, and the large bounties continually received from their mother country, (which also protected them from all their enemies,) their wealth increased as fast as their numbers. And, together with their number and their wealth, *the spirit of independency* increased also." See Jackson, *Works*, 11:131. Emphasis is mine.

41. Jackson, *Works*, 11:155.

42. Ibid.

43. Ibid. Hynson maintains that Wesley did indeed prefer a limited monarchy to other forms of government. See Leon O. Hynson, *The Wesleyan Revival: John Wesley's Ethics for Church and State* (Salem, Ohio: Schmul Publishing Co., 1999), 155-90.

44. Jackson, *Works*, 11:155.

45. Telford, *Letters*, 6:102.

46. Ibid., 6:273-74.

47. Ibid. In this letter, John indicates that Mary has accused him of adultery—a charge utterly without foundation. For more on this allegation, see Rack, *Reasonable Enthusiast*, 266.

48. Telford, *Letters*, 6:322.

49. Ibid., 6:368. (Telford's comments on Wesley's reaction to the death of his wife.)

50. Robert Southey, *The Life of Wesley; and Rise and Progress of Methodism*, 2 vols. (London: Longman, Brown, Green, and Longmans, 1846), 2:245.

51. Telford, *Letters*, 5:192.

52. W. Reginald Ward and Richard P. Heitzenrater, *The Works of John Wesley*, Bicentennial ed., vol. 22, *Journals and Diaries I* (Nashville: Abingdon Press, 1993), 286, n.42.

53. Telford, *Letters*, 5:252.

54. Ibid., 5:231.

55. Ward and Heitzenrater, *Journals and Diaries*, 22:285.

56. Nolan Harmon, ed., *The Encyclopedia of World Methodism*, vol. 2 (Nashville: The United Methodist Publishing House, 1974), 2146 (under the article "Walter Shirley").

57. Ward and Heitzenrater, 22:285-87, n. 42 (August 6, 1771). Emphasis is mine.

58. Harmon, *Encyclopedia*, 2:2146.

59. Telford, *Letters*, 5:274.

60. Ibid., 5:275.

61. Ibid., 5:282. The evangelical Calvinists, of course, viewed matters much differently and took pride in the emphasis on the holy life found in

many Puritan classics, some of which surfaced in Wesley's *Christian Library*. For a list of these Puritan authors, as well as a consideration of their contributions to the doctrine of *holiness*, see Robert C. Monk, *John Wesley: His Puritan Heritage* (Nashville: Abingdon Press, 1966), 258-62.

62. Ward and Heitzenrater, *Journals*, 23:57, n. 68.

63. Ibid., 23:56-57.

64. Jackson, *Works*, 10:377.

65. Ibid., 10:404.

66. Ibid., 10:378. Emphasis is mine. Though Wesley employs the term "Arminian" over forty times in his writings, his theological emphases can be distinguished in some important respects from that of the Dutch Reformed theologian Jacobus Arminius. Indeed, Wesley's Arminianism is best understood not in terms of the Remonstrance of 1610, but in terms of the Arminianism that surfaced in the Church of England. The English context in Wesley's thought, once again, is crucial. See Peter O. G. White, *Predestination, Policy and Polemic: Conflict and Consensus in the English Church from the Reformation to the Civil War* (Cambridge, N.Y.: Cambridge University Press, 1992).

67. Jackson, *Works*, 10:378.

68. Gerald R. Cragg, ed., *The Works of John Wesley*, Bicentennial ed., vol. 11, *The Appeals to Men of Reason and Religion* (Nashville: Abingdon Press, 1989), 11:117. Wesley so feared a deprecation of "works meet for repentance" that he omitted Article XIII of the Anglican Thirty-nine Articles ("Of Works before Justification") when he prepared an abridged version of this historic document for the Methodists. See Paul F. Blankenship, "The Significance of John Wesley's Abridgment of the Thirty-nine Articles as Seen from His Deletions," *Methodist History* 2, no. 3 (April 1964): 35-47.

69. Jackson, *Works*, 10:309.

70. Cragg, *The Appeals*, 11:106. See also 11:116. Emphasis is mine.

71. Ibid., 11:453. See also Wesley's *NT Notes*, in which he indicated that the thief on the cross even had time to perform "works meet for repentance!" See Wesley, *NT Notes*, 205 (Luke 23:40).

72. Outler, *Sermons*, 2:162-63. The same distinctions of *A Farther Appeal*, though somewhat modified (Wesley uses the terms "immediately," and "directly necessary," with respect to faith as synonyms for the *Farther Appeals'* "proximately necessary"), surfaced in this present sermon, "The Scripture Way of Salvation," in 1765.

73. Telford, *Letters*, 4:298.

74. After the publication of the Conference *Minutes* of 1770, Lady Huntingdon declared that "whoever did not wholly disavow the theses should quit her college." See Luke L. Tyerman, *The Life and Times of the*

Rev. John Wesley, M.A., Founder of the Methodists, 3 vols. (New York: Harper & Bros., 1872), 3:73.

75. Jackson, *Works*, 8:337.

76. Though in the majority of instances in which Wesley employs the language of "fearing God and working righteousness," he is not referring to justification, he nevertheless does indeed use this phrase, at times, to include justification and such usage constitutes what I have called the "narrow sense." For example, Wesley considers the spiritual estate of William Law, his one time mentor, in the following way: "That a Mystic, who denies Justification by Faith, (Mr. Law, for instance,) may be saved. But if so, what becomes of articulus stantis vel cadentis ecclesië? If so, is it not high time for us Projicere ampullas et sesquipedalia verba; and to return to the plain word, "He that feareth God, and worketh righteousness, is accepted with him? . . ." See Ward and Heitzenrater, *Journals*, 22:114-15.

77. John Wesley, *Explanatory Notes Upon the New Testament* (Salem, Ohio: Schmul Publishers), 646. In this commentary on the book of Jude, Wesley also defines a servant in a second sense as one who has the spirit of adoption; but note that this is a definition rarely used and is *not* the one that forms the first prong of the distinction the faith of a servant/the faith of a son since only the latter prong is marked by the spirit of adoption. See Wesley, *Notes*, 646.

78. Ibid., 304.

79. Ibid.

80. See Wesley's sermon "On Conscience" for more details on this aspect of prevenient grace in Outler, *Sermons*, 3:480 ff.

81. Telford, *Letters*, 6:51. During this same year, Wesley penned his *On Predestination* and the following year *Thoughts Upon Necessity*, in which he demonstrated that determinism is not the appropriate conclusion when one considers the doctrines of predestination and the sovereignty of God. In the latter treatise, for example, Wesley writes: "If all the actions and passions, and tempers of men are quite independent on their own choice, are governed by a principle exterior to themselves; then none of them is either rewardable or punishable." See Jackson, *Works*, 10:464.

82. Ward and Heitzenrater, *Journals*, 22:400.

83. Telford, *Letters*, 6:250.

84. Ibid., 6:326-27. Wesley's insistence that he knows of no gospel apart from salvation from sin is also evident in his earlier piece *A Blow at the Root: Or Christ Stabbed in the House of His Friends*, produced in 1762. See Jackson, *Works*, 10:369.

85. Outler, *Sermons*, 2:385. Emphasis is mine. This late evidence (1775) is troubling for those interpretations that would like to maintain that

Wesley dropped the matter of assurance from the proper Christian faith.

86. Harmon, *Encyclopedia*, 1:139.

87. Ibid., 1:139-40.

88. Telford, *Letters*, 6:238. For other examples of Wesley's positive estimation of "naked faith," see Jackson, *Works*, 13:2, 132.

89. Ward and Heitzenrater, *Journals*, 23:111.

10. A Church Established

1. John Telford, ed., *The Letters of John Wesley, A.M.*, 8 vols. (London: The Epworth Press, 1931), 7:30.

2. Ibid.

3. Ibid., 7:30-31.

4. Ibid., 7:31. Wesley's use of language in both his letters and sermons could, at times, be trenchant. For a rhetorical analysis of Wesley's sermons, see Harold Vaughn Whited, "A Rhetorical Analysis of the Published Sermons Preached by John Wesley at Oxford University" (Ph.D. diss., University of Michigan, 1958). Unfortunately, little has been done in terms of a rhetorical analysis of Wesley's published letters, a topic that would make an excellent study.

5. Telford, *Letters*, 7:31.

6. Ibid., 7:239. For a lively debate on the significance of the phrase "at full liberty," with respect to doctrinal standards among the American Methodists, cf. Richard P. Heitzenrater, "At Full Liberty: Doctrinal Standards in Early American Methodism," in *Mirror and Memory: Reflections on Early Methodism*, ed. Richard P. Heitzenrater (Nashville: Kingswood Books, 1989), 189-204; and Thomas C. Oden, *Doctrinal Standards in the Wesleyan Tradition* (Grand Rapids, Mich.: Francis Asbury Press of Zondervan Publishing House, 1988).

7. But if presbyters and bishops were of the same order as Wesley had maintained, in light of his reading of King and Stillingfleet, then the consecrations of Coke and Asbury as superintendents were both contradictory and pointless. See Robert Southey, *The Life of Wesley; and Rise and Progress of Methodism*, 2 vols. (London: Longman, Brown, Green, and Longmans, 1846), 2:298.

8. Telford, *Letters*, 7:238.

9. Ibid., 7:262.

10. Ibid., 7:288.

11. Frank Baker, *John Wesley and the Church of England* (Nashville: Abingdon, 1970), 243.

12. For a helpful discussion of the theological judgments entailed in Wesley's omissions, see Paul Freeman Blankenship, "The Significance of

John Wesley's Abridgement of the Thirty-nine Articles as Seen from His Deletions," *Methodist History* 2, no. 3 (1964): 35-47.

13. Baker, *Church of England*, 255.

14. Telford, *Letters*, 8:91.

15. Ibid.

16. Ibid., 8:183.

17. Ibid., 8:73.

18. W. Reginald Ward and Richard P. Heitzenrater, *The Works of John Wesley*, Bicentennial ed., vol. 23, *Diaries and Journals VI* (Nashville: Abingdon Press, 1992), 422.

19. Ibid., 8:142. See also Anthony Armstrong, *The Church of England, the Methodists, and Society, 1700–1850* (Totowa, N.J.: Rowman and Littlefield, 1973), 108-17.

20. Telford, *Letters*, 8:92.

21. Richard P. Heitzenrater, *Wesley and the People Called Methodists* (Nashville: Abingdon Press, 1995), 284.

22. Baker, *Church of England*, 218.

23. Telford, *Letters*, 7:284.

24. Ibid., 7:321.

25. Ibid., 7:384.

26. V. H. H. Green, *John Wesley* (Lanham, Md.: University Press of America, 1987), 150. Reprint of 1964 edition.

27. Albert C. Outler, ed., *The Works of John Wesley*, Bicentennial ed., vols. 1-4, *Sermons* (Nashville: Abingdon Press, 1984–1987), 4:81. Emphasis is mine. See also Wesley's observations on the 1788 Conference in Nehemiah Curnock, ed., *The Journal of the Rev. John Wesley, A.M.*, 8 vols. (London: The Epworth Press, 1938), 7:422.

28. Telford, *Letters*, 7:262.

29. Ibid., 8:58.

30. Ibid., 8:59. For additional evidence that demonstrates Wesley, in his own estimation, had not left the Church of England, see Telford, *Letters*, 7:288, 7:324, 7:332-33, 7:377, and 8:186.

31. Southey, *Life of Wesley*, 2:380.

32. Outler, *Sermons*, 4:95-96.

33. Ibid., 3:236.

34. Ibid., 2:494.

35. Ibid., 4:11. But he immediately added that being rich is "dangerous beyond expression."

36. Curnock, *Journal*, 7:436 (September 19, 1788). See also Wesley's sermon "The Mystery of Iniquity," in which he notes that the first plague that infected the Christian church was the love of money. See Outler, *Sermons*, 2:456.

37. J. Ernest Rattenbury, *Wesley's Legacy to the World* (London: The Epworth Press, 1928), 230-31.

38. J. H. Plumb, *England in the Eighteenth Century* (Baltimore: Penguin Books, 1950), 97.

39. Outler, *Sermons*, 3:527. Emphasis is mine.

40. Ward and Heitzenrater, *Works*, 23:235.

41. Outler, *Sermons*, 3:390.

42. Ibid., 3:391. Emphasis is mine.

43. Ibid., 3:393. Emphasis is mine. For a much more extensive position on this issue of wealth and valuation, see "The Soteriological Orientation of John Wesley's Ministry to the Poor," *The Asbury Theological Journal* 50, no. 1 (Spring 1995): 75-92.

44. Outler, *Sermons*, 1:519.

45. Ibid., 1:695. Emphasis is mine.

46. Ibid.

47. Telford, *Letters*, 8:51.

48. Ibid., 8:52. For a collection of primary sources with respect to the life and ministry of Charles Wesley, see John R. Tyson, comp., *Charles Wesley: A Reader* (New York: Oxford University Press, 1989).

49. Ward and Heitzenrater, *Journals*, 23:179-80.

50. Ibid., 23:287.

51. Ibid.

52. Curnock, *Journal*, 8:17.

53. Ibid., 8:35.

54. Outler, *Sermons*, 2:501. See also Kenneth J. Collins, *The Scripture Way of Salvation: The Heart of John Wesley's Theology* (Nashville: Abingdon Press, 1997), 144-52.

55. Outler, *Sermons*, 3:152.

56. Telford, *Letters*, 7:231.

57. Outler, *Sermons*, 3:452. Moreover, in his sermon "On God's Vineyard," Wesley links being a Christian with both justification and the new birth. See Outler, *Sermons*, 3:507.

58. Telford, *Letters*, 7:230. And Wesley had also counseled his niece Sarah Wesley: "If you wish not to be an *almost* but *altogether* a Christian, you will have a need of much courage and much patience. Then you will be able to do all things through Christ strengthening you." See Telford, *Letters*, 7:39 and 7:78.

59. Outler, *Sermons*, 4:49. Observe in this late period that Wesley links the faith of a servant not with the Christian faith, but with Jewish (or legal) faith.

60. Ibid., 4:121-22. For another letter, this one written to Charles, that links the power of religion with the new birth, see Telford, *Letters*, 7:217.

61. Outler, *Sermons*, 3:498.

62. Ibid., 3:130.

63. Ibid., 3:497.

64. Telford, *Letters*, 7:157.

65. Ibid., 7:95. For a more detailed argument on these matters, see Kenneth J. Collins, "The Motif of Real Christianity in the Writings of John Wesley," *The Asbury Theological Journal* 49, no. 1 (Spring 1994): 49-62.

66. Outler, *Sermons*, 3:497. Emphasis is mine.

67. Ibid., 3:498.

68. Ibid., 3:497-98. For an excellent discussion on the direct witness of the Spirit, see Arthur S. Yates, *The Doctrine of Assurance: with Special Reference to John Wesley* (London: The Epworth Press, 1952), 111ff.

69. Outler, *Sermons*, 4:35.

70. Telford, *Letters*, 7:361-62. Wesley's response to Mr. Fleury, who had claimed that Wesley pretended to extraordinary inspiration, was to associate the witness of the Spirit (assurance) as vital to the Christian faith: "I pretend to no other inspiration than that which is common to all real Christians, without which no one can be a Christian at all." See Rupert E. Davies, *The Works of John Wesley*, Bicentennial ed., vol. 9, *The Methodist Societies: History, Nature, and Design* (Nashville: Abingdon Press, 1989), 392.

71. Outler, *Sermons*, 3:497-98. Emphasis is mine. For examples of what Wesley meant by "full assurance," see Wesley, *NT Notes*, 638; Outler, *Sermons*, 3:549, 4:36; and Ward and Heitzenrater, *Journals and Diaries*, 22:436.

72. Southey, *Life of Wesley*, 1:258. Emphasis is mine. That Wesley maintains that assurance is the *common* privilege of the sons and daughters of God suggests that it is rare when assurance, marked by doubt and fear, does not soon follow the new birth.

73. For some of Wesley's uses of the term spirituality, see Outler, *Sermons*, 1:552, 568, 570; and 2:36.

74. For a model to explore in a descriptive sense the great variety of contemporary spiritualities, see Kenneth J. Collins, *Exploring Christian Spirituality: An Ecumenical Reader* (Grand Rapids, Mich.: Baker Books, 2000), 9-18.

75. Wesley writes to Freeborn Garrettson, for example, "This is an unscriptural expression, and a very fallacious rule. I wish to be, in every point, great and small, a scriptural, rational Christian." See Thomas Jackson, ed., *The Works of John Wesley*, 14 vols. (Grand Rapids, Mich.: Baker Book House, 1978), 13:73.

76. Contemporary Reformed evangelicals are, among other things, epistemologically oriented whereas the eighteenth-century Wesley, and

the tradition that followed him, was largely soteriologically oriented. Such a consideration should have been taken into account in Mark Noll's misguided criticism of Wesleyan holiness folk and Pentecostals. That is, in his critique, Noll should have first of all considered what was and remains the historic *purpose* of Methodism. See Mark A. Noll, *The Scandal of the Evangelical Mind* (Grand Rapids, Mich.: William B. Eerdmans Publishing Co., 1994), 227, 249.

77. Outler, *Sermons*, 3:260.

78. Allan H. Sager, *Gospel-Centered Spirituality: An Introduction to Our Spiritual Journey* (Minneapolis: Augsburg Fortress Press, 1990), 36.

79. Please note that I am not making the claim that the pride/humility paradigm is employed by Roman Catholicism exclusively. Catholic spirituality is more diverse than such a claim could allow. Rather, I am simply maintaining that this is a well-worked, even familiar, paradigm in Catholic circles and that it leads to a particular kind of spirituality and Christian formation.

80. Anthony C. Meisel and M. L. del Mastro, trans., *The Rule of St. Benedict* (New York: , Doubleday, 1975), 54.

81. Serge Hughes, ed., *Catherine of Genoa: Purgation and Purgatory, the Spiritual Dialogue* (New York: Paulist Press, 1979), 15.

82. Thomas à Kempis, *The Imitation of Christ*, rev. ed., trans. Joseph N. Tylenda (New York: Vintage Books, 1984), 85.

83. Jaroslav Pelikan, ed., *Luther's Works*, vol. 1, *Lectures on Genesis* (Saint Louis: Concordia Publishing House, 1955), 147.

84. Ibid., 1:147-48.

85. John T. McNeill, ed., *Calvin: Institutes of the Christian Religion*, 2 vols. (Philadelphia: Westminster Press, 1960), 1:245. Emphasis is mine.

86. Ibid., 1:246.

87. Ibid., 1:245.

88. Outler, *Sermons*, 2:477. For a work that carefully demonstrates the role of faith in Christian spiritual development, see Sondra Matthaei, *Making Disciples: Faith Formation in the Wesleyan Tradition* (Nashville: Abingdon Press, 2000).

89. Outler, *Sermons*, 2:402-3. In his sermon "The Deceitfulness of the Human Heart," Wesley associates pride with the origin of evil; but he then suggests that it, along with independence and self-will, "all centre in this atheism," or unbelief. See Outler, *Sermons*, 4:152.

90. Outler, *Sermons*, 2:163. Emphasis is mine.

91. For the earlier, largely negative uses of the phrase "naked faith," see Ward and Heitzenrater, *Journals and Diaries*, 20:143-44; 22:406; and Outler, *Sermons*, 2:212.

92. Outler, *Sermons*, 2:163.

93. Jackson, *Works*, 13:2. Emphasis is mine.

94. Telford, *Letters*, 7:295. Emphasis is mine.

95. Ibid., 7:322. Emphases are mine.

96. Outler, *Sermons*, 2:167-68.

Conclusion: "The Best of All"

1. Albert C. Outler, ed., *The Works of John Wesley*, Bicentennial ed., vols. 1-4, *Sermons* (Nashville: Abingdon Press, 1984–87), 4:143.

2. Ibid., 4:146.

3. Ibid., 4:147.

4. John Telford, ed., *The Letters of John Wesley, A.M.*, 8 vols. (London: The Epworth Press, 1931), 8:218.

5. Ibid., 8:222.

6. Telford, *Letters*, 8:234.

7. Ibid.

8. Outler, *Sermons*, 4:175.

9. Nehemiah Curnock, ed., *The Journal of the Rev. John Wesley, A.M.*, 8 vols. (London: The Epworth Press, 1938), 8:93, 8:102.

10. Outler, *Sermons*, 4:174. Emphasis is mine.

11. Telford, *Letters*, 7:76.

12. Ibid., 7:19.

13. Telford, *Letters*, 8:238.

14. Ibid., 8:211. Emphasis is mine.

15. Ibid., 8:224. In this same letter, Wesley also exclaimed: "O my Lord, for God's sake, for Christ's sake, for pity's sake suffer the poor people to enjoy their religious as well as civil liberty! I am on the brink of eternity!" See ibid., 8:225.

16. Ibid., 8:224-25.

17. Ibid., 8:231.

18. Outler, *Sermons*, 4:137.

19. Ibid., 4:138.

20. Ibid., 4:179.

21. Ibid. See also Charles Edward White, "What Wesley Practiced and Preached About Money," *Leadership: A Practical Journal for Church Leaders* 8 (Winter 1987): 27-29.

22. Outler, *Sermons*, 4:184. Emphasis is mine.

23. Telford, *Letters*, 8:265.

24. Ibid., 8:17.

25. Ibid., 8:23.

26. Ibid., 8:207. Hynson explores Wesley's views on slavery in their proper context, that is, in terms of natural law and human rights. See

Leon O. Hynson, "Wesley's 'Thoughts Upon Slavery': A Declaration of Human Rights," *Methodist History* 33, no. 1 (October 1994): 46-57.

27. Ibid., 8:199.

28. Curnock, *Journal*, 8:76.

29. Telford, *Letters*, 8:257.

30. Ibid., 8:259.

31. W. Reginald Ward and Richard P. Heitzenrater, eds., *The Works of John Wesley*, Bicentennial ed., vol. 18, *Journals and Diaries I* (Nashville: Abingdon Press, 1988), 234. Wesley heard the experiences of Mrs. Fox and Mr. Hutchins (of Pembroke College) "two living witnesses that God *can* (at least, if he *does* not always) give that faith whereof cometh salvation in a moment, as lightning falling from heaven." See Ward and Heitzenrater, *Journals and Diaries*, 18:235.

32. Ibid., 18:250.

33. Outler, *Sermons*, 2:169. Emphasis is mine.

34. Thomas Jackson, ed., *The Works of John Wesley*, 14 vols. (Grand Rapids, Mich.: Baker Book House, 1978), 10:230.

35. This means that grace as the utter favor of God informed Wesley's understanding not simply of forensic themes such as justification, but participatory ones as well such as regeneration and Christian perfection. Moreover, grace as divine favor informed the processes of redemption at every step along the way though grace as "synergistic response," as *working*, must in the nature of things recede from view, in some sense, during the crucial actualizations of grace in terms of justification, regeneration, and Christian perfection, all of which remained, for Wesley, in a very real way, the works of God *alone*, and, therefore, to be received as sheer utter *gifts*. Indeed, one is not entirely sanctified because of or on the basis of prior working or cooperation, though one must, after all, "extend the hand," so to speak, in gracious faith and receive such gifts.

36. Jackson, *Works*, 11:30.

37. Curnock, *Journal*, 8:138.

38. Ibid.

39. Ibid.

Selected Bibliography

Primary Sources

Baker, Frank, ed. *The Works of John Wesley.* Bicentennial ed. Vol. 25, *Letters I.* Nashville: Abingdon Press, 1980.

———. *The Works of John Wesley.* Bicentennial ed. Vol. 26, *Letters II.* Nashville: Abingdon Press, 1982.

Burwash, Rev. N., ed. *Wesley's Fifty-two Standard Sermons.* Salem, Ohio: Schmul Publishing Co., 1967.

Cragg, Gerald R., ed. *The Works of John Wesley.* Bicentennial ed. Vol. 11, *The Appeals to Men of Reason and Religion and Certain Related Open Letters.* Nashville: Abingdon Press, 1975.

Curnock, Nehemiah, ed. *The Journal of the Rev. John Wesley.* 8 vols. London: The Epworth Press, 1909–16.

Davies, Rupert E., ed. *The Works of John Wesley.* Bicentennial ed. Vol. 9, *The Methodist Societies, I: History, Nature, and Design.* Nashville: Abingdon Press, 1989.

Green, Richard. *The Works of John and Charles Wesley.* 2nd rev. ed. New York: AMS Press, 1976. Reprint of the 1906 edition.

Hildebrandt, Franz, and Oliver Beckerlegge, eds. *The Works of John Wesley.* Vol. 7, *A Collection of Hymns for the Use of the People Called Methodists.* Nashville: Abingdon Press, 1983.

Jackson, Thomas, ed. *The Works of Rev. John Wesley.* 14 vols. London: Wesleyan Methodist Book Room, 1829–31. Reprinted Grand Rapids, Mich.: Baker Book House, 1978.

Jarboe, Betty M., comp. *Wesley Quotations: Excerpts from the Writings of John Wesley and Other Family Members.* Metuchen, N.J.: Scarecrow Press, 1990.

Outler, Albert C., ed. *John Wesley. The Library of Protestant Thought.* New York: Oxford University Press, 1964.

————, ed. *The Works of John Wesley*. Bicentennial ed. Vols. 1-4, *Sermons*. Nashville: Abingdon Press, 1984–87.

Outler, Albert C., and Richard P. Heitzenrater, eds. *John Wesley's Sermons: An Anthology*. Nashville: Abingdon Press, 1991.

Telford, John, ed. *The Letters of the Rev. John Wesley*. 8 vols. London: The Epworth Press, 1931.

Ward, W. Reginald, and Richard P. Heitzenrater, eds. *The Works of John Wesley*. Bicentennial ed. Vols. 18-23, *Journals and Diaries*. Nashville: Abingdon Press, 1988–95.

Wesley, John. *A Christian Library, Consisting of Extracts from and Abridgements of the Choicest Pieces of Practical Divinty Which Have Been Published in the English Tongue*. 30 vols. London: T. Blanshard, 1819–27.

————. *Explanatory Notes upon the New Testament*. London: William Bowyer, 1755. Most recent reprint, Grand Rapids, Mich.: Baker Book House, 1987.

————. *Explanatory Notes upon the Old Testament*. 3 vols. Bristol: William Pine, 1765. Facsimile reprint, Salem, Ohio: Schmul Publishers, 1975.

————. *A Plain Account of Christian Perfection*. London: The Epworth Press. Philadelphia: Trinity Press International, 1990.

————. *A Plain Account of Genuine Christianity*. Library of Methodist Classics. Nashville: The United Methodist Publishing House, 1992.

————. *Primitive Physic: An Easy and Natural Method of Curing Most Diseases by John Wesley*. Library of Methodist Classics. Nashville: The United Methodist Publishing House, 1992.

Secondary Sources

Books

Abelove, Henry. *The Evangelist of Desire: John Wesley and the Methodists*. Stanford, Calif.: Stanford University Press, 1990.

Armstrong, Anthony. *The Church of England, the Methodists, and Society, 1700–1850*. Totowa, N.J.: Rowman and Littlefield, 1973.

Ayling, Stanley. *John Wesley*. Nashville: Abingdon Press, 1982.

Baker, Eric W. *A Herald of the Evangelical Revival: A Critical Inquiry into the Relation of William Law to John Wesley and the Beginnings of Methodism*. London: The Epworth Press, 1948.

Bready, J. Wesley. *This Freedom—Whence?* New York: American Tract Association, 1942.

Brown, Earl Kent. *Women of Mr. Wesley's Methodism*. New York: Edwin Mellon, 1983.

Brown-Lawson, Albert. *John Wesley and the Anglican Evangelicals of the Eighteenth Century: A Study in Cooperation and Separation with Special Reference to the Calvanistic Controversies.* Edinburgh: Pentland Press, 1994.

Burkhard, Johann Gottlieb. *Vollständige Geschichte Der Methodisten in England.* Stuttgart: Christliches Verlagshaus, 1995.

Cannon, William R. *The Theology of John Wesley, with Special Reference to the Doctrine of Justification.* Lanham, Md.: University Press of America, 1984.

Church, Leslie. *Knight of the Burning Heart: The Story of John Wesley.* London: The Epworth Press, 1938.

Clapper, Gregory S. *As If the Heart Mattered: A Wesleyan Spirituality.* Nashville: Upper Room Books, 1997.

Clark, J. C. D. *English Society 1660–1832: Religion, Ideology, and Politics During the Ancient Regime.* Cambridge: Cambridge University Press, 2000.

Collins, Kenneth J. *Exploring Christian Spirituality: An Ecumenical Reader.* Grand Rapids, Mich.: Baker Books, 2000.

———. *The Scripture Way of Salvation: The Heart of John Wesley's Theology.* Nashville: Abingdon Press, 1997.

Collins, Kenneth J., and John H. Tyson. eds. *Conversion in the Wesleyan Tradition.* Nashville: Abingdon Press, 2001.

Dallimore, Arnold A. *Susanna Wesley: The Mother of John and Charles Wesley.* Grand Rapids, Mich.: Baker Book House, 1993.

Davey, Cyril. *John Wesley and the Methodists.* Nashville: Abingdon Press, 1986.

Dobree, Bonamy. *John Wesley.* Folcraft, Pa.: Folcroft Library Edition, 1974.

Edwards, Maldwyn. *Family Circle.* London: The Epworth Press, 1961.

———. *John Wesley.* 4th ed. Madison, N.J.: General Commision on Archives, 1987.

Elmore, Paul. *The Spirit of Anglicanism.* London: S.P.C.K., 1957.

Ethridge, Willie Snow. *Strange Fires: The True Story of John Wesley's Love Affair in Georgia.* New York: Vanguard, 1971.

Fitchett, W. H. *Wesley and His Century: A Study in Spiritual Forces.* London: Smith, Elder, & Co., 1906.

Green, J. Brazier. *John Wesley and William Law.* London: The Epworth Press, 1945.

Green, V. H. H. *John Wesley.* Lanham, Md.: University Press of America, 1987. Reprint of 1964 edition.

———. *The Young Mr. Wesley.* New York: St. Martin's Press, 1961.

Harmon, Rebecca Lamar. *Susanna, Mother of the Wesleys.* Nashville: Abingdon Press, 1984.

Heitzenrater, Richard P. *The Elusive Mr. Wesley.* 2 vols. Nashville: Abingdon Press, 1984.

————. *Wesley and the People Called Methodists.* Nashville: Abingdon Press, 1995.

Henderson, D. Michael. *John Wesley's Class Meeting: A Model for Making Disciples.* Nappanee, Ind.: Evangel Publishing House, 1997.

Hindmarsh, D. Bruce. *John Newton and the English Evangelical Tradition: Between the Conversions of Wesley and Wilberforce.* Pbk. ed. Grand Rapids, Mich.: William B. Eerdmans, 2001.

Hughes, Serge, ed. *Catherine of Genoa: Purgation and Purgatory, the Spiritual Dialogue.* New York: Paulist Press, 1979.

Hulley, Leonard D. *Wesley: A Plain Man for Plain People.* Westville, South Africa: Methodist Church of South Africa, 1987.

Hynson, Leon O. *The Wesleyan Revival: John Wesley's Ethics for Church and State.* Salem, Ohio: Schmul Publishing Co., 1999.

Knight, Henry H., III. *The Presence of God in the Christian Life: John Wesley and the Means of Grace.* Metuchen, N.J.: Scarecrow Press, 1992.

Koepp, Wilhelm. *Johann Arndt.* Berlin: Protestantischer Schriftenvertrieb, 1912.

Lee, Umphrey. *John Wesley and Modern Religion.* Nashville: Abingdon-Cokesbury, 1936.

————. *The Lord's Horseman: John Wesley the Man.* New York: Abingdon Press, 1928.

Lipsky, Abram. *John Wesley: A Portrait.* New York: AMS Press, 1928.

Logan, James C. *Theology and Evangelism in the Wesleyan Heritage.* Nashville: Kingswood Books, 1994.

Lunn, Arnold. *John Wesley.* New York: Dial Press, 1929.

Macquiban, Tim. *Pure, Universal Love: Reflections on the Wesleys and Inter-Faith Dialogue.* Westminster Wesley Series No. 3. Oxford: Applied Theology Press, 1995.

Maddox, Randy L. *Responsible Grace: John Wesley's Practical Theology.* Nashville: Kingswood Books, 1994.

Marquardt, Manfred. *John Wesley's Social Ethics: Praxis and Principles.* Nashville: Abingdon Press, 1992.

Matthaei, Sondra. *Making Disciples: Faith Formation in the Wesleyan Tradition.* Nashville: Abingdon Press, 2000.

Meisel, Anthony C., and M. L. Del Mastro, eds. *The Rule of St. Benedict.* New York: An Image Book, Doubleday, 1975.

Mercer, Jerry. *Being Christian: A United Methodist Vision for the Christian Life: Based on John Wesley's Original Tract, "The Character of a Methodist."* Nashville: Discipleship Resources, 1993.

McConnell, Francis J. *John Wesley.* New York: Abingdon Press, 1939.

McNeer, May, and Lynd Ward. *John Wesley*. Nashville: Abingdon Press, 1957.

Miller, Basil. *John Wesley*. Minneapolis: Bethany House, 1969.

Monk, Robert C. *John Wesley: His Puritan Heritage*. 2nd ed. Pietist and Wesleyan Studies No. 11. Lanham, Md.: Scarecrow Press, 1999.

Moorman, J. R. H. *A History of the Church of England*. Wilton, Conn.: Morehouse-Barlow Co., 1953.

Nagler, Arthur. *Pietism and Methodism*. Nashville: Publishing House of the Methodist Episcopal Church, South, 1918.

Newton, John A. *Methodism and the Puritans*. London: Dr. William's Library Trust, 1964.

Noppen, J. P. van. *Transforming Words: The Early Methodist Revival from a Discourse Perspective*. Religions and Discourse, V. 3. Bern; New York: Peter Lang, 1999.

Overton, J. H. *John Wesley*. London: Methuen and Co., 1891.

Peers, E. Allison, trans. *John of the Cross: The Dark Night of the Soul*. New York: Doubleday, 1990.

Piette, Maximin. *John Wesley in the Evolution of Protestantism*. London: Sheed and Ward, 1938.

Plumb, J. H. *England in the Eighteenth Century*. Harmondsworth, England: Penguin Books, 1950.

Pollock, John. *John Wesley*. Oxford: Lion Publishing, 1989.

Pool, Thomas E. *John Wesley the Soul Winner*. Salem, Ohio: Schmul Pub. Co., n.d.

Porter, Roy. *England in the Eighteenth Century*. A History of England. London: The Folio Society, 1982.

Pudney, John. *John Wesley and His World*. New York: Charles Scribner's Sons, 1978.

Rack, Henry D. *Reasonable Enthusiast: John Wesley and the Rise of Methodism*. London: The Epworth Press, 1989.

Rattenbury, J. Ernest. *Wesley's Legacy to the World: Six Studies in the Permanent Values of the Evangelical Revival*. London: The Epworth Press, 1928.

Rigg, James H. *The Churchmanship of John Wesley and the Relations of Wesleyan Methodism to the Church of England*. London: Wesleyan Conference Office, 1878.

Roberts, R. Ellis. *The Church of England*. London: Francis Griffiths, 1908.

Rogal, Samuel J. *John and Charles Wesley*. New York: Macmillan, 1983.

Rowe, Kenneth E. *The Place of Wesley in the Christian Tradition*. Rev. ed. Metuchen, N.J.: Scarecrow Press, 1980.

Rupp, E. Gordon. *Religion in England, 1688–1791*. Oxford: Clarendon Press, 1986.

Sager, Allan. *Gospel-Centered Spirituality*. Minneapolis: Augsburg Fortress Press, 1990.

Schmidt, Martin. *The Young Wesley: Missionary and Theologian of Missions*. London: The Epworth Press, 1958.

———. *John Wesley: A Theological Biography*. 2 vols. Nashville: Abingdon Press, 1962–73.

Scott, Sir Percy. *John Wesleys Lehre Von Der Heiligung Vergleichen Mit Einen Lutherish-Pietistischen Beispel* [John Wesley's doctrine of salvation compared with a Lutheran-pietistic example]. Berlin: Alfred Topelman, 1939.

Simon, John S. *John Wesley and the Religious Societies*. London: The Epworth Press, 1955.

Slaatte, Howard. *Fire in the Brand: An Introduction to the Creative Work and Theology of John Wesley*. Lanham, Md.: University Press of America, 1983.

Snell, F. J. *Wesley and Methodism*. New York: Scribner, 1900.

Snyder, Howard A. *The Radical Wesley: Pattern for Church Renewal*. Grand Rapids, Mich.: Zondervan Publishing House, 1987.

Southey, Robert. *The Life of Wesley; and Rise and Progress of Methodism*. Vol. 1. London: Longman, Brown, Green, and Longmans, 1846.

Starkey, Lycurgus M. *The Work of the Holy Spirit: A Study in Wesleyan Theology*. Nashville: Abingdon Press, 1962.

Telford, John. *The Life of John Wesley*. London: Wesleyan Methodist Book Room, 1899.

Towlson, Clifford W. *Moravian and Methodist: Relationships and Influences in the Eighteenth Century*. London: The Epworth Press, 1957.

Tuttle, Robert G., Jr. *John Wesley: His Life and Theology*. Grand Rapids, Mich.: Zondervan, 1982.

Tyerman, Luke. *The Life and Times of the Rev. John Wesley, M.A.* 3 vols. New York: Burt Franklin, 1872.

Tylenda, Joseph N., trans. *Thomas à Kempis: The Imitation of Christ*. New York: Vintage Books, 1984.

Vickers, John. *John Wesley*. Fort Washington, Pa.: Christian Literature Crusade, 1977.

Vulliamy, C. E. *John Wesley*. Westwood, N.J.: Barbour and Company, 1985.

Wainwright, Geoffrey, ed. *Hymns on the Lord's Supper*. Madison, N.J.: Charles Wesley Society, 1995.

Wallace, Charles, Jr., ed. *Susanna Wesley: The Complete Writings*. New York: Oxford University Press, 1997.

Watson, Philip S. *Anatomy of a Conversion: The Message and Mission of John and Charles Wesley*. Grand Rapids, Mich.: Francis Asbury Press, 1990.

Watson, Richard. *The Life of Rev. John Wesley*. New York: Hoyt & Co., 1831.

White, James F., ed. *John Wesley's Prayer Book : The Sunday Service of the Methodists in North America*. Cleveland, Ohio: OSL Publications, 1991.

Wood, A. Skevington. *The Burning Heart: John Wesley, Evangelist*. Minneapolis: Bethany House, 1978.

Yates, Arthur S. *The Doctrine of Assurance: With Special Reference to John Wesley*. London: The Epworth Press, 1952.

Chapters in Books

Lee, Hoo-Jung. "Experiencing the Spirit in Wesley and Macarius." In *Rethinking Wesley's Theology for Contemporary Methodism*. Ed. Randy Maddox. Nashville: Abingdon Press, 1998.

Outler, Albert C. "John Wesley as a Theologian: Then as Now." In *The Wesleyan Theological Heritage: Essays of Albert C. Outler*. Ed. Thomas C. Oden and Leicester R. Longden. Grand Rapids, Mich.: Zondervan, 1991.

———. "Pietism and Enlightenment: Alternatives to Tradition." In *Christian Spirituality III*. Ed. Louis Dupre and Don Saliers. New York: Crossroad, 1989.

Stephens, W. P. "Wesley and the Moravians." In *John Wesley: Contemporary Perspectives*. Ed. John Stacey. London: The Epworth, 1988.

Stoeffler, F. Ernest. "Pietism, the Wesleys and Methodist Beginnings in America." In *Continental Pietism and Early American Christianity*. Ed. F. Ernest Stoeffler. Grand Rapids, Mich.: William. B. Eerdmans, 1976.

Watson, David L. "Aldersgate Street and the General Rules: The Form and the Power of Methodist Discipleship." In *Aldersgate Reconsidered*. Ed. Randy L. Maddox. Nashville: Kingswood Books, 1990.

Articles

Baker, Frank. "The Real John Wesley." *Methodist History* 12 (July 1974): 183-97.

———. "Investigating Wesley Family Traditions [genealogical table]." *Methodist History* 26, no. 3 (April 1988): 154-62.

———. "Wesley's Puritan Ancestry." *London Quarterly & Holborn Review* 187 (1962): 180-86.

Bassett, Paul M. "Finding the Real John Wesley." *Christianity Today* 28, no. 16 (9 November 1984): 86-88.

Brown, Dale W. "The Wesleyan Revival from a Pietist Perspective." *Wesleyan Theological Journal* 24 (1989): 7-17.

Butler, David. " 'Look for the Mother to Find the Son': The Influence of Susanna Wesley on Her Son John." *Epworth Review* 25 (1998): 90-100.

Campbell, Ted A. "Christian Tradition, John Wesley, and Evangelicalism [His View of Apostolic and Anglican Traditions]." *Anglican Theological Review* 74 (1992): 54-67.

Cho, John Chongnahm. "Adam's Fall and God's Grace: John Wesley's Theological Anthropology." *Evangelical Review of Theology* 10, no. 3 (1986): 202-13.

Collins, Kenneth J. "The Influence of Early German Pietism on John Wesley [Arndt and Francke]." *The Covenant Quarterly* 48 (1990): 23-42.

———. "John Wesley's Correspondence with His Father." *Methodist History* 26, no. 1 (October 1987): 15-26.

———. "John Wesley's Relationship with His Wife as Revealed in His Correspondence." *Methodist History* 32, no. 1 (October 1993): 4-18.

———. "Real Christianity as Integrating Theme in Wesley's Soteriology: The Critique of a Modern Myth." *The Asbury Theological Journal* 51, no. 2 (1996): 15-45.

———. "The Soteriological Orientation of John Wesley's Ministry to the Poor." *The Asbury Theological Journal* 50, no. 1 (1995): 75-92.

Drakeford, John W. "How Growing Old Looks from Within: A Study of John Wesley's Perception of the Aging Process Revealed in His Journal's 'Birthday Reflections.' " *Journal of Religion and Aging* 1, no. 2 (Winter 1984): 39-51.

Edwards, M. "Reluctant Lover; John Wesley as Suitor." *Methodist History* 12 (January 1974): 46-62.

English, John C. " 'Dear Sister': John Wesley and the Women of Early Methodism." *Methodist History* 33, no. 1 (1994): 26-33.

———. "The Cambridge Platonists in Wesley's 'A Christian Library.' " *Proceedings of the Wesley Historical Society* 36 (October 1968): 161-73.

———. "John Wesley's Indebtedness to John Norris [Epistemology and Education]." *Church History* 60 (1991): 55-69.

Estep, James Riley, Jr. "John Wesley's Philosophy of Formal Childhood Education." *Christian Education Journal* 1, no. 2 (1997): 43-52.

Frost, Brian. "Orthodoxy and Methodism." *London Quarterly & Holborn Review* 189 (1964): 13-22.

Goodwin, Charles H. "John Wesley's Indebtedness to Jonathan Edwards." *Epworth Review* 25 (1998): 89-96.

Harland, H. Gordon. "John Wesley." *Touchstone: Heritage and Theology in a New Age* 2, no. 3 (October 1984): 5-17.

Harper, K. "[William] Law and [John] Wesley." *Church Quarterly Review* 163 (1982): 61-71.

Holland, Bernard G. "The Conversions of John and Charles Wesley and Their Place in Methodist Tradition." *The Proceedings of the Wesley Historical Society* 38 (1971): 45-53, 65-71.

Holland, L. M. "John Wesley and the American Revolution." *Journal of Church and State* 5 (1963): 199-213.

Hynson, Leon O. "Wesley's 'Thoughts Upon Slavery': A Declaration of Human Rights." *Methodist History* 33, no. 1 (1994): 46-57.

Kurowski, Mark T. "The First Step Toward Grace: John Wesley's Use of the Spiritual Homilies of Macarius the Great." *Methodist History* 36, no. 2 (1998): 113-24.

Lodahl, Michael E. " 'The Witness of the Spirit': Questions of Clarification for Wesley's Doctrine of Assurance." *Wesleyan Theological Journal* 23, no. 1 and 2 (1988): 188-97.

Maddox, Randy L. "John Wesley and Eastern Orthodoxy: Influences, Convergences and Differences." *The Asbury Theological Journal* 45, no. 2 (1990): 29-53.

Maser, Frederick E. "John Wesley's Only Marriage [With reply by Frank Baker, pp. 42-45]." *Methodist History* 16 (October 1977): 33-41.

———. "Things You've Really Wanted to Know About the Wesleys." *Methodist History* 29, no. 2 (January 1991): 119-21.

O'Malley, J. Steven. "Pietistic Influence on John Wesley: Wesley and Gerhard Tersteegen." *Wesleyan Theological Journal* 31, no. 2 (1996): 48-70.

Pembroke, Neil F. "From Self-doubt to Assurance: The Psychological Roots of John Wesley's Early Spiritual Development." *Journal of Psychology and Christianity* 13 (Fall 1994): 242-53.

Raymond, Allan. "I Fear God and Honour the King: John Wesley and the American Revolution." *Church History* 45 (1976): 316-28.

Rogal, Samuel J. "John Wesley's Daily Routine." *Methodist History* 8 (October 1974): 41-51.

Sanders, Paul Samuel. "The Puritans and John Wesley." *Work and Worship* 17, no. 2 (1967): 13-19.

Smith, Warren Thomas. "The Wesleys in Georgia: An Evaluation." *The Journal of the Interdenominational Theological Center* 6 (Spring 1979): 157-67.

Turner, John M. "John Wesley: Theologian for the People." *Journal of United Reform Church History Society* 3 (1986): 320-28.

Tyson, John R. "John Wesley and William Law: A Reappraisal [Appendices]." *Wesleyan Theological Journal* 17, no. 2 (1982): 58-78.

———. "Sin, Self and Society: John Wesley's Hamartiology Reconsidered [His Sermons on Several Occasions]." *The Asbury Theological Journal* 44, no. 2 (1989): 77-89.

Wallace, Charles. "Simple and Recollected: John Wesley's Life-style." *Religion in Life* 46 (Summer 1977): 198-212.

White, Charles Edward. "What Wesley Practiced and Preached About Money." *Leadership: A Practical Journal for Church Leaders* 8 (1987): 27-29.

Wilson, Paul Scott. "Wesley's Homiletic: Law and Gospel for Preaching." *Toronto Journal of Theology* 10 (1994): 215-25.

Young, Norman. "Wesley's View of Catholic Spirit and the Ecumenical Situation Today." *Uniting Church Studies* 5 (1999): 59-66.

Yrigoyen, Charles, Jr. "John Wesley—200th Anniv. Studies." *Methodist History* 29, no. 2 (January 1991): 63-121.

Index

CPSIA information can be obtained
at www.ICGtesting.com
Printed in the USA
LVHW030823101118
596627LV00002B/57/P

9 780687 027880